Roadmap Strategies for Startups Series

BUSINESS STRUCTURES AND INCORPORATION

Roadmap Strategies for Startups Series

HOW-TO AND DO-IT-YOURSELF SERIES

BY ANN CARRINGTON

Business Structures and Incorporation

Trademark Protection and Prosecution

Writing Winning Business Plans and Investor Presentations

Meet the Author and Publisher at https://www.AuthorsDoor.com

Roadmap Strategies for Startups Series

BUSINESS STRUCTURES AND INCORPORATION

HOW-TO AND DO-IT-YOURSELF SERIES

ANN CARRINGTON

AuthorsDoor Group

an imprint of The Ridge Publishing Group

Copyright © 2021 by Ann Carrington
All rights reserved. Published by AuthorsDoor™ Group,
an imprint of The Ridge Publishing Group

The name and house mark, logo, and all other AuthorsDoor Group related marks depicted representing AuthorsDoor Group, whether registered or unregistered, are trademarks or servicemarks of The Ridge Publishing Group
www.RidgePublishingGroup.com

No part of this publication may be reproduced, or stored in a retrieval system, or transmitted in any form or by any means, electronic, mechanical, photocopying, recording, or otherwise, without written permission of the publisher. For information regarding permissions, contact The Ridge Publishing Group, Attention Permissions Department at contact@RidgePublishingGroup.com.

LIMITED OF LIABILITY DISCLAIMER OF WARRANTY: While the publisher and author have used their best efforts in preparing this book, they make no representations or warranties with respect to the accuracy or completeness of the contents of this book and specifically disclaim any implied warranties of merchantability or fitness for a particular purpose. No warranty may be created or extended by sales representatives or written sales materials. The advice and strategies contained herein may not be suitable for your situation. The publisher and author are not engaged in rendering professional services, and you should consult a professional where appropriate. Neither the publisher nor author shall be liable for any loss of profit or any other commercial damages, including but not limited to special, incidental, consequential or other damages. This book was prepared for general information and as a checklist of certain laws applicable to corporations in general. This book does not purport to cover all of the laws and related issues applicable to businesses in particular. The publisher and author undertake no responsibility to provide updates to this book.

Carrington, Ann
Business Structures and Incorporation / by Ann Carrington

Summary: A comprehensive book describing principal forms of business, exploring the considerations and strategies in making an appropriate selection, incorporation, sample forms and documents, and much more.

ISBN 978-1-884573-89-7 (Softcover)

[1. Business – Non-fiction. 2. Business Law – Non-fiction. 3. Incorporation – Non-fiction. 4. Entrepreneur – Non-fiction. 5. Legal – Non-fiction.] I. Title. II. Series.

Revised Edition: April 2021

Printed in the United States of America

TABLE OF CONTENTS

1	What Structure Makes the Most Sense?	1
2	Choice of Name	5
3	Choice of Business Entity	17
4	Sole Proprietorships	31
5	Partnerships	42
6	Limited Liability Companies	75
7	Corporations	121
8	Corporate Management	166
9	Corporate Records	188
10	Changes in Corporate Structure	218
11	Corporate Stock Matters	230
12	Capital Stock Structures	246
13	Employee and Other Matters	257
14	Tax Matters	278
15	Doing Business in Other States	283
About the Author and Publishers		290

Roadmap Strategies for Startups Series

BUSINESS STRUCTURES AND INCORPORATION

CHAPTER 1

WHAT STRUCTURE MAKES THE MOST SENSE?

One of the choices you make when starting a business and one of the most important is the type of legal organization you select for your company. This decision can affect how much you pay in taxes, the amount of paperwork your business is required to do, the personal liability you face, and your ability to borrow money. Business formation is controlled by the law of the state where your business is organized. The most common forms of business are: sole proprietorships, partnerships, corporations and limited liability companies. However, while state law controls the formation of your business, federal tax law controls how your business is taxed. In addition, federal tax law also recognizes an additional business form, the Subchapter S corporation.

This book provides a comprehensive overview describing principal forms of business, exploring the considerations and strategies in making an appropriate selection, incorporation, sample forms and documents, and much more.

Sole Proprietorship

A sole proprietorship is the most common form of business organization. It's easy to form and offers complete control to the owner. It is any unincorporated business owned entirely by one individual. In general, the owner is also personally liable for all financial obligations and debts of the business.

Sole proprietors can operate any kind of business. However, it must be a business, not an investment or hobby. It can be full-time or part-time work. This includes operating a: shop or retail trade business, large company with employees, home-based business, or one person consulting firm. Every sole proprietor is required to keep sufficient records to comply with federal tax requirements regarding business records.

BUSINESS STRUCTURES AND INCORPORATION

Generally, sole proprietors file Schedule C or C-EZ, Profit or Loss from Business, with their Form 1040. Sole proprietor farmers file Schedule F, Profit or Loss from Farming. Your net business income or loss is combined with your other income and deductions and taxed at individual rates on your personal tax return.

Sole proprietors must also pay self-employment tax on the net income reported on Schedule C or Schedule F. You may also be able to deduct one-half of SE tax on your 1040. Use Schedule SE, Self-Employment Tax, to compute this tax.

Sole proprietors do not have taxes withheld from their business income so you will generally need to make quarterly estimated tax payments if you expect to make a profit. These estimated payments include both income tax and self-employment taxes for Social Security and Medicare.

Partnership

A partnership is the relationship existing between two or more persons who join to carry on a trade or business. Each person contributes money, property, labor or skill, and expects to share in the profits and losses of the business.

A partnership does not pay any income tax at the partnership level. Partnerships file Form 1065, U.S. return of Partnership Income, to report income and expenses. This is an information return. The partnership passes the information to the individual partners on Schedule K-1, Partner's Share of Income, Credits, and Deductions. Partnerships are often referred to as pass-through or flow-through entities for this reason.

Each partner reports his share of the partnership net profit or loss on his personal Form 1040 tax return. Partners must report their share of partnership income even if a distribution is not made.

Partners are not employees of the partnership and so taxes are not withheld from any distributions. Like sole proprietors, partners generally need to make quarterly estimated tax payments if they expect to make a profit.

General partners must pay self-employment tax on their net earnings from self-employment assigned to them from the partnership. Net earnings from self-employment include an individual's share, distributed or not, of income or loss from any trade or business carried on by a partnership.

Limited partners are subject to self-employment tax only on guaranteed payments, such as professional fees for services rendered.

WHAT STRUCTURE MAKES THE MOST SENSE?

Corporation

A corporate structure is more complex than other business structures. It requires complying with more regulations and tax requirements. It may require more tax preparation services than the sole proprietorship or the partnership.

Corporations are formed under the laws of each state and are subject to corporate income tax at the federal and generally at the state level. In addition, any earnings distributed to shareholders in the form of dividends are taxed at individual tax rates on their personal tax returns.

The corporation is an entity that handles the responsibilities of the business. Like a person, the corporation can be taxed and can be held legally liable for its actions. If you organize your business as a corporation, you are generally not personally liable for the debts of the corporation. (Exceptions may exist under state law.)

When you form a corporation, you create a separate tax-paying entity. Unlike sole proprietors and partnerships, income earned by a corporation is taxed at the corporate level using corporate tax rates. Regular corporations are called C corporations because Subchapter C of Chapter 1 of the Internal Revenue Code is where you find general tax rules affecting corporations and their shareholders.

A corporation files Form 1120 or 1120-A, U.S. Corporation Income Tax Return. If a shareholder is an employee, he/she pays income tax on his/her wages, and the corporation and the employee each pay one-half of the Social Security and Medicare taxes and the corporation can deduct its half. A corporate shareholder pays only income tax for any dividends received, which may be subject to a dividends-received deduction.

Subchapter S Corporation

The Subchapter S corporation is a variation of the standard corporation. The S corporation allows income or losses to be passed through to individual tax returns, similar to a partnership. The rules for Subchapter S corporations are found in Subchapter S of Chapter 1 of the Internal Revenue Code.

An S corporation has the same corporate structure as a standard corporation. It is a legal entity, chartered under state law, and is separate from its shareholders and officers. There is generally limited liability for corporate shareholders. The difference is that the corporation files an election on Form 2553, Election by a Small Business Corporation, to be treated differently for federal tax purposes.

BUSINESS STRUCTURES AND INCORPORATION

Generally, an S corporation is exempt from federal income tax other than tax on certain capital gains and passive income. It is treated in the same way as a partnership, in that generally taxes are not paid at the corporate level.

An S corporation files Form 1120S, U.S. Corporation Income Tax Return for an S Corporation. The income flows through to be reported on the shareholders' individual returns. Schedule K-1, Shareholder's Share of Income, Credits and Deductions, is completed with Form 1120S for each shareholder. The Schedule K-1 tells shareholders their allocable share of corporate income and deductions. Shareholders must pay tax on their share of corporate income, regardless of whether it is actually distributed.

Limited Liability Company

A Limited Liability Company (LLC) is a relatively new business structure allowed by state statute.

LLCs are popular because, similar to a corporation, owners generally have limited personal liability for the debts and actions of the LLC. Other features of LLCs are more like a partnership, providing management flexibility and the benefit of pass-through taxation.

Owners of an LLC are called members. Since most states do not restrict ownership, members may include individuals, corporations, other LLCs and foreign entities. Most states also permit "single member" LLCs, those having only one owner.

A few types of businesses generally cannot be LLCs, such as banks and insurance companies. Check your state's requirements and the federal tax regulations for further information. There are special rules for foreign LLCs.

For additional information on the kinds of tax returns to file, how to handle employment taxes and possible pitfalls, refer to Publication 3402 Tax Issues for Limited Liability Companies.

Which structure best suits your business?

One form is not necessarily better than any other. Each business owner must assess his or her own needs. It may be important to seek advice from business experts and professionals when considering the advantages and disadvantages of a business entity.

CHAPTER 2

CHOICE OF NAME

Choosing a business name is one of the most important decisions you will make and is the first step in branding your business. A business name is different from your trademarks, service marks, logos, and slogans. Trademark law protects product names, logos, and trade names, even some slogans as trademarks or service marks. Copyright law protects written works, works of art, and other creative works. Patent law protects inventions and designs. Business law, however, does not fully guarantee you the exclusive use of your business name. To get close to exclusivity, you have to be first, you have to be national, and you have to be alert.

The most common misunderstanding about business names is about reserving, registering, and protecting business names. You can't reserve a business name or have exclusive use completely. Think of a business name as a lot like a personal name, many people often have the same name. So too, the first John Smith can't stop all other persons named John Smith from using that same name. Just like Chrysalis Restaurant can't make Chrysalis Hardware Store change its name, and Chrysalis Hardware Store in San Francisco can't sue Chrysalis Hardware Store in Manhattan.

The confusion starts because business names are registered by different authorities in different places, and on different levels.

- ❖ The first and simplest business name is your own name, which might be enough for John Smith using John Smith Publishing. This kind of business name normally does not require any additional paperwork.

- ❖ The second level of business names is called DBA for "doing business as" which is commonly used for sole proprietorships comprising an individual, husband and wife, or partnership. Registering a Fictitious Business Name statement within your county government gives an

BUSINESS STRUCTURES AND INCORPORATION

individual the right to operate under a business name with bank accounts, checks, etc. if yours is the first business in the county with that name. Consequently, there might still be a Chrysalis Restaurant as a DBA in any other counties within any given state.

❖ The third level of business name is the corporation, including C corporations, S corporations, and limited liability companies. The corporation is registered at the state level by filing charter documents within its state. Subsequently, no two corporations can have the exact same name in that state. Then again, there might be a Chrysalis Restaurant in other states.

Although duplicate business names are possible and common, you do still have the right to protect and defend your own business name by registering your business name with the United States Patent and Trademark Office (USPTO). In the U.S., a registered trademark or trade name trumps a non-registered first use defense within the U.S. However, in many other countries, first use trumps a registered trademark or trade name creating more confusion with our growing global economy.

Business Name Considerations

First impressions count and the business name you choose is initially the only thing customers and suppliers know about you. For example, it projects important messages to customers, staff, and suppliers, making it a critical aspect towards success. Your business name also casts a certain brand image and should reflect the personality of the organization in a way that appeals to the target market, making it suitable for the company and its target group.

Your domain name is equally as important as your business name and should also have strong business characteristics. Finding a descriptive name, which can be typed easily and quickly into the address bar of the Internet browser, is not always easy. If they are not already taken, they are usually very long. However, one should attempt to find a descriptive name, as it offers some advantages for the Google ranking and users will know instantly what to make of it. In the end, the name should identify the purpose of the company or product, search engines should love it, and the domain ".com" should still be available.

When choosing a name for your business, the name should be easy to remember, easy to pronounce or spell, as well as compact and unique at the same time. You want a name that sets you apart from your competitors, is simple, and one that will be able to fit your business for years to come.

CHOICE OF NAME

Your logo should be unique; imitating an established brand's logo should be avoided at all costs. Once your business evolves and areas such as your branding will evolve over time, updating a logo is a lot easier than updating a name. If you take the time to come up with the right business name to start with you'll reap the dividends over the years.

The email signature you use is also important. A strong email name, logo design, and slogan will allow you to attract the best opportunities.

Business Name Commercial Tie-In Checklist

- ✓ Does the name accurately reflect the business image?
- ✓ Does the name identify your business – is it descriptive?
- ✓ Is your business name short, memorable, and easy to spell?
- ✓ Does your choice of business name stand out – is it unique?
- ✓ Does the name have a strong visual element – logo, colors?

On the other hand, some of the nation's most notable brands, such as Google, Apple, Amazon and Nike chose a non-descriptive name. You might ask, "How valuable was the name Google on the first day the search engine went live?" I'm willing to bet that this unique name meant absolutely nothing to the vast majority of people online at the time. However, as the company grew, this name began to grow in prestige and value.

Many small businesses are afraid of putting a name out there that says nothing about their offering and or a name that nobody knows. Make no mistake; it will be tough in the beginning. However, if you work hard at giving your name meaning, it may very well be the very thing that gives you an edge in the end.

Nonetheless, before choosing a commercial tie-in name or a name nobody has ever heard of before, you must consider legal requirements as well. For example, you should search the various indexes of company names to ensure your chosen name is not the same as an existing registered company. You may want to start with search engine searches using Google, Yahoo!, MSN, etc. You are also advised to check your name against trademark databases within and outside the U.S.

Inasmuch, there are a number of rules which apply to company names:

Business Name Legal Requirements Checklist

- ✓ Is the business name already in use?
- ✓ Is the business name trademarked by someone else?
- ✓ Is your business domain name available?

BUSINESS STRUCTURES AND INCORPORATION

- ✓ Does your logo design exist?
- ✓ Is your slogan, catchphrase or jingle available?

The name of a business is not case sensitive. For example, the Articles of Incorporation or Certificate of Incorporation and USPTO will list the business name in capitals. But it is perfectly legal to use any combination of upper and lower case letters for the company name after formation, regardless of the format used in the charter documents and with the USPTO.

Once you have selected a business name, you should first register the name in the county or counties in which you choose "to do business in" with the County Clerk's office(s) therein. Then, if appropriate, you should also register the name in the state or states in which you choose "to do business in" with the Secretary of State's office(s) therein. You should also have a second choice name ready in case the county or state confirms your first choice name is unavailable.

Business Name County Filings

The purpose of registering a fictitious business name with the County Clerk is to ensure that consumers have access to the true names and addresses of the business owners. If conducting business as an individual, husband and wife, general partnership, co-partners, or other unincorporated association, a Fictitious Business Name Statement is not required as long as the business name contains the surname of all the owners, and does not indicate the existence of other owners. Similarly, if the business is conducted by a corporation, limited partnership (LP), limited liability partnership (LLP), or a limited liability company, a Fictitious Business Name Statement is required if the business name is not the same as the registered corporation, LP, LLP, or LLC name.

Filing Requirements

- ❖ Fictitious Business Name Statements must be filed before you begin your business or within forty days of your first transaction.
- ❖ A Fictitious Business Name Statement is effective for five years.
- ❖ Fictitious Business Name Statements must be filed in the county in which the principal place of business is based.
- ❖ An applicant may have more than one fictitious business name and there may be more than one registrant per fictitious business name.
- ❖ Registration of a Fictitious Business Name Statement does not guarantee exclusive use of that name; applicants are responsible for

CHOICE OF NAME

- ensuring that the chosen fictitious business name does not duplicate a current registration or violate any trademark protocols.
- ❖ All information in the Fictitious Business Name Statement filed with the County Clerk is public record pursuant to the California Public Record Act including the residence address.
- ❖ Be certain the information in the statement is correct and complete before filing it. Once your statement has been filed, changes to that filing cannot be made, and no refunds will be issued.

Filing FBNS Checklist

- ✓ Research the name online or in-person at the County Clerk's office.
- ✓ Obtain an application online, in-person, or by mail.
- ✓ Complete the form in black ink. The second page of the form has specific instructions on how to complete the form.
- ✓ Check the current fee.
- ✓ Choose a payment method, online, in-person or by mail.
- ✓ Your copy and publication information (if needed) will be given to you at the County Clerk's office or returned to you by mail.

Publishing Requirement

After your statement has been filed, publishing is required under the following circumstances in the state of California (Business and Professions Code 17917): (a) new Fictitious Business Name Statement filing; (b) a renewal or re-filing of Fictitious Business Name Statement with changes; (c) a renewal or re-filing of Fictitious Business Name Statement occurring more than forty days after the expiration date; (d) the filing of a Statement of Abandonment of use of fictitious business name; or (e) the filing of a Statement of Withdrawal from partnership operating under fictitious business name. California law publishing requirements include:

- ❖ The legal notice must be published a total of four times (once a week for four consecutive weeks).
- ❖ The first publication must appear within thirty days of filing date.
- ❖ California Codes Business and Professions Code 17917(d) indicates an Affidavit showing the publication of the statement shall be filed with the County Clerk where Fictitious Business Name Statement was filed within thirty days after the completion of the publication.

BUSINESS STRUCTURES AND INCORPORATION

- ❖ The newspaper may offer a service to file this Affidavit for you. You will want to check with the newspaper to receive information about the service and any associated charges.

- ❖ In other cases, the newspaper may give the Affidavit directly to you. You may bring the Affidavit to the County Clerk's office or mail it to them.

- ❖ All information on the Fictitious Business Name Statement including the residence address will be published.

If publishing is required, your statement must be published in a newspaper that has been adjudicated as one of general circulation as per California Government Code Section 6000. It is your responsibility to ascertain the current adjudication status of the newspaper you plan to use. Be sure to allow sufficient time for the newspaper to prepare your statement for publication. Failure to publish as required by law will cause your statement to expire, and will require a new statement to be filed, including the payment of another filing fee.

CHOICE OF NAME

SAMPLE
FICTITIOUS BUSINESS NAME STATEMENT FORM

BUSINESS STRUCTURES AND INCORPORATION

Business Name State Filings

Proposed names for sole proprietorships, partnerships, corporations, LLCs, as well as newly qualifying foreign (out-of-state) businesses and businesses of record preparing to change their name, should be pre-cleared through the name availability section of the Secretary of State's office of the appropriate state prior to the submittal of documents for filing. The pre-clearance and/or reservation of a business name is necessary to avoid the rejection of documents submitted to the Secretary of State for filing because of a name conflict.

Most secretaries of state maintain a consolidated list of the following: (i) names of all corporations, LLCs and limited partnerships organized under the laws of that state in good standing, (ii) names of all foreign corporations, LLCs and limited partnerships qualified to transact intrastate business in the state and in good standing, and (iii) names reserved for future issuance. Charter documents will not be accepted for filing if the stated name resembles closely, is confusingly similar to, or is the same as any name on the consolidated list.

For example, the California Secretary of State maintains a consolidated list of the following: (i) names of all California corporations in good standing, (ii) names of all foreign corporations qualified to transact intrastate business in California and in good standing, (iii) corporate names reserved under Section 201(c) of the California Corporations Code (the "Code"), (iv) names of nonqualified foreign corporations registered under Section 2101 of the Code, and (v) names that will become record names of domestic or qualified foreign corporations at some delayed effective date of a filed corporate instrument, such as a merger agreement. The Secretary of State will not accept Articles of Incorporation for filing if the stated corporate name resembles closely, is confusingly similar to, or is the same as any name on the consolidated list. Note that the Secretary of State deems the words "corporation", "incorporated" and "inc." to be one and the same word. See Code Section 201(b).

A further consideration in selecting a name is whether that name is available for use in other states where the organization will be conducting business. Most states have laws similar to that of California governing business names. State laws generally provide for the use of an "assumed" name in a foreign state when an organization's true name is not available in a state. The same considerations regarding name availability are applicable to limited partnerships and limited liability companies.

You should also give consideration at this time to trademark and trade name issues. You may also obtain trademark searches to determine if there are

CHOICE OF NAME

conflicting or similar trademark or trade names in use. In addition to searching the USPTO records, research firms, such as CORESEARCH and Thomson & Thomson, can perform these services for a fee. Giving careful consideration to these issues during the planning and organizational phase can save you considerable frustration and time and money in the future.

If a corporate, limited partnership or limited liability company name is not available because that name or a similar one is in use, it is possible to obtain the consent of the entity using the name. If you have received such consent, you file the consent with the Articles of Incorporation, Certificate of Limited Partnership, or Articles of Organization, respectively. You may obtain the address of the entity already in existence, and the name of its officers, from the Secretary of State's office.

When selecting a business name, it is advisable to check the business codes and other corporate statutes of the proposed state of incorporation for any special provisions relating to corporate names. In California, for instance, the words "bank," "trust," "trustee," or related words, may not be a part of the corporate name unless a Certificate of Approval of the Superintendent of Banks is attached to the Articles of Incorporation. The word "co-operative," or any abbreviation or derivation of that may not be part of a corporate name unless the corporation is incorporated pursuant to specified sections of the Code. For example, in some states the name of a person may not be used as a corporate name without the addition of a corporate ending or some other word or words, which show that the name is not that of the individual alone.

It should also be noted that the name of a California corporation formed as a close corporation must contain the word "corporation," "incorporated," "limited," or an abbreviation of one of such words. In addition, special rules apply for the names of professional corporations. Before selecting a name for a professional corporation, refer to the law expressly applicable to the particular professional corporation in the Business and Professions Code and to the rules and regulations of the particular state agency regulating the profession. There are also provisions governing the use of names by corporations that are organized for the furnishing of professional engineering services to be performed by licensed persons.

The availability of a name may be determined on a preliminary basis by calling the Secretary of State's office for corporations or for limited partnerships. Two names will be checked per each telephone call. (A name may not be reserved by a telephone call to the Secretary of State's office.) A telephone check is subject to later verification, and the Articles may be rejected if the telephone check was inaccurate. It is strongly recommended not to rely on verbal information obtained by telephone in proceeding to file Articles.

Filing Services

If you do not have a pre-paid account with sufficient funds already set up with the Secretary of State, it is recommended that the desired name immediately be reserved to ensure its availability through a filing service such as AmeriSearch, GKL Corporate/Search, CSC Networks/Prentice Hall Corporate Services, or CT Corporation. It is strongly advisable to obtain a minimum of three proposed names, ranked in order of preference, to facilitate reservation of a name in the event that the first choice name is not available. The use of a filing service is more expensive than using a pre-paid account.

It is recommended that you have the filing service reserve the name as noted above, which is fast and relatively inexpensive. Alternatively, you may reserve a name by a written request directly to the Secretary of State; however, this is a much slower process. A written request for name reservation may include up to four names, listed in preferred order, with a request that the first available name be reserved. There is typically a nominal charge for each name reserved and the fee must accompany the request.

Name Reservation

In California, names are reserved for sixty days from the date of issuance of a Certificate of Reservation for Corporation Name. It is possible to reserve a name for a second sixty day period after a one business day has elapsed following the expiration of the first sixty day period, provided no other person has reserved the name during the one day interim period.

In states other than California, the time period for which names will be reserved varies greatly. In Delaware, for instance, names are reserved for a period of thirty days. When a corporate name has been reserved in one or more states, it is advisable to calendar the expiration date.

* * *

It is important, but difficult, to understand the difference between the actions of a Secretary of State in allowing the use of a name and the issues involved in the use of a name or mark for purposes of identifying a good or service. The determination of a Secretary of State in approving the use of a name merely means that an entity has complied with state law that prohibits the Secretary of State from filing charter documents for a business with a name that so closely resembles the name of another business organized or qualified to do business

CHOICE OF NAME

in that state as to tend to deceive the public. Approval of a name by the Secretary of State does not imply anything other than that the proposed name has passed this statutory test.

A promising start-up business may find its business plan abruptly derailed when it receives a demand to change its name or face an injunction and penalties for trademark infringement. The business owner can avoid this problem by understanding the fundamentals of trademark law.

Trademarks and Trade Names

Trademark protection is based on a public policy determination that consumers will benefit if they can associate a particular name or mark with the person or entity that is the source of the good or service sold in connection with the name or mark. Registration or state reservation of a corporate trade name does not confer trademark rights in that mark, the first or "senior" user of a mark or name is considered the owner of that mark even if someone else has been the first to apply to register or actually register the mark.

According to basic state and federal trademark law, trademark rights are acquired by using a mark on a product and selling that product or by displaying a mark in connection with the advertisement of services. The scope of rights acquired by simple use of a mark will vary depending upon the extent to which the mark is used. For example, if a mark is used nationwide, the rights acquired in it (barring the existence if prior conflicting owners) will also be nationwide. On the other hand, use of a mark solely in a single state may result in rights only in that single state. It is possible, however to reserve nationwide rights in a mark prior to its actual use by filing an "intent-to-use" application with the USPTO. Actual use of a reserved mark must follow in order to secure the ownership rights.

Therefore, the fact that the California Secretary of State does not object to the use of a particular name as the name of a corporation does not necessarily mean that other people or entities are not already using the proposed name in connection with goods or services. If this is true, it is possible that such party would be able to prevent the California corporation from causing "confusion" in the marketplace by using the proposed name. For that reason, if it is important that the corporate name also be used as a trademark or trade name, you should have a search conducted of the existing marks in your proposed area of activity in order to determine how protectable a particular name or mark will be prior to its adoption. Legal counsel can assist you in arranging such search.

BUSINESS STRUCTURES AND INCORPORATION

Once it seems clear that no conflicts exist and the name or mark is adopted, there are various legal and administrative procedures that can be followed in order to maximize the level of protection that such name or mark will receive.

For a comprehensive glance on trademarks, including sample filings, we refer you to our book, *Trademark Protection and Prosecution* by Ann Carrington from our how-to and do-it-yourself series.

CHAPTER 3

CHOICE OF BUSINESS ENTITY

By carefully considering the forms of business entities that are available and then intelligently choosing an appropriate one, the business owner can reduce exposure to liabilities, save taxes and launch the business in a form capable of being financed and conducted efficiently. The sooner a choice is made, the more flexibility and wider selection the business owner will have. In addition, formalizing the business helps prevent misunderstandings among the participants by defining their ownership, roles and duties in the business. The primary considerations in the choice of business entity include:

- ❖ How to protect the business owner's personal assets from liabilities of the business.

- ❖ Tax strategies such as maximizing the tax benefits of start-up losses, avoiding double (or even triple) taxation, and converting ordinary income into long term capital gain, which is taxed at lower rates.

- ❖ Selecting an entity that will be attractive to investors and lenders.

- ❖ Availability of attractive equity incentives for employees and other service providers.

- ❖ Cost (start-up and ongoing).

This chapter first describes each of the principal business forms, and then explores the considerations and strategies in making an appropriate selection. A brief discussion of conducting business in other states, local licenses, and insurance follows.

A business may be conducted as a corporation, a general or limited partnership, a limited liability company or a sole proprietorship. Each state has its own laws under which businesses may organize and operate. A corporation is a distinct legal entity owned by its shareholders and managed by a board of directors. A partnership is a separate entity for some purposes but for other purposes is treated as a group of individual partners; it does not pay taxes upon its activities; instead, its partners based upon their respective interests in its profits pay taxes upon its activities. The LLC is one of the newest forms of business organization and attempts to combine the best attributes of the corporation and the partnership; if properly structured, the LLC is taxed the same as a partnership. A sole proprietorship is a business owned by one person and has little legal significance separate from its owners. Nevertheless, the sole proprietorship is probably the most prevalent form of business because of the large number of family businesses in the United States.

Most large business organizations operate as corporations, despite the tax incentives to utilize the partnership or LLC form of doing business. The principal attractions to the corporate form are the limited liability it provides to its shareholders, its familiarity and well-understood governance laws, its permanence and the ability to transfer corporate stock more easily than partnership or LLC interests (particularly in the public securities markets). In addition, many venture capital and other investment funds are unable to invest in partnerships and LLCs because their major investors are pension and profit sharing trusts and other tax-exempt entities that are subject to certain tax restrictions. The corporation is also the most familiar business entity and is governed by the most highly developed laws. However, partnerships, proprietorships and increasingly, LLCs are also widely used for smaller businesses and where tax and other considerations warrant.

Corporations

A corporation is a distinct legal entity owned by its shareholders. Unlike a partnership, a corporation may be owned by a single person who may (but need not) be the corporation's sole director and serve as any required officer. The shareholders elect the corporation's board of directors but are not otherwise active as such in the management of the corporation. The board of directors is responsible for the major corporate decisions. Day-to-day management is carried on by the corporation's officers who are appointed by, and serve at the pleasure of the board of directors.

A corporation becomes a legal entity upon the filing of its Articles of Incorporation, which in some states is known as the Certificate of Incorporation. The Articles of Incorporation is usually required to be filed with

CHOICE OF BUSINESS ENTITY

the Secretary of State's office. Items typically included in the Articles of Incorporation are a brief description of the purpose of the business, the name and address of the agent for service of process (the person to whom the state and the courts will direct papers and summonses), the capital structure of the corporation, indemnification of directors, officers, employees and other agents and limiting the liability of directors with respect to certain matters. A corporation has an unlimited life so that it is not terminated or changed on the death of a shareholder or other change in its ownership. Instead, shares are transferred upon a shareholder's death to the shareholder's heirs.

A corporation also has Bylaws which usually set forth the rules and procedures governing the management of the corporation's business and the conduct of its corporate affairs, most of which are controlled by the corporation's laws of the state of incorporation.

At the corporation's organizational meeting, which can occur as soon as the Articles of Incorporation have been filed, the incorporator named in the Articles of Incorporation appoints the first directors. The board of directors then generally elects officers, authorizes the issuance of stock to founders, establishes a bank account, and authorizes the payment of incorporation expenses. In addition, at the first meeting the board may adopt a standard form of proprietary information agreement for use by employees and consultants, a form of restricted stock purchase agreement (which typically imposes "vesting" and rights of first refusal on employee stock), an employee stock purchase and/or stock option plan, selects the fiscal year of the corporation and determines whether to elect to be taxed as an S corporation.

A closely held or closed corporation's charter documents (i.e., the Articles of Incorporation, Bylaws and organizational minutes) are largely boiler-plate and "canned" and are readily available for business owners who desire to incorporate without hiring an attorney. However, because this documentation is usually straightforward, experienced legal counsel can prepare the charter documents inexpensively. More importantly, experienced counsel's real value is less in preparing the basic documentation and more in the advice he/she can provide on choosing an appropriate capital structure, transferring assets to the corporation in the most tax efficient manner, recommending appropriate equity incentive programs, and generally avoiding pitfalls.

Unless a corporation elects to be taxed as an S corporation, it is taxed as a separate legal entity. Under current federal income tax law, a corporation is taxed on its net income (gross income less allowable deductions) at rates ranging from 15% to 35%. Property (other than money) contributed to a corporation will be subject to tax unless the person (or group of persons) contributing the property own at least 80% of the corporation. Money (or other property) distributed by a corporation to its shareholders is subject to tax again when distributed to the shareholders, with the shareholders paying that tax.

Preserving Limited Liability

The proper operation of a corporation limits the liability of the shareholders because the creditors of the corporation cannot usually reach the shareholders to satisfy the corporation's obligations. However, under the "alter ego" doctrine a court may disregard the corporate entity and hold the shareholders personally liable for the corporation's obligations, if the shareholders use the corporation to perpetuate a fraud or promote injustice. In determining whether to "pierce the corporate veil" and make the shareholders directly liable for the corporation's obligations, a court will examine many factors, such as: (i) was the corporation undercapitalized, (ii) were corporate assets used for personal reasons, (iii) were corporate assets commingled with personal assets, (iv) were the corporate and personal books kept separately, and (v) were corporate actions properly authorized by the board of directors of the shareholders.

To preserve limited liability for its shareholders, the corporation should observe at least the following procedures: (1) obtain and record shareholder and board authorization for corporate actions (an annual shareholders' meeting and regular board meetings should be conducted and accurate minutes should be prepared and maintained in the corporate records); (2) keep corporate funds separate from personal funds; (3) maintain complete and proper records for the corporation separate from personal records; (4) make it clear in all contracts with others that they are dealing with the corporation, and sign all contracts in the following manner:

> [NAME OF CORPORATION]
> By: _____
> [Name and Title]

(v) maintain an arms-length relationship between the corporation and any principal shareholder; for transactions with any of the directors or principal shareholders, or entities they have an interest in, have the board, without the vote of the interested directors, approve the transaction after all the facts material to the transaction are disclosed; and (vi) start the business with an amount of equity sufficient in light of the future capital needs of the business.

CHOICE OF BUSINESS ENTITY

Incorporating in Delaware or another State

Prior to incorporation, a business may wish to consider the relative advantages and disadvantages of incorporating in Delaware. Delaware is chosen by many larger companies that are not based in that state because of its well-developed body of corporate law which can, in certain instances; increase the power of management of the majority shareholders with respect to the minority. The choice of state of incorporation other than the state of the principal place of business usually results in somewhat greater taxes and other costs because of the need to comply with certain tax and regulatory requirements in both states. In addition, the selection of another state of incorporation may not provide the expected governance benefits, because some states subject a corporation to most of the significant limitations of the local corporation's law.

S Corporation

The Internal Revenue Code permits certain shareholders to operate as a corporation but be taxed in general without incurring corporate income tax. Such corporations, known as S corporations, generally do not pay federal income tax but pass the tax liability for their profits through to their shareholders. Consequently, profits earned by an S corporation will be taxed only once. Similarly, losses of an S corporation flow through to the shareholders and may be deducted by the shareholders on their individual tax returns (subject to certain significant limitations). Profits and losses are required to be allocated based on share ownership. The shareholders must include the profits as income when earned by the S corporation, (whether or not any amounts are distributed to shareholders). A distribution of earnings by an S corporation to its shareholders is generally not taxed a second time. In contrast, a similar distribution by a corporation other than an S corporation will be taxed twice; the C corporation must pay federal corporate income tax on profits when earned and the shareholders must treat the distribution as a dividend subject to tax.

Shareholders generally elect S corporation status when the corporation is profitable and distributes substantially all of its profits to the shareholders, or when the corporation incurs losses, and the shareholders wish to utilize the loss deductions on their personal income tax returns. Because the overall maximum individual income tax rate is higher (39.6%) than the corporate income tax rate (35%), the S corporation may not be the entity of choice if the corporation is profitable and expects to accumulate its earnings with a view to a public offering or sale of the business rather than distributing the earnings currently.

BUSINESS STRUCTURES AND INCORPORATION

There are substantial limitations upon the availability of the S corporation election and the allocation and deduction of S corporation losses by its shareholders. To qualify for S corporation status, a corporation must satisfy the following requirements:

- ❖ The corporation must have no more than 75 shareholders, all of whom are individuals, certain tax exempt organizations, qualifying trusts, or estates, and none of whom are nonresident aliens.

- ❖ The corporation must have only one class of stock (although options and differences in voting rights are generally permitted).

- ❖ The corporation may generally not own 80% or more of any other corporation unless special requirements are satisfied.

The limitation on eligible S corporation shareholders will prevent any business that intends to raise equity capital from venture capital funds, corporations or other institutional investors from qualifying as an S corporation. In addition, the requirement that an S corporation can have only one class of stock eliminates the technique most widely used by businesses that desire to issue inexpensively priced "founders stock" to service providers. Most corporations that raise money from outside investors issue two classes of stock: convertible preferred stock to the investors and common stock to the employees. The common stock is typically issued at a small fraction of the price of the preferred stock because it lacks the liquidation, dividend, voting and other preferences that the preferred stock possesses. Since an S corporation can only issue common stock, it must issue the stock to employees at the same price paid by the investors (unless sold to the founders well in advance of the sale to the investors) if the employees are to avoid being taxed on their receipt of their shares.

Accordingly, the S corporation is most commonly used for family or other closely owned businesses that obtain capital from their individual shareholders and/or debt from outside sources and do not provide equity incentives to their employees on any significant scale.

A qualified corporation may elect to be taxed as an S corporation by filing Form 2553 with the Internal Revenue Service, together with the consent of all the shareholders. This election must be filed on or before the fifteenth day of the third month of the taxable year of the corporation for which S corporation status is to be effective or at any time during the preceding taxable year. If a corporation does not meet all of the S corporation requirements each day of the year, the election will not be effective until the following year.

In other words, an S corporation is the same as any other corporation except for the manner in which it is taxed.

Partnerships

A partnership is a business carried on by at least two persons. For some purposes a partnership is treated as a distinct legal entity separate from its partners. For example, a partnership can sue and be sued, can own property in its own name, and a creditor of a partner must proceed against a partner's interest in the partnership rather than directly against the assets of the partnership. For other purposes, a partnership is treated as an aggregate of its individual partners. For example, a partnership dissolves on the death of any partner (but as discussed below, a partnership need not terminate as the result of such an event).

A partnership may be a general partnership or limited partnership. In a general partnership, each partner is a general partner and has unlimited liability for the debts of the partnership and has the power to incur obligations on behalf of the partnership within the scope of the partnership's business. As a result of this mutual agency principle, great care must be exercised in the selection of general partners. A limited partnership has one or more general partners (each of whom has the same liability and same power as a general partner in a general partnership) and one or more limited partners (whose liability is limited to the amount of its capital commitment and who must not participate in the control of the partnership or it will be treated as a general partner). Some liability concerns (such as potential claims for personal injuries or resulting from errors or omissions) can be alleviated through insurance.

Although each state has a general partnership and limited partnership act (many of which are patterned on uniform acts), the partners may generally establish their own business arrangements among themselves in the partnership agreement and override most provisions in partnership acts both in terms of how a partnership is managed and how profits and losses are allocated and distributed.

Unlike a corporation, a partnership will "dissolve" on the death or withdrawal of a partner. However, a partnership agreement can (and should) provide for alternatives to liquidation after dissolution. For example, the partnership agreement can provide for the buyout of a deceased or withdrawn partner, the election of a new general partner, and the continuation of the business of the partnership by the remaining partners. In a limited partnership, the death of a limited partner typically does not result in the liquidation of the partnership –

BUSINESS STRUCTURES AND INCORPORATION

the limited partnership interest can be passed on to the deceased limited partner's heirs.

Although partnerships require few legal formalities (not even a partnership agreement, written or oral is required for a general partnership; a limited partnership requires a filing with the Secretary of State and a written partnership agreement). For the protection of the parties, a detailed written partnership agreement is strongly suggested. As a practical matter, since a partnership is largely governed by the partnership agreement which will vary significantly with each partnership, there is more expense involved in forming a partnership than a corporation, whose governance is largely controlled by statute. Boilerplate forms should be avoided.

A key attraction of the partnership is that it pays no income tax. Income or loss flows through to each partner and is reported on each partner's individual return. Unlike an S corporation which allocates income or loss based on stock ownership, a partnership can allocate income and loss flexibly. For example, income can be allocated differently than losses. In a partnership where one partner contributes services and another contributes money, the tax losses that are generated from the expenditure of the funds contributed by the cash partner can all be allocated to the cash partner. In addition, allocations can provide for preferred returns and can change over time or as higher profit levels are achieved.

Even though partnership losses flow through to the partners based on the loss sharing arrangements in the partner agreement, there are a number of limitations that restrict the ability of a partner to deduct these losses on its personal tax return. For example, since 1986, the passive loss restrictions prevent a partner (or shareholder in an S corporation) from deducting passive losses against most income. A partner's losses from a partnership are passive losses unless the partner materially participates in the partnership's business. A limited partner will rarely be able to treat partnership losses as other than passive. Other tax limitations prevent a partner from deducting losses which exceed its tax basis or, in certain circumstances, are attributable to nonrecourse debt.

Property can generally be contributed to and distributed from a partnership without being subject to tax. This enables a partnership to convert into a corporation without tax if the incorporation is properly structured whereas the conversion of a corporation into a partnership will generally result in two levels of tax – a corporate tax and a shareholder tax.

A partnership is not particularly flexible in the sources of operating capital that are available to it. It is generally limited to capital contributed by partners and funds loaned by partners and outsiders. It is uncommon for a partnership to raise capital in public offering, in part because a publicly traded partnership is taxed as a corporation. Also, tax exempt entities (including venture capital partnerships with tax exempt entities as partners) will generally have tax difficulties in becoming a partner in a partnership that is carrying on a trade or business (as contrasted with being engaged in investment activities). Although a tax exempt organization is generally not subject to income tax, it is required to pay tax on "unrelated business income" which would include its share of any operating income of a business conducted as a partnership in which it is a partner. Most venture capital funds have tax exempt investors who required the venture capital fund to avoid incurring unrelated business income. Therefore, a business which expects to attract capital from a venture capital fund should not organize as a partnership (or LLC since a properly structured LLC is taxed the same as a partnership). Foreigners are generally disinclined to invest in a partnership (or LLC) that is carrying on an active business because their participation as a partner causes them to be treated as being engaged in a U.S. trade or business with the result that they are taxed in the U.S. on any income they recognize which is effectively connected with that trade or business.

Until recently, limited partnerships have been the entity of choice for activities such as investing in real estate or securities where flow through tax treatment is required. In addition to permitting profits and losses to flow through directly to the owners of the business, partnerships can distribute property in kind without the recognition of tax by the partnership or the partner. Many investment funds distribute highly appreciated securities to their partners after a liquidity event (e.g., an initial public offering or acquisition by a public company in a tax free reorganization) thereby allowing each partner to make an individual decision as to when to sell the securities it receives. Notwithstanding the widespread and longstanding use of limited partnerships, arrival of the LLC, which is discussed below, is resulting in many businesses that would have organized as a limited partnership organizing as an LLC in order to achieve limited liability for all members, even where they actively participate in the business.

Limited Liability Company

The limited liability company is a form of business organization which is rapidly gaining popularity in the U.S. All but a handful of states now have LLC acts which permit the organization and operation of a business as an LLC. A properly structured LLC offers its owners (referred to as "members") the pass-through federal tax treatment of a partnership, while also protecting members from personal liability for the obligations of the business. The members of the LLC have no personal liability for the obligations of the LLC (but, as is also true for corporate directors and officers, will still have personal liability for their individual acts and omissions in connection with the LLC's business).

For all practical purposes, an LLC operates as a limited partnership without the legal requirement of having a general partner who bears ultimate liability for the obligations of the partnership. An S corporation also has both the limited liability and most of the federal tax pass-through features found in the LLC, but ownership is limited to 75 shareholders, all of whom must be individuals, certain tax exempt organizations or qualifying trusts or estates and none of whom may be foreigners, and can have only one class of stock. An LLC has none of these restrictions. However, unlike a corporation, in a number of states an LLC must have at least two members.

An LLC has two principal charter documents. The first is a short (one to two pages) document filed with the Secretary of State which sets forth the name of the LLC, its address, its agent for service of process, term and whether it will be governed by the members or managers appointed by the members. This document is generally called the Articles of Organization (California).

The second charter document for an LLC is its Operating Agreement which is analogous to (and closely resembles) a partnership agreement. The Operating Agreement specifies how the LLC will be governed, the financial obligations of the members (for example, additional capital calls could be forbidden, voluntary or mandatory) and how profits, losses and distributions are shared. As with a partnership agreement, the Operating Agreement for an LLC will be tailored to suit the needs of each individual LLC, with the professional services expense for a specialized legal agreement. Again, boilerplate documents should be avoided.

The Internal Revenue Service recently issued regulations that generally allow limited liability companies and partnerships to be taxed as flow-through entities unless they elect to be taxed as corporations.

The LLC is not suitable for businesses financed by venture capital funds because of tax restrictions on the funds' tax-exempt partners. But an LLC can be very attractive for businesses financed by corporate investors and to a lesser extent (because of the passive-loss limitations) wealthy individuals. The LLC is the entity of choice for the start-up entity seeking to flow-through losses to its investors because (1) it offers the same complete liability protection to all its members as does a corporation; (2) it can have corporations and partnerships as members (unlike an S corporation) and is not subject to any of the other limitations that apply to S corporations; and (3) losses can be specially allocated entirely to the cash investors (in the S corporation losses are allocated to all the owners based on share ownership). In addition, the LLC can be incorporated tax-free at any time. For example, after the initial start-up losses have been allocated to the early round investors, the LLC could be incorporated to accommodate investment from a venture capital fund in a conventional preferred stock financing. Alternatively, incorporation could be deferred until a public offering.

Making the Selection Among the C Corporation, S Corporation, Partnership, Limited Partnership and Limited Liability Company

The two most critical factors in selecting the form of business entity are: (i) who the owners of the business will be and (ii) and how the earnings of the business will be returned to its owners.

Who Will Be the Owners?

If a business is owned by a few individuals, any of the above entities may be the appropriate business form and factors other than who the owners are will be determinative. The C corporation is usually the entity of choice if the business is going to be widely held for the following reasons:

- ❖ A corporation has unlimited life and free transferability of ownership. Although changes in its ownership resulting from transfers of stock (by a living shareholder or upon a shareholder's death) or the issuance of new shares (i.e., additional shares issued directly by the corporation) will affect the election of directors and therefore corporate management, the corporation's existence is not affected. On the other hand, free transferability of interests and unlimited life are more difficult to achieve in a partnership or LLC, and if provided for in a partnership or LLC, can adversely affect flow-through tax treatment.

- ❖ An S corporation is not suitable for a widely-held corporation because it can only have up to 75 shareholders all of whom must generally be individuals or eligible trusts for the benefit of individuals, and U.S. citizens or resident aliens.

- ❖ If the business is so widely-held that its ownership interests become publicly traded, the corporation is the entity of choice because the public markets are more receptive to offerings of corporate stock than

BUSINESS STRUCTURES AND INCORPORATION

partnership or LLC interests and because a publicly traded partnership or LLC will be taxed as a corporation (i.e., no flow-through tax treatment).

❖ If ownership interests in the business are going to be provided to employees, the C corporation will generally be the preferred entity for several reasons. First, stock ownership is easier to explain to employees than equity interests in partnerships and LLCs. Second, creating favorably priced equity incentives is easiest to accomplish in a C corporation because ownership can be held through various classes of stock. It is quite common for a corporation to issue preferred stock to investors and common stock to management and other employees. If properly structured, the common stock can be sold at a substantial discount from the preferred stock because of the special rights and preferences of the preferred stock.

For example, the preferred stock would usually have a liquidation preference equal to the price paid for the preferred stock. This preference amount must be paid if the corporation is sold or liquidated, before any funds can be paid to the holders of the common stock. The preferred stock would be convertible into common stock at the option of the holder and conversion would ordinarily occur in an upside situation where the company is successful and goes public or is sold.

Finally, the tax law provides for special "incentive" stock options where the option holder generally incurs no tax until the shares purchased on exercise of the options are sold. The gain that is ultimately recognized is taxed at the more favorable long term capital gain rates rather than as ordinary income. Incentive stock options are only available for corporations, not partnerships or LLCs. In the case of options that do not qualify as incentive stock options, the option holder recognizes ordinary income when the option is exercised in the amount of the difference between the exercise price of the option and the fair market value of the underlying stock as of the time the option is exercised.

❖ If the business raises capital from a venture capital fund, the business will usually be formed as a corporation because most venture capital funds raise money from tax exempt entities such as pension and profit sharing trusts, universities and other charitable organizations and these entities would incur taxable unrelated business taxable income if the venture fund invested in a flow-through entity such as a partnership or LLC.

CHOICE OF BUSINESS ENTITY

How Does the Business Expect to Return Its Profits to Its Owners?

A business can either distribute earnings currently to its owners or accumulate and reinvest the earnings with the goal of increasing the value of the business so that the business can either be taken public (so that the owners' equity can be sold in a stock market) or sold to another business for cash or marketable stock of the acquiring business. Current earnings are taxed as ordinary income whereas the gain on the sale of stock is taxed at the more favorable long term capital gain rates.

A tax flow-through entity such as a partnership, LLC or S corporation is the entity of choice for a business that intends to distribute earnings currently so that the earnings can be distributed without incurring a second level of tax. If a C corporation is used, earnings can be paid out without a second level of tax only if paid as salary or other reasonable compensation to shareholders who work for the business (because such compensation would be deductible by the corporation against its taxable income) thereby eliminating the corporate level tax on the earnings so distributed).

On the other hand, distributions of earnings by a corporation to its shareholders other than as compensation for services will not be deductible by the corporation and will be taxed as ordinary dividend income to its shareholders. Most small businesses which are not expected to grow into public companies and which have owners who do not work for the business (and therefore cannot receive tax deductible compensation) but who desire the distribution of the earnings of the business currently have a strong incentive to use a tax flow-through entity such as an S corporation, partnership or LLC.

- ❖ The income tax law provides an additional incentive to organize as a C corporation for the business that seeks to build long term value rather than the current distribution of earnings. Stock of a C corporation (but no other business entity including an S corporation) that qualifies as a Small Business Corporation issued after August of 1993 and which is held for at least five years, is generally eligible for a 50% capital gain deduction which reduces the effective tax rate to approximately 14% (taxpayers subject to the alternative minimum tax may incur a rate as high as 19.88%).

Conducting Business In Other States, Local Licenses, and Insurance

Before commencing operations in other states, the business should determine if such operations will require it to register as a foreign corporation, partnership or LLC in those states. Some states have significant penalties for failure to register properly. Even if it need not register as a foreign business entity, the business may be required to pay income and other taxes (including sales and use taxes) in such states for operating therein. If the business has employees located in other states, it may be subject to requirements with respect to withholding from employees' wages, workers' compensation insurance, and other regulatory requirements. If the business owns real or personal property in other states, it may be required to pay property taxes in such states.

State licensing is required for a wide variety of businesses and professions. Cities, counties, and other municipal agencies require local licenses. Since licensing requirements vary significantly among cities and counties, a business may wish to consider local licensing requirements and taxes before choosing a location for doing business.

New businesses should in most cases obtain insurance coverage for all anticipated contingencies; not only to protect the individual participants from personal liability but also to protect the assets and future retained earnings of the business. The coverage may include general liability insurance (including products liability), errors and omissions insurance for directors and officers, fire and casualty insurance, business interruption insurance, key-personnel life and disability insurance, insurance to fund share purchases in the event of the death or disability of a shareholder, and workers' compensation insurance.

CHAPTER 4

SOLE PROPRIETORSHIPS

A sole proprietorship is set up to allow an individual to own and operate a business by him or herself. A sole proprietor has total control, receives all profits from and is responsible for taxes and liabilities of the business. If a sole proprietorship is formed with a name other than the individual's name (e.g., John Smith Publishing), a fictitious business name statement must be filed with the county where the principal place of business is located. No formation documents are required to be filed with the Secretary of State. However, other state filings may be required depending on the type of business.

Sole Proprietorships Characteristics

A sole proprietorship is a form of business in which one person owns all of the assets of the business. The sole proprietorship generally does not exist as an entity apart from its owner, and so little formality is required to form it.

- ❖ Because a sole proprietorship is not an entity distinct from its owner, its owner is personally liable for the business's obligations.
- ❖ The business entity cannot continue beyond the life of the owner.
- ❖ Management is centralized (since there is only one owner), and the owner is free to transfer his interest in the sole proprietorship at will.
- ❖ All profits and losses from the business flow through directly to the owner.

Thus, if a person is interested is setting up a business with only one owner, desires little formality, is willing to risk personal assets, and wants to avoid double taxation; the sole proprietorship is worth considering as a business form.

General Sole Proprietorship Matters

Sole proprietorships are the most common form of business structure. Setting up a sole proprietorship takes minimal effort. It's also the simplest type of business structure to operate. At a minimum, you will want to take the following steps before opening your business:

- ❖ Obtain business licenses and permits for your sole proprietorship from federal, state, and local governments.

- ❖ Use the Small Business Administration as a resource.

- ❖ Make sure that you have the right to use your chosen business name by checking with the county and state governments as well as the USPTO. This way you can verify that the name has not already been taken.

- ❖ File a Fictitious Business Name Statement by registering the name of your business in the county or counties where you do business.

- ❖ Apply for a federal employer identification number with the Internal Revenue Service using Form SS-4.

- ❖ Apply for a state employer identification number with the Department of Revenue in the state in which you are forming your sole proprietorship. You need to have this number if you pay wages to employees, pay excise tax or have a Keogh retirement plan.

- ❖ Consider getting business insurance to protect your personal assets.

A sole proprietorship offers the least amount of complication in terms of start-up requirements as compared to other types of business structures (e.g., partnerships, corporations, limited liability companies, etc.). But, to ensure that your new sole proprietorship covers all legal bases and has the best chance for success before opening your business, you may wish to consult an experienced business attorney.

SOLE PROPRIETORSHIPS

SAMPLE
FEDERAL EMPLOYER IDENTIFICATION NUMBER
FORM SS-4

BUSINESS STRUCTURES AND INCORPORATION

SAMPLE
STATE EMPLOYER IDENTIFICATION NUMBER
FORM DE-1

SOLE PROPRIETORSHIPS

Business Operations and Administration

No matter what type of business you plan to start, all businesses require specific operating business procedures and requirements. Some will be government related and others will be just common sense. In addition to everyday business operations, there will be initial business start-up operations, most of them one-time requirements that need to be taken in consideration.

Select a Business Structure Checklist

- ✓ Sole Proprietorship
- ✓ Partnership (general partnership or limited partnership)
- ✓ Corporation (C corporation or S corporation)
- ✓ Limited Liability Company

Register with the Tax Authorities Checklist

- ✓ Internal Revenue Service (federal employer identification number)
- ✓ Employment Development Department (state employer identification number)
- ✓ State Board of Equalization (seller's permit)
- ✓ Business License
- ✓ Tax Calendar

Accounting and Bookkeeping Checklist

- ✓ Chart of Accounts
- ✓ Cash or Accrual Accounting
- ✓ Accounting Records and Recordkeeping
- ✓ Computers (to automate or not to automate)
- ✓ Internal Control

Payroll Taxes Checklist

- ✓ Available Publications
- ✓ Payroll Tax Rates
- ✓ State Unemployment Insurance
- ✓ Supplemental Wages
- ✓ Independent Contractors
- ✓ Summary of Payroll Tax Deposit Requirements
- ✓ Limitations on Standard Mileage Rate Method
- ✓ Annual Lease Value Table
- ✓ Other Tax Requirements

BUSINESS STRUCTURES AND INCORPORATION

Select a Year-End Checklist

- ✓ Which Month to Choose
- ✓ How to Make the Election
- ✓ Changing the Year-end

Income Taxes Checklist

- ✓ Income Tax Forms (federal, state and local income taxes)
- ✓ Estimates (federal, state and payroll taxes)
- ✓ Due Dates (corporate tax returns are due March 15th)
- ✓ Extensions
- ✓ First Corporate Return
- ✓ Tax Planning
- ✓ State Taxes (sales and use taxes)

Cash Planning and Forecasting Checklist

- ✓ Starting the Analysis
- ✓ Cash Collections
- ✓ Disbursements

Obtaining Credit and Financing Your Business Checklist

- ✓ How Do You Get the Money
- ✓ Financing Alternatives
- ✓ Debt Financing Sources
- ✓ Equity Financing Sources

Insurance Checklist

- ✓ Policies (general liability, products liability, errors and omissions, directors and officers, fire and casualty, business interruption, key-personnel life and disability, workers' compensation, etc.)
- ✓ Insurance to fund share purchases in the event of the death or disability of a shareholder.

Choose Professional Advisors Checklist

- ✓ Attorneys
- ✓ Certified Public Accountants

Business Plan

Every business can benefit from the preparation of a carefully written business plan. The purpose of the business plan is to produce a document that defines the mission, goals, strategies, initiatives, and critical action plans for each area of the company centered on market, product, organizational, and financial activities. The primary goal of the business plan is to ensure that the company's management team has a meaningful tool to enhance its capability to maximize the effectiveness of the planning, execution, and control processes and thereby maximize company performance. A secondary goal is to provide a tool for establishing annual incentive programs for management.

There are four key planning stages in the business planning process that collectively guide and govern a company's business plan:

- ❖ Primary objectives and incentives (mission statement, market goals, product goals, organization goals, and financial goals).
- ❖ Strategy development for marketing and product plans.
- ❖ Target setting.
- ❖ Budget planning.

Primary Objectives and Incentives

Primary objectives provide a model for the level of desired performance. They state the most important standards and activities that need to be achieved, as well as provide the criteria for measuring them.

Mission Statement

For example, be the world's leading provider of Internet trust services – including authentication, validation, payment, registry and registrar – that enable websites, enterprises and e-commerce service providers to conduct trusted and secure electronic commerce and communications over IP networks while: (a) Achieving and maintaining an above average return on investment for shareholders measured in terms of return on equity, earnings per share, revenue growth, and operating profit. (b) Maintaining or achieving the number one or second position in addressed market segments in terms of market share, customer satisfaction, revenue generation, product margin, product functionality, and technological leadership. (c) Treating all employees with respect and rewarding both group and individual performance that exceeds commitments and expectations.

Market Goals

For example, achieve or maintain the number one or second position in terms of market share in each addressed market segment. Utilize multiple distribution channels thereby maximizing the effectiveness of reaching and providing a high level of satisfaction to targeted customers while minimizing the dependence on a single channel. Maximize recognition of the company's brand and product offering by achieving or maintain a high profile in key industry and business events, customer events, and appropriate publications.

Product Goals

For example, ensure that all products offered work effectively together and share elements of existing core functionality. Achieve or maintain product technological, usability and functionality leadership for each product offered in terms of customer, competitive, and addressed market segment comparisons. Maintain high quality standards for all products offered as measured by the number releases and bug fixes on an individual product basis. Meet key milestones agreed upon and committed to in product road map releases throughout the year. Develop and continually update a list of key characters for each product that positions the product in the customers mind, has a tool that will enhance productivity, and or improve the security of their operations. Continue to provide a high level of customer support as determined by market segment and distribution channel requirements and measured by addressed market segment and customer standard.

Organization Goals

For example, ensure that key management controls are effectively utilized throughout the year, including: standard operating policies and procedures, annual budget, monthly financial report, and quarterly operations review. Ensure that no more than three layers of management exist between the chief executive officer and customers and employees. Ensure that management span of control is between one to two direct reports throughout the company. Achieve and or maintain an employee satisfaction level of 80% or higher as measured by annual review. Conduct quarterly employee communication meetings that clearly highlight the company's achievements and discuss challenges and update the company's internal web page with relevant information on an as needed basis. Utilize performance management techniques including individual goals as a primary tool to maximize employee performance throughout all levels in the organization. Provide training programs that enhances employee's capability to keep their skills current and the company's capability to continuously improve productivity.

Financial Goals

For example, achieve at least 80% annual revenue growth. Achieve at least 80% operating profit margin. Achieve at least 80% return on equity. Achieve continuous financial performance improvement on a year over year basis. Maximize working capital performance by maintaining days' sales outstanding at thirty days or below on average while averaging thirty days accounts payable outstanding. Ensure effective cash management by preventing build-up of cash in excess of working capital and capital expenditure requirements or cash earmarked for acquisitions. Maintain a proactive relationship with the investment community by conducting detailed updates with each major investor and financial analyst on a quarterly basis. Develop and utilize key performance indicators for each functional activity in the company to maximize performance, measure productivity, and achieve continuous improvement.

Market Segment Plan

For example, describe the target market: Who are you trying to reach? What is your company's strategic imperative in this segment (new, defend, or extend)? What is the key company asset to leverage in this segment? How big is the market? Substantiate by published research or product marketing estimates (user, revenue, and units). What are the market growth dynamics over the plan year (user, revenue, and units)? What's causing the growth, or what are reasons for slow growth (technology changes, new market entrants, or displacement of legacy system/formats)? What is the company's position in this market (revenue, units, revenue share, and unit share)?

What channel does the company use to reach this market? How must you drive that mix in the future? What is the company's positioning in this market? How are you differentiated from competitors? Who are the major players in this space? How concentrated is activity in the market? What other competitors are in adjacent markets that may enter this space?

Where are the company's strengths and weaknesses relative to each major competitor or potential competitor (technology, channels, service and support offerings, brand image and customer awareness, partnerships, or financial wherewithal)? What is your company's competitive advantage in this segment? What are the key critical action items required to achieve the planned company results (product delivery milestones, technology or product deliveries from other company groups, field operations deliverables, marketing initiatives, or partnering requirements)?

Product Development Plan

For example, describe the target market: Who are you trying to reach? What is your company's strategic imperative in this product category (hold share, gain share, or block competitors)? What is the key company asset to leverage in this product category? How big is the category? Substantiate by published research or product marketing estimates (user, revenue, or units)? What are the product category growth dynamics over the plan year (user, revenue, and units)? What's causing the growth, or what are reasons for slow growth (technology changes, new market entrants, or displacement of legacy system/formats)? What is the company's position in this product category (revenue, units, revenue share, and unit share)?

What channel does the company use to reach this customer? How must you drive that mix in the future? What is the company's positioning in this market? How are you differentiated from competitors? What are the major competing products in this space? What are the market shares and share trends in the category? What other competitors are in adjacent markets that may enter this space? How is the category evolving? Who's driving the evolution?

Where are the company's strengths and weaknesses relative to each major competitor or potential competitor (technology, features, service and support offerings, channels, brand image and customer awareness, partnerships, or financial wherewithal)? What is your company's competitive advantage in this product category? What are the key critical action items required to achieve the planned company results (product delivery milestones, technology or product deliveries from other company groups, field operations deliverables, marketing initiatives, or partnering requirements)?

What is the product definition (required functionality, current functionality, Internet technology required, external technology required, integrated with third party products and localization)? What is the pricing strategy for this product category?

Target Setting

Once the company's strategies are agreed upon, they must be translated into specific targets. Revenue by product, contribution margin by product and operating expense by functional area targets should be established for the plan year. Targets are the way senior management communicates what it expects to achieve. General principles that should be used when setting targets include: targets based on the company's overall business plan and targets tailored to each functional area. Each functional area should be responsible to invest its resources to yield the highest possible return on its resource allocation.

SOLE PROPRIETORSHIPS

Budget Planning

The financial plan should accomplish three things: (1) the financial plan pulls together the strategic, tactical, and target elements of the company; (2) the financial plan develops the pro-forma profitability of the company; and (3) the financial plan is completed at a very detailed level and consolidated at a corporate level so that management throughout the company can have continuous access to basis for which performance will be measured for their respective area of responsibility.

The heart of this planning stage is the work done by individual managers to plan activities of their own groups. Product release plans, sales plans, and market plans all fall into this category. With the strategic direction and target finalized, managers can determine the specifics to accomplish their department role and the company overall target.

Files should be distributed to each of the department manager heads for budget completion. These files should be pre-loaded with salary, focal increases, depreciation and other defined rates.

For a comprehensive book on business plans, operating plans, including sample business plans, proposals, letters of intent, resources, and much more, we recommend Writing Winning Business Plans and Investor Presentations *by Ann Carrington from our how-to and do-it-yourself series.*

CHAPTER 5

PARTNERSHIPS

A partnership is similar to a sole proprietorship except that there are at least two owners of partnership. Little formality is required to form a partnership – just an intention to carry on as co-owners a business for profit.

Partnership Characteristics

Partnerships may have a few entity characteristics (e.g., property may be held in the name of the partnership; suits can be maintained in the name of the partnership), but generally they are not treated as legal entities.

- ❖ Partners are personally liable for obligations of the partnership.
- ❖ Management generally is not centralized, but rather is spread among the partners.
- ❖ Ownership interests of partners cannot be transferred without the consent of the other partners.
- ❖ A partnership generally does not continue beyond the life of its owners (although the partners can agree to allow remaining partners to continue the partnership business after a partner leaves).
- ❖ Finally, as indicated above, profits and losses of a partnership flow through directly to the partners.

Thus, if a person is interested in forming a business with more than one owner, does not want to bother with a lot of formality, does not mind sharing management rights with co-owners, does not mind putting personal assets at risk, etc., a partnership might be an appropriate entity to form.

PARTNERSHIPS

Limited Partnerships

A limited partnership is a partnership that provides for limited liability of some investors (called limited partners), but otherwise is similar to other partnerships. A limited partnership can be formed only by compliance with the limited partnership statute. There must be at least one general partner, who has full personal liability for partnership debts and has most management rights. Thus, this form of business entity offers limited liability to most investors, centralized management (i.e., management by the general partner(s) rather than by all owners), and the flow through tax advantages of a partnership, without the 75-investor limit of an S corporation. Its downfall, however, is that at least one person must be personally liable for the business's debts.

Limited Partnership Agreement

The following agreement is not intended to be comprehensive or an absolute statement of the governing law. This agreement is not legal advice. It does not analyze any specific fact patterns from any parties but rather discusses broadly points of law, which may or may not be the most accurate, according to current case law interpretation or even case law interpretation that is very in-depth on very narrowly-presented issues. Sound legal advice arises from interaction between client and attorney in a question-and-answer dialogue where facts are provided by a client as the attorney probes for issues and then conducts appropriate research if need be to ascertain the applicable law. Anyone seeking specific advice to specific legal questions should present their facts to an attorney.

[ACRONYM OF SUCCESS] VENTURES, L.P.
LIMITED PARTNERSHIP AGREEMENT

This Agreement is made and entered into as of the ___ day of _____, 2012, by and among **ANC Management, L.L.C.**, a Delaware limited liability company (the "*General Partner*"), and each of the entities identified as a limited partner on Exhibit A (the "*Limited Partners*"), who hereby form **[Acronym of Success] Ventures, L.P.** (the "*Partnership*"), pursuant to the provisions of the Delaware Revised Uniform Limited Partnership Act (the "Act"), as follows:

ARTICLE 1
NAME, PURPOSE AND OFFICES OF PARTNERSHIP

1.1 **Name.** The name of the Partnership is [Acronym of Success] Ventures, L.P. The affairs of the Partnership shall be conducted under the Partnership name.

1.2 **Purpose.** The primary purpose of the Partnership is to make venture capital type investments principally by investing in equity or equity-oriented securities of privately-held corporations in information technology, Internet, software, communications, new media, multi-media, entertainment, telecommunications infrastructure, wireless applications and related industries. The general purposes of the Partnership are to buy, sell, hold, and otherwise invest in securities of every kind and nature and rights and options with respect thereto, including, without limitation, stock, notes, bonds and debentures; to exercise all rights, powers, privileges, and other incidents of ownership or possession with respect to securities held or owned by the Partnership; to enter into, make, and perform all contracts and other undertakings; and to engage in all activities and transactions as may be necessary, advisable, or desirable to carry out the foregoing.

    1.3   **Principal Office.** The principal office of the Partnership shall be _____, or such other place or places as the General Partner may from time to time designate. The General Partner shall provide the Limited Partners with prompt written notice of any change in the location of the Partnership's principal office.

    1.4   **Registered Agent and Office.** The name of the registered agent for service of process of the Partnership and the address of the Partnership's registered office in the State of Delaware shall be _____, or such other agent or office in the State of Delaware as the General Partner may from time to time designate.

ARTICLE 2
TERM OF PARTNERSHIP

    2.1   **Term.** The term of the Partnership shall commence upon the date of the filing of the Certificate of Limited Partnership of the Partnership with the office of the Secretary of the State of the State of Delaware and shall continue until _____, 20__, unless extended pursuant to paragraph 10.1 or sooner dissolved as provided in paragraph 10.2.

    2.2   **Events Affecting a Member of the General Partner.** Except as specifically provided in paragraph 10.2, the bankruptcy, liquidation, dissolution, reorganization, merger, sale of all or substantially all the stock or assets of, or other change in ownership or nature of the General Partner shall not dissolve the Partnership.

    2.3   **Events Affecting a Limited Partner of the Partnership.** The bankruptcy, liquidation, dissolution, reorganization, merger, sale of all or substantially all the stock or assets of, or other change in the ownership or nature of a Limited Partner shall not dissolve the Partnership.

    2.4   **Events Affecting the General Partner.** Except as specifically provided in paragraph 10.2, the bankruptcy, liquidation, dissolution, reorganization, merger, sale of all or substantially all the stock or assets of, or other change in ownership or nature of the General Partner shall not dissolve the Partnership.

ARTICLE 3
NAME AND ADMISSION OF PARTNERS

    3.1   **Name and Address.** The name and address of the General Partner and each Limited Partner (hereinafter the General Partner and the Limited Partners shall be referred to collectively as the "***Partners***" and each individually as a "***Partner***"), the amount of such Partner's Capital Commitment to the Partnership, and such Partner's Partnership Percentage are set form on Exhibit A hereto. The General Partners shall cause Exhibit A to be amended from time to time to reflect the admission of any new Partner, the withdrawal or substitution of a Partner, the transfer of interests among Partners, receipt by the Partnership of notice of any change of address of a Partner, or the change in the Partner's Capital Commitment or Partnership Percentage. An amended Exhibit A shall supersede any

PARTNERSHIPS

prior Exhibit A and become a part of this Agreement. A copy of the most recent amended Exhibit A shall be kept on file at the principal office of the Partnership.

3.2 Admission of Additional Partners.

(a)   Except as provided in paragraphs 3.2(b), 4.5(b)(ii)(2), 4.5(f) and 9.6, an additional person may be admitted as a Partner only with the consent of the General Partner and a Majority in Interest of the Limited Partners.

(b)   Notwithstanding subparagraph (a) above, additional persons may be admitted as Limited Partners with the consent of only the General Partner prior to the date six (6) months after the commencement of the Partnership, *provided* that, after such admission, the aggregate amount of capital committed for contribution by the Limited Partners, when combined with the capital commitments of any investors in any Sid by Side Fund, does not exceed _____ ($____).

(c)   Each additional person admitted as a Partner shall (i) execute and deliver to the Partnership a counterpart of this Agreement or otherwise take such actions as the General Partner shall deem appropriate in order for such additional Partner to become bound by the terms of this Agreement, and (ii) contribute that portion of its Capital Commitment which is equal to the portion of their respective Capital Commitments contributed to date by the Partnership's previously admitted Partners.

ARTICLE 4
CAPITAL ACCOUNTS, CAPITAL CONTRIBUTIONS,
AND NONCONTRIBUTING PARTNERS

4.1 Capital Accounts.
An individual Capital Account shall be maintained for each Partner.

4.2 Capital Contributions of the Limited Partners.

(a)   Each Limited Partner shall contribute capital to the Partnership upon fifteen (15) days' prior written notice; *provided* that: (a) each capital contribution shall be in accordance with Partnership Percentages, and (b) no Limited Partner shall be required to contribute any capital following the date six (6) years after the commencement of the Partnership except as may be necessary for (i) operational purposes, including payment of the management fee pursuant to Article 6, (ii) completion of transactions in process on such date, and (iii) follow-on investments in the Securities of issuers in which the Partnership already holds an interest as of the date of such proposed follow-on investment. Each capital contribution by any Limited Partner shall be made in cash.

(b)   Notwithstanding paragraph 4.2(a), no ERISA Partner (as defined in paragraph 13.1) or Governmental Plan Partner (as defined in paragraph 13.2) shall be required to contribute capital pursuant to this Agreement until such time as the Partnership shall have delivered a written notice ("***VCOC Notice***") reasonably satisfactory to each such Partner to the effect that either (i) the Partnership's first portfolio company investment qualifies, or will qualify upon its closing, as a "***venture capital investment***" within the meaning of the U.S. Department of Labor regulations ("***DOL Regulations***") such that the Partnership qualifies, as a "***venture capital operating company***" under applicable DOL Regulations, or (ii) less than twenty-five percent (25%) of the Partnership's limited partnership interests are held in the aggregate by "***benefit plan investors***", as that term is defined in the DOL Regulations. In the event that an ERISA Partner or Governmental Plan Partner has not received the VCOC Notice prior to the date on which any capital contribution would otherwise be due under paragraph 4.2(a), such Partner shall pay such capital contribution into an interest-bearing escrow account designated by the General Partner which meets the requirements for such accounts as set forth in the DOL Regulations. Upon delivery of the VCOC Notice, all amounts in such escrow account shall be delivered to the Partnership in fulfillment of the ERISA Partner's or Governmental Plan Partner's obligation under paragraph 4.2(a).

4.3 Capital Contributions of the General Partner. The General Partner shall contribute capital to the Partnership in an amount equal to one and one ninety-ninth percent (1 1/99%) of the amount contributed by the Limited Partners on each date on which any Limited Partner makes a contribution. Each capital contribution made by the General Partner shall be made in cash.

4.4 Acquisition of an Additional Interest by the General Partner. In the event that the General Partner acquires a Limited Partner's interest pursuant to the terms of this Agreement, the General Partner shall have two Partnership Percentages and two Capital Account balances for purposes of making Partnership allocations, as if such subsequently acquired interest were held by a separate entity which is a Limited Partner, although for all other purposes the General Partner shall have only one Capital Account.

4.5 Noncontributing Partners.

(a) The Partnership shall be entitled to enforce the obligations of each Limited Partner to make the contributions to capital set forth in paragraph 4.2, and the Partnership shall have all remedies available at law or in equity in the event any such contribution is not so made. If any legal proceedings relating to the failure of a Limited Partner to make such a contribution are commenced, such Limited Partner shall pay all costs and expenses incurred by the Partnership, including attorneys' fees, in connection with such proceedings.

(b) Additionally, should any Limited Partner fail to make any of the capital contributions required of it under paragraph 4.2 of this Agreement, such Partner shall be in default, and the General Partner may, in its sole discretion, elect to enforce the provisions of paragraphs 4.5(b)(i) and (ii) in connection with such a default.

(i) Should the General Partner, in its sole discretion, elect to exercise the provisions of this paragraph 4.5(b)(i), such defaulting Limited Partner shall pay the interest on the amount of the contribution to the Partnership then due at an interest rate equal to the floating commercial rate of interest publicly announced by Citibank (or its successors) as its prime rate (the "***Prime Rate***") plus four percent (4%) per annum, such interest to accrue from the date the contribution to the Partnership was required to be made pursuant to paragraph 4.2 hereof until the date the contribution is made by such defaulting Limited Partner. The accrued interest shall be paid by the defaulting Limited Partner to the partnership upon payment of such contribution. The accrued interest so paid shall not be treated as an additional contribution to the capital of the Partnership, but shall be deemed to be income to the Partnership. Until such time as the unpaid contribution and accrued interest thereon shall have been paid by the defaulting Limited Partner, the General Partner may elect to withhold any or all distributions to be made to such defaulting Limited Partner pursuant to Article 7 or Article 10.

(ii) Should the General Partner, in its sole discretion, elect to exercise the provisions fo this paragraph 4.5(b)(ii), and the default of such Limited Partner shall have continued for ten (10) or more days after notice by the General Partner to such Limited Partner of the default, the nondefaulting Limited Partners and the General

PARTNERSHIPS

Partner (the "***Optionees***") shall have the right and the option, but not the obligation, to acquire the Partnership interest of the defaulting Limited Partner (the "***Optionor***"), as follows:

(1) If the default continues for ten (10) or more days after notice of the default, the General Partner shall notify the Optionees of the default within twenty (20) days of the expiration of the aforesaid ten (10) day notice period. Such notice shall advise each Optionee of the portion and the price of the Optionor's interest available to it. The portion available to each Optionee shall be that portion of the Optionor's interest that bears the same ratio to the Optionor's entire interest as each Optionee's Partnership Percentage bears to the aggregate Partnership Percentages of all the Optionees. The aggregate price for the Optionor's interest shall be the lesser of (A) the amount of the Optionor's Capital Account calculated as of the due date of the additional contribution and adjusted to reflect the allocation of the appropriate proportion of the Partnership's unrealized gains and losses as of the due date of such defaulted contribution, and (B) the aggregate amount of the Optionor's capital contributions actually made less any distributions (valued at their fair market value on the date of distribution in accordance with paragraph 12.1) on or prior to such due date. The option granted hereunder shall be exercisable at any time after the date thirty (30) days following the date of the initial notice of default from the General Partner to the Optionor by delivery to the Optionor of a notice of exercise of option together with a nonrecourse promissory note for the purchase price and a security agreement in accordance with subparagraph (3) below.

(2) Should any Optionee not exercise in entirety its option pursuant to subparagraph (1) above (such unexercised portion, the "***Remaining Portion***"), the General Partner may, if it deems it in the best interest of the Partnership, sell the Remaining Portion to any other investor (including without limitation any nondefaulting Limited Partner) of quality, net worth and standing comparable to the other Limited Partners, on terms not more favorable to any such investor than those applicable to the Optionees' option, and upon the consent of the General Partner, any such third party investor may become a Limited Partner to the extent of the interest purchased hereunder.

(3) The price due from any Optionee or any third party investor shall be payable by a noninterest bearing, nonrecourse promissory note (in such form as the General Partner shall designate) due upon final liquidation of the Partnership. Each such note shall be secured by the portion of the Optionor's Partnership interest so purchased by its maker pursuant to a security agreement in a form designed by the General Partner and shall be enforceable by the Optionor only against such security.

(4) Upon exercise of any option hereunder, the Optionee or any third party investor, as applicable, shall be obligated (A) to contribute to the Partnership that portion of any additional capital then due from the Optionor equal to the percentage of the Optionor's interest purchased by such person and (B) to pay the same percentage of any further contributions otherwise due from such Optionor on the date such contributions are otherwise due. Each such person who purchases a portion of the Optionor's Partnership interest shall be deemed to have acquired such portion as of the due date of the additional capital contribution with respect to which the Optionor defaulted, and any distributions made after the due date on account of the Optionor's interest shall be distributed among such purchasers (and, unless the entire interest was purchased, the Optionor) in accordance with their respective interests in the Optionor's interest.

Distributions otherwise allocable to the Optionor under the preceding sentence shall first be used to offset any defaulted contribution of the Optionor still due to the Partnership. Upon completion of any transaction pursuant to this paragraph 4.5(b), the General Partner shall cause Exhibit A to be amended to reflect all necessary changes resulting therefrom including, without limitation, admission as a third party investor as a Limited Partner and adjustment of Capital Account balances, Capital Commitment amounts and partnership Percentages as of the date of Optionor's default to reflect the acquisition from Optionor of the appropriate pro rata portion of each such item. The purchase and transfer of the Partnership interest of the Optionor shall occur automatically upon exercise by any Optionee or any third party investor of its option hereunder, without any action by Optionor. Notwithstanding the foregoing, each Limited Partner agrees that in the event it fails to make any capital contribution required of it under this Agreement, it will execute any instruments or perform any other acts that are or may be necessary to effectuate and carry out the transactions contemplated by this paragraph 4.5.

(c) Notwithstanding any provision of this Agreement, if at any time before a date on which any unpaid capital contribution is payable hereunder, any ERISA Partner or Governmental Plan Partner shall obtain and deliver to the General Partner an opinion of independent legal counsel, which opinion is reasonably acceptable to the General Partner, to the effect that, as a result of applicable statutes, regulations, case law, administrative interpretations, or similar authority, the payment by such ERISA Partner or Governmental Plan Partner of such unpaid capital contribution would result, or there is a material likelihood that such payment would result, in a material violation of ERISA or any comparable state statute or in the fiduciaries of such ERISA Partner or Governmental Plan Partner being deemed under ERISA or any comparable state statute, to have delegated investment discretion over plan assets (as determined by or under ERISA or any comparable state statute) to any person or entity which is not an "investment manager" (as determined by or under ERISA or any comparable state statute), then such ERISA Partner or Governmental Plan Partner shall be released from any further obligation to make further capital contributions under paragraph 4.2, and thereafter for purposes of this Agreement such ERISA Partner's or Governmental Plan Partner's obligation to make capital contributions to the Partnership shall be deemed to be equal to the total capital contributions theretofore made by such Partner. The General Partner shall cause Exhibit A to be amended to reflect all necessary changes resulting from this subparagraph (c) including, without limitation, adjustments to such ERISA Partner's or Governmental Plan Partner's Capital Commitment and Partnership Percentage.

(d) Notwithstanding any other provision of this Agreement, if at any time before a date on which any unpaid capital contribution is payable hereunder, any Private Foundation Partner (as defined in paragraph 13.3) shall obtain and deliver to the General Partner an opinion of independent legal counsel, which opinion is reasonably acceptable to the General Partner, to the effect that, as a result of applicable statutes, regulations, case law, administrative interpretations, or similar authority, the payment by such Private Foundation Partner of such unpaid capital contribution would result, or there is a material likelihood that such payment would result, in (i) payment by the Private Foundation Partner of excise taxes imposed by Subchapter A of Chapter 42 of the Code (other than Sections 4940 and 4942 thereof), or (ii) a material breach of the fiduciary duties of its trustees under any federal or state law applicable to private foundations or any rule or regulation adopted thereunder by any agency, commission, or authority having jurisdiction,

PARTNERSHIPS

then such Private Foundation Partner shall be released from any further obligation to make further capital contributions under paragraph 4.2, and thereafter for purposes of this Agreement such Private Foundation Partner's obligation to make capital contributions to the Partnership shall be deemed to be equal to the total capital contributions theretofore made by such Partner. The General Partner shall cause Exhibit A to be amended to reflect all necessary changes resulting from this subparagraph (d) including, without limitation, adjustments to such Private Foundation Partner's Capital Commitment and Partnership Percentage.

(e) Notwithstanding any other provision of this Agreement, if at any time before a date on which any unpaid capital contribution is payable hereunder, any BHC Partner (and defined in paragraph 13.4) shall obtain and deliver to the General Partner (as defined in paragraph 13.4) shall obtain and deliver to the General Partner an opinion of independent legal counsel, which opinion is reasonably acceptable to the General Partner, to the effect that the payment by such BHC Partner of such unpaid capital contribution would result in the violation by the BHC Partner of any provision of the Bank Holding Company Act of 1956, as amended (the "***BHC Act***"), including any regulation, written interpretation or directive of any governmental authority having regulatory authority over the BHC Partner, enacted or promulgated after the date of formation of the Partnership, then such BHC Partner shall be released from any further obligation to make further capital contributions under paragraph 4.2, and thereafter for purposes of this Agreement such BHC Partner's obligation to make capital contributions to the Partnership shall be deemed to be equal to the total capital contributions theretofore made by such Partner. The General Partner shall cause Schedule A to be amended to reflect all necessary changes resulting from this subparagraph (e) including, without limitation, adjustments to such BHC Partner's Capital Commitment and Partnership Percentage.

(f) Following any release pursuant to paragraphs 4.5 (c), (d) or (e) above of any ERISA Partner, Governmental Plan Partner, Private Foundation Partner or BHC Partner, respectively, from the obligation to make any additional capital contributions to the Partnership, the General Partner may, in its sole discretion, provide notice to all Limited Partners that additional contributions to the Partnership may be requested on account of such shortfall. No Limited Partner shall be required to make any additional capital contributions as a result of such notice. If any Limited Partner makes, in its sole discretion, any additional capital contribution to the Partnership as a result of such notice, the General Partner shall cause Exhibit A to be amended to reflect all necessary changes resulting from such contribution, including, without limitation, adjustments to any such contributing Partner's Capital Commitment and Partnership Percentage.

4.6 **Suspension Period.**

(a) Notwithstanding any other provision of this Agreement, no Limited Partner shall be required to contribute capital to the Partnership in respect of its Capital Commitment during any Suspension Period (as defined in subparagraph (b)) except for:

(i) Partnership expenses, including payment of any management fee due to the General Partner;

(ii) follow-on investments in portfolio companies in which the Partnership had invested prior to commencement of the Suspension Period; and

(iii) investments which the Partnership had committed to make prior to commencement of the Suspension Period.

BUSINESS STRUCTURES AND INCORPORATION

(b) A "*Suspension Period*" shall be deemed to commence immediately in the event that both _____ and _____, each an Original manager, cease to be Managers of the General Partner or otherwise active in the affairs of the General Partner.

(c) A Suspension Period may be terminated at any time upon the affirmative vote of a Majority in Interest of the Limited Partners, regardless of whether an additional individual or entity has been approved as a new manager of the General Partner.

ARTICLE 5
PARTNERSHIP ALLOCATIONS

5.1 **Allocation of Profit or Loss.** Except as otherwise provided in this Article 5:

(a) Profit of the Partnership for each Accounting Period shall be allocated as follows:

(i) Twenty-five percent (25%) of the Partnership's Profit shall be allocated to the Capital Accounts of all of the Partners to the extent that such accounts were previously allocated a Contingent Loss that has not been restored by previous allocations pursuant to this paragraph 5.1(a)(i) or paragraph 7.5(f). Such Profit shall be allocated to a Partner's Capital Account on the basis of the proportion that the unrestored Contingent Losses contained in such Partner's Capital Account bear to the aggregate unrestored Contingent Losses contained in all Partners' Capital Accounts. Any balance of such twenty-five percent (25%) of the Partnership's Profit shall be allocated to the Capital Account of the General Partner.

(ii) Seventy-five percent (75%) of the Partnership's Profit shall be allocated to the Capital Accounts of all of the Partners in proportion to their respective Partnership Percentages.

(b) Loss of the Partnership for each Accounting Period shall be allocated as follows:

(i) Twenty-five percent (25%) of the Partnership's Loss shall be allocated to the Capital Account of the General Partner.

(ii) Seventy-five percent (75%) of the Partnership's Loss shall be allocated to the Capital Accounts of all of the Partners in proportion to their respective Partnership Percentages.

(c) All Ordinary Income and all management fees and other expenses of the Partnership for each Accounting Period shall be allocated to the Capital Accounts of all of the Partners in proportion to their respective Partnership Percentages.

5.2 **Reallocation of Contingent Losses.**

(a) Except as provided in paragraph 5.2(b), if, for any Accounting Period, after the allocations provided in this Article 5 (including any allocation required by reference to paragraph 7.5(f)) have been made, the balance of the Capital Account of the General Partner has been reduced to less than one percent (1%) of the sum of the balances of the Capital Accounts of all Partners, an amount (the "*Contingent Loss*") shall be reallocated from the General Partner's Capital Account to all of the Partner's Capital Accounts (in proportion to each Partner's respective Partnership Percentage) so that the General Partner's Capital Account balance is equal to one percent (1%) of the sum of the

PARTNERSHIPS

balances of the Capital Accounts of all Partners. For purposes of this paragraph 5.2, the General Partner's Capital Account shall not be deemed to include any amounts attributable to a Limited Partner's interest held by the General Partner, but shall be deemed to include any outstanding obligations by the General Partner to contribute capital to the Partnership.

(b) The amount of Contingent Loss that would otherwise be reallocated from the General Partner's Capital Account under paragraph 5.2(a) shall instead be allocated to the General Partner's Capital Account until allocations of Loss to the General Partner's Capital Account pursuant to this paragraph 5.2(b) equal the amount of distributions, if any, that the General Partner would have to return to the Partnership under paragraph 10.5 if the Partnership were then in liquidation.

5.3 Special Allocations.

(a) To the extent the Partnership has taxable interest income or expense with respect to any promissory note between any Partner and the Partnership as holder and maker or maker and holder pursuant to Section 483, Sections 1271 through 1288, or Section 7872 of the Code, such interest income or expense shall be specially allocated to the Partner to whom such promissory note relates, and such Partner's Capital Account adjusted if appropriate.

(b) If additional persons are admitted to the Partnership as Limited Partners subsequent to the date of its formation and prior to the date six (6) months after commencement of the Partnership pursuant to paragraph 3.2(b) ("***Additional Limited Partners***"), then organizational costs, fees (including the management fee set forth in paragraph 6.1), and expense of the Partnership that are allocated to the Partners on or after the effective date of such admission shall be allocated first to such new Partners to the extent necessary to cause such persons to be treated with respect to such items as if they had been Partners from the commencement of the Partnership's term.

5.4 Regulatory Allocations.

(a) This Agreement is intended to comply with the safe harbor provisions set forth in Treasury Regulation 1.704-1(b) and the allocations set forth in paragraph 5.4(b) (the "***Regulatory Allocations***") are intended to comply with certain requirements of Treasury Regulation Section 1.704-1(b). In the event the Regulatory Allocations result in allocations being made that are inconsistent with the manner in which the Partners intend to divide Partnership Profit and Loss as reflected in paragraphs 5.1, 5.2 and 5.3, the General Partner shall use its best efforts to adjust subsequent allocations of any items of profit, gain, loss, income or expense such that the net amount of the Regulatory Allocations and such subsequent special adjustments to each Partner is zero.

(b) The allocations provided in this Article 5 shall be subject to the following exceptions:

(i) Any loss or expense otherwise allocable to a Limited Partner which exceeds the positive balance in such Limited Partner's Capital Account shall instead be allocated first to all Partners who have positive balances in their Capital Accounts in proportion to their respective Partnership Percentages, and when all Partners' Capital Accounts have been reduced to zero, then to the General Partner; income shall first be allocated to reverse any loss allocated under this paragraph 5.4(b)(i), in reverse order of such loss allocations, until all such prior loss allocations have been reversed.

(ii) In the event any Limited Partner unexpectedly receives any adjustments, allocations, or distributions described in Treasury Regulation Section 1.704-1(b)(2)(ii)(d)(4) through (d)(6), which causes or increases a deficit balance in such Limited Partner's Capital Account, items of Partnership income and gain shall be specially allocated such Limited Partner in an amount and manner sufficient to eliminate the deficit balance in its Capital Account created by such adjustments, allocations, or distributions as quickly as possible.

(iii) For purposes of this paragraph 5.4(b), the balance in a Partner's Capital Account shall take into account the adjustments provided in Treasury Regulation Section 1.704-1(b)(2)(ii)(d)(4) through (d)(6).

5.5 Income Tax Allocations.

(a) Except as otherwise provided in this paragraph or as otherwise required by the Code and the rules and Treasury Regulations promulgated thereunder, a Partner's distributive share of Partnership income, gain, loss, deduction, or credit for income tax purposes shall be the same as is entered in the Partner's Capital Account pursuant to this Agreement.

(b) In accordance with Code Section 704(c) and the Treasury Regulations thereunder, income, gain, loss and deduction with respect to any asset contributed to the capital of the Partnership shall, solely for tax purposes, be allocated among the Partners so as to take account of any variation between the adjusted basis of such property to the Partnership for federal income tax purposes and its initial Adjusted Asset Value.

(c) In the event the Adjusted Asset Value of the Partnership asset is adjusted pursuant to the terms of this Agreement, subsequent allocations of income, gain, loss and deduction with respect to such asset shall take account of any variation between the adjusted basis of such asset for federal income tax purposes and its Adjusted Asset Value in the same manner as under Code Section 704(c) and the Treasury Regulations thereunder.

ARTICLE 6
MANAGEMENT FEE; PARTNERSHIP EXPENSES

6.1 Management Fee.

(a) The General Partner or an entity or entities designated by the General Partner shall be compensated on a quarterly basis for services rendered during the term of the Partnership by the payment by the Partnership in cash to the General Partner (or its designee) on the first day of each fiscal quarter (or portion thereof) of a management fee.

(b) The management fee for each fiscal quarter shall be an amount equal to the aggregate Capital Commitments of al Partners as of the first day of each such quarter multiplied by one-half of one percent (0.50%) (the "***Base Rate***"); *provided, however*, that (1) the Base Rate used in computing the management fee for each fiscal quarter beginning on or after _____, 20__ shall be reduced by five one-hundredths of a percent (0.05%) per fiscal quarter, an (2) thereafter, the Base Rate used in computing the quarterly management fee shall be further reduced annually by increments of five one-hundredths of one percent (0.05%); and *provided further*, that (i) the management fee for each of the Partnership's first and last fiscal quarters shall be proportionately reduced based upon the ratio the number of days in each such period bears to ninety (90), and (ii) an additional management fee shall be payable upon the date of admission of any Additional Partner to reflect the increased Capital Commitments calculated as if such Partner had been admitted to the Partnership as of the date the first Limited Partner was admitted. Notwithstanding

PARTNERSHIPS

the foregoing, in the event the term of the Partnership is extended pursuant to paragraph 10.1, then the quarterly management fee shall be an amount equal to one-quarter of one percent (0.25%) multiplied by the lower of (A) the cost basis of the assets of the Partnership, and (B) the fair market value of all assets of the Partnership, as of the first day of each fiscal quarter during such extension period.

(c) One hundred percent (100%) of the amount of any compensation paid as transaction, break-up, board or consulting fees to the General Partner or to any member or manager of the General partner from any entity in which the Partnership has an interest in connection with the General Partner's activities as General Partner (net of any unreimbursed expenses of the General Partner or any of its members or managers, and as adjusted for any similar reductions with respect to any Side by Side Fund to prevent double counting), shall be deducted in full from the management fee otherwise payable by the Partnership in the calendar quarter following the date of receipt of such fees. In the event such reduction exceeds the management fee payable for any given period, subsequent period management fees shall be reduced by such excess amount until there has been a full reduction of management fees with respect to amounts described in the foregoing sentence.

6.2 **Expenses.**

(a) From the management fee, the General Partner shall bear all normal operating expenses incurred in connection with the management of the Partnership, except for those expenses borne directly by the Partnership as set forth in subparagraphs (b), (c) and (d) below and elsewhere herein. Such normal operating expenses to be borne by the General Partner shall include, without limitation, expenditures on account of salaries, wages, travel, entertainment, and other expenses of the Partnership's employees and of the General Partner's managers and employees, rentals payable for space used by the General Partner or the Partnership, bookkeeping services and equipment, and expenses incurred in investigating and evaluating investment opportunities and in managing investments of the Partnership.

(b) The Partnership shall bear all costs and expenses incurred in the holding, purchase, sale or exchange of Securities (whether or not ultimately consummated), including, but not by way of limitation, private placement fees, finder's fees, interest on borrowed money, real property or personal property taxes on investments, brokerage fees, legal fees, audit and accounting fees, consulting fees relating to investments or proposed investments, taxes applicable to the Partnership on account of its operations, fees incurred in connection with the maintenance of bank or custodian accounts, and all expenses incurred in connection with the registration of the Partnership's Securities under applicable securities laws and regulations. The Partnership shall also bear expenses incurred by the General Partner in serving as the tax matters partner (as described in paragraph 11.6), the cost of liability and other insurance premiums, all out-of-pocket expenses of preparing and distributing reports to Partners, out-of-pocket costs associated with Partnership meetings or Advisory Committee matters, all legal and accounting fees relating to the Partnership and its activities, all costs and expense arising out of the Partnership's indemnification obligation pursuant to this Agreement, and all expenses that are not normal operating expenses.

(c) The Partnership shall bear all organization and syndication costs, fees, and expenses incurred by or on behalf of the General Partner in connection with the formation and organization of the Partnership and the General Partner, including legal

BUSINESS STRUCTURES AND INCORPORATION

and accounting fees and expense incident thereto, up to a maximum of _____ ($_____); *provided, however*, that the Partnership shall not be responsible for any private placement fee or finder's fee incurred in connection with the formation and organization of the Partnership or the General Partner.

    (d) The Partnership shall bear all liquidation costs, fees, and expenses incurred by the General Partner (or its designee) in connection with the liquidation of the Partnership at the end of the Partnership's term, specifically including but not limited to legal and accounting fees and expenses.

    (e) Each of the Partnership and the General Partner agree to reimburse the other as appropriate to give effect to the provisions of this paragraph 6.2 in the event that either such party pays an obligation which is properly the responsibility of the other.

ARTICLE 7
WITHDRAWALS BY AND DISTRIBUTIONS TO THE PARTNERS

  7.1 **Interest.** No interest shall be paid to any Partner on account of its interest in the capital of or on account of its investment in the Partnership.

  7.2 **Withdrawals by the Partners.** No Partner may withdraw any amount from its Capital Account unless such withdrawal is made pursuant to this Article 7 or Article 10.

  7.3 **Partners' Obligation to Repay or Restore.** Except as required by law or the terms of this Agreement, no Limited Partner shall be obligated at any time to repay or restore to the Partnership all or any part of any distribution made to it from the Partnership in accordance with the terms of this Article 7.

  7.4 **Mandatory Distributions.**

    (a) Each Partner shall be paid in cash within ninety (90) days after the end of each fiscal year during the original term of the Partnership an amount equal to the excess, if any, of (a) thirty percent (30%) of the net taxable income (net of taxable losses) allocated to such Partner as a result of such Partner's ownership of an interest in the Partnership for all prior fiscal years, over (b) all cash prior distributions made pursuant to this paragraph 7.4(a) or paragraph 7.5; *provided* that the General Partner shall not be required to make any such distribution if the total amount to be distributed to all Partners is less than _____ ($_____). The provisions of this paragraph 7.4(a) shall apply equally to all Partners, without regard to their tax-exempt status under the Code.

    (b) The General Partner shall distribute all Marketable Securities acquired and held by the Partnership within three (3) years after the date that such Securities become Marketable, or, in the case of Securities Marketable at the time of their acquisition by the Partnership, within three (3) years of such acquisition; *provided, however*, that with the prior consent of the Advisory Committee, such Marketable Securities may be distributed at such later date as the Advisory Committee and the General Partner shall mutually agree. All distributions of Securities pursuant to this paragraph 7.4(b) shall be subject to the applicable provisions of paragraph 7.5.

  7.5 **Discretionary Distributions.** In addition to any distributions made pursuant to paragraph 7.4 above:

    (a) The General Partner may make distributions of cash or Marketable Securities from time to time in its discretion in the following proportions: seventy-five percent (75%) to all Partners in accordance with their respective Partnership

PARTNERSHIPS

Percentages and twenty-five percent (25%) to the General Partner; *provided, however*, the General Partner shall distribute the cost basis of Securities sold to all Partners in accordance with their respective Partnership Percentages.

(b)   Notwithstanding paragraph 7.5(a), the General Partner may at any time make distributions of cash or Marketable Securities one hundred percent (100%) to all Partners in accordance with their respective Partnership Percentages.

(c)   In order to maintain its proportionate interest in the Partnership in the event of a distribution in kind pursuant to paragraph 7.5(a) above, the General Partner shall (i) make a contribution to the Partnership in cash concurrently with such distribution in an amount equal to twenty-five percent (25%) of the cost basis of the Securities distributed to all Partners in such distribution, or (ii) be obligated to contribute to the Partnership an amount equal to the amount of cash described in the foregoing clause (i), which contribution obligation shall be secured by the Securities so distributed and shall be payable upon the earlier of (A) the date two (2) years from the date of the in kind distributions giving rise to the payment obligation under this clause (ii), (B) four (4) years from the date the Securities distributed in kind became Marketable Securities, (C) the disposition of such Securities by the General Partner, or (D) the date of the Partnership's final dissolution.

(d)   Securities distributed in kind shall be subject to such conditions and restrictions as the General Partner determines are legally required or appropriate. Whenever types of classes of Securities are distributed in kind, each Partner shall receive its ratable portion of each type or class of Securities distributed in kind; *provided, however*, if any Limited Partner would receive an amount of any Security that would cause such Limited Partner to own or control in excess of the amount of such Security that it may lawfully own or control, then, upon receipt of notice to such effect from such Limited Partner, the General Partner shall vary the method of distribution, in an equitable manner, so as to avoid such excessive ownership or control.

(e)   Notwithstanding any other provision of this paragraph 7.5, prior to the dissolution of the Partnership, the Partnership shall not, without the prior approval of the Advisory Committee, make a distribution of Marketable Securities which are subject to any material restrictions on transfer as a result of applicable contractual provisions or the Securities Act (other than volume and method of sale restrictions of Rule 144 promulgated thereunder or any successor thereto).

(f)   Immediately prior to any distribution in kind, the Deemed Gain or Deemed Loss of any Securities distributed shall be allocated to the Capital Accounts of all Partners as Profit or Loss pursuant to Article 5.

(g)   Notwithstanding any other provision of this paragraph 7.5, prior to dissolution of the Partnership, the Partnership shall not make a distribution of Nonmarketable Securities.

7.6   **Withholding Obligations.**

(a)   If and to the extent the Partnership is required by law (as determined in good faith by the General Partner) to make payments ("***Tax Payments***") with respect to any Partner in amounts required to discharge any legal obligation of the Partnership or the General Partner to make payments to any governmental authority with respect to any federal, state or local tax liability of such Partner arising as a result of such Partner's interest in the Partnership, then the amount of any such Tax Payments shall be deemed to be a loan by the Partnership to such Partner, which loan shall: (i) be secured by such Partner's interest in the Partnership, (ii) bear interest at the Prime Rate (as defined in paragraph 4.5(b)(i)), and (iii) be payable upon demand.

(b) If and to the extent the Partnership is required to make any Tax Payments with respect to any distribution to a Partner, either (i) such Partner's proportionate share of such distribution shall be reduced by the amount of such Tax Payments (*provided* that such Partner's Capital Account shall be adjusted pursuant to paragraph 14.4 for such Partner's full proportionate share of the distribution), or (ii) such partner shall pay to the Partnership prior to such distribution an amount of cash equal to such Tax Payments. In the event a portion of a distribution in kind is retained by the Partnership pursuant to clause (i), such retained Securities may, in the discretion of the General Partner, either (A) be distributed to the Partners in accordance with the terms of this Article 7 including this paragraph 7.6(b), or (B) be sold by the Partnership to generate the cash necessary to satisfy such Tax Payments. If the Securities are sold, then for purposes of income tax allocations only under this Agreement, any gain or loss on such sale or exchange shall be allocated to the Partner to whom the Tax Payments relate.

ARTICLE 8
MANAGEMENT DUTIES AND RESTRICTIONS

8.1 Management. The General Partner shall have the sole and exclusive right to manage, control, and conduct the affairs of the Partnership and to do any and all acts on behalf of the Partnership, including exercise of rights to elect to adjust the tax basis of Partnership assets and to revoke such elections and to make such other tax elections as the General Partner shall deem appropriate.

8.2 No Control by the Limited Partners; No Withdrawal.

(a) No Limited Partner shall take part in the control or management of the affairs of the Partnership nor shall any Limited Partner have any authority to act for or on behalf of the Partnership or to vote on any matter relative to the Partnership and its affairs except as is specifically permitted by this Agreement. Except as specifically set forth in this Agreement, no Limited Partner shall withdraw or be required to withdraw from the Partnership.

(b) Any interest in the Partnership held for its own account by a BHC Partner that is determined at the time of admission of such BHC Partner to be in excess of 4.99% (or such greater percentage as may be permitted under the BHC Act), of the cumulative interests of all of the Limited Partners, excluding for purposes of calculating such percentage portions of any other interest that are non-voting interests pursuant to this paragraph 8.2(b) (collectively, the "***Non-Voting Interests***"), shall be a Non-Voting Interest (whether or not subsequently transferred in whole or in part to any other party except as provided in the following sentence), and shall not be entitled to vote or consent with respect to such interests, and shall be deemed to have waived any rights to vote or consent with respect to such Non-Voting Interests under the Act, which interest would otherwise be identical in all material respects with other limited partnership interests in the Partnership. Upon the admission of each additional Limited Partner to the Partnership, recalculation of the interests in the Partnership held by all BHC Partners shall be made, and only that portion of the total interest in the Partnership held by each BHC Partner that is determined as of the date of such admission to be in excess of 4.99% (or such greater percentage as may be permitted under the BHC Act) of the interests in the Limited Partners, excluding Non-Voting Interests as of such date, shall be a Non-Voting Interest. Non-Voting Interests shall

PARTNERSHIPS

not be counted as interests of Limited Partners for purposes of determining under this Agreement whether any vote required hereunder has been approved by the requisite Percentage in Interest of the Limited Partners.

8.3 **Existing Funds; Follow On funds; Side by Side Funds.**

(a) Except as provided below, each of the Original Managers of the General Partner shall, so long as each shall remain a manager of the General Partner, devote substantially all of his business time to the affairs of the Partnership, ABC Ventures, L.P. (the "***Prior Fund***") and those entities formed for the purpose of managing each of the foregoing. The foregoing notwithstanding, the Original Managers of the General Partner may (i) continue to carry out certain duties at companies where the Original Managers of the General Partner have relationships as of the commencement of the Partnership, (ii) form one or more Side by Side Funds (as defined in paragraph 8.3(b)), and (iii) form successor private equity funds on or after the earlier of (a) _____, 20__ and (b) such time as at least seventy percent (70%) of the Partnership's Committed Capital has been invested, committed or reserved for investment in portfolio companies, or applied, committed or reserved for Partnership working capital or expenses.

(b) Pursuant to paragraph 8.3(a)(ii), the General Partner and the Original Managers may form and serve as general partner (or in a similar management role) of (i) one or more entities organized to accommodate the capital investment of the members of the General Partner and its employees and their respective families, (ii) one or more investment partnerships or similar entities comprised of entities and persons having strategic or other important relationships with the Partnership and (iii) one or more investment partnerships or similar entities to accommodate the tax, regulatory or other special needs of investors who otherwise would invest as Limited Partners of the Partnership (collectively, the "***Side by Side Funds***"). In the event that any Side by Side Fund is formed, upon each purchase of Securities (other than short term obligations such as money market instruments) by the Partnership, each Side by Side Fund will simultaneously invest on the same terms as the Partnership; *provided, however* that a Side by Side Fund shall not be required to make any such investment in a Security if the General Partner receive from the issuer thereof a written notice to the effect that the issuer will not permit such Side by Side Fund to invest on the same terms as the Partnership. Each Side by Side Fund will invest a fixed percentage of each investment by the Partnership.

8.4 **Investment Opportunities and Restrictions.**

(a) Each Limited Partner hereby agrees that the General Partner may offer the right to participate in investment opportunities of the Partnership to other private investors, groups, partnerships or corporations whenever the General Partner, in its discretion, so determines, including, without limitation, subsequent funds managed by some or all of the managers of the General Partner; *provided, however*, that neither the General Partner nor its members nor their respective Affiliates shall invest personally in Securities of portfolio companies in which the Partnership holds an investment except (i) through a Side by Side Fund or (ii) where the Securities of such portfolio company are at the time of such investment Marketable Securities. Except upon the prior consent of the Advisory Committee, for so long as the Partnership may call capital pursuant to paragraph 4.2 for purposes of investing in Securities of issuers in which it does not yet hold an investment, neither the General Partner nor its members nor their respective Affiliates shall invest in any Securities of any private company in which the Partnership does not hold an investment (A) where such Securities would be within the Partnership's investment criteria or (B) where

BUSINESS STRUCTURES AND INCORPORATION

such private company directly competes with any company in which the Partnership then holds an interest, except through a Side by Side Fund.

(b) Neither the General Partner nor any of its managers nor any of their respective Affiliates may (i) buy from or sell to the Partnership any Securities without the prior approval of the Advisory Committee or (ii) lend money to the Partnership.

(c) Except as approved by the Advisory Committee, not more than ten percent (10%) of the Partnership's Committed Capital shall be invested in any single portfolio company (determined on a cost basis at the time of the investment, including follow-up costs resulting from investments in such portfolio company); *provided, however*, that such approval shall be deemed to have been given if the Advisory Committee has not notified the General Partner in writing within ten (10) days of notice of such proposed transaction. Guarantees of the indebtedness of a portfolio company by the Partnership shall be deemed to have been "*invested*" in such portfolio company for purposes of calculations under this paragraph 8.4(c).

(d) Subject to paragraph 8.4(e), the General Partner shall not borrow money or otherwise incur indebtedness on behalf of the Partnership, or guaranty indebtedness of companies in which the Partnership has invested, in an aggregate amount exceeding five percent (5%) of the Partnership's Committed Capital.

(e) The General Partner shall use reasonable efforts to operate the Partnership in a manner that will not cause any Partner subject to Section 511 of the Code to recognize unrelated business taxable income under Section 512 of the Code or unrelated debt-financing income under Section 514 of the Code ("***UBTI***"). The Partnership shall not invest in any other partnership or other non-corporate entity unless such entity is subject to similar restrictions regarding UBTI.

(f) The General Partner shall use reasonable efforts to ensure that the Partnership not enter into any transaction that would constitute participation by the Partnership or the Limited Partner in a "***prohibited transaction***" under Section 4975 of the Code.

(g) The Partnership may not carry out portfolio company investments the cost basis of which in the aggregate exceeds one hundred percent (100%) of all Capital Commitments.

(h) The prior consent of the Advisory Committee shall be required in connection with the purchase by the Partnership of the Securities of any issuer of the Securities of which are then held by the Prior Fund.

8.5 **Media Companies.**

(a) In the event that the Partnership invests in one or more companies that, directly or indirectly, own, control or operate a broadcast radio or television station, a cable or wireless cable television system, a daily newspaper or other similar enterprise subject to FCC Ownership Rules (as defined below) (collectively, "***Media Companies***"), the Partners agree that, notwithstanding any other provision of this Agreement conferring rights on the Limited Partners, the following additional limitations shall apply to any Limited Partner (the "***Exempt Limited Partners***") seeking exemption from attribution of ownership interests in such Media Companies under the attribution rules and the media multiple and cross-ownership rules of the Federal Communications Commission ("***FCC***") set forth in 47 C.F.R. paragraphs 21.912, 73.3555, 74.931(h) and 76.501 (collectively, the "***Ownership Rules***"), as the same may be modified from time to time. Such an Exempt Limited Partner shall be prohibited from:

PARTNERSHIPS

(i) acting as an employee of the Partnership if such employee's functions, directly or indirectly, relate to media enterprises of the Partnership or any Media Company in which the Partnership has invested;

(ii) serving, in any material capacity, as an independent contractor or agent with respect to the media enterprises of the Partnership or any Media Company in which the Partnership has invested;

(iii) communicating on matters pertaining to the day-to-day media operations of the Partnership or a Media Company in which the Partnership has invested with (A) an officer, director, partner, agent, representative or employee of such Media Company, or (B) the General Partner;

(iv) performing any services for the Partnership materially relating to the media activities of the Partnership or any Media Company in which the Partnership has invested;

(v) becoming actively involved in the management or operation of the Partnership's media businesses; or

(vi) voting an admission of new or additional general partners to the Partnership unless such admission may be rejected by the General Partner. The foregoing limitations are intended to insulate an Exempt Limited Partner from attribution of ownership interests in Media Companies under the Ownership Rules.

(b) An Exempt Limited Partner may, upon five (5) business days' prior written notice to the General Partner, elect to be excluded from the limitations set forth in paragraph 8.5(a)(i)-(vi) and shall thereafter be denominated a "***Non-Exempt Limited Partner***"; *provided*, that upon such election the General Partner shall review the Partnership's compliance with the Ownership Rules and take such steps as are reasonably necessary to comply therewith, and the electing Limited Partner shall cooperate in providing reasonably available information to the General Partner in such regard. A Limited partner (including a Non-Exempt Limited Partner) may, upon five (5) business days' prior written notice to the General Partner, elect to become an Exempt Limited Partner.

8.6 **Venture Capital Operating Company.** The General Partner shall use its reasonable best efforts to operate the Partnership so that it will remain at all times a "venture capital operating company" ("***VCOC***") as that term is defined in the DOL Regulations. The General Partner shall notify the Limited Partners as soon as reasonably practicable in the event the General Partner determines that the Partnership has ceased to meet the requirements to be a VCOC.

ARTICLE 9
INVESTMENT REPRESENTATION AND TRANSFER OF PARTNERSHIP INTERESTS

9.1 **Investment Representation of the Limited Partners.** This Agreement is made with each of the Limited Partners in reliance upon each Limited Partner's representation to the Partnership, which by executing this Agreement each Limited Partner hereby confirms, that its interest in the Partnership is to be acquired for investment, and not with a view to the sale or distribution of any part thereof, and that it has no present intention of selling, granting participation in, or otherwise distributing the same, and each Limited Partner understands that its interest in the Partnership has not been registered under the Securities Act and that any transfer or other disposition of the interest may not be made without registration under the Securities Act or pursuant to an applicable exemption

BUSINESS STRUCTURES AND INCORPORATION

therefrom. Each Limited Partner further represents that it does not have any contract, undertaking, agreement, or arrangement with any person to sell, transfer, or grant participations to such person, or to any third person, with respect to its interest in the Partnership.

9.2 Qualifications of the Limited Partners. Each Limited partner represents that it is an "*accredited investor*" within the meaning of that term as defined in Regulation D promulgated under the Securities Act.

9.3 Transfer by General Partner. The General Partner shall not sell, assign, mortgage, pledge or otherwise dispose of its interest in the Partnership or in its capital assets or property without the prior written consent of a Majority in Interest of the Limited Partners. Admissions of new members of the General Partner or the transfer of interests in the General Partner by its members shall not be deemed to be a sale or other disposition of the General Partner's interest in the Partnership. Notwithstanding the foregoing, in no event shall the General Partner make any transfer of an interest in the Partnership prohibited by the events described in paragraphs 9.5(a) through 9.5(h).

9.4 Transfer by Limited Partner. No Limited Partner shall sell, assign, pledge, mortgage, or otherwise dispose of or transfer its interest in the partnership without the prior written consent of the General Partner; *provided, however*, that the General Partner agrees that such consent will not be unreasonably withheld. Notwithstanding the foregoing, after delivery of the opinion of counsel hereinafter required by this Article 9, a Limited Partner may sell, assign, pledge, mortgage, or otherwise dispose of or transfer its interest in the Partnership without such consent (a) to any entity directly or indirectly holding eighty percent (80%) or more of the interests of the Limited Partner or any entity of which eighty percent (80%) or more of the beneficial ownership are held directly or indirectly, eighty percent (80%) or more of the beneficial ownership, (b) pursuant to a merger, plan of reorganization, sale or pledge of, or other general encumbrance on all or substantially all of the Limited Partner's assets, (c) as may be required by any law or regulation, (d) by testamentary disposition or intestate succession, or (e) to a trust, profit sharing plan or other entity controlled by, or for the benefit of, such Limited Partner or one or more family members. A change in any trustee or fiduciary of the Limited Partner shall not be considered to be a transfer, sale, assignment, mortgage, pledge or other disposition under this paragraph 9.4, *provided* (i) any replacement trustee or fiduciary of an ERISA Partner or a Governmental Plan Partner is also a fiduciary under ERISA (or under the state law applicable to the Governmental Plan Partner), and (ii) written notice of such change is given to the General Partner within a reasonable period of time after the effective date thereof.

9.5 Requirements for Transfer. No transfer or other disposition of the interest of the Limited Partner shall be permitted until the General Partner shall have received an opinion of counsel satisfactory to it that the effect of such transfer or disposition would not:

(a) result in the Partnership's assets being considered, in the opinion of counsel for the Partnership, as "*plan assets*" within the meaning of the Employment Retirement Income Security Act of 1974, as amended ("ERISA"), or any regulations proposed or promulgated thereunder;

(b) result in the termination of the Partnership's tax year under Section 708(b)(1)(B) of the Code;

(c) result in violation of the Securities Act or any comparable state law;

(d) require the Partnership to register as an investment company under the Investment Company Act of 1940, as amended;

(e) require the Partnership, the General Partner, or any member of the General Partner to register as an investment adviser under the Investment Advisers Act of 1940, as amended;

(f) result in a termination of the Partnership's status as a partnership for tax purposes;

(g) result in a violation of any law, rule, or regulation by the Limited Partner, the Partnership, the General Partner, or any member of the General Partner; or

(h) cause the Partnership to be deemed to be a "***publicly traded partnership***" as such term is defined in Section 7704(b) of the Code.

Such legal opinion shall be provided to the General Partner by the transferring Limited Partner or the proposed transferee. Any costs associated with such opinion shall be borne by the transferring Limited Partner or the proposed transferee. Upon request the General Partner will use its good faith diligent efforts to provide any information possessed by the Partnership and reasonably requested by a transferring Limited Partner to enable it to render the foregoing opinion.

9.6 **Substitution as a Limited Partner.** A transferee of a Limited Partner's interest pursuant to this Article 9 shall become a substituted Limited Partner only if the underlying transfer is permitted by paragraph 9.4 hereof and only if such transferee (a) elects to become a substituted Limited Partner and (b) executes, acknowledges and delivers to the Partnership such other instruments as the General Partner may deem necessary or advisable to effect the admission of such transferee as a substituted Limited Partner, including, without limitation, the written acceptance and adoption by such transferee of the provisions of this Agreement. No assignment by the Limited Partner of its interest in the Partnership shall release the assignor from its liability to the Partnership pursuant to paragraph 4.2; *provided* that if the assignee becomes a Limited Partner as provided in this paragraph 9.6, the assignor shall thereupon so be released (in the case of a partial assignment, to the extent of such assignment).

ARTICLE 10
DISSOLUTION AND LIQUIDATION OF THE PARTNERSHIP

10.1 **Extension of Partnership Term.** Upon _____, 20__, or such subsequent dates to which the Partnership term has previously been extended pursuant to this paragraph 10.1, the General Partner may extend the Partnership term from an additional one (1) year period; *provided* that in no event shall there be more than two (2) such one year extensions without the approval of a Majority in Interest of the Limited Partners. During such one (1) year extensions periods, the General Partner shall use its best efforts to convert the Partnership's Nonmarketable Securities into Marketable Securities or cash, and all Securities that become Marketable Securities during such period or periods, and all cash in excess of working capital requirements shall be promptly distributed to the Partners. The General Partner shall not purchase the Securities of any new portfolio company during such period; *provided, however,* that the General Partner may (a) purchase additional Securities of an existing portfolio company if it deems such a purchase to be in the best interests of the Partnership, and (b) exchange the Securities of an existing portfolio company for other Securities. This management fee during any extension period shall be as set forth in Article

BUSINESS STRUCTURES AND INCORPORATION

6; *provided, however*, that no management fee shall be payable for any period commencing more than twelve (12) years from the commencement of the Partnership.

    10.2   **Early Termination of the Partnership.**

        (a)   The Partnership shall dissolve, and the affairs of the Partnership shall be wound up prior to _____, 20__ (or such subsequent dates to which the Partnership term has previously been extended pursuant to paragraph 10.1):

           (i)   Ninety (90) days after the withdrawal, bankruptcy, or dissolution of the sole remaining general partner of the Partnership, unless a Majority in Interest of the Limited Partners within ninety (90) days of such event elect to continue the Partnership and appoint a new general partner effective as of the date of such event; or

           (ii)   Upon the affirmative vote of Eighty Percent (80%) in Interest of the Limited Partners in the event that a Suspension Period has commenced and remained uncured for one hundred eighty (180) days.

        (b)   In the event that the Partnership is dissolved pursuant to the provisions of this paragraph, the Partnership shall elect one or more liquidators to manage the liquidation of the Partnership in the manner described in this Article 10.

    10.3   **Winding Up Procedures.**

        (a)   Promptly upon dissolution of the Partnership (unless the Partnership is continued in accordance with this Agreement or the provisions of the Act), the affairs of the Partnership shall be wound up and the Partnership liquidated. The closing Capital Accounts of all the Partners shall be computed as of the date of dissolution as if the date of dissolution were the last day of an Accounting Period in accordance with Article 5, and then adjusted in the following manner:

           (i)   All assets and liabilities of the Partnership shall be valued as of the date of dissolution.

           (ii)   The Partnership's assets as of the date of dissolution shall be deemed to have been sold at their fair market values and the resulting Profit or Loss shall be allocated to the Partner's Capital Accounts in accordance with the provisions of Article 5.

The result of reach Partner shall be its closing Capital Account. The amount of each Partner's closing Capital Account divided by the sum of the closing Capital Accounts for all of the Partners as of such date shall be such Partner's "***Final Partnership Percentage***."

        (b)   Distributions during the winding up period may be made in cash or in kind or partly in cash and partly in kind. The General Partner or the liquidator shall use its best judgment as to the most advantageous time for the Partnership to sell Securities or to make distributions in kind. All cash and each Security distributed in kind after the date of dissolution of the Partnership shall be distributed ratably in accordance with the General Partner and the Limited Partners' Final Partnership Percentages, unless such distribution would result in a violation of a law or regulation applicable to a Limited Partner, in which event, upon receipt by the General Partner of notice to such effect, such Limited Partner may designate a different entity to receive the distribution, or designate, subject to the approval of the General Partner, an alternative distribution procedure (*provided* such alternative distribution procedure does not prejudice any of the other Partners). Each Security so distributed shall be subject to reasonable conditions and restrictions necessary or advisable in order to preserve the value of such Security or for legal reasons.

    10.4   **Payments in Liquidation.** The assets of the Partnership shall be distributed in final liquidation of the Partnership in the following order:

(a) to the creditors of the Partnership, other than Partners, in the order of priority established by law, either by payment or by establishment of reserves;

(b) to the Partners, in repayment of any loans made to, or other debts owed by, the Partnership to such Partners; and

(c) the balance, if any, to the General Partner and the Limited Partners in respect of the positive balances in their Capital Accounts in compliance with Treasury Regulation Section 1.704-1(b)(2)(ii) (b)(2); and the General Partner shall contribute to the capital of the Partnership the amount, if any, described in paragraph 10.5.

10.5 Return of Excess Distributions. Notwithstanding paragraphs 7.3 and 10.4, upon liquidation of the Partnership pursuant to this Article 10, the General Partner shall be required to pay back to the Partnership the amount by which the cumulative net profit distributions received by the General Partner over the life the Partnership (excluding amounts received by the General Partner in respect of its one percent (1%) Capital Commitment) exceeds twenty-five percent (25%) of the amount by which the Partnership's (a) cumulative Profits exceed (b) its cumulative Losses (the "***Excess Amount***"); *provided, however*, that the amount of repayment described in this paragraph 10.5 shall be reduced by the federal and state income taxes payable on the Excess Amount by the members of the General Partner (assuming for this purpose a combined federal and state tax rate of thirty percent (30%)). In the event that the assets of the General Partner are insufficient to satisfy the obligation described in the preceding sentence, each Original Manager agrees to contribute capital to the General Partner in the amount not to exceed his pro rata share of the General Partner's remaining obligation to the Partnership under this paragraph 10.5, which amounts shall be promptly contributed to the Partnership. The sum of the pro rata shares described in the preceding sentence shall be based on relative distributions received by each Original Manager from the General Partner and shall collectively equal one hundred percent (100%) of the amount to be contributed to the General Partner.

ARTICLE 11
FINANCIAL ACCOUNTING, REPORTS, MEETINGS AND VOTING

11.1 Financial Accounting; Fiscal Year. The books and records of the Partnership shall be kept in accordance with the provisions of this Agreement and otherwise in accordance with generally accepted accounting principles consistently applied, and shall be audited at the end of each fiscal year by an independent public accountant of recognized national standing selected by the General Partner. The Partnership's fiscal year shall be the calendar year.

11.2 Supervision; Inspection of Books. Proper and complete books of account of the Partnership, copies of the Partnership's federal, state and local tax returns for each fiscal year, the Schedule of Partners set forth in Exhibit A, this Agreement and the Partnership's Certificate of Limited Partnership shall be kept under the supervision of the General Partner at the principle office of the Partnership. Such books and records shall be open to inspection by the Limited Partners, or their accredited representatives, at any reasonable time during normal business hours after reasonable advance notice. Such books and records shall be maintained by the General Partner or its designee for a period of three (3) years following final dissolution of the Partnership.

11.3 Quarterly Reports. The General Partner shall transmit to the Limited Partners within forty five (45) days after the close of each of the first three quarters of each fiscal year, a summary of acquisitions and dispositions of investments made by the

BUSINESS STRUCTURES AND INCORPORATION

Partnership during such quarter, and a list of investments then held, together with a valuation of the investments then held.

11.4 Annual Report; Financial Statements of the Partnership. The General Partner shall transmit to the Limited Partners within ninety (90) days after the close of the Partnership's fiscal year audited financial statements of the Partnership prepared in accordance with the terms of this Agreement and otherwise in accordance with generally accepted accounting principles, including an income statement for the year then ended and a balance sheet as of the end of such year, a statement of changes in the Partners' Capital Accounts, and a list of investments then held. The financial statements shall be accompanied by a report from the General Partner to the Limited Partners, which shall include a status report on investments then held, a summary of acquisitions and dispositions of investments made by the Partnership during the preceding quarter and a valuation of each such investment.

11.5 Tax Returns. The General Partner shall cause the Partnership's federal, state and local tax returns and IRS Form 1065, Schedule K-1, to be prepared and delivered to the Limited Partners within ninety (90) days after the close of the Partnership's fiscal year.

11.6 Tax Matters Partner. The General Partner shall be the Partnership's tax matters partner under the Code and under any comparable provision of state law. The General Partner shall have the right to resign as tax matters partner by giving thirty (30) days' written notice to each Partner. Upon such resignation a successor tax matters partner shall be selected by the Partnership. The tax matters partner shall employ experienced tax counsel to represent the Partnership in connection with any audit or investigation of the Partnership by the Internal Revenue Service and in connection with all subsequent administrative and judicial proceedings arising out of such audit. If the tax matters partner is required by law or regulation to incur fees and expenses in connection with tax matters not affecting all the Partners, then the Partnership shall be entitled to reimbursement from those Partners on whose behalf such fees and expenses were incurred. The tax matters partner shall keep the Partners informed of all administrative and judicial proceedings, as required by Section 6223(g) of the Code, and shall furnish to each Partner, if such Partner so requests in writing, a copy of each notice or other communication received by the tax matters partner from the Internal Revenue Service, except such notices or communications are sent directly to such requesting Partner by the Internal Revenue Service. The relationship of the tax matters partner to the Limited Partners is that of a fiduciary, and the tax matters partner has fiduciary obligations to perform its duties as tax matters partner in such manner as will service the best interests of the Partnership and all of the Partnership's Partners. To the fullest extent permitted by law, but subject to the limitations and exclusions of paragraph 15.4, the Partnership agrees to indemnify the tax matters partner and its agents and save and hold them harmless, from and in respect to all (a) fees, costs and expenses in connection with or resulting from any claim, action, or demand against the tax matters partner, the General Partner or the Partnership that arise out of or in any way relate to the tax matters partner's status as tax matters partner for the Partnership, and (b) all such claims, actions, and demands and any losses or damages therefrom, including amounts paid in settlement or compromise of any such claim, action, or demand.

PARTNERSHIPS

ARTICLE 12
VALUATION

12.1 **Valuation.** Subject to the specific standards set forth below, the valuation of Securities and other assets and liabilities under this Agreement shall be at fair market value. Except as may be required under applicable Treasury Regulations, no value shall be placed on the goodwill or the name of the Partnership in determining the value of the interest of any Partner or in any accounting among the Partners.

(a) The following criteria shall be used for determining the fair market value of Securities:

(i) If traded on one or more securities exchanges or the NASDAQ National Market System, the value shall be deemed to be the average of the Securities' closing price on the principal of such exchanges during the period which includes the valuation date and the two trading days immediately preceding the valuation date.

(ii) If actively traded over the counter (other than on the NASDAQ National Market System), the value shall be deemed to be the average of the average closing bid and ask prices of such Securities during the period which includes the valuation date and the two trading days immediately preceding the valuation date.

(iii) If there is no active public market, the value shall be the fair market value thereof, as determined by the General Partner, taking into consideration the purchase price of the Securities, developments concerning the investee company subsequent to the acquisition of the Securities, any financial data and projections of the investee company provided to the General Partner, and such other factor or factors as the General Partner may deem relevant.

(b) If the General Partner in good faith determines that, because of special circumstances, the valuation methods set forth in this Article 12 do not fairly determine the value of a Security, the General Partner shall make such adjustments or use such alternative valuation method as it deems appropriate.

(c) The General Partner shall have the power at any time to determine, for all purposes of this Agreement, the fair market value of any assets and liabilities of the Partnership, subject to paragraph 12.1(d).

(d) In the event that any Limited Partner shall disagree with any valuation made by the General Partner under this Article 12, such Limited Partner shall deliver written notice to the General Partner, briefly summarizing the basis for such disagreement. The General Partner and such Limited Partner shall then meet and confer and use their good faith efforts to reach a mutually acceptable valuation. In the event that the General Partner and such Limited Partner cannot agree, then a mutually acceptable professional appraiser shall be selected to determine the valuation. The fees and expenses of any expert or experts retained in accordance with this paragraph 12.1(d) shall be borne by the Partnership.

12.2 **Advisory Committee.** The General Partner will appoint an Advisory Committee of up to five (5) members, who shall be representatives of Limited Partners of the Partnership (or of any Side by Side Fund organized pursuant to paragraph 8.3(b)(iii)) selected by the General Partner from time to time in its discretion. The duties of the Advisory Committee will include (a) consideration of any approvals sought by the General Partner pursuant to the terms of this Agreement, (b) advice regarding all matters pertaining to conflicts of interest by the Partnership, the General Partner or any of the managers of the

BUSINESS STRUCTURES AND INCORPORATION

General Partner, and (c) such advice and counsel as is requested by the General Partner in connection with the Partnership's investments and other Partnership matters. However, the General Partner will retain ultimate responsibility for asset valuations and for making all investment decisions. Any Limited Partner that has elected to be an Exempt Limited Partner pursuant to paragraph 8.5(a) shall be prohibited from participating on the Advisory Committee if and to the extent that such participation would violate or be inconsistent with any of the limitations on Exempt Limited Partners set forth in paragraph 8.5(a). The Partnership will reimburse each member for his or her reasonable out-of-pocket expenses. All actions, consents or approvals of the Advisory Committee shall require a majority of its members serving at the time such action, consent or approval is taken, which actions, consents or approvals may be carried out by telephone, facsimile or electronic mail or other means reasonably acceptable to the General Partner.

ARTICLE 13
PARTNERS SUBJECT TO SPECIAL REGULATION

13.1   ERISA Partners.

(a)   Each Limited Partner that is, or whose equity interests are at least partially owned by, an "*employee benefit plan*" (an "*ERISA Partner*") within the meaning of, and subject to the provisions of, ERISA hereby (i) acknowledges that it is its understanding that neither the Partnership, the General Partner, nor any of the Affiliates of the General Partner, are "*fiduciaries*" of such Limited Partner within the meaning of ERISA by reason of the Limited Partner investing its assets in, and being a Limited Partner of, the Partnership; (ii) acknowledges that it has been informed of and understands the investment objectives and policies of, and the investment strategies that may be pursued by, the Partnership; (iii) acknowledges that it is aware of the provisions of Section 404 of ERISA relating to the requirements for investment and diversification of the assets of employee benefit plans and trusts subject to ERISA; (iv) represents that it has given appropriate consideration to the facts and circumstances relevant to the investment by that ERISA Partner's plan in the Partnership and has determined that such investment is reasonably designed, as part of such portfolio, to further the purposes of such plan, (v) represents that, taking into account the other investments made with the assets of such plan, and the diversification thereof, such plan's investment in the Partnership is consistent with the requirements of Section 404 and other provisions of ERISA: (vi) acknowledges that it understands that current income will not be a primary objective of the Partnership; and (vii) represents that, taking into account the other investments made with the assets of such plan, the investment of assets of such plan in the Partnership is consistent with the cash flow requirements and funding objectives of such plan.

(b)   Notwithstanding any provision of this Agreement to the contrary, each ERISA Partner may elect to withdraw from the Partnership, or upon demand by the General Partner shall withdraw from the Partnership, at the time and in the manner hereinafter provided, if either the ERISA Partner or the General Partner shall obtain on opinion of counsel (which counsel shall be reasonably acceptable to both the ERISA Partner and the General Partner) to the effect that, as a result of applicable statutes, regulations, case law, administrative interpretations, or similar authority (i) the continuation of the ERISA Partner as a Limited Partner of the Partnership or the conduct of the Partnership will result, or there is a material likelihood the same will result, in a material violation of ERISA, or (ii) all or any portion of the assets of the Partnership constitutes assets of the ERISA Partner

PARTNERSHIPS

for the purposes of ERISA and are subject to the provisions of ERISA to substantially the same extent as if owned directly by the ERISA Partner. In the event of the issuance of such opinion of counsel, a copy of such opinion shall be given to all the Partners, together with the written notice of the election of the ERISA Partner to withdraw or the written demand of the General Partner for withdrawal, whichever the case may be. Thereupon, unless within one hundred twenty (120) days after receipt of such written notice and opinion the General Partner is able to eliminate the necessity for such withdrawal to the reasonable satisfaction of the ERISA Partner and the General Partner, whether by correction of the condition giving rise to the necessity of such Limited Partner's withdrawal, or the amendment of this Agreement, or otherwise, such Limited Partner shall withdraw its entire interest in the Partnership, such withdrawal to be effective upon the last day of the fiscal quarter during which such one hundred twenty (120) day period expired.

(c) In the event the General Partner receives from its counsel the legal opinion described in paragraph 13.1(b), it shall promptly give notice of such receipt to all ERISA Partners and Governmental Plan Partners. In the event any ERISA Partner or Governmental Plan Partner receives from its counsel the legal opinion described in paragraph 13.1(b), such ERISA or Governmental Plan Partner shall promptly give notice of such receipt to the General Partner.

(d) The withdrawing Limited Partner shall be entitled to receive within one hundred twenty (120) days after the date of such withdrawal an amount equal to the fair value of such Partner's interest as of the effective date of such withdrawal (calculated by treating all Partnership assets as though sold at fair market value as determined under paragraph 12.1 with any resulting net Profit or Loss allocated in accordance with Article 5.

(e) Any distribution or payment to a withdrawing Limited Partner pursuant to this paragraph may, in the sole discretion of the General Partner, be made in cash, in Securities, in the form of a promissory note, or any combination thereof. The terms of any such promissory note shall be mutually agreed upon the General Partner and the withdrawing Limited Partner.

13.2 **Governmental Plan Partners.** Notwithstanding any provision of the Agreement to the contrary, any Limited Partner that is either (i) a "***governmental plan***" as defined in Title 29, Section 1002(32) of the United States Code, (ii) an employee benefit plan subject to regulation under applicable state laws that are similar in purpose and intent to ERISA, or (iii) whose equity interests are at least partially owned by any party described in the foregoing clauses (i) or (ii) (a "***Governmental Plan Partner***"), may elect to withdraw from the Partnership, or upon demand by the General Partner shall withdraw from the Partnership, if either the Governmental Plan Partner or the General Partner shall obtain an opinion of counsel (which counsel shall be reasonably acceptable to both the Governmental Plan Partner and the General Partner) to the effect that the Governmental Plan Partner, the Partnership, or the General Partner (including its Affiliates) would be in violation, or there is a material likelihood the same would result, of any statute or regulation of the state of residence of the Governmental Plan Partner or any political subdivision of such state, enacted or promulgated after the date of formation of the Partnership, as a result of the Governmental Plan Partner continuing as a Limited Partner. In the event of the issuance of the opinion of counsel referred to in the preceding sentence, the withdrawal of and disposition of the Governmental Plan Partner's interest in the Partnership shall be governed by paragraph 13.1, as if the Governmental Plan Partner were an ERISA Partner.

BUSINESS STRUCTURES AND INCORPORATION

13.3 Private Foundation Partners. Notwithstanding any provision of the Agreement to the contrary, any Limited Partner that is, or whose equity interests are at least partially owned by, a "*private foundation*" as described in Section 509 of the Code (a "*Private Foundation Partner*"), may elect to withdraw from the Partnership, or upon demand by the General Partner shall withdraw from the Partnership, if either the Private Foundation Partner or the General Partner shall obtain an opinion of counsel (which counsel shall be reasonably acceptable to both the Private Foundation Partner and the General Partner) to the effect that such withdrawal is necessary in order for the Private Foundation Partner to avoid (a) excise taxes imposed by Subchapter A of Chapter 42 of the Code (other than Securities 4940 and 4942 thereof), or (b) a material breach of the fiduciary duties of its trustees under any federal or state law applicable to private foundations or any rule or regulation adopted thereunder by any agency, commission, or authority having jurisdiction. In the event of the issuance of the opinion of counsel referred to in the preceding sentence, the withdrawal of and disposition of the Private Foundation Partner's interest in the Partnership shall be governed by paragraph 13.1, as if the Private Foundation Partner were an ERISA Partner.

13.4 Bank Holding Company Act Partners. Notwithstanding any provision of the Agreement to the contrary, any Limited Partner that is subject to the BHC Act (a "*BHC Partner*") may elect to withdraw from the partnership if the BHC Partner shall obtain an opinion of counsel (which counsel shall be reasonably acceptable to the General Partner) to the effect that the BHC Partner would be in violation of any provision of the BHC Act, including any regulation, written interpretation or directive of any governmental authority having regulatory authority over the BHC Partner, enacted or promulgated after the date of formation of the Partnership, as a result of the BHC Partner continuing as a Limited Partner. In the event of the issuance of the opinion of counsel referred to in the preceding sentence, the withdrawal of the disposition of the BHC Partner's interest in the Partnership shall be governed by paragraph 13.1 of the Agreement, as if the BHC Partner were an ERISA Partner.

ARTICLE 14
CERTAIN DEFINITIONS

14.1 Accounting Period. An Accounting Period shall be (a) a calendar year if there are no changes in the Partners' respective interests in the Profits or Losses of the Partnership during such calendar year except on the first day thereof, or (b) any other period beginning on the first day of a calendar year, or any other day during a calendar year upon which occurs a change in such respective interests, and ending on the last day of a calendar year, or on the day preceding an earlier day upon which any change in such respective interests shall occur.

14.2 Adjusted Asset Value. The Adjusted Asset Value with respect to any asset shall be the asset's adjusted basis for federal income tax purposes, except as follows:

(a) The initial Adjusted Asset Value of any asset contributed by a Partner to the Partnership shall be the gross fair market value of such asset at the time of contribution, as determined by the contributing Partner and the Partnership.

(b) In the discretion of the General Partner, the Adjusted Asset Values of all Partnership assets may be adjusted to equal their respective gross fair market values, as determined by the General Partner, and the resulting unrealized profit or loss allocated to the Capital Accounts of the Partners pursuant to Article 5, upon distribution by the Partnership to a Partner of more than a *de minimis* amount of Partnership assets, unless all Partners receive simultaneous distributions of either undivided interests in the distributed property or identical Partnership assets in proportion to their interests in Partnership distributions as provided in paragraphs 7.4, 7.5 and 7.6.

(c) The Adjusted Asset Values of all Partnership assets shall be adjusted to equal their respective gross fair market values, as determined by the General Partner, and the resulting unrealized profit or loss allocated to the Capital Accounts of the Partners pursuant to Article 5, as of the termination of the Partnership either by expiration of the Partnership's term or the occurrence of an event described in paragraph 10.2.

14.3 Affiliate. An Affiliate of any person shall mean (a) any person that directly, or indirectly through one or more intermediaries, controls, or is controlled by or is under common control with the person specified or (b) such person's immediate family members (excluding family members who do not reside in the same household).

14.4 Capital Account. The Capital Account of each Partner shall consist of its original capital contribution, (a) increased by any additional capital contributions, its share of income or gain that is allocated to it pursuant to this Agreement, and the amount of any Partnership liabilities that are assumed by it or that are secured by any Partnership property distributed to it, and (b) decreased by the amount of any distributions to or withdrawals by it, its share of expense or loss that is allocated to it pursuant to this Agreement, and the amount of any of its liabilities that are summed by the Partnership or that are secured by any property contributed by it to the Partnership. The foregoing provision and the other provisions of this Agreement relating to the maintenance of Capital Accounts are intended to comply with Treasury Regulation Section 1.704-1(b)(2)(iv), and shall be interpreted and applied in the manner consistent with such Regulations. In the event the General Partner shall determine that it is prudent to modify the manner in which the Capital Accounts, or any debits or credits thereto, are computed in order to comply with such Regulations, the General Partner may make such modification, *provided* that it is not likely to have more than an insignificant effect on the total amounts distributable to any Partner pursuant to Article 7 and Article 10.

14.5 Capital Commitment. A Partner's Capital Commitment shall mean the amount that such Partner has agreed to contribute to the capital of the Partnership as set forth opposite such Partner's name on Exhibit A hereto. The Partnership's Committed Capital shall equal the sum of the aggregate Capital Commitments of all Partners.

14.6 Code. The Code is the Internal Revenue Code of 1986, as amended from time to time (or any corresponding provisions of succeeding law).

14.7 Deemed Gain or Deemed Loss. The Deemed Gain from any in kind distribution of Securities shall be equal to the excess, if any, of the fair market value of the Securities distributed (valued as of the date of distribution in accordance with paragraph 12.1), over the aggregate Adjusted Asset Value of the Securities distributed. The Deemed Loss from any in kind distribution of Securities shall be equal to the excess, if any, of the aggregate Adjusted Asset Value of the Securities distributed over the fair market value of the Securities distributed (valued as of the date of distribution in accordance with paragraph 12.1).

14.8 Marketable; Marketable Securities; Marketability. These terms shall refer to Securities that are (a) traded on a national securities exchange or over the counter or (b) currently the subject of an effective Securities Act registration statement. Notwithstanding the foregoing, a Security shall not be deemed to be a Marketable Security if, in the good faith judgment of the General Partner, the market on which such Security trades is not adequate to permit an orderly sale of all shares of such Security held by the Partnership within a reasonable time period.

14.9 **Nonmarketable Securities.** Nonmarketable Securities are all Securities other than Marketable Securities.

14.10 **Ordinary Income.** Ordinary Income shall mean all income received by the Partnership from commercial paper, certificates of deposit, treasury bills, and other money market investments with maturities of less than twelve (12) months, and all interest income and dividends, or other non-liquidating corporate distributions which are not a return of capital for federal income tax purposes.

14.11 **Original Managers.** Original Managers shall refer to _____, _____ and _____.

14.12 **Partnership Percentage.** The Partnership Percentage for each Partner shall be the percentage set forth opposite each Partner's name on Exhibit A hereto.

14.13 **Percentage in Interest; Majority in Interest.** A specified fraction or percentage in interest of the Partners or of the Limited Partners shall mean Partners or Limited Partners of the Partnership, and of any Side by Side Fund organized pursuant to paragraph 8.3(b)(iii), whose capital commitments, stated as a percentage of the aggregate capital commitments of the Partnership and of any such Side by Side Fund, equal to exceed the required fraction or percentage in interest of all such Partners or Limited Partners; *provided, however*, that where expressly stated, a specified fraction or percentage in interest of the Partners or of the Limited Partners shall mean Partners or Limited Partners whose Partnership Percentages equal or exceed the required fraction or percentage of the Partnership Percentages of all such Partners or Limited Partners of this Partnership. A Majority in Interest shall mean more than fifty percent (50%) in interest. Any limited partnership interest owned or controlled by the General Partner shall be deemed not to be outstanding for purposes of any determination under this Agreement of a particular percentage in interest of the Limited Partners.

14.14 **Profit or Loss.** Profit or Loss shall be an amount computed for each Accounting Period as fo the last day thereof that is equal to the Partnership's taxable income or loss for such Accounting Period, determined in accordance with Section 703(a) of the Code (for this purpose, all items of income, gain, loss, or deduction required to be stated separately pursuant to Code Section 703(a)(1) shall be included in taxable income or loss), with the following adjustments:

(a) Any income of the Partnership that is exempt from federal income tax and not otherwise taken into account in computing Profit or Loss pursuant to this paragraph shall be added to such taxable income or loss;

(b) Any expenditures of the Partnership described in Code Section 705(a)(2)(B) or treated as Code Section 705(a)(2)(B) expenditures pursuant to Treasury Regulation Section 1.704-1(b)(2)(iv)(i) and not otherwise taken into account in computing Profit or Loss pursuant to this paragraph shall be subtracted from such taxable income or loss;

(c) Gain or loss resulting from any disposition of a Partnership asset with respect to which gain or loss is recognized for federal income tax purposes shall be computed by reference to the Adjusted Asset Value of the asset disposed of rather than its adjusted tax basis;

PARTNERSHIPS

(d) The difference between the gross fair market value of all Partnership assets and their respective Adjusted Asset Values shall be added to such taxable income or loss in the circumstances described in paragraph 14.2;

(e) Items which are specially allocated pursuant to paragraphs 5.1(c) and 5.3 shall not be taken into account in computing Profit or Loss; and

(f) The amount of any Deemed Gain or Deemed Loss on any Securities distributed in kind shall be added to or subtracted from (as the case may be) such taxable income or loss.

14.15 **Securities.** Securities shall mean securities of every kind and nature and rights and options with respect thereto, including stock, notes, bonds, debentures, evidences of indebtedness and other business interests of every type, including partnerships, joint ventures, proprietorships and other business entities.

14.16 **Securities Act.** Securities Act shall mean the Securities Act of 1933, as amended.

14.17 **Treasury Regulations.** Treasury Regulations shall mean the Income Tax Regulations promulgated under the Code, as such Regulations may be amended from time to time (including corresponding provisions of succeeding Regulations).

ARTICLE 15
OTHER PROVISIONS

15.1 **Governing Law.** This Agreement shall be governed by and construed under the laws of the State of Delaware as applied to agreements among the residents of such state made and to be performed entirely within such state in accordance with the provisions of the Act.

15.2 **Limitation of Liability of the Limited Partners.** Except as required by law, no Limited Partner shall be bound by, nor be personally liable for, the expenses, liabilities, or obligations of the Partnership in excess of its capital commitment to the Partnership.

15.3 **Exculpation.** Neither the tax matters partner, the General Partner, the members of the General Partner, the members of the Advisory Committee nor their respective agents or Affiliates shall be liable to the Limited Partners or the Partnership for honest mistakes of judgment, or for action or inaction, taken in good faith for a purpose that was reasonably believed to be in the best interests of the Partnership, or for losses due to such mistakes, action, or inaction, or to the negligence, dishonesty, or bad faith of any employee, broker, or other agent of the Partnership, *provided* that such employee, broker, or agent was selected, engaged, or retained with reasonable care. The General Partner and such persons may consult with counsel and accountants in respect of Partnership affairs and be fully protected and justified in any action or inaction that is taken in accordance with the advice or opinion of such counsel or accountants, *provided* that they shall have been selected with reasonable care. Notwithstanding any of the foregoing to the contrary, the provisions of this paragraph and the immediately following paragraph shall not be construed so as to relieve (or attempt to relieve) any person of any liability by reason of willful misconduct, recklessness or gross negligence or to the extent (but only to the extent) that such liability may not be waived, modified, or limited under applicable law, but shall be construed so as to effectuate the provisions of such paragraphs to the fullest extent permitted by law.

15.4 **Indemnification.** The Partnership agrees to indemnify, out of the assets of the Partnership only, the General Partner, the members of the General Partner, the

BUSINESS STRUCTURES AND INCORPORATION

members of the Advisory Committee, the tax matters partner and their agents and Affiliates to the fullest extent permitted by law and to save and hold them harmless from and in respect of all (a) reasonable fees, costs, and expenses, including legal fees, paid in connection with or resulting from any claim, action, or demand against the General Partner, the members of the General Partner, the tax matters partner, the Partnership and their agents that arise out of or in any way relate to the Partnership, its properties, business, or affairs and (b) such claims, actions, and demands and any losses or damages resulting from such claims, actions, and demands, including amounts paid in settlement or compromise (if recommended by attorneys for the Partnership) of any such claim, action or demand; *provided, however*, that this indemnity shall not extend to conduct not undertaken in good faith to promote the best interests of the Partnership or the portfolio companies of the Partnership, nor to any conduct which constitutes recklessness, willful misconduct or gross negligence. Expenses incurred by any indemnified person in defending a claim or proceeding covered by this paragraph shall be paid by the Partnership in advance of the final disposition of such claim or proceeding, *provided* the indemnified person undertakes to repay such amount if it is ultimately determined that such person was not entitled to be indemnified. The provisions of this paragraph 15.4 shall remain in effect as to each indemnified person whether or not such indemnified person continues to serve in the capacity that entitled such person to be indemnified. Without limiting the generality of this paragraph 15.4, each indemnified person shall use reasonable efforts to pursue indemnification, insurance or other similar rights from portfolio companies of the partnership and to permit the Partnership to be subrogated to the indemnified person's rights with respect to any such portfolio company indemnification, insurance or other similar rights.

    15.5 **Arbitration.** Any controversy or claim arising out of or relating to this Agreement, or the breach thereof, except with respect to the valuation of Partnership assets, shall be settled by arbitration in _____, _____ in accordance with the rules, then obtaining, of the American Arbitration Association, and judgment upon the award rendered may be entered in any court having jurisdiction thereof.

    15.6 **Execution and Filing of Documents.** This Agreement may be executed in two or more counterparts, each of which shall be deemed an original but all of which together shall constitute one and the same instrument.

    15.7 **Other Instruments and Acts.** The Partners agree to execute any other instruments or perform any other acts that are or may be reasonably necessary to effectuate and carry on the partnership created by this Agreement.

    15.8 **Binding Agreement.** This Agreement shall be binding upon the transferees, successors, assigns, and legal representatives of the Partners.

    15.9 **Notices.** Any notice or other communication that one Partner desires to give to another Partner shall be in writing, and shall be deemed effectively given upon personal delivery or three (3) days after deposit in any United States mail box, by registered or certified mail, postage prepaid, upon confirmed transmission by facsimile, or upon confirmed delivery by overnight commercial courier service, addressed to the other Partner at the address shown on Exhibit A or at such other address as a Partner may designate by ten (10) days' advance written notice to the other Partners.

    15.10 **Power of Attorney.** By signing this Agreement, each Limited Partner designates and appoints the General Partner its true and lawful attorney, in its name, place, and stead to make, execute, sign, and file the Certificate of Limited Partnership and any amendment thereto and such other instruments, documents, or certificates that may from

PARTNERSHIPS

time to time be required of the Partnership by the laws of the United States of America, the laws of the state of the Partnership's formation, or any other state in which the Partnership shall conduct its affairs in order to qualify or otherwise enable the Partnership to conduct its affairs in such jurisdictions. Such attorney is not hereby granted any authority on behalf of the Limited Partners to amend this Agreement except that as attorney for each of the Limited Partners, the General Partner shall have the authority to amend this Agreement and the Certificate of Limited Partnership (and to execute any amendment to the Agreement or the Certificate of Limited Partnership on behalf of itself and as attorney in fact for each of the Limited Partners) as may be required to effect:

(a) Admission of additional Partners pursuant to Article 3;

(b) Transfers of Limited Partnership interests pursuant to Article 9;

(c) Extensions of the Partnership term pursuant to Article 10; and

(d) Withdrawal of Partners pursuant to Article 13.

This power of attorney granted by each Limited Partner shall expire as to such Partner immediately after the dissolution of the Partnership or the amendment of the Partnership's Exhibit A to reflect the complete withdrawal of such Partner as a Partner of the Partnership.

15.11 Amendment.

(a) Except as provided by the immediately preceding paragraph and subject to paragraph 15.11(b), this Agreement may be amended only with the written consent of the General Partner and a Majority in Interest of the Limited Partners.

(b) Notwithstanding paragraph 15.11(a), (i) no amendment to the provisions of paragraphs 4.5(c), 4.5(d), 4.5(e) or Article 13 may be made without the consent of each ERISA Partner, Governmental Plan Partner, Private Foundation Partner and BHC Partner who may be adversely affected by such amendment, and (ii) no amendment to paragraph 8.4(e) may be made without the consent of a Majority in Interest of those Limited Partners who are tax exempt under the Code (including those Limited Partners whose interests are at least partially owned by any tax exempt person).

(c) Notwithstanding paragraphs 15.11(a) and (b), no amendment of this Agreement may (i) modify an provision requiring the consent of more than a majority in Interest o the Limited Partners without the consent of such higher Percentage in Interest, or (ii) modify the method of making Partnership allocations or distributions, modify the method of determining the Partnership Percentage of any Partner, reduce any Partner's Capital Account, modify any provision of this Agreement pertaining to limitations on liability of the Limited Partners, or (iii) change the restrictions contained in this paragraph 15.11(c), unless each Partner materially adversely affected thereby in a manner different than the other Partners has expressly consented in writing to such amendment.

(d) The Partnership's or General Partner's (or its managers', members' or employees') noncompliance with any provision hereof in any single transaction or event may be waived in writing by a Majority in Interest of Limited Partners to the extent such consent would be required to amend such provision pursuant to paragraph 15.11(a). No waiver shall be deemed a waiver of any subsequent event of noncompliance.

15.12 Entire Agreement. This Agreement constitutes the full, complete, and final agreement of the Partners and supersedes all prior written or oral agreements between the Partners with respect to the Partnership.

BUSINESS STRUCTURES AND INCORPORATION

15.13 Titles; Subtitles. The titles and subtitles used in this Agreement are used for convenience only and shall not be considered in the interpretation of this Agreement.

15.14 Partnership Name. The Partnership shall have the exclusive right to use the Partnership name as long as the Partnership continues. Upon termination of the Partnership, the Partnership shall assign whatever rights it may have in such name to the General Partner. No value shall be placed upon the name or the goodwill attached to it for the purpose of determining the value of any Partner's Capital Account or interest in the Partnership.

IN WITNESS WHEREOF, the Partners have executed this Agreement as of the date first written above.

GENERAL PARTNER:
ANC MANAGEMENT, L.L.C.

By: _____
    Managing Partner

LIMITED PARTNER:

_____
(Print name of investing entity)
By: _____
Name: _____
Title: _____

"THE SECURITIES EVIDENCED BY THIS PARTNERSHIP AGREEMENT HAVE NOT BEEN REGISTERED UNDER THE SECURITIES ACT OF 1933, AS AMENDED, AND MAY NOT BE SOLD, TRANSFERRED, ASSIGNED OR HYPOTHECATED UNLESS THERE IS AN EFFECTIVE REGISTRATION STATEMENT UNDER THE 1933 ACT COVERING SUCH SECURITIES OR THE GENERAL PARTNER RECEIVES AN OPINION OF COUNSEL FOR THE HOLDER OF THESE SECURITIES REASONABLY SATISFACTOR TO THE GENERAL PARTNER, STATING THAT SUCH SALE, TRANSFER, ASSIGNMENT OR HYPOTHECATION IS EXEMPT FROM THE REGISTRATION AND PROSPECTUS DELIVERY REQUIREMENTS OF THE 1933 ACT."

Each of the undersigned acknowledges his respective obligations under paragraph 10.5 of this Agreement.

_____
_____

CHAPTER 6

LIMITED LIABILITY COMPANIES

The limited liability company (LLC) is a relatively new form of business entity designed to offer the limited liability of a corporation and the flow through tax advantages of a partnership. Like a corporation, it may be formed only by filing appropriate documents with the state, but otherwise it is a very flexible business form: owners may choose centralized management or owner management, free transferability of ownership or restricted transferability, etc.

LLC Characteristics

An LLC is an entity designed to be taxed like a partnership but offer its owners (called members) the limited liability that shareholders of a corporation enjoy. Under current tax laws, unless an LLC requests to be taxed as a corporation, it will receive partnership tax treatment (i.e., the LLC will not be treated as a taxable entity; its profits and losses flow through the LLC to its owners).

❖ **S Corporation and Limited Partnership Comparisons** – If a person is seeking a business format that offers limited personal liability and an opportunity to control the business, an LLC may be better than a S corporation (a corporation that elects to be taxed as a partnership under the Tax Code), because an LLC is not subject to the limitations of S Corporations (e.g., S corporations are limited to 75 or fewer shareholders, there can be only one class of stock, etc). Similarly, an LLC may be better than a limited partnership because limited partnership acts require that there be at least one general partner who is personally liable for the partnership's obligations; no member need be personally liable for the obligations of an LLC.

BUSINESS STRUCTURES AND INCORPORATION

- ❖ **Controlling Law—Statute vs. Operating Agreement** – Although LLCs are governed by statute, the statute provides that LLC members can adopt operating agreements with provisions different from the LLC statute, and generally the operating agreement will control.
- ❖ **Distinct Entity** – An LLC is treated as an entity distinct from its members. It may hold property in its own name, sue or be sued, etc.

LLC Operating Agreement

The following agreement is not intended to be comprehensive or an absolute statement of the governing law. This agreement is not legal advice. It does not analyze any specific fact patterns from any parties but rather discusses broadly points of law, which may or may not be the most accurate, according to current case law interpretation or even case law interpretation that is very in-depth on very narrowly-presented issues. Sound legal advice arises from interaction between client and attorney in a question-and-answer dialogue where facts are provided by a client as the attorney probes for issues and then conducts appropriate research if need be to ascertain the applicable law. Anyone seeking specific advice to specific legal questions should present their facts to an attorney.

OPERATING AGREEMENT
OF
SMITH VENTURES, LLC
A CALIFORNIA LIMITED LIABILITY COMPANY

THE SECURITES REPRESENTED BY THIS AGREEMENT HAVE NOT BEEN REGISTERED UNDER THE SECURITIES ACT OF 1933 NOR REGISTERED NOR QUALIFED UNDER ANY STATE SECURITEIS LAWS. SUCH SECURITIES MAY NOT BE OFFERED FOR SALE, SOLD, DELIVERED AFTER SALE, TRANSFERRED, PLEDGED, OR HYPOTHECATED UNLESS QUALIFED AND REGISTERED UNDER APPLICABLE STATE AND FEDERAL SECURITIES LAWS OR UNLESS, IN THE OPINION OF COUNSEL SATISFACTORY TO THE COMPANY, SUCH QUALIFICATION AND REGISTRATION IS NOT REQUIRED. ANY TRANSFER OF THE SECURITIES REPRESENTED BY THIS AGREEMENT IS FUTHER SUBJECT TO OTHER RESTRICTIONS, TERMS AND CONDITONS WHICH ARE SET FORTH HEREIN.

OPERATING AGREEMENT
OF
SMITH VENTURES, LLC
A CALIFORNIA LIMITED LIABILITY COMPANY

This Operating Agreement is made and entered into as of the ____ day of _____, 20__, by and between John Smith and Jane Smith. John Smith and Jane Smith are hereinafter sometimes collectively referred to as the "Members" and individually as the "Member").

LIMITED LIABILITY COMPANIES

RECITALS

A. On _____, 20__, the Articles of Organization for SMITH VENTURES, LLC, a California limited liability company ("Company"), were filed with the California Secretary of State.

B. The Members desire to adopt this Operating Agreement.

AGREEMENT

ARTICLE 1

DEFINITIONS

When used in this Agreement, the following terms shall have the meanings set forth below (all terms used in this Agreement that are not defined in this Article shall have the meanings set forth elsewhere in this Agreement):

1.1 "Act" shall mean the Beverly-Killea Limited Liability Company Act, codified in the California Corporations Code, Section 17000 et seq., as the same may be amended from time to time.

1.2 "Affiliate" shall mean any individual, partnership, corporation, trust or other entity or association, directly or indirectly, through one or more intermediaries, controlling, controlled by, or under common control with the Member. The term "control," as used in the immediately preceding sentence, means, with respect to a corporation or limited liability company the right to exercise, directly or indirectly, more than fifty percent (50%) of the voting rights attributable to the controlled corporation or limited liability company, and, with respect to any individual, partnership, trust, other entity or association, the possession, directly or indirectly, of the power to direct or cause the direction of the management or policies of the controlled entity.

1.3 "Agreement" shall mean this Operating Agreement, as originally executed and as amended from time to time.

1.4 "Articles" shall mean the Articles of Organization for the Company originally filed with the California Secretary of State and as amended from time to time.

1.5 "Bankruptcy" shall mean: (i) the filing of an application by a Member for his, her, or its consent to, the appointment of a trustee, receiver, or custodian of his, her, or its other assets; (ii) the entry of an order for relief with respect to a Member in proceedings under the United States Bankruptcy Code, as amended or superseded from time to time; (iii) the making by a Member of a general assignment for the benefit of creditors; (iv) the entry of an order, judgment, or decree by any court of competent jurisdiction appointing a trustee, receiver, or custodian of the assets of a Member unless the proceedings and the person appointed are dismissed within ninety (90) days; or (v) the failure by a Member generally to pay his, her, or its debts as the debts become due within the meaning of Section 303(h)(1) of the United States Bankruptcy Code, as determined by the Bankruptcy Court, or the admission in writing of his, her, or its inability to pay his, her, or its debts as they become due.

1.6 "Capital Account" shall mean with respect to any Member the Capital Account which the Company establishes and maintains for such Member pursuant to Section 3.

1.7 "Capital Contribution" shall mean the total value of cash and fair market value of property (including promissory notes or other obligation to contribute cash

BUSINESS STRUCTURES AND INCORPORATION

or property) contributed and/or services rendered, or to be rendered to the Company by Members.

1.8 "Code" shall mean the Internal Revenue Code of 1986, as amended from time to time, the provisions of succeeding law, and to the extent applicable, the Regulations.

1.9 "Company" shall mean the SMITH VENTURES, LLC, a California limited liability company.

1.10 "Company Minimum Gain" shall have the meaning ascribed to the term "Partnership Minimum Gain" in the Regulations Section 1.704-2(d).

1.11 "Corporations Code" shall mean the California Corporation Code, as amended from time to time, and the provisions of succeeding law.

1.12 "Dissociation Event" shall mean with respect to any Member one or more of the following: the withdrawal, death, bankruptcy or dissolution of the Member.

1.13 "Distributable Cash" shall mean the amount of cash which the Manager reasonably deems available for distribution, taking into account all Company debts, liabilities, and obligations of the Company then due, amounts which the Manager deems necessary to place into reserves for customary and usual expenses with respect to the Company's business, and anticipated repairs and maintenance to Company assets.

1.14 "Economic Interest" shall mean a Member's or Economic Interest Owner's share of one or more of the Company's Net Profits, Net Losses, and distributions of the Company's assets pursuant to this Agreement and the Act, but shall not include any other rights of a Member, including, without limitation, the right to vote or participate in the management, or any right to information concerning the business and affairs of Company. Unless otherwise provided in this Agreement, a Member's or Economic Interest Owner's Economic Interest in the Company's Net Profits, Net Losses, and distributions shall be such Member's or Economic Interest Owner's Percentage Interest as defined in Section 1.

1.15 "Economic Interest Owner" shall mean the owner of an Economic Interest who is not a Member.

1.16 "Fiscal Year" shall mean the Company's Fiscal Year, which shall be the calendar year.

1.17 "Former Member" shall mean a Member who withdraws from the Company in accordance with Section 4. For purposes of Sections 9 through 9, a "Former Member" is any Member who is obligated to sell his or her interest in the Company to the Remaining Members and/or the Company.

1.18 "Former Member's Interest" shall mean a Former Member's Membership Interest in the Company.

1.19 "Majority Interest" shall mean one or more Members who own Percentage Interests which taken together exceed fifty percent (50%) of the aggregate of all Percentage Interests.

1.20 "Management Agreement" shall mean the agreement between the Company and Jane Smith, whereby Jane Smith shall be compensated for performance of her duties as Manager.

1.21 "Manager" shall mean one or more Managers. Specifically, "Manager" shall mean Jane Smith, or any other Person that succeeds her in that capacity.

1.22 "Member" shall mean each Person who (i) is an initial signatory to this Agreement, has been admitted to the Company as a Member in accordance with the Articles

LIMITED LIABILITY COMPANIES

or this Agreement or is an assignee who has become a Member in accordance with Article 8, and (ii) has not withdrawn or, if other than an individual, dissolved.

1.23 "Member Nonrecourse Debt" shall have the meaning ascribed to the term "Partner Nonrecourse Debt" in Regulations Section 1.704-2(b)(4).

1.24 "Member Nonrecourse Deductions" shall mean items of Company loss, deduction, or Code Section 705(a)(2)(B) expenditures which are attributable to Member Nonrecourse Debt.

1.25 "Membership Interest" shall mean a Member's entire interest in the Company including the Member's Economic Interest, the right to vote on or participate in the management, and the right to receive information concerning the business and affairs, of the Company. Unless otherwise provided in this Agreement, the Percentage Interest of a Member's Membership Interest shall be such Member's Percentage Interest as defined in Section 1.

1.26 "Net Profits" and "Net Losses" shall mean, for each taxable year of the Company (or other period for which Net Profits or Net Losses must be computed), the Company's taxable income or loss determined in accordance with Code Section 703(a), with the following adjustments: (a) All items of income, gain, loss, deduction, or credit required to be stated separately pursuant to Code Section 703(a)(1) shall be included in computing taxable income or loss; (b) Any tax-exempt income of the Company, not otherwise taken into account in computing taxable income or loss, shall be included in computing Net Profits or Net Losses; (c) Any expenditures of the Company described in Code Section 705(a)(2)(B) (or treated as such pursuant to Regulations Section 1.704-1(b)(2)(iv)(i)) and not otherwise taken into account in computing Net Profits or Net Losses, shall be subtracted from taxable income or loss; (d) Gain or loss resulting from any taxable disposition of Company property shall be computed by reference to the book value as adjusted under Regulations Section 1.704-1(b) (for purposes of this Section 1 "adjusted book value") of the property disposed of, notwithstanding the fact that the adjusted book value differs from the adjusted basis of the property for federal income tax purposes; (e) In lieu of the depreciation, amortization or cost recovery deductions allowable in computing taxable income or loss, there shall be taken into account the depreciation computed based upon the adjusted book value of the asset; and (f) Notwithstanding any other provision of this definition, any items which are specially allocated pursuant to Section 6 shall not be taken into account in computing Net Profits or Net Losses.

1.27 "Nonrecourse Liability" shall have the meaning set forth in Regulations Section 1.752-1(a)(2).

1.28 "Percentage Interest" shall mean the percentage of a Member set forth opposite the name of such Member under the column "Percentage Interest" in **Exhibit A** hereto, as such percentage may be adjusted from time to time pursuant to the terms of this Agreement.

1.29 "Person" shall mean an individual, general partnership, limited partnership, limited liability company, corporation, trust, estate, real estate investment trust association or any other association or business entity.

1.30 "Regulations" shall, unless the context clearly indicates otherwise, mean the regulations currently in force as final or temporary that have been issued by the United States Department of Treasury pursuant to its authority under the Code.

BUSINESS STRUCTURES AND INCORPORATION

1.31 "Remaining Members" shall, upon the occurrence of a Dissociation Event as defined in Section 1, mean all the Members except the Member subject to the Dissociation Event.

1.32 "Secretary of State" shall mean the Secretary of State for the State of California and its delegates responsible for the administration of the Act.

1.33 "Tax Matters Partner" shall be Jane Smith or her successor as designated below.

ARTICLE 2
ORGANIZATIONAL MATTERS

2.1 Formation. Pursuant to the Act, the Members have formed a California limited liability company under the laws of the State of California by filing the Articles of Organization with the Secretary of State and entering into this Agreement. The rights and liabilities of the Members shall be determined pursuant to the Act and this Agreement. To the extent that the rights or obligations of any Member are different by reason of any provision of this Agreement than they would be in the absence of such provisions, this Agreement shall, to the extent permitted by the Act, control.

2.2 Name. The name of the Company shall be "SMITH VENTURES, LLC". The business of the Company may be conducted under that name or, upon compliance with applicable laws, any other name that the Manager deems appropriate or advisable. The Manager shall file any fictitious name certificates and similar filings, and any amendments thereto, that the Manager considers appropriate or advisable.

2.3 Term. The term of this Company commenced on the date the Articles of Organization were filed with the Secretary of State and shall continue until the Company is dissolved as provided herein, or _____, 20__, whichever shall first occur, provided, however, the term may be extended beyond such date by the unanimous agreement of the Members.

2.4 Office and Agent. The Company shall continuously maintain an office and registered agent in the State of California as required by the Act. The principal office of the Company shall be as the Manager may determine. The Company also may have such offices, anywhere within and without the State of California, as the Manager from time to time may determine, or the business of the Company may require. The initial registered office and agent of the Company shall be stated in the Articles or as otherwise determined by the Manager.

2.5 Addresses of the Members and Manager. The respective addresses of the Members and the Manager are set forth on **Exhibit A**.

2.6 Purpose of Company. The purpose of the Company is to engage in any lawful business for which a limited liability company may be organized under the Act.

LIMITED LIABILITY COMPANIES

ARTICLE 3
CAPITAL CONTRIBUTIONS

3.1   Initial Capital Contributions. Upon execution of this Agreement, each of the Original Members shall have contributed to the Company as such Member's initial Capital Contribution cash in the amounts set forth in **Exhibit A**, attached hereto and incorporated herein by reference. In exchange for each Member's initial Capital Contribution, the Member received (i) a Membership Interest in the Company as set forth opposite such Member's name in **Exhibit A**, and (ii) a credit to such Member's Capital Account equal to the sum of the cash and the fair market value of the property contributed.

3.2   Additional Capital Contributions. No Member shall be required to make any additional Capital Contributions. Upon a determination by the Manager that additional Capital Contributions are necessary or appropriate for the conduct of the Company's business, including without limitation, expansion or diversification, the Members may be permitted to make additional Capital Contributions if and to the extent they so desire. In that event, the Members shall have the opportunity, but not the obligation, to participate in such additional Capital Contributions on a pro rata basis in accordance with their Membership Interests. Each Member shall receive a credit to such Member's Capital Account in the amount of any additional capital which the Member contributes to the Company, and such Member shall receive an additional Membership Interest determined by the value of the Additional Capital Contribution in relation to the value of the Company as a whole. The value of the Company as a whole shall be determined at the time the Additional Capital Contribution is made pursuant to the appraisal mechanism stated in Section 9 below. Immediately following such Capital Contributions, the Manager shall amend this Agreement to adjust the Membership Interests and Economic Interests to reflect the new relative proportions of the Capital Accounts of the Members and Economic Interest Owners. Notwithstanding anything to the contrary, such an amendment shall not require the vote or approval of the Members.

3.3   Capital Accounts. The Company shall establish an individual Capital Account for each Member and Economic Interest Owner. The Company shall determine and maintain each Capital Account in accordance with Regulations Section 1.704-1(b)(2)(iv). If a Member or an Economic Interest Owner transfers all or a part of his, her, or its Economic Interest in accordance with this Agreement, such Member's or Economic Interest Owner's Capital Account attributable to the transferred Economic Interest shall carry over to the new owner of such Economic Interest pursuant to Regulations Section 1.704-1(b)(2)(iv)(1).

3.4   No Interest. No Member or Economic Interest Owner shall be entitled to receive any interest on his, her, or its Capital Contributions.

3.5   Valuation of Company Assets. The book values of all Company assets shall be adjusted to equal their respective fair market values (taking Code Section 7701(g) into account), as reasonably determined by the Manager, upon the occurrence of any of the following events: (i) a contribution of money or property (other than a de minimis amount) to the Company by a new or existing Member as consideration for a Membership Interest; (ii) a distribution of money or property (other than a de minimis amount) by the Company to a Member as consideration for a Membership Interest; and (iii) the liquidation of the Company within the meaning of Regulations Section 1.704-1(b)(2)(ii)(g). Any such adjustments shall be reflected by corresponding adjustments to the Capital Accounts which

BUSINESS STRUCTURES AND INCORPORATION

reflect the manner in which the unrealized income, gain, loss, or deduction inherent in such property (that has not been reflected in the Capital Accounts previously) would be allocated among the Members if there were a taxable disposition of such assets for such fair market values.

ARTICLE 4
MEMBERS

4.1 <u>Limited Liability</u>. Except as set forth in this Agreement, no Member shall be personally liable for any debt, obligation, or liability of the Company, whether that liability or obligation arises in contract, tort, or otherwise.

4.2 <u>Admission of Additional Members</u>. The Manager may admit to the Company additional Members, from time to time, subject to the following: (a) The Manager consents to the admission; (b) The additional Member shall make a Capital Contribution in such amount and on such terms as the Manager determines to be appropriate based upon the needs of the Company, the net value of the Company's assets, the Company's financial condition, and the benefits anticipated to be realized by the additional Member; and (c) No additional Member shall be admitted if the effect of such admission would be to terminate the Company within the meaning of Code Section 708(b).

Notwithstanding the foregoing, substitute Members may only be admitted in accordance with Article 8. The Manager shall amend this Agreement to reflect the admission of additional Members and such amendment shall not require the vote or approval of the Members.

4.3 <u>Withdrawals</u>. No Member may withdraw from the Company without the consent of the Manager. If a withdrawal is consented to, such Member's Membership Interest shall be subject to purchase and sale as provided in Section 9.

4.4 <u>Termination of Membership Interest</u>. Upon (i) the transfer of all or a portion of a Member's Membership Interest in violation of this Agreement, (ii) the occurrence of a Dissociation Event of a Member which does not result in the admission of a substitute Member pursuant to Section 8 as to such Member's Membership Interest, or (iii) the withdrawal of a Member in accordance with Section 4, the Membership Interest of such Member may be purchased by the Company or Remaining Members as provided herein, or, if not so purchased, such Membership Interest shall become an Economic Interest and the balance of the rights associated with the Membership Interest (including without limitation, the right of the Member to vote or participate in the management of the business, property and affairs of the Company) may, in the sole discretion of the Manager, be purchased by the Company pursuant to Section 8.

4.5 <u>Transactions With The Company</u>. Subject to any limitations set forth in this Agreement and with the prior approval of the Manager after full disclosure of the Member's involvement, a Member may engage in any transaction (including, without limitation, the purchase, sale, lease or exchange of any property, or the lending of funds, or the rendering of any service, or the establishment of any salary, other compensation or other terms of employment) with the Company. Subject to other applicable law, such Member has the same rights and obligations with respect thereto as a Person who is not a Member.

4.6 <u>Remuneration To Members</u>. Except as otherwise authorized in, or pursuant to, this Agreement, no Member is entitled to remuneration for acting in the Company business, subject to the entitlement of Members winding up the affairs of the Company to reasonable compensation pursuant to Section 11. Notwithstanding the prior sentence and subject to the provisions of Section 4, the Company shall pay the Members for services rendered to the Company to the extent that the Members are not required to render such services themselves without charge to the Company.

  4.7 Members Are Not Agents. Pursuant to Section 5 and the Articles, the management of the Company is vested in the Manager. No Member, acting solely in the capacity of a Member, is an agent of the Company nor can any Member in such capacity bind nor execute any instrument on behalf of the Company.

  This Section supersedes any authority granted to the Members pursuant to Section 17157 of the Act. Any Member who takes any action or binds the Company in violation of this Section shall be solely responsible for any loss and expense incurred by the Company as a result of the unauthorized action and shall indemnify and hold the Company harmless with respect to the loss or expense.

  4.8. Voting Rights. Except as expressly provided in this Agreement or the Articles, Members shall have no voting, approval or consent rights. Members who are not the subject of a Dissociation Event or who have not assigned their Membership Interests shall have the right to approve or disapprove matters as specifically stated in this Agreement, including the following: (a) Those matters specified in Section 5; (b) Any other matter expressly set forth in this Agreement; and (c) Such other matters as the Manager may from time to time elect to submit to the vote of the Members, provided however, that the Manager shall not be obligated to submit any matter to the vote of the Members except as otherwise provided in this Agreement.

  4.9 Meetings of Members. No annual or regular meetings of Members are required.

ARTICLE 5

MANAGEMENT AND CONTROL OF THE COMPANY

  5.1 Management of the Company by Manager.

    (a) Exclusive Management by Manager. The business, property and affairs of the Company shall be managed exclusively by the Manager, who may, but need not, be Members. Except for situations in which the approval of the Members is expressly required by the Act, the Articles or this Agreement, the Manager shall have full, complete and exclusive authority, power, and discretion to manage, and control the business, property and affairs of the Company, to make all decisions regarding those matters and to perform any and all other acts or activities customary or incident to the management of the Company's business, property and affairs.

    (b) Agency Authority of Manager. Subject to Section 5, the Manager (if only one) or each Manager (if there are more than one Managers), acting alone, is authorized to (i) endorse checks, drafts, and other evidence of indebtedness made payable to the order of the Company, but only for the purpose of deposit into the Company's accounts, (ii) sign all checks, drafts, and other instruments obligating the Company to pay money, and (iii) sign all contracts obligations, or any other instrument or document on behalf of the Company. Notwithstanding anything to the contrary, the Manager may, subject to any limitations that the Manager deems necessary or appropriate, authorize one or more agents of the Company, which may or may not be employees or Members of the Company, to (i) endorse checks, drafts, and other evidence of indebtedness made payable to the order of the Company, but only for the purpose of deposit into the Company's accounts, and (ii) sign checks, drafts, and other instruments obligating the Company to pay money.

(c) <u>Meetings of Managers</u>. Meetings of Managers, if there are more than one Manager, are not required.

5.2 Election of Managers.

(a) <u>Number, Term, and Qualifications</u>. The Company shall initially have one (1) Manager. Jane Smith shall be and is hereby appointed the initial Manager. Upon the death, resignation or removal of Jane Smith, John Smith shall be the successor Manager. If John Smith predeceases Jane Smith or is unable to perform his duties as successor Manager upon the death, resignation or removal of Jane Smith for some other reason, then the successor Manager shall be elected pursuant to subsection (d) of this Section.

The number of Managers of the Company shall be fixed from time to time by the affirmative vote or written consent of Members holding a Majority Interest, provided that if the number of Managers is increased from one (1) to more than one (1), the Articles shall be amended to delete the statement that the Company has only one (1) Manager. At no time shall there be less than one (1) Manager. Unless a Manager resigns or is removed, each Manager shall hold office until a successor shall have been elected and qualified. Successor Managers shall be elected by the affirmative vote or written consent of Members holding a Majority Interest. A Manager need not be a Member, an individual, a resident of the State of California, or a citizen of the United States.

(b) <u>Resignation</u>. Any Manager may resign at any time by giving written notice to the Members and the remaining Managers, if any. Any such resignation shall be without prejudice to the rights, if any, of the Company under any contract to which the resigning Manager is a party. The resignation of any Manager shall take effect upon receipt of that notice or at such later time as shall be specified in the notice; and, unless otherwise specified in the notice, the acceptance of the resignation shall not be necessary to make it effective. The resignation of a Manager who is also a Member shall not affect the Manager's rights as a Member and shall not constitute a withdrawal of a Member.

(c) <u>Removal</u>.

(i) Except as set forth in this Section, the Members shall have no power to remove or expel a Manager. A Manager may only be removed by the vote of Members holding a majority of the Percentage Interest (including the Percentage Interest of such Manager in her capacity as a Member) upon default in the performance of her obligations as a Manager. The following acts and/or omissions shall constitute a default by a Manager: the failure to perform any duty or act required of the Manager by this Agreement or the Act, or the performance of any act prohibited by this Agreement or the Act, provided that the Manager (1) shall have received written notice from the remaining Members of such default, and (2) shall not have cured such default, if it is a monetary default, within thirty (30) days thereafter, or (3) shall not have commenced to cure or remedy such default, if it is a non-monetary default, within thirty (30) days thereafter, and (4) shall not have thereafter pursued any such correction to completion with diligence and continuity and corrected such default within a reasonable time.

(ii) Upon the occurrence of an event of default of a Manager as specified above, the Remaining Members may remove the Manager by giving said Manager written notice of removal. Notice of removal shall be served on the Manager either by certified or registered mail, return receipt requested, or by personal service, and shall set forth the effective date of the removal.

LIMITED LIABILITY COMPANIES

(iii) Any removal shall be without prejudice to the rights, if any, of the Manager under any employment or management contract and, if the Manager is also a Member, shall not affect the Manager's rights as a Member or constitute a withdrawal of a Member.

(d) <u>Vacancies</u>. Any vacancy occurring for any reason in the number of Managers may be filled by the affirmative vote or written consent of a Majority Interest of Members.

5.3 <u>Powers of Manager</u>. Without limiting the generality of Section 5, but subject to Section 5 and to the express limitations set forth elsewhere in this Agreement, the Manager shall have all necessary powers to manage and carry out the purposes, business, property, and affairs of the Company and to make all decisions affecting such business and affairs, including, without limitation, the power to exercise on behalf of the Company all powers described in Corporations Code Section 17003, including without limitation, the power to: (a) Acquire, purchase, renovate, improve, alter, rebuild, demolish, replace, and own property or assets that the Manager determines is necessary or appropriate or in the interest of the business of the Company, and to acquire options for the purchase of any such property; (b) Sell, exchange, lease, or otherwise dispose of the property and assets owned by the Company, or any part thereof, or any interest therein; (c) Guarantee the payment of money or the performance of any contract or obligation of any Person; (d) Sue on, defend, or compromise any and all claims or liabilities in favor of or against the Company; and/or submit any or all such claims or liabilities to arbitration; (e) Make contracts and guarantees, incur liabilities, act as surety, and borrow money; (f) Issue notes, bonds, and other obligations and secure any of them by mortgage or deed of trust or security interest of any or all of the Company's assets; (g) Retain legal counsel, auditors, and other professionals in connection with the Company business and to pay therefore such remuneration as the Manager may determine; (h) Care for and distribute funds to the Members by way of cash flow, income, return of capital, or otherwise, all in accordance with the provisions of this Agreement, and perform all matters in furtherance of the objectives of the Company or this Agreement; (i) Employ from time to time, at the expense of the Company, on such terms and for such compensation as the Manager may determine, but subject to this Agreement, Persons to render services to the Company; (j) Pay or cause to be paid all expenses, fees, charges, taxes, and liabilities incurred or arising in connection with the Company, or in connection with the management thereof, including without limitation, such expenses and charges for the services of the Company employees, accountants, attorneys, and other agents or independent contractors, and such other expenses and charges as the Manager deems is necessary or advisable to incur; and (k) Make elections for federal, state and local tax purposes, including without limitation, any election permitted by applicable law to (i) adjust the basis of the Company property pursuant to Code Sections 754, 734(b), and/or 743(b), and/or comparable provisions of state or local law in connection with the transfer of Membership Interests; and (ii) extend the statute of limitations for assessment of tax deficiencies against Members with respect to adjustments to the Company's federal, state or local tax returns.

The expression of any power or authority of the Manager in this Agreement shall not in any way limit or exclude any other power or authority which is not specifically or expressly set forth in this Agreement. If there is more than one (1) Manager, the rights and powers of the Manager hereunder shall be exercised by such Manager in such manner as they may agree, including without limitation by delegating responsibility for conduct of

BUSINESS STRUCTURES AND INCORPORATION

Company business or any portion thereof to any one (1) or more of the Managers. Any such delegation of responsibility or authority to one (1) or more Managers may be revoked at any time by the Remaining Managers. In the absence of any agreement among such persons, no Manager may exercise any of such rights and powers without the consent of a majority (in number) of the Managers. Furthermore, any provision in this Agreement requiring the consent of the Managing Manager shall mean the consent of a majority (in number) of the Managers unless otherwise expressly stated.

   5.4 <u>Limitations on Power of Manager</u>. Notwithstanding any other provisions of this Agreement, the Manager shall have no authority hereunder to cause the Company to engage in the following transactions without first obtaining the affirmative vote or written consent of a Majority Interest (or such greater Percentage Interests set forth below) of the Members: (a) The merger of the Company with another limited liability company, limited partnership, general partnership or other Person (provided (i) in no event shall a Member be required to become a general partner in a merger with a limited partnership without his, her, or its express consent or unless the agreement of merger provides each Member with dissenter's rights described in the Act, and (ii) in a merger of the Company with a general partnership, if the Members become personally liable for any obligations as a result of the merger, the principal terms of the agreement of merger must be approved by all of the Members unless the agreement of merger provides that all Members will have dissenter's rights provided in the Act); (b) An alteration of the primary purpose of the Company as set forth in Section 2; (c) Any act which would make it impossible to carry on the ordinary business of the Company; (d) Any other transaction described in this Agreement as requiring the vote, consent, or approval of the Members; or (e) Entering into any amendment of the Articles or this Agreement (except as otherwise provided in this Agreement) shall require the unanimous vote, consent, or approval of the Members.

   5.5 <u>Members Have No Managerial Authority</u>. The Members shall have no power to participate in the management of the Company except as expressly authorized by this Agreement or the Articles and except as expressly required by the Act. Unless expressly and duly authorized in writing to do so by the Manager, no Member shall have any power or authority to bind or act on behalf of the Company in any way, to pledge its credit, or to render it liable for any purpose.

   5.6 <u>Performance of Duties; Liability of Manager</u>. A Manager shall not be liable to the Company or to any Member for any loss or damage sustained by the Company or any Member, unless the loss or damage shall have been the result of fraud, deceit, gross negligence, reckless or intentional misconduct, or a knowing violation of law by the Manager.

   5.7 <u>Devotion of Time</u>. The Manager is not obligated to devote all of her time or business efforts to the affairs of the Company. The Manager shall devote whatever time, effort, and skill as she deems appropriate for the operation of the Company.

   5.8 <u>Competing Activities</u>. The Manager and her Affiliates may engage or invest in any business activity of any type or description, including without limitations those that might be the same as or similar to the Company's business and that might be in director or indirect competition with the Company. Any such activity may be engaged in independently or with others, and may include without limitation the conduct of the same business as that of the Company for the account of any one or all of such Persons. Neither the Company nor any Member shall have any right in or to such other ventures or activities, or to the income or proceeds derived there from. The Manager shall not be obligated to present any investment opportunity or prospective economic advantage to the Company, even if the opportunity is of the character that, if presented to the Company, could be taken by the Company. The Manager shall have the right to hold any investment opportunity or prospective economic advantage for their own account or to recommend such opportunity to Persons other than the Company. The Members acknowledge that the Manager and her Affiliates own and/or manage other businesses, including businesses that may compete with the Company and for the Manager's time. The Members hereby waive any and all rights and claims which they may otherwise have against the Manager and her Affiliates as a result of any such activities.

5.9 Transactions between the Company and a Manager. Notwithstanding that it may constitute a conflict of interest, the Manager may, and may cause her Affiliates to, engage in any transaction (including, without limitation, the purchase, sale, lease, or exchange of any property, or the lending of funds, or the rendering of any service, or the establishment of any salary, other compensation, or other terms of employment) with the Company so long as such transaction is not expressly prohibited by this Agreement and so long as the terms and conditions of such transaction on an overall basis, are fair and reasonable to the Company and are at least as favorable to the Company as those that are generally available from Persons capable of similarly performing them and in similar transactions between parties operating at arm's length.

A transaction between a Manager and/or his, her, or its Affiliates, on the one hand, and the Company, on the other hand, shall be conclusively determined to constitute a transaction on terms and conditions, on an overall basis, fair and reasonable to the Company and at least as favorable to the Company as those generally available in a similar transaction between parties operating at arm's length if Members holding a majority of the Percentage Interests of Members having no interest in such transaction (other than their interest as Members) affirmatively vote or consent in writing to approve the transaction. Notwithstanding the foregoing, the Manager shall not have any obligation in connection with any such transaction between the Company and the Manager or an Affiliate of the Manager, to seek the consent of the Members having no interest in such transaction.

5.10 Payments to Manager. Except as otherwise authorized in, or pursuant to, this Section, this Agreement or the Management Agreement, neither the Manager nor her Affiliates are entitled to remuneration for services rendered or goods provided to the Company. The Manager and her Affiliates shall receive only the following payments: (a) Services Performed by Manager or Affiliates. The Company shall pay a Manager and/or her Affiliates for services rendered or goods provided to the Company pursuant to the Management Agreement. (b) Expenses. The Company shall reimburse the Manager and Affiliates for the actual cost of goods and materials used for or by the Company.

5.11 Limited Liability of Manager. No person who is a Manager of the Company shall be personally liable under any judgment of a court, or in any other manner, for any debt, obligation, or liability of the Company, whether that liability or obligation arises in contract, tort, or otherwise, solely by reason being a Manager of the Company.

ARTICLE 6
ALLOCATIONS OF NET PROFITS AND NET LOSSES AND DISTRIBUTIONS

6.1 Allocations of Net Profit and Net Loss.

(a) *Net Loss*. Subject to the limitation set forth in Section 6, Net Loss for each Fiscal Year shall be allocated to the Members and Economic Interest Owners in accordance with their Economic Interests.

(b) *Loss Limitation*. Notwithstanding Section 6, loss allocations to a Member or Economic Interest Owner shall be made only to the extent that such loss allocations will not create a deficit Capital Account balance for that Member or Economic Interest Owner in excess of an amount, if any, equal to such Member's or Economic Interest Owner's share of Company Minimum Gain that would be realized on a foreclosure of the Company's property. Any loss not allocated to a Member or Economic Interest Owner because of the foregoing provision shall be allocated to the other Members and Economic Interest Owners (to the extent the other Members and Economic Interest Owners are not limited in respect of the allocation of losses under this Section). Any loss reallocated under this Section shall be taken into account in computing subsequent allocations of income and losses pursuant to this Article, so that the net amount of any item so allocated and the income and losses allocated to each Member or Economic Interest Owner pursuant to this Article, to the extent possible, shall be equal to the net amount that would have been allocated to each such Member or Economic Interest Owner pursuant to this Article if no reallocation of losses had occurred under this Section.

(c) *Net Profit*. Subject to allocations under Section 6 and 6, Net Profit shall be allocated to the Members and Economic Interest Owners in accordance with their Economic Interests.

6.2 *Special Allocations*.

(a) *Minimum Gain Chargeback*. Notwithstanding Section 6, if there is a net decrease in Company Minimum Gain during any Fiscal Year, each Member and Economic Interest Owner shall be specially allocated items of Company income and gain for such Fiscal Year (and, if necessary, in subsequent Fiscal Years) in an amount equal to the portion of such Member's or Economic Interest Owner's share of the net decrease in Company Minimum Gain that is allocable to the disposition of Company property subject to a Nonrecourse Liability which share of such net decrease shall be determined in accordance with Regulations Section 1.704-2(g)(2). Allocations pursuant to this Section shall be made in proportion to the amounts required to be allocated to each Member and Economic Interest Owner under this Section. The items to be so allocated shall be determined in accordance with Regulations Section 1.704-2(f). This Section is intended to comply with the minimum gain chargeback requirement contained in Regulations Section 1.704-2(f) and shall be interpreted consistently therewith.

(b) *Chargeback of Minimum Gain Attributable to Member Nonrecourse Debt*. Notwithstanding Section 6 of this Agreement, if there is a net decrease in Company Minimum Gain attributable to a Member Nonrecourse Debt, during any Fiscal Year, each Member and Economic Interest Owner who has a share of the Company Minimum Gain attributable to such Member Nonrecourse Debt (which share shall be determined in accordance with Regulations Section 1.704-2(i)(5)) shall be specially allocated items of Company income and gain for such Fiscal Year (and, if necessary, in subsequent Fiscal Years) in an amount equal to that portion of such Member's or Economic Interest Owner's share of the net decrease in Company Minimum Gain attributable to such Member Nonrecourse Debt that is allocable to the disposition of Company property subject to such Member Nonrecourse Debt (which share of such net decrease shall be determined in accordance with Regulations Section 1.704-2(i)(5)). Allocations pursuant to this Section shall

LIMITED LIABILITY COMPANIES

be made in proportion to the amounts required to be allocated to each Member and Economic Interest Owner under this Section. The items to be so allocated shall be determined in accordance with Regulations Section 1.704-2(i)(4). This Section is intended to comply with the Minimum Gain Chargeback requirement contained in Regulations Section 1.704-2(i)(4) and shall be interpreted consistently therewith.

(c) <u>Nonrecourse Deductions</u>. Notwithstanding Section 6, any Nonrecourse Deductions (as defined Regulations Section 1.704-2(b)(1)) for any Fiscal Year or other period shall be specially allocated to the Members and Economic Interest Owners in proportion to their Economic Interests.

(d) <u>Member Nonrecourse Deductions</u>. Notwithstanding Section 6, those items of Company loss, deduction, or Code Section 705(a)(2)(B) expenditures which are attributable to Member Nonrecourse Debt for any Fiscal Year or other period shall be specially allocated to the Member or Economic Interest Owner who bears the economic risk of loss with respect to the Member Nonrecourse Debt to which such items are attributable in accordance with Regulations Section 1.704-1(i).

(e) <u>Qualified Income Offset</u>. Notwithstanding Section 6, if a Member or Economic Interest Owner unexpectedly receives any adjustments, allocations, or distributions described in Regulations Section 1.704-1(b)(2)(ii)(d)(4), (5) or (6), or any other event creates a deficit balance in such Member's Capital Account in excess of such Member's or Economic Interest Owner's share of Company Minimum Gain, items of Company income and gain shall be specially allocated to such Member or Economic Interest Owner in an amount and manner sufficient to eliminate such excess deficit balance as quickly as possible. Any special allocations of items of income and gain pursuant to this Section shall be taken into account in computing subsequent allocations of income and gain pursuant to this Article so that the net amount of any item so allocated and the income, gain, and losses allocated to each Member and Economic Interest Owner pursuant to this Article to the extent possible, shall be equal to the net amount that would have been allocated to each such Member and Economic Interest Owner pursuant to the provisions of this Section if such unexpected adjustments, allocations, or distributions had not occurred.

6.3 <u>Tax Allocations</u>.

(a) <u>General Tax Allocations</u>. Except as otherwise provided in this Agreement, every item of income, gain, loss, deduction, or credit of the Company shall be allocated for income tax purposes to each Member and Economic Interest Owner insofar as possible in accordance with the allocation of Net Profits and Net Losses for book accounting purposes.

(b) <u>Contributed Property</u>. In accordance with Code Section 704(c) and the Regulations thereunder, income, gain, loss and deduction with respect to any property contributed to the capital of the Company shall, solely for tax purposes, be allocated among the Members and Economic Interest Owners so as to take account of any variation between the adjusted basis of such property to the Company for federal income tax purposes and its fair market value on the date of contribution.

(c) <u>Method of Allocations</u>. The Manager shall make any elections or other decisions relating to tax allocations in a manner that reasonably reflects the intention of this Agreement. Allocations pursuant to this Section are solely for purposes of federal, state, and local taxes and shall not affect, or in any way be taken into account in computing, any Person's Capital Account or share of Net Profits, Net Losses, other items or distributions pursuant to any provision of this Agreement.

6.4   <u>Allocation of Net Profits and Losses and Distributions in Respect of a Transferred Interest</u>. If any Economic Interest is transferred, or is increased or decreased by reason of the admission of a new Member or otherwise, during any Fiscal Year of the Company, each item of income, gain, loss, deduction, or credit of the Company for such Fiscal Year shall be assigned pro rata to each day in the particular period of such fiscal year to which such item is attributable (i.e., the day on or during which it is accrued or otherwise incurred) and the amount of each such item so assigned to any such day shall be allocated to the Member or Economic Interest Owner based upon his, her or its respective Economic Interest at the close of such day.

However, for the purpose of accounting convenience and simplicity, the Company shall treat a transfer of, or an increase or decrease in, an Economic Interest which occurs at any time during a calendar month as having been consummated on the last day of such calendar month, regardless of when during the month such transfer, increase, or decrease actually occurs.

Notwithstanding any provision above to the contrary, gain or loss of the Company realized in connection with a sale or other disposition of any of the assets of the Company shall be allocated solely to the parties owning Economic Interests as of the date of such sale or other disposition occurs.

6.5   <u>Obligations of Members to Report Allocations</u>. The Members are aware of the income tax consequences of the allocations made by this Article and hereby agree to be bound by the provisions of this Article in reporting their shares of Company income and loss for income tax purposes.

ARTICLE 7
DISTRIBUTIONS

7.1   <u>Distribution of Cash by the Company</u>. Subject to applicable law and any limitations contained elsewhere in this Agreement, the Manager shall from time to time, at her own discretion, distribute Distributable Cash to the Members and Economic Interest Owners, which distributions shall to the Members and Economic Interest Owners in proportion to their Economic Interests.

All such distributions shall be made only to the Persons who, according to the books and records of the Company, are the holders of record of the Economic Interests in respect of which such distributions are made on the actual date of distribution. Neither the Company nor any Manager shall incur any liability for making distributions in accordance with this Section.

7.2   <u>Form of Distribution</u>. A Member or Economic Interest Owner, regardless of the nature of the Member or Economic Interest Owner's Capital Contribution, has no right to demand and receive any distribution from the Company in any form other than money. No Member or Economic Interest Owner may be compelled to accept from the Company a distribution of any asset in kind in lieu of a proportionate distribution of money being made to other Members and Economic Interest Owners. Except upon a dissolution and the winding up of the Company, no Member or Economic Interest Owner may be compelled to accept a distribution of any asset in kind.

7.3   <u>Return of Distributions</u>. Except for distributions made in violation of the Act or this Agreement, no Member or Economic Interest Owner shall be obligated to return any distribution to the Company or pay the amount of any distribution for the account of the Company or to any creditor of the Company. The amount of any distribution returned to the Company by a Member or Economic Interest Owner or paid by a Member or Economic Interest Owner for the account of the Company or to a creditor of the Company shall be added to the account or accounts from which it was subtracted when it was distributed to the Member or Economic Interest Owner.

ARTICLE 8
TRANSFER AND ASSIGNMENT OF INTERESTS

8.1 Transfer and Assignment of Interests. Except as otherwise provided in this Article, a Member may not transfer, assign, convey, sell, or encumber all or any part of such Member's Membership Interest without the consent of the Manager. Until the transferee of the Membership Interest or any portion thereof is admitted as a substitute Member pursuant to Section 8.3, the transferee shall have no right to vote or participate in the management of the business, property and affairs of the Company or to exercise any rights of a Member. Such transferee shall only be entitled to become an Economic Interest Owner and thereafter shall only receive the share of one or more of the Company's Net Profits, Net Losses and distributions of the Company's assets to which the transferor of such Economic Interest would otherwise be entitled. After the consummation of any transfer of any part of a Membership Interest, the Membership Interest so transferred shall continue to be subject to the terms and provisions of this Agreement and any further transfers shall be required to comply with all the terms and provisions of this Agreement.

8.2 Restrictions on Transfer of Interests. In addition to other restrictions found in this Agreement, no Member shall transfer, assign, convey, sell, encumber or in any way alienate all or any part of his, her, or its Membership Interest: (i) without compliance with the Securities Act of 1933, as amended, the California Corporate Securities Law of 1968, as amended, or any other applicable securities laws, and (ii) if the Membership Interest to be transferred, assigned, sold or exchanged, when added to the total of all other Membership Interests sold or exchanged in the preceding twelve (12) consecutive months prior thereto, would cause the termination of the Company under the Code, as determined by the Manager. Any transfer in violation of this Section shall be null and void and the purported transferee shall not become either a Member or an Economic Interest Holder.

8.3 Substitution of Members. A transferee of a Membership Interest shall have the right to become a substitute Member only if: (i) the requirements of Section 8 relating to securities and tax requirements hereof are met; (ii) such Person executes an instrument satisfactory to the Manager accepting and adopting the terms and provisions of this Agreement; (iii) such Person executes or causes to be executed such additional documents that the Manager deems necessary or appropriate including, without limitation, a Consent of Spouse; (iv) such Person pays any reasonable expenses in connection with his, her, or its admission as a new Member, as determined by the Manager; and (v) the Manager consents to the substitution of the Member. The admission of a substitute Member shall not result in the release of the Member who assigned the Membership Interest from any liability that such Member may have to the Company. The Manager shall amend this Agreement to reflect the admission of a substitute Member pursuant to this Section and such amendment shall not require the vote or approval of the Members.

8.4 Transfers to Certain Family Members and Affiliates. Notwithstanding Section 8, the Membership Interest of any Member may be transferred subject to compliance with Section 8, by the Member by (i) gift, sale, or inheritance to any Member, or to the parent, children, grandchildren, sibling, or other issue of a Member or to a trust for any of aforementioned group, or to a trust to provide income to a spouse so long as the remainder interest is to pass to any of the aforementioned group, or (ii) to any Affiliate of the Member; it being agreed that in executing this Agreement, each Member has consented to such transfer. A transferee pursuant to this Section shall be an Economic Owner until and unless such transferee becomes a substitute Member pursuant to Section 8. Notwithstanding anything to the contrary in this Section and Section 8, a transferee of a Membership Interest who is already a Member, an Affiliate of a Member, or a trust for the benefit of a Member shall automatically become a substitute Member with respect to the transferred Membership Interest.

  8.5 Effective Date of Transfer. The transfer of all or any portion of a Membership Interest shall be effective as of the date provided in Section 6 following the date upon which the requirements of Sections 8 and 8 have been met. Any transferee of a Membership Interest shall take subject to the restrictions on transfer imposed by this Agreement.

  8.6 Rights of Legal Representative. If a Member who is an individual dies or is adjudged by a court of competent jurisdiction to be incompetent to manage the Member's person or property, the Member's executor, administrator, guardian, conservator, or other legal representative may exercise all of the Member's rights for the purpose of settling the Member's estate or administering the Member's property, including any power the Member has under the Articles or this Agreement to give an assignee the right to become a Member. If a Member is a corporation, trust, or other entity and is dissolved or terminated, the powers of that Member may be exercised by his, her, or its legal representative or successor.

  8.7 Option to Purchase Membership Rights. Upon and contemporaneously with any transfer, assignment, conveyance or sale (whether arising out of an attempted charge upon that Member's Economic Interest by judicial process, a foreclosure by a creditor of the Member or otherwise) of a Member's Economic Interest (or portion thereof) which does not at the same time transfer the balance of the rights associated with the Membership Interest transferred by the Member (including, without limitation, the rights of the Member to vote or participate in the management of the business, property and affairs of the Company), the Company, in the sole discretion of the Manager, shall have the option to purchase from the Member, and if exercised, the Member shall sell to Company for a purchase price of _____ ($_____), all remaining rights and interest retained by the Member that immediately before the transfer, assignment, conveyance or sale were associated with the transferred Economic Interest. The Manager, in her sole discretion, may assign the Company's option rights hereunder to any Member. Such purchase and sale shall not, however, result in the release of the Member from any liability to the Company as a Member nor a forfeiture of his, her, or its Economic Interest.

  Each Member hereby acknowledges and agrees that the option granted to the Company to purchase all remaining rights and interests retained by a Member who transfers his, her, or its Economic Interest (or portion thereof) which does not at the same time transfer the balance of the rights associated with the Membership Interest is not unreasonable under the circumstances existing as of the date hereof.

  8.8 Right of First Refusal. Each time a Member or Economic Interest Owner ("Transferor") proposes to transfer, assign, convey, sell, encumber or in any way alienate all or any part of his, her, or its Membership or Economic Interest ("Interest") (or as required by operation of law or other involuntary transfer to do so), other than pursuant

LIMITED LIABILITY COMPANIES

to Section 8, such Transferor shall first offer such Interest to the Company and the non-transferring Members in accordance with the following provisions: (a) Transferor shall deliver a written notice to the Company and the non-transferring Members stating (i) Transferor's bona fide intention to transfer such Interest, (ii) the name and address of the proposed transferee, (iii) the Interest to be transferred, and (iv) the purchase price in terms of payment for which the Transferor proposes to transfer such Interest. (b) Within thirty (30) days after receipt of the notice described above, or, if the transfer is by gift or inheritance, within thirty (30) days after the determination of the purchase price, each non-transferring Member shall notify the Manager in writing of his, her, or its desire to purchase a portion of the Interest being so transferred. The failure of any Member to submit a notice within the applicable period shall constitute an election on the part of that Member not to purchase any of the Interest which may be so transferred. Each Member so electing to purchase shall be entitled to purchase a portion of such Membership Interest in the same proportion that the Percentage Interest of such Member bears to the aggregate of the Percentage Interests of all of the Members electing to so purchase the Interest being transferred. In the event any Member elects to purchase none or less than all of his or her pro rata share of such Interest, then the other Members can elect to purchase more than their pro rata share. (c) If the Members fail to purchase the entire Interest being transferred, the Company may purchase any remaining share of such Interest. (d) Within ninety (90) days after receipt of the notice described above or the determination of the purchase price if a transfer by gift or inheritance, the Company and the Members electing to purchase such Interest shall have the first right to purchase or obtain such Interest upon the price and terms of payment designated in such notice. If such notice provides for the payment of non-cash consideration, the Company and such purchasing Members each may elect to pay the consideration in cash equal to the good faith estimate of the present fair market value of the non-cash consideration offered as determined by the Manager. (e) If the Transferor proposes to transfer the Interest by gift or inheritance to Persons other than those set forth in Section 8 and the Company and/or the non-transferring Members elect to purchase the Interest as set forth in this Section, then the purchase price and the terms shall be determined pursuant to purchase terms set forth in Sections 9 and 9 through 9. (f) If the Company or the non-transferring Members elect not to purchase or obtain all of the Interest designated in such notice, then the Transferor may transfer the Interest described in the notice to the proposed transferee, providing such transfer (i) is completed within thirty (30) days after the expiration of the Company's and the non-transferring Members' right to purchase such Interest, (ii) is made on terms no less favorable to the Transferor than as designated in the notice, and (iii) the requirements of Sections 8 and 8 relating to unanimous consent of non-transferring Members, securities and tax requirements hereof are met. If such Membership Interest is not so transferred, the Transferor must give notice in accordance with this Section prior to any other or subsequent transfer of such Membership Interest.

   8.9 Dissolution of Marriage. In the event of any dissolution of marriage of any married Member decreed by a court of competent jurisdiction, the Membership Interest shall be allocated and distributed between such Member ("Divorced Member") and his or her spouse pursuant to a court order or agreement, assignment, stipulation or otherwise ("Event of Divorce"); provided, however, that (i) no spouse shall become a Member of the Company by virtue of an Event of Divorce; (ii) any such spouse shall only be an Economic Owner; (iii) as between the Divorced Member and his or her spouse, if such Divorced Member retains a Membership Interest in the Company following such transfer of

BUSINESS STRUCTURES AND INCORPORATION

Economic Interest to his or her spouse, such Divorced Member shall, pursuant to Corporations Code Section 17301(a)(4), continue to have the exclusive right and authority to act as a Member with respect to the Economic Interest allocated or distributed to such Divorced Member's spouse; (iv) if the Divorced Member transfers his or her entire Membership Interest in the Company to the spouse, then neither the Divorced Member nor the spouse shall have any rights or authority to act as a Member and the Company shall have an option to purchase pursuant to Section 8 the balance of the rights associated with the Membership Interest not transferred to the spouse (including, without limitation, the rights of a Member to vote or participate in the management of the business, property and affairs of the Company); and (v) any action, consent or approval taken or given or any document or instrument executed by such Member on his or her own behalf (and on behalf of the spouse as an Economic Owner hereunder) shall be binding upon such Member and his or her spouse, and the other Members and any third party shall be entitled to rely on any action so taken by such Member in accordance herewith.

Notwithstanding anything to the contrary, an Event of Divorce shall be a transfer for purposes of Section 8 of that portion of the Divorced Member's Membership Interest allocated and distributed to his or her spouse. The Company and the non-transferring Members shall have the right to purchase such Membership Interest and all terms and conditions of Section 8 shall apply, except that (i) the purchase price shall be the value of the Membership Interest stipulated, agreed to or established in the settlement agreement, court order, or consent, whichever is applicable, or if none, determined in accordance with Section 9, and (ii) the purchase price shall be paid in cash.

ARTICLE 9
CONSEQUENCES OF WITHDRAWAL, DEATH, DISSOLUTION, OR BANKRUPTCY OF MEMBER

9.1 <u>Dissociation</u>. The occurrence of a Dissociation Event shall not dissolve the Company.

9.2 <u>Withdrawal</u>. Upon the withdrawal of a Member in accordance with Section 4, the Company may elect to purchase the withdrawing Member's Membership Interest pursuant to the terms set forth in this Article or may allow the Remaining Members to do so pursuant to Section 9. If the Company elects to purchase the withdrawing Member's Membership Interest, the Manager shall give the withdrawing Member notice of the Company's election to purchase such withdrawing Member's Membership Interest within thirty (30) days following affirmative vote or written consent of the remaining Members consenting to the withdraw pursuant to Section 4.

9.3 <u>Purchase Price</u>. If the Company and/or the remaining Members elect to purchase the Former Member's Interest, the Company and the Former Member or the Former Member's legal representative shall set the purchase price ("Purchase Price") for the Former Member's Interest by mutual agreement. If the parties cannot agree within thirty (30) days of the event triggering the obligation to purchase and/or sale, then the Purchase Price of the Former Member's Interest shall be determined by appraisal.

Within fifteen (15) days following the expiration of the thirty (30) day period, the Company and the Former Member or the Former Member's legal representative each shall appoint an independent appraiser to give an opinion as to the value of the Former Member's Interest. If either party fails to so designate an appraiser, the appraisal of the one (1) appraiser appointed shall be conclusive. Each appraiser shall deliver such written opinion to the

LIMITED LIABILITY COMPANIES

Manager and to the Former Member or the Former Member's legal representative within thirty (30) days after his or her appointment.

If the two opinions of value differ by not more than ten percent (10%) of the higher opinion of value, then the value of the Former Member's Interest shall be deemed to be the average of the two opinions of value. If the two opinions of value differ by more than ten percent (10%) of the higher opinion of value, then the appraisers shall, within ten (10) days after delivery of their opinions of value, jointly select a third qualified appraiser who shall review the previous two appraisals, perform his or her own independent appraisal, and then select a value for the Former Member's Interest that is not higher than the higher nor lower than the lower of the first two opinions of value. The third appraiser shall deliver his or her written opinion of value to the Company and the Former Member or the Former Member's legal representative within thirty (30) days after appointment, and it shall be binding on the parties as the value of the Former Member's Interest.

The decision of the appraisers as provided hereinabove shall be final, conclusive and binding on all parties. The Manager shall notify all the remaining Members of the Purchase Price within ten (10) days after the Purchase Price is determined pursuant to this Section. Each of the parties shall pay one-half of all reasonable and proper costs and expenses of the appraisals; provided however, that each party shall bear his, her or its respective attorneys' fees incurred in connection with the appraisal procedure. The Members intend and hereby agree that all of the appraisers acting hereunder, however appointed shall be qualified by profession and/or experience to make the evaluation required hereunder. Also, the Members intend and hereby agree that any appraisal of a Former Member's Interest in the Company shall take into consideration all appropriate discounts.

9.4   Notice of Intent to Purchase. Within thirty (30) days after the remaining Members have been notified as to the Purchase Price of the Former Member's Interest determined in accordance with Section 9, each Remaining Member shall notify the Manager in writing of his, her, or its desire to purchase a portion of the Former Member's Interest. The failure of any Remaining Member to submit a notice within the applicable period shall constitute an election on the part of the Member not to purchase any of the Former Member's Interest. Each Remaining Member so electing to purchase shall be entitled to purchase a portion of the Former Member's Interest in the same proportion that the Percentage Interest of the Remaining Member bears to the aggregate of the Percentage Interests of all of the Remaining Members electing to purchase the Former Member's Interest. If any Remaining Member elects to purchase none or less than all of his, her, or its pro rata share of the Former Member's Interest, then the Remaining Members can elect to purchase more than their pro rata share. If the Remaining Members fail to purchase the entire interest of the Former Member, the Company shall purchase any remaining share of the Former Member's Interest.

9.5   Payment of Purchase Price. The Purchase Price shall be paid by the Company or the Remaining Members, as the case may be, by either of the following methods, each of which may be selected separately by the Company or the Remaining Members: (a) The Company or the Remaining Members shall at the closing pay in cash the total Purchase Price for the Former Member's Interest; or (b) The Company or the Remaining Members shall pay at the closing one-fifth (1/5) of the Purchase Price in which case the balance of the Purchase Price shall then be paid in four equal annual principal installments, plus accrued interest, and be payable each year on the anniversary date of the closing. The unpaid principal balance shall accrue interest at the current applicable federal rate as provided in the Code for the month in which the initial payment is made, but the Company and the Remaining Members shall have the right to prepay in full or in part at any time without penalty. The obligation to pay the balance due shall be evidenced by a promissory note, and if purchased by a Remaining Member, secured by a pledge of the Membership Interest being purchased.

9.6   Closing of Purchase of Former Member's Interest. The closing for the sale of a Former Member's Interest pursuant to this Article shall be held at the principal office of Company no later than sixty (60) days after the determination of the Purchase Price, except that if the closing date falls on a Saturday, Sunday, or California legal holiday, then the closing shall be held on the next succeeding business day. At the closing, the Former Member or such Former Member's legal representative shall deliver to the Company or the Remaining Members an instrument of transfer (containing warranties of title and no encumbrances) conveying the Former Member's Interest. The Former Member or such Former Member's legal representative, the Company and the Remaining Members shall do all things and execute and deliver all papers as may be necessary to fully consummate such sale and purchase in accordance with the terms and provisions of this Agreement.

9.7   Purchase Terms Varied by Agreement. Nothing contained herein is intended to prohibit Members from agreeing upon other terms and conditions for the purchase by the Company or any Member of the Membership Interest of any Member in the Company desiring to retire, withdraw or resign, in whole or in part, as a Member.

ARTICLE 10
ACCOUNTING, RECORDS, REPORTING BY MEMBERS

10.1   Books and Records. The books and records of the Company shall be kept, and the financial position and the results of its operations recorded, in accordance with the accounting methods followed for federal income tax purposes. The books and records of the Company shall reflect all the Company transactions and shall be appropriate and adequate for the Company's business. The Company shall maintain at its principal office in California all of the following: (a) A current and past list of the full name and last known business or residence address of each Member and Economic Interest Owner set forth in alphabetical order, together with the Capital Contributions, Capital Account and Percentage Interest of each Member and Economic Interest Owner; (b) A current list of the full name and business or residence address of each Manager; (c) A copy of the Articles and any and all amendments thereto together with executed copies of any powers of attorney pursuant to which the Articles or any amendments thereto have been executed; (d) Copies of the Company's federal, state, and local income tax or information returns and reports, if any, for the six (6) most recent taxable years; (e) A copy of this Agreement and any and all amendments thereto together with executed copies of any powers of attorney pursuant to which this Agreement or any amendments thereto have executed; (f) Copies of the financial statements of the Company, if any, for the six (6) most recent Fiscal Years; and (g) The Company's books and records as they relate to the internal affairs of the Company for at least the current and past four (4) Fiscal Years.

10.2   Delivery to Members and Inspection.

(a)   Upon the request of any Member for purposes reasonably related to the interest of that Person as a Member, the Manager shall promptly deliver to the requesting Member, at the expense of the Company, a copy of the information required to be maintained by Sections 10, 10 and 10.

LIMITED LIABILITY COMPANIES

(b) Each Member has the right, upon reasonable request for purposes reasonably related to the interest of the Person as a Member, to: (i) inspect and copy during normal business hours any of the Company records described in Sections 10 through 10; and (ii) obtain from the Company, promptly after their becoming available, a copy of the Company's federal, state, and local income tax or information returns for each Fiscal Year.

(c) Any request, inspection or copying by a Member under this Section may be made by that Person or that Person's agent or attorney.

(d) The Manager shall promptly furnish to a Member a copy of any amendment to the Articles or this Agreement executed by the Manager pursuant to a power of attorney from the Member.

10.3 <u>Annual Statements</u>.

(a) The Manager shall cause to be prepared at least annually, at Company expense, information necessary for the preparation of the Members' and Economic Interest Owners' federal and state income tax returns. The Manager shall send or cause to be sent to each Member or Economic Interest Owner within ninety (90) days after the end of each taxable year such information as is necessary to complete federal and state income tax or information returns, and a copy of the Company's federal, state, and local income tax or information returns for that year.

(b) The Manager shall cause to be filed at least annually with the California Secretary of State the statement required under Corporations Code Section 17060.

10.4 <u>Filings</u>. The Manager, at Company expense, shall cause the income tax returns for the Company to be prepared and timely filed with the appropriate authorities. The Manager, at Company expense, shall also cause to be prepared and timely filed, with appropriate federal and state regulatory and administrative bodies, amendments to, or restatements of, the Articles and all reports required to be filed by the Company with those entities under the Act or other then current applicable laws, rules, and regulations. If a Manager required by the Act to execute or file any document fails, after demand, to do so within a reasonable period of time or refuses to do so, any other Manager or Member may prepare, execute and file that document with the Secretary of the State.

10.5 <u>Bank Accounts</u>. The Manager shall maintain the funds of the Company in one or more separate bank accounts in the name of the Company, and shall not permit the funds of the Company to be commingled in any fashion with the funds of any other Person.

10.6 <u>Accounting Decisions and Reliance on Others</u>. All decisions as to accounting matters, except as otherwise specifically set forth herein, shall be made by the Manager. The Manager may rely upon the advice of the Company's accountants as to whether such decisions are in accordance with accounting methods followed for federal income tax purposes.

10.7 <u>Tax Matters for the Company Handled by Manager and Tax Matters Partner</u>. The Manager shall from time to time cause the Company to make such tax elections as they deem to be in the best interests of the Company and the Members. The Tax Matters Partner, as defined in Code Section 6231, shall represent the Company (at the Company's expense) in connection with all examinations of the Company's affairs by tax authorities, including resulting judicial and administrative proceedings, and shall expend the Company funds for professional services and costs associated therewith. The Tax Matters Partner shall oversee the Company tax affairs in the overall best interest of the Company. If for any

BUSINESS STRUCTURES AND INCORPORATION

reason the Tax Matters Partner can no longer serve in that capacity or ceases to be a Member or Manager, as the case may be, Members holding a Majority Interest may designate another to be Tax Matters Partner.

ARTICLE 11
DISSOLUTION AND WINDING UP

11.1 Dissolution. The Company shall be dissolved, its assets shall be disposed of, and its affairs wound up on the first to occur of the following: (a) Upon the happening of any event of dissolution specified in the Articles; (b) Upon the entry of a decree of judicial dissolution pursuant to Section 17351 of the Corporations Code; or (c) Upon the vote of Members holding a Majority Interest and the consent of all the Managers.

11.2 Certificate of Dissolution. As soon as possible following the occurrence of any of the events specified in Section 11, the Managers who have not wrongfully dissolved the Company, or, if none, a Member shall execute a Certificate of Dissolution in such form as shall be prescribed by the California Secretary of State and file the Certificate as required by the Act.

11.3 Winding Up. Upon the occurrence of any event specified in Section 11, the Company shall continue solely for the purpose of winding up its affairs in an orderly manner, liquidating its assets, and satisfying the claims of its creditors. The Managers who have not wrongfully dissolved the Company, or, if none, the Members shall (i) be responsible for overseeing the winding up and liquidation of Company, (ii) take full account of the liabilities of Company and assets, (iii) either cause its assets to be sold or distributed, and if sold as promptly as is consistent with obtaining the fair market value thereof, and (iv) cause the sale proceeds and/or the assets, to the extent sufficient therefore, to be applied and distributed as provided in Section 11. The Persons winding up the affairs of the Company shall give written notice of the commencement of winding up by mail to all known creditors and claimants whose addresses appear on the records of the Company. The Manager or Members winding up the affairs of the Company shall be entitled to reasonable compensation for such services.

11.4 Distributions in Kind. Except as provided in Section 7, any non-cash asset distributed to one or more Members shall first be valued at its fair market value to determine the Net Profit or Net Loss that would have resulted if such asset were sold for such value, such Net Profit or Net Loss shall then be allocated pursuant to Article 6, and the Members' Capital Accounts shall be adjusted to reflect such allocations. The amount distributed and charged to the Capital Account of each Member receiving an interest in such distributed asset shall be the fair market value of such interest (net of any liability secured by such asset that such Member assumes or takes subject to). The fair market value of such asset shall be determined by the Manager or by the Members or if any Member objects by an independent appraiser (any such appraiser must be recognized as an expert in valuing the type of asset involved) selected by the Manager or liquidating trustee and approved by the Members.

11.5 Order of Payment of Liabilities Upon Dissolution.

(a) After determining that all known debts and liabilities of the Company in the process of winding up, including, without limitation, debts and liabilities to Members who are creditors of the Company, have been paid or adequately provided for, the remaining assets shall be distributed to the Members in accordance with their positive Capital Account balances, after taking into account income and loss allocations for the

LIMITED LIABILITY COMPANIES

Company's taxable year during which liquidation occurs. Such liquidating distributions shall be made by the end of the Company's taxable year in which the Company is liquidated, or, if later, within ninety (90) days after the date of such liquidation.

(b) The payment of a debt or liability, whether the whereabouts of the creditor is known or unknown, has been adequately provided for if payment thereof has been assumed or guaranteed in good faith by one or more financially responsible persons or by the United States government or any agency thereof, and the provision, including the financial responsibility of the Person, was determined in good faith and with reasonable care by the Manager or Members to be adequate at the time of any distribution of the assets pursuant to this Section. This Section shall not prescribe the exclusive means of making adequate provision for debts and liabilities.

11.6 Compliance with Regulations. All payments to the Members upon the winding-up and dissolution of Company shall be made strictly in accordance with the positive Capital Account balance limitation and other requirements of Regulations Section 1.704-1(b)(2)(ii)(d).

11.7 Limitations on Payments Made in Dissolution. Except as otherwise specifically provided in this Agreement, each Member shall only be entitled to look solely at the assets of Company for the return of his, her, or its positive Capital Account balance and shall have no recourse for his, her, or its Capital Contribution and/or share of Net Profits (upon dissolution or otherwise) against the Manager or any other Member except as provided in Article 12.

11.8 Certificate of Cancellation. Upon the completion of the winding up of the affairs and distribution of all of the assets of the Company as provided in this Article or when a domestic limited liability company is not the surviving entity, the Manager or Members who filed the Certificate of Dissolution shall cause to be filed in the office of, and on a form prescribed by, the Secretary of State, a certificate of cancellation of the Articles.

11.9 No Action Causing Dissociation. Except as expressly permitted in this Agreement, a Member shall not take any action that directly causes a Dissociation Event.

ARTICLE 12

INDEMNIFICATION AND INSURANCE

12.1 Indemnification of Any Agents. The Company shall indemnify any Member or Manager and may indemnify any other Person who was or is a party or is threatened to be made a party to any threatened, pending or completed action, suit or proceeding by reason of the fact that he, she, or it is or was a Member, Manager, officer, employee or other agent of the Company or that, being or having been such a Member, Manager, officer, employee or agent, he, she, or it is or was serving at the request of the Company as a manager, director, officer, employee or other agent of another limited liability company, corporation, partnership, joint venture, trust or other enterprise (all such persons being referred to hereinafter as an "agent"), to the fullest extent permitted by applicable law in effect on the date hereof and to such greater extent as applicable law may hereafter from time to time permit.

12.2 Insurance. The Company shall have the power to purchase and maintain insurance on behalf of any Person who is or was an agent of the Company against any liability asserted against such Person and incurred by such Person in any such capacity, or arising out of such Person's status a an agent, whether or not the Company would have

BUSINESS STRUCTURES AND INCORPORATION

the power to indemnify such Person against such liability under the provisions of Section 12 or under applicable law.

ARTICLE 13
INVESTMENT REPRESENTATIONS

Each Member hereby represents and warrants to, and agrees with, the Manager, the other Members, and the Company as follows:

13.1 Preexisting Relationship or Experience.

(a) Such Member has a preexisting personal or business relationship with the Company, the Manager or control persons; or

(b) By reason of such Member's business or financial experience, or by reason of the business or financial experience of his, her, or its financial advisor who is unaffiliated with and who is not compensated, directly or indirectly, by the Company or any Affiliate or selling agent of the Company, he, she, or it is capable of evaluating the risks and merits of an investment in the Membership Interest and of protecting his, her, or its own interests in connection with this investment.

13.2 No Advertising. Such Member has not seen, received, been presented with, or been solicited by any leaflet, public promotional meeting, newspaper or magazine article or advertisement, radio or television advertisement, or any other form of advertising or general solicitation with respect to the sale of the Membership Interest.

13.3 Investment Intent. Such Member is acquiring the Membership Interest for investment purposes for his, her, or its own account only and not with a view to or for sale in connection with any distribution of all or any part of the Membership Interest. No other person will have any direct or indirect beneficial interest in or right to the Membership Interest.

13.4 Purpose of Entity. If the Member is a corporation, partnership, limited liability company, trust, or other entity, it was not organized for the specific purpose of acquiring the Membership Interest.

13.5 Residency. Such Member is a resident of the State of California.

13.6 Economic Risk. Such Member is financially able to bear the economic risk of an investment in the Membership Interest, including the total loss thereof.

13.7 No Registration of Membership Interest. Such Member acknowledges that the Membership Interest has not been registered under the Securities Act of 1933, as amended (the "Securities Act"), or qualified under the California Corporate Securities Law of 1968, as amended, or any other applicable securities laws in reliance, in part, on such Member's representations, warranties, and agreements herein.

13.8 Membership Interest in Restricted Security. Such Member understands that the Membership Interest is a "restricted security" under the Securities Act in that the Membership Interest will be acquired from the Company in a transaction not involving a public offering, and that the Membership Interest may be resold without registration under the Securities Act only in certain limited circumstances and that otherwise the Membership Interest must be held indefinitely.

13.9 No Obligation to Register. Such Member represents, warrants, and agrees that the Company and the Manager are under no obligation to register or qualify the Membership Interest under the Securities Act or under any state securities law, or to assist such Member in complying with any exemption from registration and qualification.

LIMITED LIABILITY COMPANIES

13.10   No Disposition in Violation of Law.   Without limiting the representation set forth above, and without limiting Article 8 of this Agreement, such Member will not make any disposition of all or any part of the Membership Interest which will result in the violation by such Member or by the Company of the Securities Act, the California Corporate Securities Law of 1968, or any other applicable securities laws. Without limiting the foregoing, such Member agrees not to make any disposition of all or any part of the Membership Interest unless and until: (a) There is then in effect a registration statement under the Securities Act covering such proposed disposition and such disposition is made in accordance with such registration statement and any applicable requirements of state securities laws; or (b) Such Member has notified the Company of the proposed disposition and has furnished the Company with a detailed statement of the circumstances surrounding the proposed disposition, and if reasonably requested by the Manager, such Member has furnished the Company with a written opinion of counsel, reasonably satisfactory to the Company, that such disposition will not require registration of any securities under the Securities Act or the consent of or a permit from appropriate authorities under any applicable state securities law.

13.11   Legends.   Such Member understands that the certificates (if any) evidencing the Membership Interest may bear one or all of the following legends: (a) "THE SECURITIES REPRESENTED BY THIS AGREEMENT HAVE NOT BEEN REGISTERED UNDER THE SECURITIES ACT OF 1933 NOR REGISTERED NOR QUALIFED UNDER ANY STATE SECURITIES LAWS. SUCH SECURITES MAY NOT BE OFFERED FOR SALE, SOLD, DELIVERED AFTER SALE, TRANSFERRED, PLEDGED, OR HYPOTHECATED UNLESS QUALIFED AND REGISTERED UNDER APPLICABLE STATE AND FEDERAL SECURITIES LAWS OR UNLESS, IN THE OPINION OF COUNSEL SATISFACTORY TO THE COMPANY, SUCH QUALIFICATION AND REGISTRATION IS NOT REQUIRED. ANY TRANSFER OF THE SECURITIES REPRESENTAED BY THIS AGREEMENT IS FURTHER SUBJECT TO OTHER RESTRICTIONS, TERMS, AND CONDITIONS WHICH ARE SET FORTH HEREIN." (b) Any legend required by applicable sate securities laws.

13.12   Investment Risk.   Such Member acknowledges that the Membership Interest is a speculative investment which involves a substantial degree of risk or loss by the Member of such Member's entire investment in the Company, that such Member understands and takes full cognizance of the risk factors related to the purchase of the Membership Interest, and that the Company is newly organized.

13.13   Investment Experience.   Such Member is an experienced investor in unregistered and restricted securities of speculative and high-risk ventures.

13.14   Restrictions on Transferability.   Such Member acknowledges that there are substantial restrictions on the transferability of the Membership Interest pursuant to this Agreement, that there is no public market for the Membership Interest and none is expected to develop, and that, accordingly, it may not be possible for the Member to liquidate such Member's investment in the Company.

13.15   Information Reviewed.   Such Member has received and reviewed all information the Member considers necessary or appropriate for deciding whether to purchase the Membership Interest. Such Member has had an opportunity to ask questions and receive answers from the Company and its officers, Manager and employees regarding the terms and conditions of purchase of the Membership Interest and regarding the business, financial affairs, and other aspects of the Company and has further had the opportunity to obtain all information (to the extent the Company possesses or can acquire such information without unreasonable effort or expense) which such Member deems necessary to evaluate the investment and to verify the accuracy of information otherwise provided to such Member.

13.16   No Representations By Company. Neither any Manager, any agent or employee of the Company or of any Manager, nor any other Person has at any time expressly or implicitly represented, guaranteed, or warranted to such Member that the Member may freely transfer the Membership Interest, that a percentage of profit and/or amount or type of consideration will be realized as a result of an investment in the Membership Interest, that past performance or experience on the part of the Manager or his Affiliates or any other person in any way indicates the predictable results of the ownership of the Membership Interest or of the overall Company business, that any cash distributions from Company operations or otherwise will be made to the Members by any specific date or will be made at all, or that any specific tax benefits will accrue as a result of an investment in the Company.

13.17   Consultation with Attorney. Such Member has been advised to consult with such Member's own attorney regarding all legal matters concerning an investment in the Company and the tax consequences of participating in the Company, and has done so, to the extent such Member considers necessary.

13.18   Tax Consequences. Such Member acknowledges that the tax consequences to the Member's investment in the Company will depend on the Member's particular circumstances, and neither the Company, the Manager, the Members, nor the partners, shareholders, agents, officers, directors, employees, Affiliates, or consultants of any of them will be responsible or liable for the tax consequences to him, her, or it of an investment in the Company. Such Member will look solely to, and rely upon, such Member's own advisers with respect to the tax consequences of this investment.

13.19   No Assurance of Tax Benefits. Such Member acknowledges that there can be no assurance that the Code or the Regulations will not be amended or interpreted in the future in such a manner so as to deprive the Company and the Members of some or all of the tax benefits they might now receive, nor that some of the deductions claimed by the Company or the allocations of items of income, gain, loss, deduction, or credit among the Members may not be challenged by the Internal Revenue Service.

13.20   Indemnity. Such Member shall indemnify and hold harmless the Company, each and every Manager, each and every other Member, and any officers, directors, shareholders, employees, partners, agents, attorneys, registered representatives, and control persons of any such entity who was or is a party or is threatened to be made a party to any threatened, pending, or completed action, suit, or proceeding, whether, civil, criminal, administrative, or investigative, by reason of or arising from any misrepresentation or misstatement of facts or omission to represent or state facts made by such Member including, without limitation, the information in this Agreement, against losses, liabilities, and expenses of the Company, each and every Manager, each and every other Member, and any officers, directors, shareholders, employees, partners, attorneys, accountants, agents, registered representatives, and control persons of any such Person (including attorneys' fees, judgments, fines, and amounts paid in settlement, payable as incurred) incurred by such Person in connection with such action, suit, proceeding, or the like.

LIMITED LIABILITY COMPANIES

ARTICLE 14
MISCELLANEOUS

14.1 Complete Agreement. This Agreement and the Articles constitute the complete and exclusive statement of agreement among the Members and Manager with respect to the subject matter herein and therein and replace and supersede all prior written and oral agreements or statements by and among the Members and Manager or any of them. No representation, statement, condition or warranty not contained in this Agreement or the Articles will be binding on the Members or Manager or have any force or affect whatsoever. To the extent that any provision of the Articles conflict with any provision of this Agreement, the Articles shall control.

14.2 Binding Effect. Subject to the provisions of this Agreement relating to transferability, this Agreement will be binding upon and inure to the benefit of the Members, and their respective successors and assigns.

14.3 Parties in Interest. Except as expressly provided in the Act, nothing in this Agreement shall confer any rights or remedies under or by reason of this Agreement on any Persons other than the Members and Manager and their respective successors and assigns, nor shall anything in this Agreement relieve or discharge the obligation or liability of any third person to any party to this Agreement, nor shall any provision give any third person any right of subrogation or action over or against any party to this Agreement.

14.4 Pronouns; Statutory References. All pronouns and all variations thereof shall be deemed to refer to the masculine, feminine, or neuter, singular or plural, as the context in which they are used may require. Any reference to the Code, the Regulations, the Act, Corporations Code or other statutes or laws will include all amendments, modifications, or replacements of the specific sections and provisions concerned.

14.5 Headings. All headings herein are inserted only for convenience and ease of reference and are not to be considered in the construction or interpretation of any provision of this Agreement.

14.6 Interpretation. In the event any claim is made by any Member relating to any conflict, omission or ambiguity in this Agreement, no presumption or burden of proof or persuasion shall be implied by virtue of the fact that this Agreement was prepared by or at the request of a particular Member or his, her, or its counsel.

14.7 References to this Agreement. Numbered or lettered articles, sections and subsections herein contained refer to articles, sections and subsections of this Agreement unless otherwise expressly stated.

14.8 Jurisdiction. Each Member hereby consents and acknowledges that this Agreement is executed and intended to be performed in the State of California, and the laws of that state shall govern its interpretation and effect. Any disputes between or among the then Members concerning enforcement of the terms of this Agreement shall be tried in the United States District Court for the Northern District Court of California in San Jose or the Santa Clara County Superior or Municipal Court. Each Member further agrees that personal jurisdiction over him, her, or it may be effected by service of process by certified mail addressed as provided in Section 14 of this Agreement, and when so made shall be as if served upon him, her, or it personally within the State of California.

14.9 Exhibits. All Exhibits attached to this Agreement are incorporated and shall be treated as if set forth herein.

BUSINESS STRUCTURES AND INCORPORATION

14.10   Severability. If any provision of this Agreement or the application of such provision to any Person or circumstance shall be held invalid, the remainder of this Agreement or the application of such provision to Persons or circumstances other than those to which it is held invalid shall not be affected thereby.

14.11   Additional Documents and Acts. Each Member agrees to execute and deliver such additional documents and instruments and to perform such additional acts as may be necessary or appropriate to effectuate, carry out and perform all of the terms, provisions, and conditions of this Agreement and the transactions contemplated hereby.

14.12   Notices. Any notice to be given or to be served upon the Company or any party hereto in connection with this Agreement must be in writing (which may include facsimile), and will be deemed to have been given and received when delivered to the address specified by the party to receive the notice. Such notices will be given to a Member or Manager at the address specified in **Exhibit A** hereto. Any party may, at any time by giving five (5) days prior written notice to the other parties, designate any other address in substitution of the foregoing address to which such notice will be given.

14.13   Amendments. Except as specifically provided in Sections 4, 8 and elsewhere in this Agreement, all amendments to this Agreement will be in writing and signed by all the Members. All amendments to the Articles shall require the vote, approval or consent of all the Members.

14.14   Covenant of Capacity to Sign. All Members covenant that they possess all necessary capacity and authority to sign and enter this Agreement. All individuals signing this Agreement for a Member which is a corporation, a partnership, or other legal entity, or signing under a power of attorney or as a trustee, guardian, conservator, or in any other legal capacity, covenant that they have the necessary capacity and authority to act for, sign, and bind the respective entity or principal on whose behalf they are signing. If a Member is not a natural person, neither the Company nor any Member will (i) be required to determine the authority of the individual signing this Agreement to make any commitment or undertaking on behalf of such entity or to determine any fact or circumstance bearing upon the existence of the authority of such individual, or (ii) be responsible for the application or distribution of proceeds paid or credited to individuals signing this Agreement on behalf of such entity.

14.15   No Interest in Company Property; Waiver of Action for Partition. No Member or Economic Interest Owner has any interest in specific property of the Company. Without limiting the foregoing, each Member and Economic Interest Owner irrevocably waives during the term of the Company any right that he, she, or it may have to maintain any action for partition with respect to the property of the Company.

14.16   Multiple Counterparts. This Agreement may be executed in two or more counterparts, each of which shall be deemed an original, but all of which shall constitute one and the same instrument.

14.17   Attorneys' Fees. In the event that any dispute between the Company and the Members or among the Members should result in litigation or arbitration, the prevailing party in such dispute shall be entitled to recover from the other party all reasonable fees, costs and expenses of enforcing any right of the prevailing party, including without limitation, reasonable attorneys' fees and expenses. In addition to the foregoing award for attorneys' fees, the prevailing party shall be entitled to its attorneys' fees incurred in any post-judgment proceedings to enforce any such judgment. The provisions set forth in this section shall survive the merger of these provisions into any judgment.

LIMITED LIABILITY COMPANIES

14.18 *Time is of the Essence*. All dates and times in this Agreement are of the essence.

14.19 *Remedies Cumulative*. The remedies under this Agreement are cumulative and shall not exclude any other remedies to which any person may be lawfully entitled.

14.20 *Special Power of Attorney*.

(a) *Attorney In Fact*. Each Member hereby grants the Manager a special power of attorney irrevocably making, constituting, and appointing the Manager as the Member's attorney in fact, with all power and authority to act in the Member's name and on the Member's behalf to execute, acknowledge and deliver and swear to in the execution, acknowledgment, delivery and filing of the following documents: (i) Promissory notes, security agreements, and/or UCC-1 financing statements (and all amendments thereto) to be delivered in connection of such Member's failure to make a capital contribution if required; (ii) Assignments of Membership Interest or other documents of transfer to be delivered in connection with the purchase or other transfer of a Membership Interest pursuant to Section 8, 8, 8 or 9; or (iii) Any other instrument or document that may be reasonably required by the Manager in connection with any of the foregoing or to reflect any reduction in the Member's Capital Account, Percentage Interest, Economic Interest or Membership Interest.

(b) *Irrevocable Power*. The special power of attorney granted pursuant to this Section (i) is irrevocable, (ii) is coupled with an interest, and (iii) shall survive a Member's death, incapacity or dissolution.

(c) *Signatures*. The Manager may exercise the special power of attorney granted in this Section by a facsimile signature of any Manager or by the signature of any Manager.

IN WITNESS WHEREOF, all of the Members of SMITH VENTURES, LLC, a California limited liability company, have executed this Agreement, effective as of the date written above.

MEMBERS:

Jane Smith   **John Smith**

Exhibit A

MEMBER INFORMATION

Member Names	Member Addresses	Capital Account	Percentage Interest
John Smith	1234 Street Address City, State and Zip code	$	50%
Jane Smith	1234 Street Address City, State and Zip code	$	50%
		$	100%

BUSINESS STRUCTURES AND INCORPORATION

MANAGER INFORMATION

Manager Name	Manager Address
Jane Smith	1234 Street Address
	City, State and Zip code

Management Agreement

The following agreement is not intended to be comprehensive or an absolute statement of the governing law. This agreement is not legal advice. It does not analyze any specific fact patterns from any parties but rather discusses broadly points of law, which may or may not be the most accurate, according to current case law interpretation or even case law interpretation that is very in-depth on very narrowly-presented issues. Sound legal advice arises from interaction between client and attorney in a question-and-answer dialogue where facts are provided by a client as the attorney probes for issues and then conducts appropriate research if need be to ascertain the applicable law. Anyone seeking specific advice to specific legal questions should present their facts to an attorney.

LIMITED LIABILITY COMPANIES

SMITH VENTURES, LLC
AND
JANE SMITH
MANAGEMENT AGREEMENT

THIS MANAGEMENT AGREEMENT (this "Agreement") is made on _____, 20__ **BETWEEN**:

    A.   **SMITH VENTURES, LLC**, a California limited liability company, whose registered office is at _____ (the "SVLLC"); and

    B.   Jane Smith of **SMITH VENTURES, LLC**, a California limited liability company, whose registered office is at _____ (the "Manager").

WHEREAS the SVLLC wishes to appoint the Manager, and the Manager has agreed to act as the manager of the SVLLC and its Investments (as defined below) upon the following terms and conditions.

IT IS AGREED as follows:

ARTICLE I

DEFINITION OF TERMS

1.1   In this Agreement the following words and expressions shall have the following meanings respectively:

    1.1.1   "**Affiliate**" shall mean, with respect to any Person, any other Person with regard to which the Person is controlling, controlled or commonly controlled. For purposes of the preceding sentence, "control" shall mean the power to direct the principal business management and activities of a Person, whether through ownership of voting securities, by agreement, or otherwise.

    1.1.2   "**Articles**" means the articles of organization of the SVLLC as amended from time to time and any reference herein to an Article shall be taken to refer to the Articles unless otherwise specified.

    1.1.3   "**Bank**" shall mean _____.

    1.1.4   "**Bankruptcy**" shall mean, with respect to a Person: (i) an assignment of all or substantially all of the assets of such Person for the benefit of its creditors generally; (ii) the commencement of any bankruptcy or insolvency case or proceeding against such Person which shall continue and remain unsuspended and in effect for a period of sixty (60) days; (iii) the filing by such Person of a petition, answer or consent seeking relief under any bankruptcy, insolvency or similar law; or (iv) the occurrence of any other event that is deemed to constitute bankruptcy for purposes of any applicable laws.

    1.1.5   "**Board of Directors**" shall mean the Board of Directors of the SVLLC.

    1.1.6   "**Business Day**" shall mean any day (other than a Saturday, Sunday or any statutory public holiday) when banks in the United States are open for normal business.

    1.1.7   "**Cause**" shall mean any act that both (i) constitutes fraud, a felony relating to the Manager's role as a Member or Manager or involving moral turpitude, gross negligence in the management of the SVLLC, or a willful breach of a fiduciary duty arising under this Agreement and (ii) in the reasonable judgment of eighty percent (80%) in interest of the Members of the SVLLC, clearly reflects an unfitness to serve in a management capacity with regard to the SVLLC.

BUSINESS STRUCTURES AND INCORPORATION

1.1.8 "**Close of Business**" shall mean 5:00 p.m., local time, in California.

1.1.9 "**Custodial Account**" shall mean that certain custodial account held by the Bank and opened by the SVLLC in accordance with the Custodial Agreement.

1.1.10 "**Custodial Agreement**" shall mean that certain Agreement on Custody of Venture Capital Account made by and among the SVLLC, the Manager, and the Bank.

1.1.11 "**Deposit Assets**" shall mean the assets that the SVLLC entrusts to the Bank's safeguarding according to the Custodial Agreement and other forms of assets derived from the operation or increment of the value of such assets, including all kinds of properties, creditors' rights and interests that also include the increment of SVLLC.

1.1.12 "**Fair Market Value**" shall have the meaning set forth on **Exhibit A**.

1.1.13 "**Fiscal Year**" shall mean the period beginning from January 1 to December 31.

1.1.14 "**Investment**" shall mean each and every investment that SVLLC makes from time to time and the assets and rights acquired by SVLLC, which are analogous to investment by nature, including Portfolio Securities.

1.1.15 "**Manager**" shall mean one or more Managers. Specifically, "Manager" shall mean Jane Smith, or any other Person that succeeds her in that capacity.

1.1.16 "**Managers Committee**" shall mean the committee of SVLLC managers that is set up pursuant to Clause 3.6 of this Agreement.

1.1.17 "**Person**" shall mean any individual or legal entity including but not limited to a partnership, corporation, limited liability company, non-corporate entity, trust, joint venture, government organ, or other domestic and overseas entities.

1.1.18 "**Portfolio Company**" shall mean any corporation or other business entity which is an issuer of securities held by SVLLC.

1.1.19 "**Portfolio Securities**" shall mean securities (including any interest in any non-publicly traded securities and promissory notes) issued by Portfolio Companies and held by SVLLC.

1.1.20 "**SVLLC Agreement**" shall mean that certain Joint Venture Agreement signed by and among the members of the SVLLC regarding the joint investment into and the establishing of the SVLLC.

1.1.21 "**SVLLC Fund Amount**" shall mean an amount that (as of the time of determination) is equal to the excess of the sum of: (i) the amount of cash (or Fair Market Value of property) released from the Custodial Account and paid to an account controlled by the investors of the SVLLC.

1.1.22 "**Unanimous Approval**" shall mean the approval of all Persons present or represented at a meeting and entitled to vote, provided that in respect of any proposal which was not described in the notice of meeting issued for such meeting, unanimous approval shall mean the approval of all Persons entitled to vote thereon whether or not present at such meeting.

1.2 In this Agreement, a reference to a Clause or Schedule, unless the context otherwise requires, is a reference to a clause of or a schedule to this Agreement.

1.3 The Schedules form part of this Agreement and shall have the same force and effect as if set out in the body of this Agreement and references to this Agreement include the Schedules.

1.4 The headings in this Agreement shall not affect the interpretation of this Agreement.

LIMITED LIABILITY COMPANIES

1.5 Any reference to the Manager includes a reference to its or their duly authorized agents or delegates.

ARTICLE 2
TERM OF AGREEMENT

2.1 The Agreement shall come into force as of the date the Articles were filed with the California Secretary of State, and the term of the Agreement shall be seven (7) years; *provided, however*, the Manager may extend the term of the Agreement for up to three periods of one year each.

ARTICLE 3
APPOINTMENT AND FUNCTIONS OF THE MANAGER

3.1 SVLLC hereby appoints the Manager to manage the day-to-day business and affairs of SVLLC and to manage the Investments on the terms contained in this Agreement.

3.2 Subject to Clause 3.6 hereof, without prejudice to the generality of Clause 3.1 above, the duties to be performed by the Manager on behalf of SVLLC shall include:

3.2.1 sourcing, identifying and evaluating suitable Investments for SVLLC;

3.2.2 introducing, deciding and establishing the Investments on behalf of SVLLC;

3.2.3 managing the investment activities, including but not limited to purchasing (or otherwise acquiring), selling (or otherwise disposing of) and invest in investments, moneys and other assets;

3.2.4 liaising with SVLLC and keeping SVLLC informed on matters relating to the Investments;

3.2.5 withdrawing from the Deposit Assets from time to tome to pay the Manager as contemplated under this Agreement or reimburse the Manager for expenditures incurred by the Manager on SVLLC 's behalf in connection with carrying out the Manager's obligations under this Agreement;

3.2.6 arranging for the payment and disbursements on behalf of SVLLC for (a) fees and taxes and other liabilities that may be imposed on SVLLC by competent governmental authorities, (b) fees and expenses incurred in connection with Clause 5 of this Agreement, and (c) other liabilities of SVLLC incurred in connection with transactions contemplated by this Agreement or in the ordinary course of business;

3.2.7 collecting the interests and dividends and other income and revenues derived from the investment made with the Deposit Assets on behalf of SVLLC;

3.2.8 releasing to SVLLC that portion of the Deposit Assets and Investments to which SVLLC is entitled pursuant to the Custodial Agreement;

3.2.9 supervising the record and maintenance of SVLLC's financial report;

3.2.10 introducing Portfolio Companies to SVLLC which will offer the Portfolio Company directed start-up services, including but not limited to, employee training, technique support, management service, business consultation (as appropriate) and arrange the appointment of the liaising with partners, directors and officers of each such Portfolio Company;

3.2.11 assisting with the winding-up and dissolution of SVLLC in accordance with the Articles following the expiration of the term of SVLLC or the occurrence of the cause(s) for termination as specified in the Articles; and

BUSINESS STRUCTURES AND INCORPORATION

3.2.12 subject to other provisions of this Agreement, doing all things as may be reasonably requested by the Board (either in writing to the Manager or by a resolution of the Board) in relation to the business of SVLLC.

3.3 Without prejudice to the generality of Clause 4.2, the Manager is hereby granted sole and absolute authority, power and control over the Custodial Account and in the name of SVLLC to perform the following on a fully discretionary basis:

3.3.1 to issue orders and instructions with respect to the acquisition and disposition of investments, moneys and other assets of SVLLC;

3.3.2 to maintain the documents and certificates concerning the ownership of the Investments;

3.3.3 to exercise rights attaching to the investments by SVLLC;

3.3.4 to effect foreign exchange transactions on behalf of and for the Custodial Account of SVLLC in connection with any purchase, other acquisition, sale or other disposal of Investments;

3.3.5 to negotiate, enter into, and perform all contracts, agreements and other undertakings as may in the opinion of the Manager be necessary or advisable or incidental to the carrying out of the objectives of this Agreement (including the entering into of guarantees (exclusive of any financial guarantees) and undertaking in connection with an investment);

3.3.6 to negotiate the borrowing requirements of SVLLC and the provision of any underwriting and guarantees (exclusive of any financial guarantees) by SVLLC;

3.3.7 generally to do all other things as may in the Manager's opinion be reasonably required to manage the Deposit Assets and the Investments; and

3.3.8 to assist with execution of all relevant documentation to be entered into by, or at the request of, SVLLC.

3.4 The Manager is hereby authorized to manage the Custodial Account and the Investments in its sole and absolute discretion and SVLLC shall not interfere with the decisions made by the Manager.

3.5 Manager shall establish a Managers Committee in accordance with Clause 3.6. The Managers Committee's principal responsibility will be to administrate the Manager's fulfillment of its responsibility under Clause 3 of this Agreement, including but not limited to matters related to investment, management, disposal and withdrawal of the Investments. The Managers Committee shall meet regularly as appropriate and shall devote such time and energy as is reasonably necessary to diligently manage SVLLC business and affairs. It is understood that the members of the Managers Committee will fulfill their responsibilities pursuant to this Clause 3 from both within and outside of the United States.

3.6 The Managers Committee shall be comprised of one (2) members, namely John Smith and Jane Smith. All decisions of the Managers Committee shall be adopted by Unanimous Approval of the individual members of the Managers Committee. The individual members of the Managers Committee agree that the exercise of their collective powers and discretion as individual members of Managers Committee conferred under this Agreement shall be made through the Managers Committee.

3.7 SVLLC may appoint representatives to attend the regular meetings of the Managers Committee, to be informed of the investment decisions and operations of SVLLC, to participate in discussions and to table a proposal. However, SVLLC has no voting right and/or veto power with respect to any decision of the Managers Committee. Upon the Manager's request, SVLLC may recommend personnel to be employed by the Manager as a permanent employee (he or she has to quit the previous job). The ultimate decision whether to employ the recommended person shall, however, be in the sole and absolute discretion of the Manager.

3.8   Any change in the membership or composition of the Managers Committee shall be approved, in writing, by the Board of Directors of the SVLLC.

ARTICLE 4
COMMITMENT AND AUTHORIZATION OF THE SVLLC

4.1   The SVLLC promise it shall deposit into the Custodial Account amounts sufficient to meet its obligations. The SVLLC hereby represents and warrants that it does not have (and will not have): (i) any assets other than the Deposit Assets and Investments held in the Custodial Account; or (ii) any Profits or Losses other than those which are attributable to the assets listed in the immediately preceding clause (i).

4.2   To ensure that the Manager is fully authorized by SVLLC to fulfill its obligation hereunder, unless otherwise regulated by this Agreement, the Manager is hereby fully delegated the sole and absolute authority to manage the Deposit Assets and the Investments and to administer the daily operation and management of each Investment.

4.3   The SVLLC promises to appoint those directors of each Portfolio Company for which the SVLLC is entitled to appoint directors from among the candidates recommended by the Manager and to require them to exercise their powers as directors as directed by the Manager.

4.4   The SVLLC shall sign and deliver the documents relating to any Investment provided by the Manager, and provide all other required documents and signatures as the Manager may reasonably require.

ARTICLE 5
CONTINUATION AND EXERCISE OF RIGHTS OF MANAGER

5.1   The powers, rights, and authorities of the Manager herein contained are continuing ones and shall remain in full force and effect until revoked by termination of this Agreement and such revocation shall not affect any powers, rights, or authorities of the Manager exercised prior to the Manager's receipt of notice of such revocation.

ARTICLE 6
FEES AND EXPENSES

6.1   In consideration of the services to be performed by the Manager hereunder, SVLLC shall pay to the Manager throughout the term of this Agreement an annual management fee (the "**Management Fee**"). The Management Fee shall be payable quarterly in advance and shall be pro-rated on a daily basis for short fiscal periods, and additionally pro-rated on a daily basis at any time that there is an adjustment of the SVLLC Capital Commitment. The first payment of Management Fee shall be made at the signing of this Agreement. The annual Management Fee shall be equal to three percent (3%) of the SVLLC Capital Commitment. Commencing with the first complete fiscal year following the fifth anniversary after the filing of the Articles, the annual Management Fee rate shall be reduced by one quarter of one percentage (0.25%) point per year, but shall not in any event be reduced to less than one and one half percent (1.5%) of SVLLC's Capital Commitment. In addition, in the event of any increase in SVLLC's Capital Commitment, the SVLLC shall

BUSINESS STRUCTURES AND INCORPORATION

pay the Manager corresponding management fees, expenses and other expenditures in the amount and manner regulated in this article.

6.2   SVLLC shall reimburse or cause to be reimbursed to the Manager without set-off or deduction the following reasonable costs and expenses:

      6.2.1   Any expenses which are not generally treated as normal operating expenses of the Manager (including salaries and benefits provided to employees of the Manager or its Affiliates, rent, communications, travel and similar expenses, investment and business consultant fees, and other expenses incurred in investigating, evaluating or monitoring investment opportunities) for fulfilling its obligations under this Agreement; and

      6.2.2   Any SVLLC Expenses.

The SVLLC hereby warrants that the Manager has the right to draw the above-mentioned Management Fee, expenses and expenditures from the Deposit Assets and Investments pursuant to the Custodial Agreement.

6.3   The Management Fee and all other sums reimbursable or payable to the Manager under this Clause 6 shall be paid by SVLLC in priority to any other fees, costs and expenses of SVLLC (other than those priorities specifically required by applicable law).

ARTICLE 7
ACCOUNTING, VALUATIONS, RECORDS AND REPORTS

7.1   The Manager shall keep, or cause to be kept, on behalf of SVLLC such books, records, and Custodial Account statements as may be required to give a complete record of all transactions carried out by SVLLC on the recommendation of the Manager in relation to the investment and divestment of the Investments, and as will enable semi-annual progress reports of SVLLC to be prepared.

7.2   The Manager shall prepare and send to SVLLC on a or before September 1 (or if September 1 is not a Business Day, the immediately following Business Day) of each Fiscal Year of SVLLC a semi-annual progress report which includes a statement of Investments and other property and assets of SVLLC, details of Investments purchased, sold and otherwise disposed of during the relevant period and the cost and value of each Investment at the end of June 30 of such Fiscal Year and un-audited Custodial Account statements of SVLLC for the relevant period.

7.3   The Manager shall prepare, or shall assist with the preparation of, the audited Custodial Account statements of SVLLC, which shall be distributed with the report described in Clause 7.4 below.

7.4   On or before March 15 (or if March 15 is not a Business Day, the immediately following Business Day) following each Fiscal year of SVLLC, the Manager shall prepare, or arrange for the preparation of, and send to an annual report which includes a statement of Investments and other property and assets of SVLLC, details of the Investments purchased, sold and otherwise disposed of during the relevant period and the cost and value of each Investment at the end of December 31 of such Fiscal Year.

7.5   SVLLC shall promptly provide all reasonable information and such other reasonable assistance to the Manager as may be reasonably requested by the Manager, in performing its obligations under this Clause 7.

LIMITED LIABILITY COMPANIES

ARTICLE 8
POWER OF DELEGATION

8.1 The Manager may only delegate its powers to members of the Managers Committee.

8.2 Notwithstanding the foregoing, the Manager shall be entitled to retain, at its own expense, the services of investment advisers, to advise it on the Investments of SVLLC.

ARTICLE 9
TERM OF SVLLC

9.1 The term of the SVLLC shall be as set forth in its Articles; *provided* that such term shall expire no earlier than the term of this Agreement.

ARTICLE 10
REGULATORY COMPLIANCE

10.1 The Manager, in performing its obligations hereunder, shall use its reasonable best efforts to comply at all times with all applicable laws and with the terms of all licenses, permissions, authorizations and consents necessary to enable it to perform such obligations.

10.2 The parties shall reasonably co-operate with each other to reduce the imposition of taxes to the maximum extent possible. Notwithstanding the provisions of this Agreement to the contrary, the relationship between the Manager and SVLLC as evidenced by this Agreement shall be treated for federal, state and local income tax purposes in the United States as if SVLLC and its Investments' were a single partnership and all of the equity holders of SVLLC (which, solely for this purpose shall include the Manager) and its Investments' were constituent partners thereof. A Party shall not file (and each party hereby represents that it has not filed) any income tax election or other document in the United States that is inconsistent with the immediately preceding sentence.

ARTICLE 11
EXERCISE OF RIGHTS ATTACHED TO INVESTMENTS

11.1 Any rights conferred by Investments shall be exercised in such manner as the Manager may determine to be appropriate in its sole and absolute discretion. SVLLC shall from time to time upon request from the Manager execute and deliver or cause to be executed and delivered to the Manager or its nominee(s) such powers of attorney or proxies as may reasonably be required authorizing such attorneys or proxies to exercise any rights or otherwise act in respect of all or any part of the investments.

ARTICLE 12
LIABILITY AND INDEMNITY

12.1 None of the members of the Managers Committee, the Manager, or their respective directors, officers, employees or agents shall be liable to SVLLC, any Affiliate of SVLLC or any Shareholders for any action taken or not taken by them or for any action taken or not taken by any other person with respect to SVLLC or in respect of the Investments or Portfolio Companies provided that the Manager shall remain liable for its own respective acts and omissions arising from or in any way related to the fraud, negligence, willful default, willful violation of any applicable law or regulation or bad faith on the part of the Manager or any of its directors, officers, employees or agents acting as such.

12.2   SVLLC hereby indemnifies, and agrees to indemnify, upon demand, each of the members of the Managers Committee, the Manager, and each of their respective directors, officers, employees or agents against any losses, claims, demands, damages, liabilities (including liabilities in contract and in tort), proceedings, costs and expenses (including legal and other expenses reasonably incurred in connection with any of the foregoing) to which such Person may become subject by reason of its actual or alleged management of, or involvement in, the affairs of SVLLC (including such Person's involvement as an officer or director of a Portfolio Company); provided that this indemnity shall not apply in cases of fraud, negligence, willful default, willful violation of any applicable laws or regulation or bad faith on the part of the person seeking indemnification under this Clause 12.2.

ARTICLE 13
TERMINATION

13.1   Except when any of the following events occur, the Agreement shall not be terminated before the expiration of the term set forth in Clause 2: (a) As set forth in a written agreement executed after discussion by both Parties; (b) Bankruptcy, dissolution or liquidation of either Party; or (c) Any incident of force majeure under Clause 19, which materially frustrates the clear purposes of this Agreement.

13.2   On termination of this Agreement the Manager shall be entitled to receive all fees and other moneys accrued due but not yet paid to it up to the date of such termination as provided in this Agreement and shall repay on a pro rata basis fees and other moneys paid to it in respect of any period after the date of such termination. In addition to amounts payable under this Clause 13.2, SVLLC shall also pay to the Manager all such expenses referred to in Clause 6 to the extent to which the Manager is obliged to continue to make such payments beyond the date of termination of this Agreement.

13.3   After termination of this Agreement and subject to Clause 13.2, the Manager shall release to SVLLC the remaining Investments and Deposit Assets.

13.4   Upon termination of this Agreement, the Manager shall promptly deliver to SVLLC or as they shall direct, all books of Custodial Account, records, registers, correspondence and documents relating to the affairs of or belonging to SVLLC in the possession of or under the control of the Manager.

13.5   Clause 3.2.11 shall survive the termination of this Agreement. The termination of this Agreement shall be without prejudice to accrued rights and liabilities and any provisions expressed to survive the termination hereof.

ARTICLE 14
CONFIDENTIALITY

14.1   Each party to this Agreement shall, with respect to the other parties, maintain the full confidentiality, and not to disclose, any confidential information received by it regarding the business and affairs of the others. Each party further undertakes to the other parties not to make use of such confidential information other than for the purposes of this Agreement; *provided, however,* that such party may disclose such information to its employees, partners, directors, officers, advisers, agents or other Persons appointed or retained under Clause 8 to the extent necessary to fulfill the purposes of this Agreement, in which event it shall procure that any such employees, partners, directors, officers, advisers, agents or other persons are made aware of and comply with the obligations of confidentiality under this Agreement.

14.2 Clause 14.1 shall not apply to any information if:

14.2.1 the information is or becomes available to the public (other than through a breach of Clause 14.1);

14.2.2 the information is already known to the recipient, as evidenced by written records maintained in the ordinary course of its business, at the time it is furnished by the other party;

14.2.3 the information becomes known or available to a party from a Person other than the other party and such Person is not under an obligation of confidentiality or such information is independently developed by the recipient;

14.2.4 disclosure is required by law, regulation, a court of competent jurisdiction or any government authority; or

14.2.5 the disclosure of such information to a specified recipient has been agreed upon by the other party in writing provided that such information may only be disclosed subject to obtaining undertakings from such recipient to keep such information confidential.

14.3 The Manager shall be permitted to refer to the appointment made hereunder in its or other corporate literature.

ARTICLE 15
RELIANCE ON DOCUMENTS

15.1 Wherever pursuant to any provision of this Agreement any notice, instruction or other communication is to be given by, or on behalf of, SVLLC to the Manager, the Manager may accept as sufficient evidence thereof:

15.1.1 a document signed or purporting to be signed on behalf of SVLLC by such Person or Persons whose signature the Manager is for the time being authorized by SVLLC to accept; or

15.1.2 a message by telex, electronic mail or facsimile transmitted by, or on behalf of, SVLLC by such Person or Persons whose messages the Manager are for the time being authorized by SVLLC to accept, and the Manager shall not be obligated to accept any document or message signed or transmitted or purporting to be signed or transmitted by any other Person.

ARTICLE 16
NOTICES

16.1 Any and all notices, requests, demands and other communications required or otherwise contemplated to be made under this Agreement shall be in writing, in the English language, and shall be deemed to have been duly given in the absence of evidence of earlier receipt: (i) if delivered personally at the address set out below, when received; (ii) if transmitted by facsimile to the number set out below, upon receipt of an error-free transmittal report by the sender; (iii) if by international courier service, on the fourth (4th) business day (being a day on which banks in the United States are normally open for business) following the date of deposit with such courier service, or such earlier delivery date as may be confirmed to the sender by such courier service; or (iv) if sent by first class prepaid mail (airmail if overseas) on the seventh (7th) day following that on which the letter containing the same is posted, and in providing such service it shall be sufficient to demonstrate that such communication was properly addressed, stamped and posted by first class prepaid mail (airmail if overseas).

BUSINESS STRUCTURES AND INCORPORATION

16.2   Notices, requests, demands and other communications required or otherwise contemplated to be made under this Agreement shall be delivered or sent as follows:

    16.2.1   If to SVLLC:
            Address:
            Telephone:
            Facsimile:
            Attention:

    16.2.2   If to Jane Smith:]
            Address:
            Telephone:
            Facsimile:
            Attention:

ARTICLE 17

CONFLICTS OF INTEREST AND SERVICES TO OTHERS

17.1   SVLLC recognizes and accepts that the functions and duties which the Manager undertakes on behalf of SVLLC shall not be exclusive and the Manager or any Affiliate or shareholder of the Manager may perform similar functions and duties for others.

17.2   SVLLC understands and agrees that the Manager and their Affiliates and shareholders may give advice and take action in the performance of their respective duties owed to any of their respective partners or associates which may differ from the advice given to or the nature of action recommended for SVLLC.

17.3   Notwithstanding any provisions of this Agreement to the contrary, the Manager or its Affiliates may cause one or more affiliated directed start-ups to enter into "Incubation Services Agreements" with one or more Portfolio Companies pursuant to which such incubators will provide office space and equipment as well as a variety of incubation services (collectively, the "Incubation Services") to such Portfolio Companies in exchange for cash and securities issued by such Portfolio Companies; *provided, however,* that, except to the extent the Manager or its beneficial owners have a residual interest in any employee bonus pool of any such incubator formed to hold securities issued by such Portfolio Companies in exchange for such Incubation Services, neither the Manager nor its beneficial owners shall have any beneficial interest in any such securities. For purpose of the preceding sentence, a "residual interest in any employee bonus pool" shall mean an interest in that position of any such pool, if any, which is forfeited by specific employees of such incubator pursuant to vesting arrangements. The SVLLC further acknowledges that the beneficial owners of the Manager: (i) may be involved in the management of the incubators; (ii) may own substantially all of the equity interests of the incubators; and (iii) may receive cash compensation from the incubators.

ARTICLE 18

ASSIGNMENT

18.1   No party hereto shall be entitled to assign or otherwise part with any interest in this Agreement or any of its rights or obligations hereunder in the form of lien, transfer or any other forms and any such lien, transfer or any other forms of transfer shall be null and void. Notwithstanding the above specific provisions and demonstration of intention of both parties, however, if due to implementation of the applicable law there is any result of transferring of any of the rights or interests hereunder then the transferee shall be subject to limitations, obligations and liabilities (including but limited to any obligation to return payments made under this Agreement and any duty to maintain the confidentiality of information) associated with interest transferred hereunder.

ARTICLE 19
FORCE MAJEURE

19.1 No party to this Agreement shall be treated as being in breach of its obligations under this Agreement if its failure to perform any such obligation is due solely to an event of force majeure (including, without limitation, act of God, storm, fire, flood, earthquake and other natural disasters, strike, lock-out, industrial dispute, legislation, governmental regulation or restriction, riot, civil war, civil disturbance, coup d'etat, international hostilities, are or any other cause) outside the reasonable control of that party. The party affected by such event of force majeure shall not later than seven (7) days after the commencement of such event give the other parties' notice of the event and shall use all reasonable means to resume full performance of its obligations under this Agreement as soon as possible.

ARTICLE 20
AMENDMENTS

20.1 Amendments to this Agreement shall be made only by written instrument signed by both parties. If all or part of this Agreement cannot be performed due to change of the laws or regulations or other policies, then the parties hereto shall, on the basis of friendly consultation, amend this Agreement according to the relevant laws and regulations and policies.

ARTICLE 21
SEVERABILITY

21.1 If any provision of this Agreement is found to be invalid or unenforceable, then such provision shall be construed, to the extent feasible, so as to render the provision enforceable and to provide for the consummation of the transactions contemplated hereby on substantially the same terms as originally set forth herein, and if no feasible interpretation would save such provision, it shall be severed from the remainder of this Agreement, which shall remain in full force and effect unless the severed provision is essential to the rights or benefits received by any party. In such event, the parties shall use their best efforts to negotiate, in good faith, a substitute, valid and enforceable provision or agreement which most nearly affects the parties' intent in entering this Agreement.

ARTICLE 22
GOVERNING LAW AND JURISDICTION

22.1 This Agreement is governed by, and shall be construed in accordance with the laws of the State of California.

ARTICLE 23
DISPUTE SETTLEMENT

23.1 Any dispute, controversy or claim arising out of or relating to this Agreement shall be resolved in accordance with the procedures specified in this Clause, which shall be the sole and exclusive procedure for the settlement of any such disputes.

23.2 Negotiation among the Parties:

BUSINESS STRUCTURES AND INCORPORATION

23.2.1   The parties shall attempt in good faith to resolve any disputes arising out of or relating to this Agreement promptly by negotiation between the appointed representatives of the Manager and SVLLC.

23.2.2   If the dispute has not been resolved by the parties within thirty (30) days from the date of the disputing party's notice, or if the parties fail to meet within fifteen (15) days from the date of such notice, either party may initiate arbitration as provided hereinafter.

23.2.3   All negotiations pursuant to this Clause are on a confidential and without prejudice basis and shall be treated as compromise and settlement negotiations.

23.3   Arbitration:

23.3.1   The parties hereby agree that any dispute, controversy or claim arising out of or relating to this Agreement, or the breach or alleged breach thereof, or affecting this Agreement in any way, shall be resolved exclusively through arbitration held in Santa Clara, California, pursuant to the rules from the American Arbitration Association. The decision of the arbitrators shall be binding upon both parties in accordance with its then-effective arbitration procedural rules. Enforcement of an award arising in connection therewith may be entered in any court having jurisdiction thereof. The parties expressly acknowledge that, under the preceding sentence, they are waiving their right to seek a trial with regard to all matters for which arbitration is required. Any arbitration, mediation, court action, or other adjudicative proceeding arising out of or relating to this Agreement shall be held in the Santa Clara County are or, if such proceeding cannot be lawfully held in such location, as near thereto as applicable law permits. The parties hereby formally subject themselves exclusively to the venue, and personal and subject matter jurisdiction, of the courts located in the California Santa Clara County area for the purpose of: (i) enforcement of an award arising in connection with the arbitration set forth in this Clause 23.3.1; and (ii) the adjudication of any dispute, controversy or claim arising out of or relating to this Agreement for which arbitration is not required.

23.3.2   The provisions under this Clause 23 shall be independent and shall continue to have effect after termination and rescission of this Agreement.

23.4   Continued Performance:

23.4.1   Each party is required to continue to perform its obligations under this Agreement until the final resolution of any dispute arising out of or relating to this Agreement has been worked out.

ARTICLE 24

COUNTERPARTS

24.1   This Agreement may be executed in two or more counterparts, each of which shall be deemed an original, but all of which shall constitute one and the same instrument.

ARTICLE 25

WAIVER

25.1   No waiver of any default or breach hereunder shall be construed to constitute a waiver of such rights and any separate or part exercise of any right hereunder shall not construct any barrier to any future exercise of such rights. No rights of any party hereto will be deemed to be waived unless such waiver is in writing and signed by the authorized representative of the party intending to be bound.

LIMITED LIABILITY COMPANIES

IN WITNESS WHEREOF the parties hereto have caused this Agreement to be executed the day and year first above written.

SVLLC
By:
_____

John Smith
Member

JANE SMITH
By:
_____

Jane Smith
Managing Member

<u>**Exhibit A**</u>

"**Fair Market Value**" shall mean, as of the time of determination, the value of the asset in question as determined by the Manager (the "Valuation Party") in its sole and absolute discretion unless otherwise set forth herein. SVLLC shall be notified of such Fair Market Value determination within ninety (90) days of such determination; *provided, however*, a notice stating Fair Market Value shall not be required to be delivered more than once per calendar quarter. If, within thirty (30) days after a notice described in the immediately preceding sentence is mailed or otherwise furnished to SVLLC, a group of SVLLC equity holders whose aggregate capital interests in SVLLC exceed two-thirds (2/3) of the total capital interests in SVLLC held by all SVLLC equity holders (a "Two-Thirds-Interest") notifies the Valuation Party of their objection to the valuation of one or more assets set forth in such notice, the Valuation Partner shall re-determine the value of such assets and shall notify SVLLC of the results of such re-determination. If, within thirty (30) days after such notice, a Two-Thirds-Interest notifies the Valuation Party of their objection to such re-determined value and the Valuation Party thereafter declines to adjust such value in a manner that eliminated continued objection by a Two-Thirds-Interest, the value of the assets in question shall be determined in accordance with the Appraisal Procedure set forth below.

For purposes of this Agreement, "Appraisal Procedure" shall refer to the following steps: (i) The Valuation Party and SVLLC shall each provide the other with notice of their proposed value for the asset(s) in question; (ii) The Valuation Party and SVLLC shall each select an independent appraiser acceptable to the other party (which acceptance shall not be unreasonably withheld); (iii) The two appraisers shall jointly select a third appraiser; (iv) The third appraiser shall determine which of the proposed values is closest to the actual fair market value of the asset(s) in question (as of the time for which such value is to be determined); and (v) Such closest value shall be deemed to be the Fair Market Value of the asset(s) in question (as of the time for which such valuation has been determined) for all purposes under this Agreement.

Special Rules: (a) If there is an adjustment to the valuation of a Security following an objection by SVLLC, SVLLC Amount shall be adjusted accordingly, as determined by the Valuation Party in its reasonable discretion. However, no such valuation adjustment shall give rise to any recall, rescission, or reapportionment of any payment made prior to the time of such adjustment. (b) In determining SVLLC Amount, or in any accounting, no value shall be placed on the goodwill, going concern value, name, records, files, statistical data or similar assets of SVLLC not normally reflected in the accounting records of such fund, but there shall be taken into consideration any items of income earned but not yet received, expenses incurred but not yet paid, liabilities fixed or contingent, and prepaid expenses to the extent not otherwise reflected in the books of account as well as the Fair Market Value of options or commitments to purchase or sell Securities pursuant to agreements entered into on or prior to the valuation date.

CHAPTER 7

CORPORATIONS

The corporation is a form of business ownership that has advantages and disadvantages over other forms of business ownership. There are even a number of forms of corporations, each with its own advantages and disadvantages. Thus, the first issue to be addressed in corporate law is how the corporate form differs from other business entities and how the various corporate forms differ from each other.

Corporation Characteristics

A corporation is a legal entity distinct from its owners. Creation of such an entity generally requires filing certain documents with the Secretary of State. Running a corporation generally requires more formality than is required to run most other type of business entities. Corporations generally have the following characteristics:

- ❖ **Limited Liability for Owners, Directors, and Officers** – The owners of a corporation (called shareholders or stockholders) generally are not personally liable for the obligations of the corporation; neither are the corporation's directors or officers. Generally only the corporation itself can be held liable for corporate obligations. The owners risk only the investment that they make in the business to purchase their ownership interests (shares). Thus, if a person wants to set up a business entity that protects his or her personal assets from the possibility of being seized to satisfy obligations of the business, a corporation would be a good business form to consider.

- ❖ **Central Management** – Generally, the right to manage a corporation is not spread out among the shareholders, but rather is centralized in a board of directors, who usually delegate the day-to-day management duties to officers. Thus, if a person wants to avoid conflicts with co-

BUSINESS STRUCTURES AND INCORPORATION

owners regarding management of the business, a corporation may be a good form of business to choose.

- ❖ **Free Transferability of Ownership** – Generally, ownership of a corporation is freely transferable; a shareholder can sell his or her shares to whomever he/she wants, whenever he/she wants, at whatever price he/she wants in most circumstances. Thus, if a person wants to set up a business entity that will enable him/her to easily bring in new investors in exchange for ownership interest, the corporate form is worth considering.

- ❖ **Continuity of Life** – A corporation may exist perpetually and generally is not affected by changes in ownership (i.e., sale of shares). Thus, if a person wants to create a business entity that can exist apart from and beyond its current owners; the corporate form is worth considering.

- ❖ **Taxation** – C Corporation and S Corporation taxation:

Generally, a corporation is taxed as an entity distinct from its owners; i.e., it must pay income taxes on any profits that it makes, and generally shareholders do not have to pay income tax on the corporation's profits until the profits are distributed. (Under the tax laws, such a corporation is known as a C corporation.) The corporate tax rate generally is lower than the personal tax rate, and so this arrangement can be advantageous to persons who want to delay the realization of income. However, this advantage comes at a price – double taxation – because when the corporation does make distributions to shareholders, the distributions are treated as taxable income to the shareholders even though the corporation has already paid taxes on its profits.

The tax laws also permit certain corporations to elect to be taxed like partnerships and yet retain the other advantages (see above) of the corporate form. Such corporations are called S corporations under the laws. Partnerships and S corporations are not subject to double taxation – profits and losses flow through the entity to the owners. This may be advantageous when losses are expected for the first few years that the business will be operating, since it allows the owners to offset the losses against their current incomes. It also may result in lower overall taxes on profits because there is no double taxation. However, there are a number of restrictions on S corporations (e.g., stock can be held by no more than 75 persons, generally shareholders must be individuals, there can be only one class of stock, etc.).

CORPORATIONS

Where to Incorporate

If the place of business of the company is not in California (e.g., New York), Delaware is often the preferred state of incorporation choice of domicile.

If the place of business of the company is in California, the major obstacle to incorporating in Delaware is not the cost of two franchise fees, but rather the complexities dictated by Section 2115 of the California Corporations Code (the "pseudo foreign corporation" section). There are a variety of issues with respect to corporate governance, legal opinions and dissenters' rights that are difficult and may be expensive for the client to resolve if Section 2115 is applicable. Section 2115 applies if (i) more than half of the corporation's business activities are in California (using the payroll, property and sales factors of the Revenue and Taxation code section 25129) and (ii) more than half of the corporation's voting securities are held of record by persons having California addresses.

Therefore, if the business will initially or likely in the early years have more than fifty percent of its shares held by non-California residents, it is often recommended that the business incorporate in Delaware. Thus, where venture capitalists with non-California offices are investors, you may want to encourage the venture fund to list the non-California office as the location for purposes of the shareholder list. However, if the business is not likely to ever get outside the provisions of Section 2115, then California incorporation is usually recommended.

If you are still undecided and cannot predict where your shareholder base will be in the future, typical businesses would take the position to incorporate in California and reincorporate in Delaware at the time of an initial public offering (IPO) if that should occur.

General Corporate Matters

Promptly after incorporation, the corporation is required to file certain reports and tax returns with various federal, state and local governmental agencies. While the corporation may not be required to complete all of the times set forth below, we have described them in order to provide you with a checklist and ready reference source outlining certain matters which newly formed companies should bear in mind. Changes at the various governmental offices occur frequently, and the various reports, tax returns and other requirements may also change. You may wish to consult with an attorney regarding any new changes in the law. You should also check with your accountant to make sure that all items are properly prepared and filed in a timely fashion.

BUSINESS STRUCTURES AND INCORPORATION

Articles of Incorporation

Upon the filing of the Articles of Incorporation with the California Secretary of State, the existence of your corporation begins. The California Corporations Code provides a fairly modern and simplified system on this and many other aspects of corporate law. Note that the Articles simply provide that "the purpose of this corporation is to engage in any lawful act or activity for which a corporation may be organized" in California, which excludes only the trust company business, banking business and the practice of a profession permitted to be incorporated by law. In addition, the Articles provide for indemnification of the directors and potentially the executive officers, to the fullest extent not prohibited by California law.

SAMPLE ARTICLES OF INCORPORATION

OF

_____

I.

The name of this corporation is _____.

II.

The purpose of this corporation is to engage in any lawful act or activity for which a corporation may be organized under the General Corporation Law of California other than the banking business, the trust company business or the practice of a profession permitted to be incorporated by the California Corporations Code.

III.

[OPTION 1:

The corporation is authorized to issue only one class of stock, to be designated Common Stock. The total number of shares of Common Stock presently authorized is _____ (____) [par value _____ (____) per share]*

* Companies may wish to state a par value for the shares (although not required under California law) as this may be useful in the foreign qualification process in the future.

OPTION 2:

This corporation is authorized to issue two classes of stock to be designated, respectively, "Common Stock" and "Preferred Stock." The total number of shares which the corporation is authorized to issue is _____ (____) shares. _____ (____) shares shall be Common Stock [par value _____ (____)]* and _____ (____) shares shall be Preferred Stock [par value _____ (____) per share]*

* Companies may wish to state a par value for the shares (although not required under California law) as this may be useful in the foreign qualification process in the future.

The Preferred Stock may be issued from time to time in one or more series. The Board of Directors is hereby authorized, to fix or alter the dividend rights, dividend rate, conversion rights, voting rights, rights and terms of redemption (including sinking fund provisions), redemption price or prices, and the liquidation preferences of any wholly unissued series of Preferred Stock, and the number of shares constituting any such series and the designation thereof, or any of them and to increase or decrease the number of shares of any series subsequent to the issuance of shares of that series, but not below the number of shares of such series then outstanding. In case the number of shares of any series shall be so decreased, the shares constituting such decrease shall resume the status that they had prior to the adoption of the resolution originally fixing the number of shares of such series.]

IV.

The liability of the directors of this corporation for monetary damages shall be eliminated to the fullest extent permissible under California law.

(a) This corporation is authorized to provide indemnification of agents (as defined in Section 317 of the California Corporations Code) for breach of duty to the corporation and its shareholders through bylaw provisions or through agreements with the agents, or through shareholder resolutions, or otherwise, in excess of the indemnification otherwise permitted by Section 317 of the Corporations Code, subject to the limits on such excess indemnification set forth in Section 204 of the Corporations Code.

(b) Any repeal or modification of this Article shall only be prospective and shall not affect the rights under this Article in effect at the time of the alleged occurrence of any act or omission to act giving rise to liability or indemnification.

V.

The name and address in the State of California of this corporation's initial agent for service of process is:

_____

_____

_____, California _____

IN WITNESS WHEREOF, for the purpose of forming this corporation under the laws of the State of California, the undersigned, as sole incorporator of this corporation, has executed these Articles of Incorporation this _____ day of _____, 20__.

_____
[INCORPORATOR'S NAME]
Sole Incorporator

Options

1. For Professional Corporation – Article II should be changed pursuant to Section 202(b)(ii) of the Corporations Code.

2. For "Close Corporation" Article II should contain the words: "this corporation is a close corporation," and an additional article containing the words: "All of the corporation's issued shares of all classes shall be held of record by not more than _____ persons." (See Section 158 of the Corporations Code.)

BUSINESS STRUCTURES AND INCORPORATION

3. For Corporations subject to Banking Law or Insurance Code, refer to Section 202(b)(2) and (3), respectively, of the Corporations Code.

4. Permissible but optional provisions for Articles of Incorporation are contained in Section 204 of the Corporations Code.

Action by Written Consent of Sole Incorporator

This action effects the appointment of the initial directors of the corporation by the organizer of the corporation, the sole incorporator, i.e., the incorporator must appoint first Board.

SAMPLE ACTION BY WRITTEN CONSENT OF
SOLE INCORPORATOR OF
_____

The undersigned, being the sole incorporator of _____, a California corporation (the "Company"), pursuant to Section 210 of the California Corporations Code, hereby adopts the following resolution by written consent:

APPOINTMENT OF DIRECTORS

  RESOLVED, that, effective as of this date, the following persons be, and they hereby are, appointed as the initial directors of the Company to serve until the first annual meeting of shareholders or until their successors are duly elected and qualified:

_____
_____
_____

  IN WITNESS WHEREOF, the undersigned has executed this Action by Written Consent as of the _____ day of _____, 20__.

_____
Sole Incorporator

Bylaws

You will want to read the Bylaws thoroughly, since they contain the basic internal rules for operating as a corporation. The Bylaws cover such subjects as the manner, place and time for calling and holding meetings of shareholders and directors, powers of the directors, duties and obligations of corporate officers and indemnification of directors and potentially executive officers. For example, in the sample Bylaws below, it provides that the transfer or sale of stock will be subject to a right of first refusal. Such a provision is customary in a small corporation; however, you should check with legal counsel to be sure that it is intended.

SAMPLE BYLAWS
OF

_____

(A CALIFORNIA CORPORATION)

ARTICLE I
OFFICES

Section 1. **Principal Office.** The principal executive office of the corporation shall be located at such place as the Board of Directors may from time to time authorize. If the principal executive office is located outside this state, and the corporation has one or more business offices in this state, the Board of Directors shall fix and designate a principal business office in the State of California.

Section 2. **Other Offices.** Additional offices of the corporation shall be located at such place or places, within or outside the State of California, as the Board of Directors may from time to time authorize.

ARTICLE II
CORPORATE SEAL

Section 3. **Corporate Seal.** If the Board of Directors adopts a corporate seal such seal shall have inscribed thereon the name of the corporation and the state and date of its incorporation. If and when a seal is adopted by the Board of Directors, such seal may be engraved, lithographed, printed, stamped, impressed upon, or affixed to any contract, conveyance, certificate for shares, or other instrument executed by the corporation.

ARTICLE III
SHAREHOLDERS' MEETINGS AND VOTING RIGHTS

Section 4. **Place of Meetings.** Meetings of shareholders shall be held at the principal executive office of the corporation, or at any other place, within or outside the State of California, which may be fixed either by the Board of Directors or by the written consent of all persons entitled to vote at such meeting, given either before or after the meeting and filed with the Secretary of the Corporation.

Section 5. **Annual Meeting.** The annual meeting of the shareholders of the corporation shall be held on any date and time which may from time to time be designated by the Board of Directors. At such annual meeting, directors shall be elected and any other business may be transacted which may properly come before the meeting.

BUSINESS STRUCTURES AND INCORPORATION

Section 6. Postponement of Annual Meeting. The Board of Directors and the President shall each have authority to hold at an earlier date and/or time, or to postpone to a later date and/or time, the annual meeting of shareholders.

Section 7. Special Meetings.

(a) Special meetings of the shareholders, for any purpose or purposes, may be called by the Board of Directors, the Chairman of the Board of Directors, the President, or the holders of shares entitled to cast not less than ten percent (10%) of the votes at the meeting.

(b) Upon written request to the Chairman of the Board of Directors, the President, any vice president or the Secretary of the corporation by any person or persons (other than the Board of Directors) entitled to call a special meeting of the shareholders, such officer forthwith shall cause notice to be given to the shareholders entitled to vote, that a meeting will be held at a time requested by the person or persons calling the meeting, such time to be not less than thirty-five (35) nor more than sixty (60) days after receipt of such request. If such notice is not given within twenty (20) days after receipt of such request, the person or persons calling the meeting may give notice thereof in the manner provided by law or in these Bylaws. Nothing contained in this Section 7 shall be construed as limiting, fixing or affecting the time or date when a meeting of shareholders called by action of the Board of Directors may be held.

Section 8. Notice of Meetings. Except as otherwise may be required by law and subject to subsection 7(b) above, written notice of each meeting of shareholders shall be given to each shareholder entitled to vote at that meeting (see Section 15 below), by the Secretary, assistant secretary or other person charged with that duty, not less than ten (10) (or, if sent by third class mail, thirty (30)) nor more than sixty (60) days before such meeting.

Notice of any meeting of shareholders shall state the date, place and hour of the meeting and,

(a) in the case of a special meeting, the general nature of the business to be transacted, and no other business may be transacted at such meeting;

(b) in the case of an annual meeting, the general nature of matters which the Board of Directors, at the time the notice is given, intends to present for action by the shareholders;

(c) in the case of any meeting at which directors are to be elected, the names of the nominees intended at the time of the notice to be presented by management for election; and

(d) in the case of any meeting, if action is to be taken on any of the following proposals, the general nature of such proposal:

(1) a proposal to approve a transaction within the provisions of California Corporations Code, Section 310 (relating to certain transactions in which a director has a direct or indirect financial interest);

(2) a proposal to approve a transaction within the provisions of California Corporations Code, Section 902 (relating to amending the Articles of Incorporation of the corporation);

(3) a proposal to approve a transaction within the provisions of California Corporations Code, Sections 181 and 1201 (relating to reorganization);

(4) a proposal to approve a transaction within the provisions of California Corporations Code, Section 1900 (winding up and dissolution);

CORPORATIONS

(5) a proposal to approve a plan of distribution within the provisions of California Corporations Code, Section 2007 (relating to certain plans providing for distribution not in accordance with the liquidation rights of preferred shares, if any).

At a special meeting, notice of which has been given in accordance with this Section, action may not be taken with respect to business, the general nature of which has not been stated in such notice. At an annual meeting, action may be taken with respect to business stated in the notice of such meeting, given in accordance with this Section, and, subject to subsection 8(d) above, with respect to any other business as may properly come before the meeting.

Section 9. Manner of Giving Notice. Notice of any meeting of shareholders shall be given either personally or by first-class mail, or, if the corporation has outstanding shares held of record by 500 or more persons (determined as provided in California Corporations Code Section 605) on the record date for such meeting, third-class mail, or telegraphic or other written communication, addressed to the shareholder at the address of that shareholder appearing on the books of the corporation or given by the shareholder to the corporation for the purpose of notice. If no such address appears on the corporation's books or is given, notice shall be deemed to have been given if sent to that shareholder by first-class mail or telegraphic or other written communication to the corporation's principal executive office, or if published at least once in a newspaper of general circulation in the county where that office is located. Notice shall be deemed to have been given at the time when delivered personally or deposited in the mail or sent by telegram or other means of written communication.

If any notice addressed to a shareholder at the address of that shareholder appearing on the books of the corporation is returned to the corporation by the United States Postal Service marked to indicate that the United States Postal Service is unable to deliver the notice to the shareholder at that address, all future notices shall be deemed to have been duly given without further mailing if these shall be available to the shareholder on written demand by the shareholder at the principal executive office of the corporation for a period of one (1) year from the date of the giving of the notice.

An affidavit of mailing of any notice or report in accordance with the provisions of this Section 9, executed by the Secretary, Assistant Secretary or any transfer agent, shall be prima facie evidence of the giving of the notice.

Section 10. Quorum and Transaction of Business.

(a) At any meeting of the shareholders, a majority of the shares entitled to vote, represented in person or by proxy, shall constitute a quorum. If a quorum is present, the affirmative vote of the majority of shares represented at the meeting and entitled to vote on any matter shall be the act of the shareholders, unless the vote of a greater number or voting by classes is required by law or by the Articles of Incorporation, and except as provided in subsection (b) below.

(b) The shareholders present at a duly called or held meeting of the shareholders at which a quorum is present may continue to do business until adjournment, notwithstanding the withdrawal of enough shareholders to leave less than a quorum, provided that any action taken (other than adjournment) is approved by at least a majority of the shares required to constitute a quorum.

(c) In the absence of a quorum, no business other than adjournment may be transacted, except as described in subsection (b) above.

Section 11. Adjournment and Notice of Adjourned Meetings. Any meeting of shareholders may be adjourned from time to time, whether or not a quorum is present, by the affirmative vote of a majority of shares represented at such meeting either in person or by proxy and entitled to vote at such meeting.

In the event any meeting is adjourned, it shall not be necessary to give notice of the time and place of such adjourned meeting pursuant to Sections 8 and 9 of these Bylaws; provided that if any of the following three events occur, such notice must be given:

  (a) announcement of the adjourned meeting's time and place is not made at the original meeting which it continues or

  (b) such meeting is adjourned for more than forty- five (45) days from the date set for the original meeting or

  (c) a new record date is fixed for the adjourned meeting.

At the adjourned meeting, the corporation may transact any business which might have been transacted at the original meeting.

Section 12. Waiver of Notice, Consent to Meeting or Approval of Minutes.

  (a) Subject to subsection (b) of this Section, the transactions of any meeting of shareholders, however called and noticed, and wherever held, shall be as valid as though made at a meeting duly held after regular call and notice, if a quorum is present either in person or by proxy, and if, either before or after the meeting, each of the persons entitled to vote but not present in person or by proxy signs a written waiver of notice or a consent to holding of the meeting or an approval of the minutes thereof.

  (b) A waiver of notice, consent to the holding of a meeting or approval of the minutes thereof need not specify the business to be transacted or transacted at nor the purpose of the meeting; provided that in the case of proposals described in subsection (d) of Section 8 of these Bylaws, the general nature of such proposals must be described in any such waiver of notice and such proposals can only be approved by waiver of notice, not by consent to holding of the meeting or approval of the minutes.

  (c) All waivers, consents and approvals shall be filed with the corporate records or made a part of the minutes of the meeting.

  (d) A person's attendance at a meeting shall constitute waiver of notice of and presence at such meeting, except when such person objects at the beginning of the meeting to transaction of any business because the meeting is not lawfully called or convened and except that attendance at a meeting is not a waiver of any right to object to the consideration of matters which are required by law or these Bylaws to be in such notice (including those matters described in subsection (d) of Section 8 of these Bylaws), but are not so included if such person expressly objects to consideration of such matter or matters at any time during the meeting.

Section 13. Action by Written Consent Without a Meeting. Any action which may be taken at any meeting of shareholders may be taken without a meeting and without prior notice if written consents setting forth the action so taken are signed by the holders of the outstanding shares having not less than the minimum number of votes that would be necessary to authorize or take such action at a meeting at which all shares entitled to vote thereon were present and voted.

Directors may not be elected by written consent except by unanimous written consent of all shares entitled to vote for the election of directors; provided that any vacancy on the Board of Directors (other than a vacancy created by removal) which has not been filled by the board of directors may be filled by the written consent of a majority of outstanding shares entitled to vote for the election of directors.

Any written consent may be revoked pursuant to California Corporations Code Section 603(c) prior to the time that written consents of the number of shares required to authorize the proposed action have been filed with the Secretary. Such revocation must be in writing and will be effective upon its receipt by the Secretary.

If the consents of all shareholders entitled to vote have not been solicited in writing, and if the unanimous written consent of all such shareholders shall not have been received, the Secretary shall give prompt notice of any corporate action approved by the shareholders without a meeting to those shareholders entitled to vote on such matters who have not consented thereto in writing. This notice shall be given in the manner specified in Section 9 of these Bylaws. In the case of approval of (i) a transaction within the provisions of California Corporations Code, Section 310 (relating to certain transactions in which a director has an interest), (ii) a transaction within the provisions of California Corporations Code, Section 317 (relating to indemnification of agents of the corporation), (iii) a transaction within the provisions of California Corporations Code, Sections 181 and 1201 (relating to reorganization), and (iv) a plan of distribution within the provisions of California Corporations Code, Section 2007 (relating to certain plans providing for distribution not in accordance with the liquidation rights of preferred shares, if any), the notice shall be given at least ten (10) days before the consummation of any action authorized by that approval.

Section 14. Voting. The shareholders entitled to vote at any meeting of shareholders shall be determined in accordance with the provisions of Section 15 of these Bylaws, subject to the provisions of Sections 702 through 704 of the California Corporations Code (relating to voting shares held by a fiduciary, in the name of a corporation, or in joint ownership). Voting at any meeting of shareholders need not be by ballot; *provided, however,* that elections for directors must be by ballot if balloting is demanded by a shareholder at the meeting and before the voting begins.

Every person entitled to vote at an election for directors may cumulate the votes to which such person is entitled, *i.e.*, such person may cast a total number of votes equal to the number of directors to be elected multiplied by the number of votes to which such person's shares are entitled, and may cast said total number of votes for one or more candidates in such proportions as such person thinks fit; *provided, however,* no shareholder shall be entitled to so cumulate such shareholder's votes unless the candidates for which such shareholder is voting have been placed in nomination prior to the voting and a shareholder has given notice at the meeting, prior to the vote, of an intention to cumulate votes. In any election of directors, the candidates receiving the highest number of votes, up to the number of directors to be elected, are elected.

Except as may be otherwise provided in the Articles of Incorporation or by law, and subject to the foregoing provisions regarding the cumulation of votes, each shareholder shall be entitled to one vote for each share held.

Any shareholder may vote part of such shareholder's shares in favor of a proposal and refrain from voting the remaining shares or vote them against the proposal, other than elections to office, but, if the shareholder fails to specify the number of shares such shareholder is voting affirmatively, it will be conclusively presumed that the shareholder's approving vote is with respect to all shares such shareholder is entitled to vote.

No shareholder approval, other than unanimous approval of those entitled to vote, will be valid as to proposals described in subsection 8(d) of these Bylaws unless the general nature of such business was stated in the notice of meeting or in any written waiver of notice.

BUSINESS STRUCTURES AND INCORPORATION

Section 15. Persons Entitled to Vote or Consent. The Board of Directors may fix a record date pursuant to Section 60 of these Bylaws to determine which shareholders are entitled to notice of and to vote at a meeting or consent to corporate actions, as provided in Sections 13 and 14 of these Bylaws. Only persons in whose name shares otherwise entitled to vote stand on the stock records of the corporation on such date shall be entitled to vote or consent.

If no record date is fixed:

(a) The record date for determining shareholders entitled to notice of or to vote at a meeting of shareholders shall be at the close of business on the business day next preceding the day notice is given or, if notice is waived, at the close of business on the business day next preceding the day on which the meeting is held;

(b) The record date for determining shareholders entitled to give consent to corporate action in writing without a meeting, when no prior action by the Board of Directors has been taken, shall be the day on which the first written consent is given;

(c) The record date for determining shareholders for any other purpose shall be at the close of business on the day on which the Board of Directors adopts the resolution relating thereto, or the sixtieth (60th) day prior to the date of such other action, whichever is later.

A determination of shareholders of record entitled to notice of or to vote at a meeting of shareholders shall apply to any adjournment of the meeting unless the Board of Directors fixes a new record date for the adjourned meeting; *provided, however,* that the Board of Directors shall fix a new record date if the meeting is adjourned for more than forty-five (45) days from the date set for the original meeting.

Shares of the corporation held by its subsidiary or subsidiaries (as defined in California Corporations Code, Section 189(b)) are not entitled to vote in any matter.

Section 16. Proxies. Every person entitled to vote or execute consents may do so either in person or by one or more agents authorized to act by a written proxy executed by the person or such person's duly authorized agent and filed with the Secretary of the corporation; provided that no such proxy shall be valid after the expiration of eleven (11) months from the date of its execution unless otherwise provided in the proxy. The manner of execution, suspension, revocation, exercise and effect of proxies is governed by law.

Section 17. Inspectors of Election. Before any meeting of shareholders, the Board of Directors may appoint any persons, other than nominees for office, to act as inspectors of election at the meeting or its adjournment. If no inspectors of election are so appointed, the chairman of the meeting may, and on the request of any shareholder or a shareholder's proxy shall, appoint inspectors of election at the meeting. The number of inspectors shall be either one (1) or three (3). If inspectors are appointed at a meeting on the request of one or more shareholders or proxies, the majority of shares represented in person or proxy shall determine whether one (1) or three (3) inspectors are to be appointed. If any person appointed as inspector fails to appear or fails or refuses to act, the chairman of the meeting may, and upon the request of any shareholder or a shareholder's proxy shall, appoint a person to fill that vacancy.

These inspectors shall:

    (a) Determine the number of shares outstanding and the voting power of each, the shares represented at the meeting, the existence of a quorum, and the authenticity, validity, and effect of proxies;

    (b) Receive votes, ballots, or consents;

    (c) Hear and determine all challenges and questions in any way arising in connection with the right to vote;

    (d) Count and tabulate all votes or consents;

    (e) Determine when the polls shall close;

    (f) Determine the result; and

    (g) Do any other acts that may be proper to conduct the election or vote with fairness to all shareholders.

ARTICLE IV
BOARD OF DIRECTORS

    Section 18. Powers. Subject to the provisions of law or any limitations in the Articles of Incorporation or these Bylaws, as to action required to be approved by the shareholders or by the outstanding shares, the business and affairs of the corporation shall be managed and all corporate powers shall be exercised, by or under the direction of the Board of Directors. The Board of Directors may delegate the management of the day-to-day operation of the business of the corporation to a management company or other person, provided that the business and affairs of the corporation shall be managed and all corporate powers shall be exercised under the ultimate direction of the Board of Directors.

    Section 19. Number of Directors. The authorized number of directors of the corporation shall be _____ (___), until changed by a duly adopted amendment to these Bylaws approved by the affirmative vote of a majority of the outstanding shares entitled to vote; provided, an amendment reducing the number of directors to less than _____ (___), cannot be adopted if votes cast against its adoption at a meeting or shares not consenting to it in the case of action by written consent are equal to more than 16-2/3 percent of the outstanding shares entitled to vote. No reduction of the authorized number of directors shall remove any director prior to the expiration of such director's term of office.

    Section 20. Election of Directors, Term, Qualifications. The directors shall be elected at each annual meeting of shareholders to hold office until the next annual meeting. Each director, including a director elected or appointed to fill a vacancy, shall hold office either until the expiration of the term for which elected or appointed and until a successor has been elected and qualified, or until his death, resignation or removal. Directors need not be shareholders of the corporation.

    Section 21. Resignations. Any director of the corporation may resign effective upon giving written notice to the Chairman of the Board, the President, the Secretary or the Board of Directors of the corporation, unless the notice specifies a later time for the effectiveness of such resignation. If the resignation specifies effectiveness at a future time, a successor may be elected pursuant to Section 23 of these Bylaws to take office on the date that the resignation becomes effective.

    Section 22. Removal. The Board of Directors may declare vacant the office of a director who has been declared of unsound mind by an order of court or who has been convicted of a felony.

The entire Board of Directors or any individual director may be removed from office without cause by the affirmative vote of a majority of the outstanding shares entitled to vote on such removal; *provided, however,* that unless the entire Board is removed, no individual director may be removed when the votes cast against such director's removal, or not consenting in writing to such removal, would be sufficient to elect that director if voted cumulatively at an election at which the same total number of votes cast were cast (or, if such action is taken by written consent, all shares entitled to vote were voted) and the entire number of directors authorized at the time of such director's most recent election were then being elected.

Section 23. Vacancies. A vacancy or vacancies on the Board of Directors shall be deemed to exist in case of the death, resignation or removal of any director, or upon increase in the authorized number of directors or if shareholders fail to elect the full authorized number of directors at an annual meeting of shareholders or if, for whatever reason, there are fewer directors on the Board of Directors, than the full number authorized. Such vacancy or vacancies, other than a vacancy created by the removal of a director, may be filled by a majority of the remaining directors, though less than a quorum, or by a sole remaining director. A vacancy created by the removal of a director may be filled only by the affirmative vote of a majority of the shares represented and voting at a duly held meeting at which a quorum is present (which shares voting affirmatively also constitute at least a majority of the required quorum) or by the written consent of shareholders pursuant to Section 13 hereinabove. The shareholders may elect a director at any time to fill any vacancy not filled by the directors. Any such election by written consent, other than to fill a vacancy created by removal, requires the consent of a majority of the outstanding shares entitled to vote. Any such election by written consent to fill a vacancy created by removal requires the consent of all of the outstanding shares entitled to vote.

If, after the filling of any vacancy by the directors, the directors then in office who have been elected by the shareholders constitute less than a majority of the directors then in office, any holder or holders of an aggregate of five percent (5%) or more of the shares outstanding at that time and having the right to vote for such directors may call a special meeting of shareholders to be held to elect the entire Board of Directors. The term of office of any director shall terminate upon such election of a successor.

Section 24. Regular Meetings. Immediately after each annual meeting of shareholders, and at such place fixed by the Board of Directors, or if no such place is fixed at the place of the annual meeting, the Board of Directors shall hold a regular meeting for the purposes of organization, the appointment of officers and the transaction of other business. Other regular meetings of the Board of Directors shall be held at such times, places and dates as fixed in these Bylaws or by the Board of Directors; *provided, however,* that if the date for such a meeting falls on a legal holiday, then the meeting shall be held at the same time on the next succeeding full business day. Regular meetings of the Board of Directors held pursuant to this Section 24 may be held without notice.

Section 25. Electronic Participation. So long as permitted by statute, directors may participate in a meeting through any means of communication, including conference telephone, electronic video screen communication, or other communications equipment. Participating in a meeting pursuant to this section constitutes presence in person at that meeting if each participating director is provided the means to communicate with all of the other directors concurrently and (a) the meeting is held by conference telephone or video conferencing or other communications mode enabling participants to determine, through voice or image recognition, that a participant is or is not a director entitled to participate in the meeting or (b) another communications device (such as a computer modem) is used in conjunction with another method (determined in the discretion of the chairperson of the meeting) enabling participants to determine that a participant is or is not a director entitled to participate in the meeting. Such verification method may include use of passwords or similar codes for gaining access to the meeting or encryption and authentication technology approved in the discretion of the chairperson.

Section 26. Special Meetings. Special meetings of the Board of Directors for any purpose may be called by the Chairman of the Board or the President or any vice president or the Secretary of the corporation or any two (2) directors.

Section 27. Notice of Meetings. Notice of the date, time and place of all meetings of the Board of Directors, other than regular meetings held pursuant to Section 24 above shall be delivered personally, orally or in writing, or by telephone, including a voice messaging system or other system or technology designed to record and communication messages, telegraph, facsimile, electronic mail or other electronic means, to each director, at least forty-eight (48) hours before the meeting, or sent in writing to each director by first-class mail, charges prepaid, at least four (4) days before the meeting. Such notice may be given by the Secretary of the corporation or by the person or persons who called a meeting. Such notice need not specify the purpose of the meeting. Notice of any meeting of the Board of Directors need not be given to any director who signs a waiver of notice of such meeting, or a consent to holding the meeting or an approval of the minutes thereof, either before or after the meeting, or who attends the meeting without protesting prior thereto or at its commencement such director's lack of notice. All such waivers, consents and approvals shall be filed with the corporate records or made a part of the minutes of the meeting.

Section 28. Place of Meetings. Meetings of the Board of Directors may be held at any place within or without the state which has been designated in the notice of the meeting or, if not stated in the notice or there is no notice, designated in the Bylaws or by resolution of the Board of Directors.

Section 29. Action by Written Consent Without a Meeting. Any action required or permitted to be taken by the Board of Directors may be taken without a meeting, if all members of the Board of Directors individually or collectively consent in writing to such action. Such written consent or consents shall be filed with the minutes of the proceedings of the Board of Directors. Such action by written consent shall have the same force and effect as a unanimous vote of such directors.

Section 30. Quorum and Transaction of Business. A majority of the authorized number of directors shall constitute a quorum for the transaction of business. Every act or decision done or made by a majority of the directors present at a meeting duly held at which a quorum is present shall be the act of the Board of Directors, unless the law, the Articles of Incorporation or these Bylaws specifically require a greater number. A meeting at which a quorum is initially present may continue to transact business, notwithstanding withdrawal of directors, if any action taken is approved by at least a majority of the number of directors constituting a quorum for such meeting. In the absence of a quorum at any meeting of the Board of Directors, a majority of the directors present may adjourn the meeting, as provided in Section 31 of these Bylaws.

Section 31. Adjournment. Any meeting of the Board of Directors, whether or not a quorum is present, may be adjourned to another time and place by the affirmative vote of a majority of the directors present. If the meeting is adjourned for more than twenty-four (24) hours, notice of such adjournment to another time or place shall be given prior to the

BUSINESS STRUCTURES AND INCORPORATION

time of the adjourned meeting to the directors who were not present at the time of the adjournment.

Section 32. Organization. The Chairman of the Board shall preside at every meeting of the Board of Directors, if present. If there is no Chairman of the Board or if the Chairman is not present, a Chairman chosen by a majority of the directors present shall act as chairman. The Secretary of the corporation or, in the absence of the Secretary, any person appointed by the Chairman shall act as secretary of the meeting.

Section 33. Compensation. Directors and members of committees may receive such compensation, if any, for their services, and such reimbursement for expenses, as may be fixed or determined by the Board of Directors.

Section 34. Committees. The Board of Directors may, by resolution adopted by a majority of the authorized number of directors, designate one or more committees, each consisting of two (2) or more directors, to serve at the pleasure of the Board of Directors. The Board of Directors, by a vote of the majority of authorized directors, may designate one or more directors as alternate members of any committee, to replace any absent member at any meeting of such committee. Any such committee shall have authority to act in the manner and to the extent provided in the resolution of the Board of Directors, and may have all the authority of the Board of Directors in the management of the business and affairs of the corporation, except with respect to:

(a) the approval of any action for which shareholders' approval or approval of the outstanding shares also is required by the California Corporations Code;

(b) the filling of vacancies on the Board of Directors or any of its committees;

(c) the fixing of compensation of directors for serving on the Board of Directors or any of its committees;

(d) the adoption, amendment or repeal of these Bylaws;

(e) the amendment or repeal of any resolution of the Board of Directors which by its express terms is not so amendable or repealable;

(f) a distribution to shareholders, except at a rate or in a periodic amount or within a price range determined by the Board of Directors; or

(g) the appointment of other committees of the Board of Directors or the members thereof.

Any committee may from time to time provide by resolution for regular meetings at specified times and places. If the date of such a meeting falls on a legal holiday, then the meeting shall be held at the same time on the next succeeding full business day. No notice of such a meeting need be given. Such regular meetings need not be held if the committee shall so determine at any time before or after the time when such meeting would otherwise have taken place. Special meetings may be called at any time in the same manner and by the same persons as stated in Sections 26 and 27 of these Bylaws for meetings of the Board of Directors. The provisions of Sections 25, 28, 29, 30, 31 and 32 of these Bylaws shall apply to committees, committee members and committee meetings as if the words "committee" and "committee member" were substituted for the word "Board of Directors", and "director", respectively, throughout such sections.

CORPORATIONS

ARTICLE V
OFFICERS

Section 35. Officers. The corporation shall have a Chairman of the Board or a President or both, a Secretary, a Chief Financial Officer and such other officers with such titles and duties as the Board of Directors may determine. Any two or more offices may be held by the same person.

Section 36. Appointment. All officers shall be chosen and appointed by the Board of Directors; *provided, however,* the Board of Directors may empower the chief executive officer of the corporation to appoint such officers, other than Chairman of the Board, President, Secretary or Chief Financial Officer, as the business of the corporation may require. All officers shall serve at the pleasure of the Board of Directors, subject to the rights, if any, of an officer under a contract of employment.

Section 37. Inability to Act. In the case of absence or inability to act of any officer of the corporation or of any person authorized by these Bylaws to act in such officer's place, the Board of Directors may from time to time delegate the powers or duties of such officer to any other officer, or any director or other person whom it may select, for such period of time as the Board of Directors deems necessary.

Section 38. Resignations. Any officer may resign at any time upon written notice to the corporation, without prejudice to the rights, if any, of the corporation under any contract to which such officer is a party. Such resignation shall be effective upon its receipt by the Chairman of the Board, the President, the Secretary or the Board of Directors, unless a different time is specified in the notice for effectiveness of such resignation. The acceptance of any such resignation shall not be necessary to make it effective unless otherwise specified in such notice.

Section 39. Removal. Any officer may be removed from office at any time, with or without cause, but subject to the rights, if any, of such officer under any contract of employment, by the Board of Directors or by any committee to whom such power of removal has been duly delegated, or, with regard to any officer who has been appointed by the chief executive officer pursuant to Section 36 above, by the chief executive officer or any other officer upon whom such power of removal may be conferred by the Board of Directors.

Section 40. Vacancies. A vacancy occurring in any office for any cause may be filled by the Board of Directors, in the manner prescribed by this Article of the Bylaws for initial appointment to such office.

Section 41. Chairman of the Board. The Chairman of the Board, if there be such an officer, shall, if present, preside at all meetings of the Board of Directors and shall exercise and perform such other powers and duties as may be assigned from time to time by the Board of Directors or prescribed by these Bylaws. If no President is appointed, the Chairman of the Board is the general manager and chief executive officer of the corporation, and shall exercise all powers of the President described in Section 42 below.

Section 42. President. Subject to such powers, if any, as may be given by the Board of Directors to the Chairman of the Board, if there be such an officer, the President shall be the general manager and chief executive officer of the corporation and shall have general supervision, direction, and control over the business and affairs of the corporation, subject to the control of the Board of Directors. The President may sign and execute, in the name of the corporation, any instrument authorized by the Board of Directors, except when the signing and execution thereof shall have been expressly delegated by the Board of Directors or by these Bylaws to some other officer or agent of the corporation. The President shall have all the general powers and duties of management usually vested in the president of a corporation, and shall have such other powers and duties as may be prescribed from time to time by the Board of Directors or these Bylaws. The President shall have discretion to prescribe the duties of other officers and employees of the corporation in a manner not inconsistent with the provisions of these Bylaws and the directions of the Board of Directors.

Section 43. Vice Presidents. In the absence or disability of the President, in the event of a vacancy in the office of President, or in the event such officer refuses to act, the Vice President shall perform all the duties of the President and, when so acting, shall have all the powers of, and be subject to all the restrictions on, the President. If at any such time the corporation has more than one vice president, the duties and powers of the President shall pass to each vice president in order of such vice president's rank as fixed by the Board of Directors or, if the vice presidents are not so ranked, to the vice president designated by the Board of Directors. The vice presidents shall have such other powers and perform such other duties as may be prescribed for them from time to time by the Board of Directors or pursuant to Sections 35 and 36 of these Bylaws or otherwise pursuant to these Bylaws.

Section 44. Secretary. The Secretary shall:

(a) Keep, or cause to be kept, minutes of all meetings of the corporation's shareholders, Board of Directors, and committees of the Board of Directors, if any. Such minutes shall be kept in written form.

(b) Keep, or cause to be kept, at the principal executive office of the corporation, or at the office of its transfer agent or registrar, if any, a record of the corporation's shareholders, showing the names and addresses of all shareholders, and the number and classes of shares held by each. Such records shall be kept in written form or any other form capable of being converted into written form.

(c) Keep, or cause to be kept, at the principal executive office of the corporation, or if the principal executive office is not in California, at its principal business office in California, an original or copy of these Bylaws, as amended.

(d) Give, or cause to be given, notice of all meetings of shareholders, directors and committees of the Board of Directors, as required by law or by these Bylaws.

(e) Keep the seal of the corporation, if any, in safe custody.

(f) Exercise such powers and perform such duties as are usually vested in the office of secretary of a corporation, and exercise such other powers and perform such other duties as may be prescribed from time to time by the Board of Directors or these Bylaws.

If any assistant secretaries are appointed, the assistant secretary, or one of the assistant secretaries in the order of their rank as fixed by the Board of Directors or, if they are not so ranked, the assistant secretary designated by the Board of Directors, in the absence or disability of the Secretary or in the event of such officer's refusal to act or if a vacancy exists in the office of Secretary, shall perform the duties and exercise the powers of the Secretary and discharge such duties as may be assigned from time to time pursuant to these Bylaws or by the Board of Directors.

Section 45. Chief Financial Officer. The Chief Financial Officer shall:

(a) Be responsible for all functions and duties of the treasurer of the corporation.

(b) Keep and maintain, or cause to be kept and maintained, adequate and correct books and records of account for the corporation.

(c) Receive or be responsible for receipt of all monies due and payable to the corporation from any source whatsoever; have charge and custody of, and be responsible for, all monies and other valuables of the corporation and be responsible for deposit of all such monies in the name and to the credit of the corporation with such depositaries as may be designated by the Board of Directors or a duly appointed and authorized committee of the Board of Directors.

(d) Disburse or be responsible for the disbursement of the funds of the corporation as may be ordered by the Board of Directors or a duly appointed and authorized committee of the Board of Directors.

(e) Render to the chief executive officer and the Board of Directors a statement of the financial condition of the corporation if called upon to do so.

(f) Exercise such powers and perform such duties as are usually vested in the office of chief financial officer of a corporation, and exercise such other powers and perform such other duties as may be prescribed by the Board of Directors or these Bylaws.

If any assistant financial officer is appointed, the assistant financial officer, or one of the assistant financial officers, if there are more than one, in the order of their rank as fixed by the Board of Directors or, if they are not so ranked, the assistant financial officer designated by the Board of Directors, shall, in the absence or disability of the Chief Financial Officer or in the event of such officer's refusal to act, perform the duties and exercise the powers of the Chief Financial Officer, and shall have such powers and discharge such duties as may be assigned from time to time pursuant to these Bylaws or by the Board of Directors.

Section 46. Compensation. The compensation of the officers shall be fixed from time to time by the Board of Directors, and no officer shall be prevented from receiving such compensation by reason of the fact that such officer is also a director of the corporation.

ARTICLE VI
CONTRACTS, LOANS, BANK ACCOUNTS, CHECKS AND DRAFTS

Section 47. Execution of Contracts and Other Instruments. Except as these Bylaws may otherwise provide, the Board of Directors or its duly appointed and authorized committee may authorize any officer or officers, agent or agents, to enter into any contract or execute and deliver any instrument in the name of and on behalf of the corporation, and such authorization may be general or confined to specific instances. Except as so authorized or otherwise expressly provided in these Bylaws, no officer, agent, or employee shall have any power or authority to bind the corporation by any contract or engagement or to pledge its credit or to render it liable for any purpose or in any amount.

Section 48. Loans. No loans shall be contracted on behalf of the corporation and no negotiable paper shall be issued in its name, unless and except as authorized by the Board of Directors or its duly appointed and authorized committee. When so authorized by the Board of Directors or such committee, any officer or agent of the corporation may affect loans and advances at any time for the corporation from any bank, trust company, or other institution, or from any firm, corporation or individual, and for such loans and advances may make, execute and deliver promissory notes, bonds or other evidences of indebtedness of the corporation and, when authorized as aforesaid, may mortgage, pledge, hypothecate or transfer any and all stocks, securities and other property, real or personal, at any time held by the corporation, and to that end endorse, assign and deliver the same as security for the payment of any and all loans, advances, indebtedness, and liabilities of the corporation. Such authorization may be general or confined to specific instances.

Section 49. Bank Accounts. The Board of Directors or its duly appointed and authorized committee from time to time may authorize the opening and keeping of general and/or special bank accounts with such banks, trust companies, or other depositaries as may be selected by the Board of Directors, its duly appointed and authorized committee or by any officer or officers, agent or agents, of the corporation to whom such power may be delegated from time to time by the Board of Directors. The Board of Directors or its duly appointed and authorized committee may make such rules and regulations with respect to said bank accounts, not inconsistent with the provisions of these Bylaws, as are deemed advisable.

Section 50. Checks, Drafts, Etc. All checks, drafts or other orders for the payment of money, notes, acceptances or other evidences of indebtedness issued in the name of the corporation shall be signed by such officer or officers, agent or agents, of the corporation, and in such manner, as shall be determined from time to time by resolution of the Board of Directors or its duly appointed and authorized committee. Endorsements for deposit to the credit of the corporation in any of its duly authorized depositaries may be made, without counter-signature, by the President or any vice president or the Chief Financial Officer or any assistant financial officer or by any other officer or agent of the corporation to whom the Board of Directors or its duly appointed and authorized committee, by resolution, shall have delegated such power or by hand-stamped impression in the name of the corporation.

ARTICLE VII
CERTIFICATES FOR SHARES AND THEIR TRANSFER

Section 51. Certificate for Shares. Every holder of shares in the corporation shall be entitled to have a certificate signed in the name of the corporation by the Chairman or Vice Chairman of the Board or the President or a Vice President and by the Chief Financial Officer or an assistant financial officer or by the Secretary or an assistant secretary, certifying the number of shares and the class or series of shares owned by the shareholder. Any or all of the signatures on the certificate may be facsimile. In case any officer, transfer agent or registrar who has signed or whose facsimile signature has been placed upon a certificate shall have ceased to be such officer, transfer agent or registrar before such certificate is issued, it may be issued by the corporation with the same effect as if such person were an officer, transfer agent or registrar at the date of issue.

In the event that the corporation shall issue any shares as only partly paid, the certificate issued to represent such partly paid shares shall have stated thereon the total consideration to be paid for such shares and the amount paid thereon.

Section 52. Transfer on the Books. Upon surrender to the Secretary or transfer agent (if any) of the corporation of a certificate for shares of the corporation duly endorsed, with reasonable assurance that the endorsement is genuine and effective, or accompanied by proper evidence of succession, assignment or authority to transfer and upon compliance with applicable federal and state securities laws and if the corporation has no statutory duty to inquire into adverse claims or has discharged any such duty and if any applicable law relating to the collection of taxes has been complied with, it shall be the duty of the corporation, by its Secretary or transfer agent, to cancel the old certificate, to issue a new certificate to the person entitled thereto and to record the transaction on the books of the corporation.

Section 53. Lost, Destroyed and Stolen Certificates. The holder of any certificate for shares of the corporation alleged to have been lost, destroyed or stolen shall notify the corporation by making a written affidavit or affirmation of such fact. Upon receipt of said affidavit or affirmation the Board of Directors, or its duly appointed and authorized committee or any officer or officers authorized by the Board so to do, may order the issuance of a new certificate for shares in the place of any certificate previously issued by the corporation and which is alleged to have been lost, destroyed or stolen. However, the Board of Directors or such authorized committee, officer or officers may require the owner of the allegedly lost, destroyed or stolen certificate, or such owner's legal representative, to give the corporation a bond or other adequate security sufficient to indemnify the corporation and its transfer agent and/or registrar, if any, against any claim that may be made against it or them on account of such allegedly lost, destroyed or stolen certificate or the replacement thereof. Said bond or other security shall be in such amount, on such terms and conditions and, in the case of a bond, with such surety or sureties as may be acceptable to the Board of Directors or to its duly appointed and authorized committee or any officer or officers authorized by the Board of Directors to determine the sufficiency thereof. The requirement of a bond or other security may be waived in particular cases at the discretion of the Board of Directors or its duly appointed and authorized committee or any officer or officers authorized by the Board of Directors so to do.

Section 54. Issuance, Transfer and Registration of Shares. The Board of Directors may make such rules and regulations, not inconsistent with law or with these Bylaws, as it may deem advisable concerning the issuance, transfer and registration of certificates for shares of the capital stock of the corporation. The Board of Directors may appoint a transfer agent or registrar of transfers, or both, and may require all certificates for shares of the corporation to bear the signature of either or both.

ARTICLE VIII
INSPECTION OF CORPORATE RECORDS

Section 55. Inspection by Directors. Every director shall have the absolute right at any reasonable time to inspect and copy all books, records, and documents of every kind of the corporation and any of its subsidiaries and to inspect the physical properties of the corporation and any of its subsidiaries. Such inspection may be made by the director in person or by agent or attorney, and the right of inspection includes the right to copy and make extracts.

Section 56. Inspection by Shareholders.
  (a) **Inspection of Corporate Records.**
    (1) A shareholder or shareholders holding at least five (5%) percent in the aggregate of the outstanding voting shares of the corporation or who hold at least one percent of such voting shares and have filed a Schedule 14B with the United States Securities and Exchange Commission relating to the election of directors of the corporation shall have an absolute right to do either or both of the following: (i) inspect and copy the record of shareholders' names and addresses and shareholdings during usual business hours upon five

BUSINESS STRUCTURES AND INCORPORATION

(5) business days' prior written demand upon the corporation; or (ii) obtain from the transfer agent, if any, for the corporation, upon five business days' prior written demand and upon the tender of its usual charges for such a list (the amount of which charges shall be stated to the shareholder by the transfer agent upon request), a list of the shareholders' names and addresses who are entitled to vote for the election of directors and their shareholdings, as of the most recent record date for which it has been compiled or as of a date specified by the shareholder subsequent to the date of demand.

(2) The record of shareholders shall also be open to inspection and copying by any shareholder or holder of a voting trust certificate at any time during usual business hours upon written demand on the corporation, for a purpose reasonably related to such holder's interest as a shareholder or holder of a voting trust certificate.

(3) The accounting books and records and minutes of proceedings of the shareholders and the Board of Directors and of any committees of the Board of Directors of the corporation and of each of its subsidiaries shall be open to inspection, copying and making extracts upon written demand on the corporation of any shareholder or holder of a voting trust certificate at any reasonable time during usual business hours, for a purpose reasonably related to such holder's interests as a shareholder or as a holder of such voting trust certificate.

(4) Any inspection, copying, and making of extracts under this subsection (a) may be done in person or by agent or attorney.

(b) Inspection of Bylaws. The original or a copy of these Bylaws shall be kept as provided in Section 44 of these Bylaws and shall be open to inspection by the shareholders at all reasonable times during office hours. If the principal executive office of the corporation is not in California, and the corporation has no principal business office in the state of California, a current copy of these Bylaws shall be furnished to any shareholder upon written request.

Section 57. Written Form. If any record subject to inspection pursuant to Section 56 above is not maintained in written form, a request for inspection is not complied with unless and until the corporation at its expense makes such record available in written form.

ARTICLE IX
MISCELLANEOUS

Section 58. Fiscal Year. Unless otherwise fixed by resolution of the Board of Directors, the fiscal year of the corporation shall end on the 31st day of December in each calendar year.

Section 59. Annual Report.

(a) Subject to the provisions of Section 59(b) below, the Board of Directors shall cause an annual report to be sent to each shareholder of the corporation in the manner provided in Section 9 of these Bylaws not later than one hundred twenty (120) days after the close of the corporation's fiscal year. Such report shall include a balance sheet as of the end of such fiscal year and an income statement and statement of changes in financial position for such fiscal year, accompanied by any report thereon of independent accountants or, if there is no such report, the certificate of an authorized officer of the corporation that such statements were prepared without audit from the books and records of the corporation. When there are more than 100 shareholders of record of the corporation's shares, as determined by Section 605 of the California Corporations Code, additional information as required by Section 1501(b) of the California Corporations Code shall also be contained in such report, provided that if the corporation has a class of securities registered under Section 12 of the United States Securities Exchange Act of 1934, that Act shall take precedence. Such report shall be sent to shareholders at least fifteen (15) (or, if sent by third-class mail, thirty-five (35)) days prior to the next annual meeting of shareholders after the end of the fiscal year to which it relates.

If and so long as there are fewer than 100 shareholders of record of the corporation's shares, the requirement of sending of an annual report to the shareholders of the corporation is hereby expressly waived.

Section 60. Record Date. The Board of Directors may fix a time in the future as a record date for the determination of the shareholders entitled to notice of or to vote at any meeting or entitled to receive payment of any dividend or other distribution or allotment of any rights or entitled to exercise any rights in respect of any change, conversion or exchange of shares or entitled to exercise any rights in respect of any other lawful action. The record date so fixed shall not be more than sixty (60) days nor less than ten (10) days prior to the date of the meeting nor more than sixty (60) days prior to any other action or event for the purpose of which it is fixed. If no record date is fixed, the provisions of Section 15 of these Bylaws shall apply with respect to notice of meetings, votes, and consents and the record date for determining shareholders for any other purpose shall be at the close of business on the day on which the Board of Directors adopts the resolutions relating thereto, or the sixtieth (60th) day prior to the date of such other action or event, whichever is later.

Only shareholders of record at the close of business on the record date shall be entitled to notice and to vote or to receive the dividend, distribution or allotment of rights or to exercise the rights, as the case may be, notwithstanding any transfer of any shares on the books of the corporation after the record date, except as otherwise provided in the Articles of Incorporation, by agreement or by law.

Section 61. Bylaw Amendments. Except as otherwise provided by law or Section 19 of these Bylaws, these Bylaws may be amended or repealed by the Board of Directors or by the affirmative vote of a majority of the outstanding shares entitled to vote, including, if applicable, the affirmative vote of a majority of the outstanding shares of each class or series entitled by law or the Articles of Incorporation to vote as a class or series on the amendment or repeal or adoption of any bylaw or Bylaws; *provided, however,* after issuance of shares, a bylaw specifying or changing a fixed number of directors or the maximum or minimum number or changing from a fixed to a variable board or vice versa may only be adopted by approval of the outstanding shares as provided herein.

Section 62. Construction and Definition. Unless the context requires otherwise, the general provisions, rules of construction, and definitions contained in the California Corporations Code shall govern the construction of these Bylaws.

Without limiting the foregoing, "shall" is mandatory and "may" is permissive.

BUSINESS STRUCTURES AND INCORPORATION

ARTICLE X
INDEMNIFICATION

Section 63. Indemnification of Directors, Officers, Employees and Other Agents.

(a) **Directors and Executive Officers.** The corporation shall indemnify its directors and executive officers to the fullest extent not prohibited by the California General Corporation Law; *provided, however,* that the corporation may limit the extent of such indemnification by individual contracts with its directors and executive officers; and, *provided, further,* that the corporation shall not be required to indemnify any director or executive officer in connection with any proceeding (or part thereof) initiated by such person or any proceeding by such person against the corporation or its directors, officers, employees or other agents unless (i) such indemnification is expressly required to be made by law, (ii) the proceeding was authorized by the board of directors of the corporation or (iii) such indemnification is provided by the corporation, in its sole discretion, pursuant to the powers vested in the corporation under the California General Corporation Law.

(b) **Other Officers, Employees and Other Agents.** The corporation shall have the power to indemnify its other officers, employees and other agents as set forth in the California General Corporation Law.

(c) **Determination by the Corporation.** Promptly after receipt of a request for indemnification hereunder (and in any event within ninety (90) days thereof) a reasonable, good faith determination as to whether indemnification of the director or executive officer is proper under the circumstances because such director or executive officer has met the applicable standard of care shall be made by:

(1) a majority vote of a quorum consisting of directors who are not parties to such proceeding;

(2) if such quorum is not obtainable, by independent legal counsel in a written opinion; or

(3) approval or ratification by the affirmative vote of a majority of the shares of this corporation represented and voting at a duly held meeting at which a quorum is present (which shares voting affirmatively also constitute at least a majority of the required quorum) or by written consent of a majority of the outstanding shares entitled to vote; where in each case the shares owned by the person to be indemnified shall not be considered entitled to vote thereon.

(d) **Good Faith.**

(1) For purposes of any determination under this bylaw, a director or executive officer shall be deemed to have acted in good faith and in a manner he reasonably believed to be in the best interests of the corporation and its shareholders, and, with respect to any criminal action or proceeding, to have had no reasonable cause to believe that his conduct was unlawful, if his action is based on information, opinions, reports and statements, including financial statements and other financial data, in each case prepared or presented by: (i) one or more officers or employees of the corporation whom the director or executive officer believed to be reliable and competent in the matters presented; (ii) counsel, independent accountants or other persons as to matters which the director or executive officer believed to be within such person's professional competence; and (iii) with respect to a director, a committee of the Board upon which such director does not serve, as to matters within such committee's designated authority, which committee the director

believes to merit confidence; so long as, in each case, the director or executive officer acts without knowledge that would cause such reliance to be unwarranted.

(2) The termination of any proceeding by judgment, order, settlement, conviction or upon a plea of nolo contendere or its equivalent shall not, of itself, create a presumption that the person did not act in good faith and in a manner which he reasonably believed to be in the best interests of the corporation and its shareholders or that he had reasonable cause to believe that his conduct was unlawful.

(3) The provisions of this paragraph (d) shall not be deemed to be exclusive or to limit in any way the circumstances in which a person may be deemed to have met the applicable standard of conduct set forth by the California General Corporation Law.

(e) **Expenses.** The corporation shall advance, prior to the final disposition of any proceeding, promptly following request therefor, all expenses incurred by any director or executive officer in connection with such proceeding upon receipt of an undertaking by or on behalf of such person to repay said amounts if it shall be determined ultimately that such person is not entitled to be indemnified under this bylaw or otherwise.

Notwithstanding the foregoing, unless otherwise determined pursuant to paragraph (f) of this bylaw, no advance shall be made by the corporation if a determination is reasonably and promptly made by the Board of Directors by a majority vote of a quorum consisting of directors who were not parties to the proceeding (or, if no such quorum exists, by independent legal counsel in a written opinion) that the facts known to the decision making party at the time such determination is made demonstrate clearly and convincingly that such person acted in bad faith or in a manner that such person did not believe to be in the best interests of the corporation and its shareholders.

(f) **Enforcement.** Without the necessity of entering into an express contract, all rights to indemnification and advances to directors and executive officers under this bylaw shall be deemed to be contractual rights and be effective to the same extent and as if provided for in a contract between the corporation and the director or executive officer. Any right to indemnification or advances granted by this bylaw to a director or executive officer shall be enforceable by or on behalf of the person holding such right in the forum in which the proceeding is or was pending or, if such forum is not available or a determination is made that such forum is not convenient, in any court of competent jurisdiction if (i) the claim for indemnification or advances is denied, in whole or in part, or (ii) no disposition of such claim is made within ninety (90) days of request therefor. The claimant in such enforcement action, if successful in whole or in part, shall be entitled to be paid also the expense of prosecuting his claim. The corporation shall be entitled to raise as a defense to any such action that the claimant has not met the standards of conduct that make it permissible under the California General Corporation Law for the corporation to indemnify the claimant for the amount claimed. Neither the failure of the corporation (including its board of directors, independent legal counsel or its shareholders) to have made a determination prior to the commencement of such action that indemnification of the claimant is proper in the circumstances because he has met the applicable standard of conduct set forth in the California General Corporation Law, nor an actual determination by the corporation (including its board of directors, independent legal counsel or its shareholders) that the claimant has not met such applicable standard of conduct, shall be a defense to the action or create a presumption that claimant has not met the applicable standard of conduct.

BUSINESS STRUCTURES AND INCORPORATION

(g) **Non-Exclusivity of Rights.** To the fullest extent permitted by the corporation's Articles of Incorporation and the California General Corporation Law, the rights conferred on any person by this bylaw shall not be exclusive of any other right which such person may have or hereafter acquire under any statute, provision of the Articles of Incorporation, Bylaws, agreement, vote of shareholders or disinterested directors or otherwise, both as to action in his official capacity and as to action in another capacity while holding office. The corporation is specifically authorized to enter into individual contracts with any or all of its directors, officers, employees or agents respecting indemnification and advances, to the fullest extent permitted by the California General Corporation Law and the corporation's Articles of Incorporation.

(h) **Survival of Rights.** The rights conferred on any person by this bylaw shall continue as to a person who has ceased to be a director or executive officer and shall inure to the benefit of the heirs, executors and administrators of such a person.

(i) **Insurance.** The corporation, upon approval by the board of directors, may purchase insurance on behalf of any person required or permitted to be indemnified pursuant to this bylaw.

(j) **Amendments.** Any repeal or modification of this bylaw shall only be prospective and shall not affect the rights under this bylaw in effect at the time of the alleged occurrence of any action or omission to act that is the cause of any proceeding against any agent of the corporation.

(k) **Employee Benefit Plans.** The corporation shall indemnify the directors and officers of the corporation who serve at the request of the corporation as trustees, investment managers or other fiduciaries of employee benefit plans to the fullest extent permitted by the California General Corporation Law.

(l) **Saving Clause.** If this bylaw or any portion hereof shall be invalidated on any ground by any court of competent jurisdiction, then the corporation shall nevertheless indemnify each director and executive officer to the fullest extent permitted by any applicable portion of this bylaw that shall not have been invalidated, or by any other applicable law.

(m) **Certain Definitions.** For the purposes of this bylaw, the following definitions shall apply:

(1) The term **"proceeding"** shall be broadly construed and shall include, without limitation, the investigation, preparation, prosecution, defense, settlement and appeal of any threatened, pending or completed action, suit or proceeding, whether civil, criminal, administrative, arbitrative or investigative.

(2) The term **"expenses"** shall be broadly construed and shall include, without limitation, court costs, attorneys' fees, witness fees, fines, amounts paid in settlement or judgment and any other costs and expenses of any nature or kind incurred in connection with any proceeding, including expenses of establishing a right to indemnification under this bylaw or any applicable law.

(3) The term the **"corporation"** shall include, in addition to the resulting corporation, any constituent corporation (including any constituent of a constituent) absorbed in a consolidation or merger which, if its separate existence had continued, would have had power and authority to indemnify its directors, officers, and employees or agents, so that any person who is or was a director, officer, employee or agent of such constituent corporation, or is or was serving at the request of such constituent corporation as a director, officer, employee or agent of another corporation, partnership,

CORPORATIONS

joint venture, trust or other enterprise, shall stand in the same position under the provisions of this bylaw with respect to the resulting or surviving corporation as he would have with respect to such constituent corporation if its separate existence had continued.

(4) References to a **"director," "officer," "employee,"** or **"agent"** of the corporation shall include, without limitation, situations where such person is or was serving at the request of the corporation as a director, officer, employee, trustee or agent of another corporation, partnership, joint venture, trust or other enterprise.

ARTICLE XI
RIGHT OF FIRST REFUSAL

Section 64. Right of First Refusal. No shareholder shall sell, assign, pledge, or in any manner transfer any of the shares of stock of the corporation or any right or interest therein, whether voluntarily or by operation of law, or by gift or otherwise, except by a transfer which meets the requirements hereinafter set forth in this bylaw:

(a) If the shareholder desires to sell or otherwise transfer any of his shares of stock, then the shareholder shall first give written notice thereof to the corporation. The notice shall name the proposed transferee and state the number of shares to be transferred, the proposed consideration, and all other terms and conditions of the proposed transfer.

(b) For thirty (30) days following receipt of such notice, the corporation shall have the option to purchase all (but not less than all) of the shares specified in the notice at the price and upon the terms set forth in such notice; *provided, however,* that, with the consent of the shareholder, the corporation shall have the option to purchase a lesser portion of the shares specified in said notice at the price and upon the terms set forth therein. In the event of a gift, property settlement or other transfer in which the proposed transferee is not paying the full price for the shares, and that is not otherwise exempted from the provisions of this Section 64, the price shall be deemed to be the fair market value of the stock at such time as determined in good faith by the Board of Directors. In the event the corporation elects to purchase all of the shares or, with consent of the shareholder, a lesser portion of the shares, it shall give written notice to the transferring shareholder of its election and settlement for said shares shall be made as provided below in paragraph (d).

(c) The corporation may assign its rights hereunder.

(d) In the event the corporation and/or its assignee(s) elect to acquire any of the shares of the transferring shareholder as specified in said transferring shareholder's notice, the Secretary of the corporation shall so notify the transferring shareholder and settlement thereof shall be made in cash within thirty (30) days after the Secretary of the corporation receives said transferring shareholder's notice; provided that if the terms of payment set forth in said transferring shareholder's notice were other than cash against delivery, the corporation and/or its assignee(s) shall pay for said shares on the same terms and conditions set forth in said transferring shareholder's notice.

(e) In the event the corporation and/or its assignees(s) do not elect to acquire all of the shares specified in the transferring shareholder's notice, said transferring shareholder may, within the sixty-day period following the expiration of the option rights granted to the corporation and/or its assignees(s) herein, transfer the shares specified in said transferring shareholder's notice which were not acquired by the corporation and/or its assignees(s) as specified in said transferring shareholder's notice. All shares so sold by said transferring shareholder shall continue to be subject to the provisions of this bylaw in the same manner as before said transfer.

BUSINESS STRUCTURES AND INCORPORATION

(f) Anything to the contrary contained herein notwithstanding, the following transactions shall be exempt from the provisions of this bylaw:

(1) A shareholder's transfer of any or all shares held either during such shareholder's lifetime or on death by will or intestacy to such shareholder's immediate family or to any custodian or trustee for the account of such shareholder or such shareholder's immediate family or to any limited partnership of which the shareholder, members of such shareholder's immediate family or any trust for the account of such shareholder or such shareholder's immediate family will be the general of limited partner(s) of such partnership. "Immediate family" as used herein shall mean spouse, lineal descendant, father, mother, brother, or sister of the shareholder making such transfer.

(2) A shareholder's bona fide pledge or mortgage of any shares with a commercial lending institution, provided that any subsequent transfer of said shares by said institution shall be conducted in the manner set forth in this bylaw.

(3) A shareholder's transfer of any or all of such shareholder's shares to the corporation or to any other shareholder of the corporation.

(4) A shareholder's transfer of any or all of such shareholder's shares to a person who, at the time of such transfer, is an officer or director of the corporation.

(5) A corporate shareholder's transfer of any or all of its shares pursuant to and in accordance with the terms of any merger, consolidation, reclassification of shares or capital reorganization of the corporate shareholder, or pursuant to a sale of all or substantially all of the stock or assets of a corporate shareholder.

(6) A corporate shareholder's transfer of any or all of its shares to any or all of its shareholders.

(7) A transfer by a shareholder which is a limited or general partnership to any or all of its partners or former partners.

In any such case, the transferee, assignee, or other recipient shall receive and hold such stock subject to the provisions of this bylaw, and there shall be no further transfer of such stock except in accord with this bylaw.

(g) The provisions of this bylaw may be waived with respect to any transfer either by the corporation, upon duly authorized action of its Board of Directors, or by the shareholders, upon the express written consent of the owners of a majority of the voting power of the corporation (excluding the votes represented by those shares to be transferred by the transferring shareholder). This bylaw may be amended or repealed either by a duly authorized action of the Board of Directors or by the shareholders, upon the express written consent of the owners of a majority of the voting power of the corporation.

(h) Any sale or transfer, or purported sale or transfer, of securities of the corporation shall be null and void unless the terms, conditions, and provisions of this bylaw are strictly observed and followed.

(i) The foregoing right of first refusal shall terminate on either of the following dates, whichever shall first occur:

(1) On _____, 20___; or

(2) Upon the date securities of the corporation are first offered to the public pursuant to a registration statement filed with, and declared effective by, the United States Securities and Exchange Commission under the Securities Act of 1933, as amended.

(j) The certificates representing shares of stock of the corporation shall bear on their face the following legend so long as the foregoing right of first refusal remains in effect:

"THE SHARES REPRESENTED BY THIS CERTIFICATE ARE SUBJECT TO A RIGHT OF FIRST REFUSAL OPTION IN FAVOR OF THE CORPORATION AND/OR ITS ASSIGNEE(S), AS PROVIDED IN THE BYLAWS OF THE CORPORATION."

ARTICLE XII
LOANS OF OFFICERS AND OTHERS

Section 65. Certain Corporate Loans and Guaranties. If the corporation has outstanding shares held of record by 100 or more persons on the date of approval by the Board of Directors, the corporation may make loans of money or property to, or guarantee the obligations of, any officer of the corporation or its parent or any subsidiary, whether or not a director of the corporation or its parent or any subsidiary, or adopt an employee benefit plan or plans authorizing such loans or guaranties, upon the approval of the Board of Directors alone, by a vote sufficient without counting the vote of any interested director or directors, if the Board of Directors determines that such a loan or guaranty or plan may reasonably be expected to benefit the corporation. Notwithstanding the foregoing, the corporation shall have the power to make loans permitted by the California Corporations Code.

Organizational Meeting

Under California law, the Board of Directors may act in a formal meeting of the Board or by unanimous written consent in lieu of an organizational meeting. The sample minutes and consent below covers all of the steps necessary to complete the incorporation process. The minutes and consent covers ratification by the Board of the actions taken by the Incorporator, including the election of officers, authorization of the payment of incorporation expenses, issuance of stock, establishment of a corporate bank account, approval of agreements and other important matters. In particular, we note the following:

- ❖ It is essential to establish the corporation as a separate entity for liability and tax purposes. Accordingly, the provisions of the initial stock issuances are important in order to provide the corporation with adequate capital to meet the needs of the business.

- ❖ The minutes and consent calls for the selection of a calendar or fiscal year for the corporation. The corporation may elect to be taxed on either a calendar year or a fiscal year basis, but it must be the same for both California and federal taxes. If reasons dictate otherwise, you can, prior to filing the corporation's first tax return, change the fiscal year end to any other month you'd like so long as the initial fiscal year end is not more than twelve months from the date of incorporation.

BUSINESS STRUCTURES AND INCORPORATION

S corporations and personal service corporations may be more limited in the choice of a fiscal year.

❖ The standard form resolutions establishing a corporation bank account and providing for bank borrowing are necessary in the corporation's financial dealings. Each bank has a standard form, and, if you already have selected a bank, the form for the bank or banks you select should be attached to the minutes. Note that the banking resolutions adopted in the minutes and consent are purposely broad in nature and are designed to permit the corporation to open new bank accounts from time to time with any bank the corporation should choose, without the necessity of returning to the Board of Directors for specific approval. However, such resolutions are not designed to authorize the borrowing of money or the creation of lease lines, which should be specifically authorized by the Corporation's Board of Directors.

❖ In addition to the above matters, you may wish to adopt a corporate seal. While this is no longer formally required by statute, the seal provides a means of verifying the execution of certain documents on behalf of the corporation. The most common example is the affixing of the seal on a corporation's stock certificates.

SAMPLE UNANIMOUS WRITTEN CONSENT OF THE BOARD OF DIRECTORS IN LIEU OF ORGANIZATIONAL MEETING OF

_____

The undersigned, constituting all of the members of the Board of Directors of _____, a California corporation (the "Company"), hereby adopt the following resolutions by unanimous written consent pursuant to Section 307(b) of the California Corporations Code.

APPOINTMENT OF DIRECTORS

RESOLVED, that the Action by Written Consent of Sole Incorporator attached hereto as Exhibit A appointing the Company's initial directors, be, and it hereby is, ratified and approved.

CORPORATIONS

ARTICLES OF INCORPORATION

      RESOLVED, that the Articles of Incorporation of the Company filed with the California Secretary of State on _____, 20__ be, and they hereby are, ratified and affirmed.

ELECTION OF OFFICERS

      RESOLVED, that the following persons be, and they hereby are, elected as officers of the Company, to serve until the next annual meeting or until their successors are duly elected and qualified:

President	_____
Chief Executive Officer	_____
Chief Financial Officer	_____
Secretary	_____

ADOPTION OF BYLAWS

      RESOLVED, that the Bylaws attached hereto as Exhibit B be, and they hereby are, adopted as the Bylaws of and for the Company; and

      RESOLVED FURTHER, that the Secretary of the Company be, and he hereby is, authorized and directed to execute a Certificate of Secretary regarding the adoption of the Bylaws, to insert the Bylaws in the Company's Minute Book and to see that a copy of the Bylaws is kept at the Company's principal office, as required by law.

CORPORATE SEAL

      RESOLVED, that the form of corporate seal shown below be, and it hereby is adopted as the seal of the Company.

EMPLOYER TAX IDENTIFICATION NUMBER

      RESOLVED, that the appropriate officers of the Company be, and each of them hereby is, authorized and are directed to apply to the Internal Revenue Service for an employer's identification number on Form SS-4.

EMPLOYMENT DEVELOPMENT DEPARTMENT IDENTIFICATION NUMBER

      RESOLVED, that the appropriate officers of the Company be, and each of them hereby is, authorized and are directed to apply to the Employment Development Department for an identification number on Form DE-1.

WITHHOLDING TAXES

      RESOLVED, that the Chief Financial Officer be, and hereby is, authorized and directed to consult with the bookkeeper, auditors and attorneys of the Company in order to be fully informed as to, and to collect and pay promptly when due, all withholding taxes which the Company may now be (or hereafter become) liable.

STATEMENT BY DOMESTIC STOCK CORPORATION

      RESOLVED, that the appropriate officers of the Company shall file with the Secretary of State of California pursuant to Section 1502 of the California Corporations Code a statement of the names of the Chief Executive Officer, Secretary, Chief Financial Officer and incumbent directors, together with a statement of the location and address of the principal office of the Company, and designating _____ as agent for service of process.

BUSINESS STRUCTURES AND INCORPORATION

DESIGNATION OF DEPOSITORY

  RESOLVED, that the Chief Executive Officer, the President and the Chief Financial Officer of the Company be, and each of them hereby is, authorized:

  (a) To designate one or more banks or similar financial institutions as depositories of the funds of the Company;

  (b) To open, maintain and close general and special accounts with any such depositories;

  (c) To cause to be deposited, from time to time, in such accounts with any such depository, such funds of the Company as such officers deem necessary or advisable, and to designate or change the designation of the officer or officers or agent or agents of the Company authorized to make such deposits and to endorse checks, drafts and other instruments for deposit;

  (d) To designate, change or revoke the designation, from time to time, of the officer or officers or agent or agents of the Company authorized to sign or countersign checks, drafts or other orders for the payment of money issued in the name of the Company against any funds deposited in any of such accounts;

  (e) To authorize the use of facsimile signatures for the signing or countersigning of checks, drafts or other orders for the payment of money, and to enter into such agreements as banks and similar financial institutions customarily require as a condition for permitting the use of facsimile signatures; and

  (f) To make such general and special rules and regulations with respect to such accounts as they may deem necessary or advisable, and to complete, execute and certify any customary printed blank signature card forms in order to exercise conveniently the authority granted by this resolution and any resolutions printed on such cards are deemed adopted as a part of this resolution.

  RESOLVED FURTHER, that all form resolutions required by any such depository be, and they hereby are, adopted in such form used by such depository, and that the Secretary be, and hereby is, (i) authorized to certify such resolutions as having been adopted by this Unanimous Written Consent and (ii) directed to insert a copy of such form resolutions in the Minute Book immediately following this Unanimous Written Consent; and

  RESOLVED FURTHER, that any such depository to which a certified copy of these resolutions has been delivered by the Secretary of the Company be, and it hereby is, authorized and entitled to rely upon such resolutions for all purposes until it shall have received written notice of the revocation or amendment of these resolutions adopted by the Board of Directors of the Company.

FISCAL YEAR

  RESOLVED, that the fiscal year of the Company shall end on the 31st day of the month of December of each year.

CORPORATIONS

PRINCIPAL OFFICE

    RESOLVED, that the principal executive office of the Company shall be at _____, in the County of _____, California.

MANAGEMENT POWERS

    RESOLVED, that the officers of the Company be, and each of them hereby is, authorized to sign and execute in the name and on behalf of the Company all applications, contracts, leases and other deeds and documents or instruments in writing of whatsoever nature that may be required in the ordinary course of business of the Company and that may be necessary to secure for operation of the corporate affairs, governmental permits and licenses for, and incidental to, the lawful operations of the business of the Company, and to do such acts and things as such officers deem necessary or advisable to fulfill such legal requirements as are applicable to the Company and its business.

STOCK CERTIFICATES

    RESOLVED, that the stock certificates representing Common Stock of the Company be in substantially the form of Stock Certificate attached hereto as Exhibit C; that each such Certificate shall bear the name of the Company, the number of shares represented thereby, the name of the owner of such shares and the date such shares were issued; and

    RESOLVED FURTHER, that such Stock Certificates shall be consecutively numbered beginning with No. 1; shall be issued only when the signature of the President and Secretary, or other such officers as provided in the California Corporations Code, are affixed thereto; and that such Certificates may also bear other wording related to the ownership, issuance and transferability of the shares represented thereby.

SALE OF COMMON STOCK

    RESOLVED, that the officers of the Company be, and each of them hereby is, authorized and directed, for and on behalf of the Company, to sell and issue an aggregate of _____ (_____) shares of its Common Stock at a purchase price of _____ ($_____) per share, payable in cash, as follows:

Name of Purchaser	Total Number of Shares	Purchase Price
_____	_____	_____
_____	_____	_____
_____	_____	_____

    RESOLVED FURTHER, that the Board of Directors of the Company hereby determines, after due consideration of all relevant factors, that the fair market value of the Company's Common Stock as of the date hereof is equal to _____ ($_____) per share;

    RESOLVED FURTHER, which the form of Stock Purchase Agreement attached hereto as Exhibit D, be and it hereby is, adopted, ratified and approved;

    RESOLVED FUTHER, that the sale and issuance of Common Stock to each of the above-named individuals shall be conditioned upon the receipt by the Company of (a) the purchase price for said stock and (b) an executed Stock Purchase Agreement, including executed copies of

BUSINESS STRUCTURES AND INCORPORATION

any and all documents attached thereto as exhibits, substantially in the form attached hereto; provided, however, that the President of the Company be, and hereby is, authorized and directed to amend, alter or revise the form of Stock Purchase Agreement as he in his sole discretion deems necessary or appropriate to accurately reflect the terms of the contemplated sale of Common Stock to each individual purchaser;

RESOLVED FURTHER, that the shares of Common Stock authorized to be sold and issued by the Company shall be offered and sold in accordance with the terms of the exemption from qualification provided by Section 25102(f) of the California Corporations Code;

RESOLVED FURTHER, that the President and Secretary of the Company be, and each of them hereby is, authorized and directed, for and on behalf of the Company, to execute a form of notice of such issuance and to cause such notice, when duly executed, to be filed with the California Commissioner of Corporations;

RESOLVED FURTHER, that the shares of Common Stock authorized to be sold and issued by the Company shall be offered and sold in accordance with the terms of the exemption from registration provided by Rule 701 promulgated under the Securities Act of 1933, as mended/Section 4(2) of the Securities Act of 1933, as amended; and

RESOLVED FURTHER, that the officers of the Company be, and each of them hereby is, authorized and directed, for and on behalf of the Company, to take such further action and execute such additional documents as each may deem necessary or appropriate to carry out the purposes of the above resolutions.

RATIFICATION

RESOLVED, that all prior acts done on behalf of the Company by the sole incorporator or agents be, and the same hereby are, ratified and approved as acts of the Company.

INCORPORATION EXPENSES

RESOLVED, that the officers of the Company be, and each of them hereby is authorized and directed to pay the expenses of the incorporation and organization of the Company.

ADDITIONAL FILINGS

RESOLVED, that the appropriate officers of the Company be, and each of them hereby is, authorized and directed, for and on behalf of the Company, to make such filings and applications, to execute and deliver such documents and instruments, and to do such acts and things as such officer deems necessary or advisable in order to obtain such licenses, authorizations and permits as are necessary or desirable for the Company's business, and to fulfill such legal requirements as are applicable to the Company and its business and to complete the organization of the Company.

This consent may be signed in one or more counterparts, each of which shall be deemed an original, and all of which together shall constitute one instrument. This consent shall be filed with the minutes of the proceedings of the Board of Directors of the Company.

IN WITNESS WHEREOF, the undersigned have executed this Action by Unanimous Written Consent as of the ___ day of _____, 20___.

Respectfully submitted,

_____
Officer

_____

CORPORATIONS

Officer
_____

Officer
_____

Officer
_____

SAMPLE CERTIFICATE OF SECRETARY
I HEREBY CERTIFY THAT:

    I am the duly elected and acting Secretary of _____, a California corporation (the "Company"); and

    Attached hereto is a complete and accurate copy of the Bylaws of the Company as duly adopted by the Board of Directors by Unanimous Written Consent dated _____, 20__ and said Bylaws are presently in effect.

    IN WITNESS WHEREOF, I have hereunto subscribed my name and affixed the seal of the Company this _____ day of _____, 20__.

Respectfully submitted,

_____
Secretary

S Corporation Election

The Internal Revenue Code permits shareholders of S corporations to operate their business as a corporation but be taxed in general as a partnership. S corporations generally do not pay federal income tax but pass the tax liability for their profits and losses through to their shareholders. Consequently, profits earned by an S corporation will be taxed only once. The shareholders must include the profits as income when earned by the S corporation, (whether or not any amounts are distributed to shareholders). A distribution of earnings by an S corporation to its shareholders is generally not taxed a second time. In contrast, a similar distribution by a C corporation will be taxed twice; the corporation must pay federal corporate income tax on profits earned, and the shareholders must treat the distribution as a dividend subject to tax.

Shareholders generally elect S corporation status when the corporation is profitable and distributes substantially all of its profits to the shareholders, or when the corporation incurs losses, and the shareholders wish to utilize the loss deductions on their personal income tax statements. However, because the overall maximum individual income tax rate (39.6%) is higher than the corporate income tax rate (35%), using an S corporation may not be the best choice if the corporation is profitable and expects to accumulate its earnings, rather than distribute them currently. There are substantial limitations upon the availability of the S corporation election and the allocation and deduction of S corporation losses by its shareholders.

BUSINESS STRUCTURES AND INCORPORATION

To qualify as an S corporation, a corporation must meet certain eligibility requirements and must strictly comply with the certain procedures for the election of S corporation status. Specifically, for treatment as an S corporation, the corporation must meet the following criteria:

- ❖ The corporation must be organized under the laws of the U.S. (or any state or territory thereof) and may not be a member of an affiliated group of corporations;

- ❖ There may be no more than 75 shareholders, all of whom are individuals, certain tax exempt organizations, qualifying trusts or estates and none of whom are nonresident aliens; and

- ❖ There may be only one class of stock outstanding (although options and differences in voting rights are generally permitted).

Once the election is made, the corporation must continue to satisfy such requirements to maintain S corporation status. The election must be made on the current version of Form 2553 and must be timely filed with the Internal Revenue Service. In addition, the election must be made by an existing corporation on or before the fifteenth day of the third month of the corporation's taxable year. Thus, for existing calendar year corporations, the election must generally be made by March 15th to be effective that year.

With respect to a newly formed corporation, the two month and fifteen-day time period begins to run on the earlier of the first day upon which the corporation (i) has assets, (ii) has shareholders, or (iii) begins to do business. The filing by the corporation of Articles of Incorporation is a prerequisite to making the election. In the case of a new corporation whose first year begins mid-month, the regulations of the Internal Revenue Service define a "month" to mean the period commencing with the beginning of the first day of the taxable year and ending with the close of the day preceding the numerically corresponding day of the succeeding calendar month.

If the election is not made by a corporation until after the two month and fifteen-day time period, the election will not be effective until the following year (and will only be effective if the corporation met the S corporation requirements at the time the election was filed).

Anyone who has an interest in the stock of the prospective S corporation must consent to the election. The spouse of a shareholder who has a community property interest in the shareholder's stock or the income from it must consent to the election. Persons with interests in the stock as tenants in common, joint tenants, or tenants by the entirety must each consent to the election, and the deemed owners of any trusts must consent to the election. Shareholder consents should generally be made on Form 2553 itself. However, separate consents which contain the information on Form 2553 may be attached.

In general, a corporation which makes a federal election is deemed to have made California S corporation election on the same date as the federal election. However, the corporation must report the federal election to the Franchise Tax Board (i) before the sixteenth day of the third month of the income tax year for which the California election is to take effect, or (ii) within two and one-half months after qualifying to do business in California, whichever is later.

To report the federal election, the corporation must complete California Form 3560, attach a copy of federal Form 2553 and file them with the Franchise Tax Board. When completing Form 3560, the corporation should only fill in Part I; Part II, box 1; and Part IV of the form. However, the requirements for electing California S corporation status were modified by California Revenue and Taxation Code Section 23801. Pursuant to this amendment, Form 3560 was significantly revised by the Franchise Tax Board. Consequently, if a federal S corporation does not want to be treated as a California S corporation, it must elect California C corporation status by completing Part I; Part II, box 2; and Part IV of California Form 3560 and filing such form with the Franchise Tax Board within the California Filing Period.

If a corporation elects to be treated as a California S corporation and has one or more shareholders who are nonresidents of California or are trusts with one or more nonresident fiduciaries, then (i) each nonresident shareholder of fiduciary must file with the corporation's California income tax return (Form 100S) a statement of consent by that shareholder of fiduciary to be subject to the jurisdiction of the State of California to tax the shareholder's pro rata share of the income attributable to California sources, and (ii) the corporation must include with its income tax return a list of its shareholders on California Form 3830.

BUSINESS STRUCTURES AND INCORPORATION

SAMPLE
ELECTION BY A SMALL BUSINESS CORPORATION
FORM 2553

Form 2553 (Rev. December 2007)
Department of the Treasury
Internal Revenue Service

Election by a Small Business Corporation
(Under section 1362 of the Internal Revenue Code)
► See Parts II and III on page 3 and the separate instructions.
► The corporation can fax this form to the IRS (see separate instructions).

OMB No. 1545-0146

Note. This election to be an S corporation can be accepted only if all the tests are met under **Who May Elect** on page 1 of the instructions; all shareholders have signed the consent statement; an officer has signed below; and the exact name and address of the corporation and other required form information are provided.

Part I Election Information

Type or Print

Name (see instructions)

Number, street, and room or suite no. (If a P.O. box, see instructions.)

City or town, state, and ZIP code

A Employer identification number

B Date incorporated

C State of incorporation

D Check the applicable box(es) if the corporation, after applying for the EIN shown in **A** above, changed its ☐ name or ☐ address

E Election is to be effective for tax year beginning (month, day, year) (see instructions) . . . . . ► ___/___/___

Caution. A corporation (entity) making the election for its first tax year in existence will usually enter the beginning date of a short tax year that begins on a date other than January 1.

F Selected tax year:
(1) ☐ Calendar year
(2) ☐ Fiscal year ending (month and day) ► ___
(3) ☐ 52-53-week year ending with reference to the month of December
(4) ☐ 52-53-week year ending with reference to the month of ► ___

If box (2) or (4) is checked, complete Part II

G If more than 100 shareholders are listed for item J (see page 2), check this box if treating members of a family as one shareholder results in no more than 100 shareholders (see test 2 under **Who May Elect** in the instructions) ► ☐

H Name and title of officer or legal representative who the IRS may call for more information

I Telephone number of officer or legal representative ( )

If this S corporation election is being filed with Form 1120S, I declare that I had reasonable cause for not filing Form 2553 timely, and if this election is made by an entity eligible to elect to be treated as a corporation, I declare that I also had reasonable cause for not filing an entity classification election timely. See below for my explanation of the reasons the election or elections were not made on time (see instructions).

Sign Here ► Under penalties of perjury, I declare that I have examined this election, including accompanying schedules and statements, and to the best of my knowledge and belief, it is true, correct, and complete.

Signature of officer _____ Title _____ Date _____

For Paperwork Reduction Act Notice, see separate instructions.   Cat. No. 18629R   Form **2553** (Rev. 12-2007)

CORPORATIONS

SAMPLE
S CORPORATION ELECTION OR TERMINATION/REVOCATION
FORM 3560

TAXABLE YEAR **2 0 _ _** **S Corporation Election or Termination/Revocation**   **CALIFORNIA FORM 3560**

Effective for taxable year beginning month ____ day ____ year 20____, and ending month ____ day ____ year ____

Part I
- California corporation number
- Federal employer identification number
- Corporation name
- Address / PMB no.
- City / State / ZIP Code

Part II
Check the applicable box. See instructions.
- ☐ 1. Report a new federal S corporation election.
- ☐ 2. Elect to remain or to become a California C corporation.
- ☐ 3. Elect California S corporation status by a federal S corporation.
- ☐ 4. Report a federal S corporation termination/revocation.
- ☐ 5. Terminate (revoke) California S corporation status only.
- ☐ 6. Correct an untimely, invalid, or an inadvertent termination of an S corporation election.

Part III
- A. Federal tax year ending (month and day)
- B. California taxable year ending (month and day)
- C. Principal business activity code
- Principal product or service
- D. Date of federal election or California revocation (mo., day, and year)
- E. Date of incorporation (mo., day, and year)
- F. State of incorporation
- G. Date of qualification in California (mo., day, and year)

H. Is the corporation a continuation of any form of predecessor? .... ☐ Yes ☐ No
If "Yes," state name of predecessor, type of organization, period of its existence, and California corporation number, if any ▶ ____

I. Selected taxable year: Annual return will be filed for taxable year ending (month and day) ▶ ____
The selected taxable year must be a permitted taxable year. See Specific Line Instructions.

J. Name of each shareholder, person having a community property interest in the corporation's stock, and each tenant in common, joint tenant, and tenant by the entirety on the date of the election. A husband and wife (and their estates) are counted as one shareholder in determining the number of shareholders, without regard to the manner in which stock is owned.

K. Shareholders' Consent Statement. We, the undersigned shareholders, consent to the corporation's election to be treated as:
- ☐ An "S corporation" under R&TC Section 23801(a)(4) (IRC Section 1362(a)).
- ☐ A "C corporation" under R&TC Section 23801(a)(4) or 23801(f) (IRC Section 1362(d)).

(Shareholders must sign and date below)*

Signature	Date	L. Stock owned (Number of shares / Dates acquired)	M. Social security number or federal employer identification number	N. Shareholder's taxable year end (month and day)

Attach additional sheets if necessary.

* For the consent statement of a shareholder to be valid, the consent statement of each shareholder's spouse having a community property interest in the corporation's stock, and each tenant in common, joint tenant, and tenant by the entirety must either appear above or be attached to this form with each of the above party's signatures.

Part IV
Under penalties of perjury, I declare that I have examined this form, including accompanying schedules and statements, and to the best of my knowledge and belief, it is true, correct, and complete.

Signature of Officer ▶
Title / Date / Telephone ( )

For Privacy Act Notice, get form FTB 1131.   356001109   FTB 3560 c2 2001

BUSINESS STRUCTURES AND INCORPORATION

Finally, California S corporation rules are not identical to the federal rules. For example, California imposes a two and one-half percent corporate level tax on the taxable income of every S corporation. The federal rules do not.

Employer Identification Numbers

An employer must obtain both federal and state employer identification numbers in order to complete required filings with federal and state tax authorities, regardless of whether or not the corporation has any employees.

Federal Tax ID Number

The federal identification number may be obtained by filing Form SS-4 with the Internal Revenue Service or, for expedited service, by calling the Internal Revenue Service directly. The application for the number must be filed on or before the seventh day after the date business commences, if the applicant pays wages; otherwise, it must be filed in time for the number to be included in any return, statement or other document.

State Tax ID Number

For example, the California state identification number may be obtained by filing Form DE-1 with the California Employment Development Department ("EDD").

Statement by Domestic Stock Corporation

California law requires corporations, limited liability companies and common interest development associations to update the records of the California Secretary of State on an annual or biennial basis by filing a statement of information, called a Statement by Domestic Stock Corporation to remain a corporation in good standing and to avoid paying a penalty and the suspension of its corporate franchise.

The California mailer format for statement of information filing reminders and related notices has been changed from the standard paper and envelope format to a new postcard format.

CORPORATIONS

SAMPLE

STATEMENT OF DOMESTIC STOCK CORPORATION

BUSINESS STRUCTURES AND INCORPORATION

SAMPLE
STATEMENT OF INFORMATION

State of California
Secretary of State

Statement of Information
(Domestic Stock and Agricultural Cooperative Corporations)
FEES (Filing and Disclosure): $25.00.
If this is an amendment, see instructions.
IMPORTANT – READ INSTRUCTIONS BEFORE COMPLETING THIS FORM

1. CORPORATE NAME

2. CALIFORNIA CORPORATE NUMBER

This Space for Filing Use Only

No Change Statement (Not applicable if agent address of record is a P.O. Box address. See instructions.)
3. If there have been any changes to the information contained in the last Statement of Information filed with the California Secretary of State, or no statement of information has been previously filed, this form must be completed in its entirety.
☐ If there has been no change in any of the information contained in the last Statement of Information filed with the California Secretary of State, check the box and proceed to **Item 17**.

Complete Addresses for the Following (Do not abbreviate the name of the city. Items 4 and 5 cannot be P.O. Boxes.)

4.	STREET ADDRESS OF PRINCIPAL EXECUTIVE OFFICE	CITY	STATE	ZIP CODE
5.	STREET ADDRESS OF PRINCIPAL BUSINESS OFFICE IN CALIFORNIA, IF ANY	CITY	STATE CA	ZIP CODE
6.	MAILING ADDRESS OF CORPORATION, IF DIFFERENT THAN ITEM 4	CITY	STATE	ZIP CODE

Names and Complete Addresses of the Following Officers (The corporation must list these three officers. A comparable title for the specific officer may be added; however, the preprinted titles on this form must not be altered.)

7.	CHIEF EXECUTIVE OFFICER/	ADDRESS	CITY	STATE	ZIP CODE
8.	SECRETARY	ADDRESS	CITY	STATE	ZIP CODE
9.	CHIEF FINANCIAL OFFICER/	ADDRESS	CITY	STATE	ZIP CODE

Names and Complete Addresses of All Directors, Including Directors Who are Also Officers (The corporation must have at least one director. Attach additional pages, if necessary.)

10.	NAME	ADDRESS	CITY	STATE	ZIP CODE
11.	NAME	ADDRESS	CITY	STATE	ZIP CODE
12.	NAME	ADDRESS	CITY	STATE	ZIP CODE

13. NUMBER OF VACANCIES ON THE BOARD OF DIRECTORS, IF ANY

Agent for Service of Process If the agent is an individual, the agent must reside in California and Item 15 must be completed with a California street address, a P.O. Box address is not acceptable. If the agent is another corporation, the agent must have on file with the California Secretary of State a certificate pursuant to California Corporations Code section 1505 and Item 15 must be left blank.

14. NAME OF AGENT FOR SERVICE OF PROCESS

15. STREET ADDRESS OF AGENT FOR SERVICE OF PROCESS IN CALIFORNIA, **IF AN INDIVIDUAL** CITY STATE CA ZIP CODE

Type of Business
16. DESCRIBE THE TYPE OF BUSINESS OF THE CORPORATION

17. BY SUBMITTING THIS STATEMENT OF INFORMATION TO THE CALIFORNIA SECRETARY OF STATE, THE CORPORATION CERTIFIES THE INFORMATION CONTAINED HEREIN, INCLUDING ANY ATTACHMENTS, IS TRUE AND CORRECT.

DATE   TYPE/PRINT NAME OF PERSON COMPLETING FORM   TITLE   SIGNATURE

SI-200 (REV 01/2012)   APPROVED BY SECRETARY OF STATE

CORPORATIONS

Business Licenses

If your business is located in a city, contact the city officer for information regarding business licensing requirements and fees. In addition, check to see if the county requires zoning and general plan conformance for all uses established in the unincorporated areas, including businesses and commercial use.

Other Requirements, Permits, and Information

Depending on the proposed business or use, additional approvals, permits and/or licenses may be required from other governmental agencies. For example, in the state of California:

1. **Department of Environmental Health** – Requirements for food handling and serving facilities.

2. **Internal Revenue Service** – Information on obtaining a tax identification number, social security tax, federal business income tax, self-employment tax, excise tax, filing tax returns, and other federal tax issues: 55 South Market Street, San Jose, CA 95113, 1-800-829-1040, www.irs.ustreas.gov

3. **Franchise Tax Board** – Information regarding California state income and business taxes, corporate franchise taxes: 96 North Third Street, San Jose, CA 95113, 1-800-852-5711, www.ftb.ca.gov

4. **State Board of Equalization** – Use and sales tax permits (resale numbers, sellers' permits, resale permits); diesel fuel, cigarette, alcohol, and hazardous waste taxes: 250 South Second Street, San Jose, CA 95113, 408-277-1231, www.boe.ca.gov

5. **Secretary of State** – Registration of corporations, limited liability companies, limited partnerships, trademarks, service marks, and unincorporated and non-profit associations: 1500 11th Street, Sacramento, CA 95814, 916-653-6814, www.ss.ca.gov

6. **Secretary of State – California Business Portal** – A central location to access business-related functions and filings with the state, including a step-by-step guide to starting a business in California: Secretary of State – California Business Portal, www.ss.ca.gov/business/business.htm

7. **Employment Development Department – Employment Tax Branch** – California payroll taxes, unemployment, and disability

BUSINESS STRUCTURES AND INCORPORATION

taxes: 906 Ruff Drive, San Jose, CA 95110, 888-745-3886, www.edd.cahwnet.gov

8. **Department of Consumer Affairs** – Information relating to licensing requirements at the state level for specific business entities and professions: 400 R Street, Suite 1080, Sacramento, CA 95814, 1-800-952-5210, www.dca.ca.gov

9. **Contractors State License Board** – Tests and issues licenses for contractors whose projects will cost $500.00 or more: 100 Paseo de San Antonio, Room 319, San Jose, CA 95113, 408-277-1244, www.cslb.ca.gov

10. **Alcoholic Beverage Control** – Issues alcoholic beverage licenses – www.abc.ca.gov

11. **Santa Clara County Planning Office** – Zoning and land use information, permits for special events and certain professions: 70 West Hedding Street, 7th Floor, San Jose, CA 95110, 408-299-5770, www.sccplanning.org

12. **Santa Clara County Department of Environmental Health** – Permits for food facilities and other health/environment related business and activities: 1555 Berger Drive, Suite 300, San Jose, CA 95112, 408-918-3400, www.ehinfo.org

13. **Santa Clara County Assessor's Office** – Information on business property tax assessments: 70 West Hedding Street, 4th Floor, San Jose, CA 95110, 408-299-5400, www.scc-assessor.org

14. **California Small Business Helpline** – Offers recorded messages on starting a business, management and technical assistance programs, financing, small business conferences, publications, and other sources of information available to small businesses: 1-800-303-6600, 24 hours a day

15. **Commerce and Economic Development Program** – Provide information on business and community resources, including information on the California Office of Small Business: www.commerce.ca.gov/state/ttca/ttca_homepage.jsp

16. **U.S. Small Business Administration (SBA)** – Offers assistance and information on a wide range of small business issues, including

CORPORATIONS

SBA loans: 455 Market Street, 6th Floor, San Francisco, CA 94105, 415-744-6779, www.sba.gov

CHAPTER 8

CORPORATE MANAGEMENT

The board of directors constitutes the centralized management of the corporation, but the shareholders (who are the real owners) are responsible for electing directors and for controlling other significant matters in corporate management. In close corporations, shareholders often play a more active role in the management of the corporation. Shareholders may, through pooling agreements and voting trusts, exercise their voting control as a group. Their voting strength may be supplemented and protected by inspection rights, preemptive rights, and cumulative voting provisions. Shareholders may receive a return on their investment through dividends, and they may bring derivative actions on behalf of the corporation to enforce corporate rights.

The board of directors is ultimately responsible for the management of the corporation. The board of directors appoints, and delegates authority to, the corporation's officers. The officers handle the corporation's day-to-day affairs, including the execution of documents and instruments, under the direction of the board of directors. The corporation's Bylaws generally describe the principal duties and responsibilities of the officers of the corporation.

Each member of the board of directors, in fulfilling his/her duties, is charged with a duty of care and a duty of loyalty to the corporation. As such, each director must act in good faith and in a manner such director believes to be in the best interests of the corporation. Directors must act with such care as an ordinarily prudent person in a like position would use under similar circumstances. In doing so, the directors may rely on the advice of independent experts, but they must make a reasonable inquiry into the facts on which such experts base their advice.

CORPORATE MANAGEMENT

Likewise, the director must not usurp an opportunity which properly belongs to the corporation. In this regard a director must bear in mind that the corporation must first be offered any opportunity which falls within the realm of the corporation's business prior to a director undertaking to benefit personally from such opportunity.

The California Corporations Code specifically requires that the corporation's board of directors approve certain corporate actions. To approve corporate actions, the board of directors typically adopts resolutions by unanimous written consent or by vote at a directors' meeting (which may be held by telephone or other electronic means). The Bylaws of the corporation describe procedures for obtaining unanimous written consent and calling and holding director's meetings; you should review the Bylaws whenever you have a question concerning such procedures. Forms of actions by written consent should be kept in the minute book, with the other corporate records of the corporation. The board of directors generally may take action at a properly noticed meeting at which a majority of the authorized number of directors (a quorum) is present upon a vote by a majority of those present.

Special rules apply where a director has an interest in the matter to be approved. Transactions involving directors should be evaluated to determine whether the transaction is fair to the Corporation, and the material terms and director's interest are fully disclosed to and ratified by shareholders or by non-interested directors acting in good faith.

Actions that generally require directors' approval include (among others):

- ❖ Election of corporate officers.
- ❖ Amendments to the repeal of the Bylaws.
- ❖ Election of directors to fill vacancies on the Board.
- ❖ Issuance, sale or transfer of shares of stock.
- ❖ Calling of meetings of shareholders.
- ❖ Declaration of dividends and other shareholder distributions.
- ❖ Certain amendments to the Articles of Incorporation.
- ❖ Sale, lease, conveyance, exchange, transfer or other disposition of corporate property and assets.
- ❖ Corporate borrowing and lending.

BUSINESS STRUCTURES AND INCORPORATION

- ❖ Designation of corporate banks and authorized signatories.
- ❖ Adoption of business policies and plans.

It is also good corporate practice for the board of directors to adopt resolutions authorizing any other significant corporate action or transaction.

Controlling shareholders of a corporation owe the same fiduciary duty to the corporation and to the minority shareholders as does a director (i.e., to use their ability to control the corporation in a fair, just and reasonable manner).

The California Corporations Code also requires shareholder approval of certain fundamental corporate actions. To approve corporate action, the shareholders typically adopt resolutions by written consent or by vote at an annual or special meeting of shareholders. The Bylaws also describe the procedures the corporation must follow for obtaining shareholder written consent and calling and holding annual and special meetings of shareholders.

Actions that generally require shareholder approval include (among others):

- ❖ Certain amendments to the Articles of Incorporation.
- ❖ Amendment of the Bylaws to specify or change a fixed number of authorized directors, or the minimum or maximum number of directors.
- ❖ Election or removal of director.
- ❖ Sale of all or substantially all of the corporation's property assets.
- ❖ Mergers, reorganizations or dissolution of the corporation.
- ❖ Transactions between the corporation and one of its directors or an entity in which a director has a material financial interest.
- ❖ In some circumstances, loans by the corporation of money or property to, and guarantees of obligations of, one of its officers or directors.

In practical terms, it will not always be evident whether you and the other principals of the corporation should take action as officer, director or shareholder, or in several capacities. The easiest solution, although it is not always the best solution, is to see (and document) both Board and shareholder approval of any major action the corporation is considering taking.

CORPORATE MANAGEMENT

Management Rights of Shareholders

The power to manage the corporation generally is vested in the directors, who delegate the power to make day-to-day decisions to officers. Generally, the shareholders have no direct control in management of the corporation's business. However, a number of states allow the Articles of Incorporation, the Bylaws, or a shareholder agreement to dispense with the board and vest management power in the shareholders if all shareholders consent and the corporation's shares are not listed on a national securities exchange.

In a broad sense, shareholder management is exercised through shareholder voting rights on important corporate matters. All modern corporate statutes provide that the following powers are vested in the shareholders:

- ❖ Initial directors are named in the Articles of Incorporation and those directors serve until the next board of directors is elected by the shareholders. Most jurisdictions allow shareholders to vote to remove a director with or without cause before expiration of his/her term, but this right does not exist if the Articles of Incorporation provide that the directors can be removed only for cause.

- ❖ A number of states permit the initial Bylaws to be adopted by the board of directors, and the power to alter, amend, or repeal the Bylaws is vested in the board of directors but the power may be reserved to the shareholders by the Articles of Incorporation. Typically, the Bylaws will include the duties and authority of corporate officers, formalities for shareholders' and directors' meetings, the mechanics of shareholder voting, and provisions for the issuance and transfer of stock.

- ❖ Shareholder approval is required in cases of merger, consolidation, sale of corporate assets out of the ordinary course of business, dissolution, and for other extraordinary corporate matters. Similarly, amendments to the Articles of Incorporation usually require shareholder approval.

Shareholders' Meetings

Corporations must hold annual meetings of the shareholders, the primary purpose of which is the election of directors. A number of jurisdictions provide that if the annual meeting is not held within the earlier of six months after the end of the corporation's fiscal year or fifteen months after its last annual meeting, a court may, on the application of any shareholder, summarily order the meeting to be held.

Special shareholders' meetings may be called during the year to conduct business requiring shareholder approval. Special meetings typically may be called by the board of directors, the president, the holders of 1/10 or more of all shares entitled to vote, or other persons so authorized in the Articles of Incorporation or Bylaws (place of meetings, notice requirements, eligibility to vote, and proxies are provided for in the corporate Bylaws).

Meetings of shareholders may be held within or outside the state. The Bylaws may specify either the place of the meetings or the manner in which the place will be selected. If no place is stated or fixed, the meetings are to be held at the corporation's registered office.

Generally, written notice of the shareholders' meetings – special or annual – must be sent to the shareholders within a stated period of time.

Pre-emptive Rights

When the corporation proposes to issue additional shares of stock, the current shareholders often want to purchase some shares in order to maintain their proportional voting strength. Under certain circumstances, shareholders have a pre-emptive right to purchase a portion of the new issue.

The traditional rule is that unless otherwise provided in the Articles, a holder of common stock has a judicial pre-emptive right to purchase a pro rata portion of unissued or treasury stock that the corporation proposes to issue for cash. The modern trend denies pre-emptive rights unless specifically granted in the Articles.

Pre-emptive rights may be limited only to issuance of stock authorized after a shareholder has purchased his/her stock. There are no pre-emptive rights in stock that was previously authorized but unissued. Neither would there be any pre-emptive rights if such rights had been abolished in the Articles or Bylaws. In some jurisdictions, however, pre-emptive rights apply to a latter issue of the originally authorized stock if considerable time has elapsed, or if there has been a considerable change in corporate circumstances between the first and second issues. In some states, there are pre-emptive rights in previously authorized shares that were not sold as part of the original issue.

There are no pre-emptive rights if they have been eliminated in the Articles. Unless otherwise provided in the Articles, there are no pre-emptive rights in stock issued for services or property; only in stock issued for cash. Therefore, an acquisition of the assets of another corporation for stock will not create pre-emptive rights in the shareholders of the acquiring corporation. Unless provided

CORPORATE MANAGEMENT

otherwise in the Articles, there are no pre-emptive rights in shares sold to employees, provided that the sale is approved by the shareholders.

The board of directors may fix the price and terms of the shares. The pre-emptive right is usually only an opportunity to acquire shares at such price and on such terms as the directors provide.

Shareholder Agreements

Shareholders may enter into several types of agreements in an effort to protect their voting power, proportionate stock ownership, or other special interests in the corporation. Although most shareholder agreements are encountered in the close corporation (where the stock is held by a few individuals and is not actively traded); most of these agreements could be used in any corporation.

Voting Trusts and Pooling Agreements

The voting trust and the shareholder pooling agreement are devices used to concentrate shareholder voting control for the purpose of affecting corporate policy in the manner most advantageous to the shareholders in the trust or agreement.

A voting trust is an agreement among shareholders under which all the shares owned by the parties to the agreement are transferred to a trustee, who votes the shares and distributes the dividends in accordance with the provisions of the voting trust agreement. The voting trustee becomes the legal (though not the equitable) owner of the shares and his/her name is entered in the corporate stock transfer book. In addition to being a device for maintaining control of a corporation, the voting trust is a method used to circumvent the prohibition against irrevocable proxies.

A pooling (or voting) agreement has the same objective as a voting trust – that is, to consolidate votes for control. The pooling agreement is simply an agreement among shareholders to vote their shares as the majority of signers directs. Arbitration is usually provided if disagreement results. A critical difference between pooling agreements and voting trusts is that there is no formal separation of voting power and beneficial ownership in poling agreements. Thus, statutory limitations on voting trusts probably do not apply to the pooling agreement.

Restrictions on Transfer of Stock

An effective method of control within the close corporation is to reasonably restrict the transfer of shares. Typical shareholder agreements regarding restrictions on transfer of shares specify that no shareholder will sell shares to an outsider without first offering the shares to the corporation or to the other shareholders.

Agreements Affecting Action by Directors

The board of directors has unfettered authority to determine corporate policy and manage the corporation. Therefore, insofar as shareholder agreements infringe on director discretion, they may be invalid. Several states have enacted special close corporation statutes that validate such agreements provided that the agreements controlling the votes of the directors have a valid business purpose and provided that all of the shareholders have agreed to it (e.g., assuming unanimous shareholder approval, it would be proper to control the directors' choice of who the corporate officers would be). In addition, a number of states have provisions, such as section 8.01 of the Revised Model Business Corporations Act, that provide that the managerial authority of the board may be reduced by provision in the Articles of Incorporation.

Inspection of Books and Records

By statute in most jurisdictions, shareholders have the right to inspect corporate books and records. Judicially, the shareholders' right to inspect is limited only to the requirements that inspection be at proper time and place and for a proper purpose. The judicial right to inspect and the statutory right to inspect coexist in most jurisdictions, since statutes seldom specify all corporate books and records subject to inspection under the judicial rights.

Scope of Right to Inspect

Statutory authority for shareholder inspection usually specifies which books the shareholders may inspect. Even if the statutes do not specifically grant the right to inspect certain records the right may exist by courts. Generally, judicially the shareholder may inspect any books relevant to the business affairs of the corporation.

Judicially, the shareholder has the burden of proving that the purpose of the inspection is proper. The statutory right to inspect requires at least some statement of purpose, and either the shareholder must prove a proper purpose or the corporation must prove that the purpose is improper. Where proper purpose is a condition precedent to the shareholder's right to inspect, the question will always be one of fact. The examination of corporate books and records to learn names and addresses of other shareholders to wage a proxy fight is a proper purpose.

The record holder of shares of the corporation may inspect in every jurisdiction. Most state statutes further provide that holders of voting trust certificates may inspect the corporate records. Experts (e.g., accountants, statisticians, etc.) or other agents (e.g., attorneys) may accompany the shareholder. Several jurisdictions require written demand on the corporation stating the purpose of the shareholder inspection. By statute and judicially shareholders are permitted to copy corporate records or make extracts of any documents in connection with any inspection.

Limitation or Loss of Right to Inspect

The right of a shareholder to inspect the corporate records cannot be limited by the Articles of Incorporation or the Bylaws. However, a shareholder who has offered for sale a list of shareholders, or who has aided or abetted any person in procuring a list of shareholder, or who has improperly used any information secured through a prior examination of the corporate books may be disqualified from further inspection of the books. Many statutes limit such misconduct to two years preceding the current demand to inspect.

Various penalties are prescribed for the corporation or its officers who have failed or refused to produce corporate records for shareholder inspection. Most penalties are stated in terms of a dollar amount. Note that directors also have a right to inspect the books for proper purposes, as do former directors (e.g., if they need the information to defend a suit).

Shareholder Suits

Shareholders enjoy a dual personality. They are entitled to enforce their own claims against the corporation, officers, directors, or majority shareholders by direct action. Shareholders are also the guardians of the corporation's causes of action, provided no one else in the corporation will assert them. In this sense, shareholders my sue derivatively to enforce the corporate cause of action provided that they meet the requirements specified by law and provided they have made necessary demands on the corporation or the directors to enforce the cause of action. In either capacity, direct or derivative action, the shareholder may sue for him/herself and for others similarly situated.

Distributions

Under most state statutes, the board of directors has discretion to declare distributions to shareholders, including dividends, in the form of cash, property, or its own shares.

BUSINESS STRUCTURES AND INCORPORATION

Capital Accounts

Since the modern approach has eliminated the par value concept, there is no restriction on the source of funds that may be used to pay dividends. In states not following this approach, there are restrictions on dividend sources – the funds can come from only certain types of capital accounts: (1) stated capital – this is the sum of the par value of the shares issued, plus the amount allocated to stated capital at the time of issuance of shares without par value, plus any other amounts transferred to the stated capital account; (2) paid-in (capital) surplus – this is the sum of amounts received in excess of par value upon the issuance of stock, plus amounts allocated to paid-in surplus upon the issuance of shares without par value, minus any decrease as the result of certain transactions, e.g., payment of preferred dividends (only if no earned surplus available); (3) earned surplus (retained earnings) – this is the sum of accumulated profits from operations minus any amounts paid as dividends or transferred to paid-in surplus or stated capital as a result of stock dividends; and (4) revaluation surplus – the surplus arises from the revaluation of assets.

Legality of Payment

For the payment of a dividend to be legal, it must meet three tests: (i) the corporation must be solvent; (ii) payment must not violate any provisions in the Articles of Incorporation; and (iii) payment may not violate any statute concerning the source of funds for payment.

Cash and Property Dividends

The declaration of dividends is within the discretion of the board of directors, and it requires a very strong case to induce a court of equity to order the directors to declare a dividend. In addition, a court will enjoin payment of dividends where: (1) Such payments discriminate between members of the same class of stock (dividends must be declared equally for each share of stock in a class); or (2) Such payments violate the preferences of a preferred class of shareholders.

With respect to preferred shareholders, a corporation need not give each shareholder an equal right to receive distributions. Shares may be divided into classes with varying rights. Common preference terms include: preferred shares (noncumulative), cumulative preferred shares, cumulating if earned preferred shares, and participating preferred shares.

Stock Dividends

These are dividends in the corporation's own authorized but unissued shares. Since no assets are distributed, the solvency of the corporation remains the same, and there is no damage to creditors and shareholders as in cash dividends. Once a cash dividend has been declared, it generally may not be revoked. The declaration gives the shareholders the rights of ordinary creditors. However, dividends may be revoked if the corporation was insolvent or lacked sufficient surplus. Stock dividends, however, may be revoked at any time before being paid.

Dividends are declared payable to persons named in the corporate records as shareholders on a particular date – known as the record date. If shares have been sold prior to the record date but have not been transferred on the corporation's books, the corporation pays the record owner (i.e., the seller), and the beneficial owner of the shares (i.e., the purchaser) must look to the seller for payment.

Re-acquisition of Shares

The Articles may grant the corporation the right to redeem shares from shareholders at a set price (a forced sale), or the corporation may repurchase shares from shareholders who voluntarily offer to sell their shares back to the corporation. Both redemptions and repurchases are treated as distributions; thus both are subject to the legality of payment rules for distributions, including the fund restrictions in par value states. However, most states permit corporations to reacquire their shares, notwithstanding the surplus account restrictions, to: (1) Eliminate fractional shares; (2) Collect or compromise indebtedness to the corporation; (3) Pay dissenting shareholders entitled to payment for their shares; or (4) Retire redeemable shares by redemption below the redemption price.

Unlawful Distributions

If funds are not legally available, or if the corporation is insolvent, or would become insolvent by the payment of cash dividends, the issuance of a distribution to shareholders will render the directors personally liable for effecting the transaction. Likewise, there is some authority that the shareholders may be liable for the amount of the unlawful distribution received, although notice or knowledge of the illegality of the transaction may be required.

Shareholders' Liabilities

Generally, shareholders may act in their own personal interests and have no fiduciary duty to the corporation or their fellow shareholders. Shareholder liability generally is limited to the liabilities discussed above for: (1) unpaid or watered stock; (2) a pierced corporate veil; or (3) absence of de facto corporation. Shareholders in a close corporation are generally held to owe each other the same duty of loyalty and utmost good faith that is owed by partners to each other. As well, certain limitations have emerged with respect to shareholders who hold a controlling interest. A controlling shareholder must refrain from using his/her control to obtain a special advantage or to cause the corporation to take action that unfairly prejudices the minority shareholders.

Board of Directors

The board of directors of the corporation has general responsibility for the management of the business and the affairs of the corporation. The directors are vested with the duty to manage the corporation to the best of their ability, and they are expected to use good business judgment. However, they are not insurers of business success. A court will not interfere with the directors' management decisions in the absence of fraud, illegal conduct, or an irrational business judgment.

Director Qualification and Action

- In most jurisdictions, there need be only one director. Other jurisdictions require at least three directors. The Articles of Incorporation or Bylaws may require as many directors as desired, without limitation.

- Initial directors may be named in the Articles of Incorporation. The initial directors hold office until the first annual meeting of the shareholders or until their successors have been elected and qualified.

- The directors are elected at each annual meeting of the shareholders, subject to contrary provisions in the Articles. If a corporation does not hold an annual meeting of shareholders, the directors remain in office until their successors are elected. Directors who are elected must accept the office (expressly or implicitly) in order to qualify.

- Many jurisdictions permit the classification of directors, allowing the entire board to be divided into two or three classes, with each class as nearly equal in number as possible, and their term of office expiring in staggered years from one to three. This procedure permits the continuity in corporate policy by maintaining seasoned members of the board in office.

The Articles of Incorporation or Bylaws may prescribe reasonable qualifications for directors. In the absence of any requirements by statute, articles, or Bylaws, the directors need not be shareholders in the corporation or residents of any particular state.

CORPORATE MANAGEMENT

In most states, vacancies may be filled by the shareholders or the directors, but if the vacant office was held by a director elected by a voting group of shareholders, only the holders of shares of that voting group are entitled to vote to fill the vacancy if it is filled by the shareholders.

Directors may be removed for cause by the shareholders in all jurisdictions. Most jurisdictions permit the removal of a director by the shareholders with or without cause, although some states allow this right to be limited by the Articles of Incorporation. The shareholders have the power to remove the entire board or any lesser number.

Directors' Meetings

Directors may act in regular or special meetings. Special meetings are called in accordance with the provisions of the Bylaws, which may designate certain persons who are entitled to call the meetings, and usually prescribe the notice required.

The board of directors is usually required to hold an organization meeting after the corporation is formed. The statutes requiring directors' organizational meetings also prescribe the notice required. The Bylaws govern the notice requirements for directors' meetings other than the organizational meeting. In most jurisdictions, unless the Articles of Incorporation or Bylaws provide otherwise, regular meetings of the board may be held without notice, but notice is required for special meetings.

A director's attendance at a meeting usually constitutes waiver of any notice required in the Bylaws, unless attendance is for the sole purpose of protesting the lack of notice. Otherwise, directors may waive notice by a written waiver given before, during, or after the meeting.

A majority of the board of directors constitutes a quorum for the meeting unless the Articles of Incorporation or the Bylaws require a higher number. A quorum must be present at the time the vote is taken for the vote to constitute a valid act of the board. Thus, even if a quorum is present at the beginning of a meeting, a group of minority directors may, by leaving, remove the quorum and thereby prevent further board action. Recall that the rule is different for shareholders' meetings.

The board of directors may act by a majority vote unless the Articles of Incorporation, or the Bylaws require a higher vote. That is, a majority of those present, if there is a quorum, can pass resolutions. If there are not enough directors in office to make a quorum, the remaining directors can take no action except to elect new directors to fill the vacancies.

Voting agreements among the directors are void as against public policy. Directors are bound to use their individual business judgment in their capacity as directors. Any agreement tending to sterilize the independent director discretion is invalid. In addition, unlike shareholders, directors may not vote by proxy.

Action by Directors

The board of directors is vested with the responsibility for control of all of the affairs of the corporation. While some corporations may involve their directors in day-to-day activities, the daily business affairs are usually controlled by the officers, who are selected by the board of directors and serve at their pleasure. Action by the board of directors must be taken in accordance with the statute, and usually involves a resolution, properly adopted at a board of directors meeting, setting forth the appropriate action and establishing the corporate policy. The directors must function as a board. A single director has no authority to bind the corporation.

Among the specific duties of directors are the election, removal, and supervision of officers; adoption, amendment, and repeal of Bylaws; fixing management compensation; and initiating extraordinary corporate action. The directors can make contracts binding the corporation for a period extending beyond their terms. Thus, a long-term employment contract approved by the board is enforceable against the corporation (unless for an unreasonably long time; e.g., lifetime contracts). A future board has the power to fire an employee despite a long-term contract, but the employee might have a damage action against the corporation.

Delegation of Authority

The board of directors is not expected to participate in the daily business affairs of the corporation. Rather, most statutes authorize the delegation of management functions for daily business affairs to the officers or to executive committees.

Unless the Articles of Incorporation or Bylaws provide otherwise, the board of directors may create one or more committees, with two or more members, and appoint members of the board of directors to serve on them. The board of directors remains responsible for the actions of the committee and is responsible for supervision of the committee. In addition, the board may delegate most of its operating authority to committees. However, most statutes provide that certain powers, such as declaration of dividends or amendment of the Bylaws, cannot be delegated to a committee.

The officers' duties are normally prescribed by statute and the corporate Bylaws. Any authority delegated to the officers comes from the board of directors, who remain responsible for supervision of the officers.

Directors' Duties and Liabilities

The directors' management duties are typical fiduciary duties, including the duty of due care, the duty of loyalty, and the duty to protect the interests of the other intra-corporate parties. Directors are required to observe all statutory requirements of the state of incorporation and the state where the corporation is authorized to do business, and to exercise their good business judgment.

Duty of Care

The directors' duty of care is a catch-all fiduciary duty by which the directors are expected to exercise good business judgment and to use ordinary care and prudence in the operation of the corporation.

The standard of directors' due care is usually defined in terms that are similar to those used in tort negligence cases. The general standard is that a director shall perform in good faith and in a manner the director reasonably believes to be in the best interest of the corporation and with the care an ordinary prudent person in a like position would use under similar circumstances. Directors are not expected to insure the success of the business organization; rather, they are liable only for negligent acts omissions in the performance of their duties (e.g., failure to obtain fire insurance, hiring a treasurer without looking into his/her record, where the treasurer turns out to be a convicted embezzler, etc.)

Courts have frequently considered the actual participation of the director in the management affairs of the corporation. There is authority that a part-time director who is uncompensated will not be held to a normal standard of care. Of course, a director who enters a dissent to corporate action in the minutes to directors' meetings will not be liable for that action.

Generally, directors are insulated from liability for the consequences of a business judgment if they exercised due care, acted in good faith, and had a rational basis for the decision. This puts the decision-making in the proper place, with the directors rather than the courts, except for unusually circumstances. However, a director who has preached his/her duty of care may be held personally liable only for losses suffered by the corporation as the direct and proximate result of his/her breach of duty. (Note, that in a number of jurisdictions, a director's personal liability for breach of fiduciary duty as a director may be eliminated or limited in the Articles.)

Courts have held directors liable if they cause the corporation to violate a statute – even though they exercised good business judgment in so doing. For example, illegal campaign contributions, brides, etc. The burden of proof to show negligence is on the plaintiff – and as a practical matter, the burden is heavy. This is in contrast to the duty of loyalty where the burden is on the defendant.

Defenses available to directors include: (1) good faith reliance on expert advice to an action for breach of the duty of care; (2) absence from the meeting at which the actionable conduct occurred if the director had a valid excuse, and may be a defense even without an excuse if the director did not habitually skip meetings; (3) some courts have recognized factors such as age, inexperience, non-residence, etc., as defenses, while other permit the director to show that he/she was a mere figurehead – but should not automatically be considered a valid defense; and (4) if the shareholders unanimously ratify the negligent act, this will preclude any attack on the transaction (except possibly by creditors).

Duty of Loyalty
A director owes a duty of loyalty to his corporation and will not be permitted to profit at the corporation's expense. This rule often is at issue when a director (i) has a personal interest in a corporate transaction, (ii) takes advantage of an opportunity in which his/her corporation had an interest or expectancy, (iii) enters into a competing business, or (iv) the director uses inside information while purchasing securities.

Judicially, if a corporation entered into a transaction in which a director had a personal interest, the transaction would be deemed void because of the conflict of interest. However, nearly all states have moved away from this approach and will uphold transactions in which a director has a personal interest if: (i) the material facts of the transaction were disclosed to or known by the board and they approved the transaction, (ii) the material facts of the transaction were disclosed or known by the shareholders and they approved the transaction, or (iii) the transaction was fair.

Generally, a director's fiduciary duty of loyalty prohibits the director from engaging in business properly belonging to the corporation. The primary reason for this rule is that business dealings outside the corporation subject the director to a potential conflict of interest that may result in an exercise of discretion other than that in the best interests of the corporation. The corporate opportunity

CORPORATE MANAGEMENT

doctrine requires the director first to give the corporation an opportunity to act. In determining what business dealings are corporate opportunities, the courts focus primarily on whether the corporation might itself have taken the deal, so that the transaction created a potential conflict between the interests of the director and those of the corporation.

Nonetheless, directors are permitted to engage in unrelated businesses, but a clear conflict of interest may arise if the director's personal business is in direct competition with the corporation.

Finally, directors, as well as other corporate insiders, might be liable for fraud for trading corporate securities on the basis of inside information. However, the extent of liability for judicial fraud for misstating facts to the other party to a transaction is questionable. However, there is clearly no duty to disclose all facts to the other party unless found: (i) misleading because the facts were incomplete, ((ii) failed to disclose a fact that was not readily discoverable by the other party and was so basic that the other party would have expected it to have been disclosed, (iii) actively concealed facts from the other party, or (iv) officer or director breached a fiduciary duty to the plaintiff.

State Statute Liability of Directors and Officers

State securities laws have imposed strict rules upon directors and others, especially with respect to their dealings in the stock of their corporations. Directors may be liable under various state statutes, the most important of which include the local corporation code and the securities law (state blue sky law).

All state blue sky laws contain antifraud provisions, very similar to the federal securities acts, and the director may be liable for any violations of the state provisions. The Uniform Securities Act, which has been adopted by several states, copies rule 10b-5 almost in its entirety. The substantive effect of the Uniform Act Section 101 is exactly the same as rule 10b-5.

Compensation and Indemnification of Officers and Directors

Compensation of directors or officers raises issues similar to those involved in contracts of an interested director. Directors or officers who work for the corporation are selling services to it; and the price paid for those services must be authorized by the directors and fair to the corporation.

A director, however, is not entitled to compensation for his/her services as a director unless, before the services are rendered, the Bylaws, a shareholders' resolution, or an independent board of directors authorizes compensation. The amount of compensation authorized for directors and officers must also be fair, i.e., reasonably related to the value of services rendered. If it is not, the compensation may be challenged as a waste of corporate assets.

However, excessive compensation can be approved by unanimous shareholder action if no creditor is prejudiced, but a mere majority of shareholders may not waste or make a gift of corporate assets by ratifying excessive compensation. On the other hand, compensation for past services rendered by an officer or director is viewed with suspicions, e.g., a generous retirement plan or bonus given at the end of the director's career.

A director or officer is entitled to reimbursement from the corporation for expenditures for corporate purposes. It is less clear, however, whether a director or officer may be indemnified for liabilities and expenses incurred in litigation for conduct undertaken in an official capacity.

Officers

The officers are agents of the corporation and receive their power to manage from the directors. Unlike directors, officers are employees of the corporation (a director is an employee only if the director accepts duties that make him/her an employee). Most statutes authorize a president, one or more vice presidents, a secretary, one or more assistant secretaries, a treasurer, and one or more assistant treasurers. Some modern statutes use titles such as chief executive officer and chief financial officer. In many jurisdictions the same person may not hold certain office concurrently, such as that of president and secretary. Most jurisdictions do not prescribe any particular qualifications for officers, but Bylaws may.

Powers

The ordinary rules of agency determine the authority and powers of the officers and agents. Authority may be actual or apparent. When actual, an officer has whatever authority is expressly granted to the officer and whatever authority may be implied from the express grant. Apparent when the corporation holds out an officer as possessing certain authority, thereby inducing others reasonably to believe that the authority exists, the officer has apparent authority to act and to bind the corporation even though actual authority to do so has not been granted. For example, an officer who continues to serve after his appointment has expired may possess apparent authority.

CORPORATE MANAGEMENT

Unauthorized actions may become binding on the corporation because of ratification, adoption, or estoppel. The corporation is also liable (civilly or criminally) for actions by its officers within the scope of their authority, even if the particular act in question was not specifically authorized. The officer is also liable along with the corporation for his torts or crimes.

Election and Removal

The election and removal of officers is within the discretion of the board of directors. The first officers are usually elected by the board of directors at their organizational meeting in jurisdictions where an organizational meeting of the directors must be held. In any case, the officers are elected by the directors by formal action in a directors' meeting.

With respect to removal, the officers usually may be removed by the board with or without cause, considering the best interests of the corporation. However, the removal of an officer in violation of his employment contract is without prejudice to the recovery of damages for breach of the contract rights. Consequently, the corporation may be liable in damages for the untimely removal of an officer.

Duties and Liabilities

Corporate officers, like corporate directors, are subject to fiduciary duties. Officers are agents of their corporation and, like any other agents, will be liable for contracts and obligations incurred by them in violation of their agency authority.

Corporate Governance Principles and Practices

Sample corporate governance principles and practices memo to board members, summarizing their roles and responsibilities:

CORPORATE GOVERNANCE PRINCIPLES AND PRACTICES MEMO

The primary responsibilities of the board of directors of _____ (the "Company") are to oversee the exercise of corporate powers and to ensure that the Company's business and affairs are managed to meet its stated goals and objectives. The Board recognizes its responsibility to engage, and provide for the continuity of, executive management that possesses the character, skills and experience required to attain the Company's goals and to ensure that nominees for the Board possess appropriate qualifications and reflect a reasonable diversity of backgrounds and perspectives.

Directors will fulfill the following responsibilities and requirements:
- Represent the collective interests of all stockholders of the Company;
- Discharge Board duties in good faith, with due care and in a manner

BUSINESS STRUCTURES AND INCORPORATION

he/she reasonably believes to be in the best interests of the Company;
- Possess independence, objectivity and the highest degree of integrity on an individual and collective basis;
- Be dedicated to understanding the business of the Company and issues presented to the Board;
- Be committed to active, objective, thoughtful, constructive and independent participation at meetings of the Board and its committees;
- Bring to the Board's deliberations their collective breadth of business, professional and personal experience to represent the interests of shareholders;
- Review fundamental operating, financial and other corporate plans, strategies and objectives;
- Evaluate on a regular and timely basis the qualitative and quantitative performance of the Company and its senior management;
- Review the process of providing appropriate financial and operation information, internally and externally;
- Assure adherence to proper policies of corporate conduct, including compliance with applicable laws, regulations, business and ethical standards;
- Assure compliance with requirements for timely, accurate and complete disclosure of information in filings with the Securities and Exchange Commission such as proxy statements and reports on Form 10-K or 10-Q (e.g., disclosure regarding nominating committee functions and communications between security holders and boards of directors);
- Assure maintenance of proper accounting, financial and other appropriate controls; and
- Evaluate and take steps to improve the overall effectiveness of the Board.

The Board has the responsibility to organize its functions and conduct its business in the manner it deems most effective and efficient, consistent with its duties of good faith, due care and loyalty. In that regard, the Board has adopted a set of flexible policies to guide its governance practices in the future. These practices, set forth below, will be regularly re-evaluated by the Board's Corporate Governance and Nominating Committee in light of changing circumstances in order to continue serving the best interests of shareholders. Accordingly, the summary of current practices is not a fixed policy or resolution by the Board, but merely a statement of current practices that is subject to continuing assessment and change.

1. <u>Size of the Board</u>

The Board of Directors currently has [_____] members. The number will vary from time to time depending on circumstances, but the Board's intention is to [maintain its size in a range] between [_____] and [_____] members. A significant majority of the Board members are and will continue to be independent directors.

2. <u>Board Definition of What Constitutes Independence for Directors</u>

No relationship between any director and the Company should be of a nature that could compromise the independence of any Board member in governing the affairs of the Company. The determination of what constitutes independence for a director in any individual situation shall be made by the Board in light of the totality of the facts and circumstances relating to such situation, including whether the director is a current or past

CORPORATE MANAGEMENT

employee of the Company, and in compliance with the requirements of NASDAQ's applicable listing standards and other applicable rules and regulations.

[3.   Independent Lead Director

The Board may elect an independent director to serve as Lead Director. The Lead Director will facilitate and preside over meetings of independent directors in executive session. Also, the Lead Director may serve as the focal point for directors regarding the resolution of any conflicts with the chief executive officer, or with other directors, and for coordinating feedback to the chief executive officer on behalf of directors regarding business issues and corporate governance.]

4.   Number of Committees

The present Board committees are: the Audit Committee, the Compensation Committee and the Corporate Governance and Nominating Committee. Members of all committees are non-employees of the Company and shall be "independent" under applicable NASDAQ guidelines. The Board considers its current committee structure to be appropriate but the number and scope of committees may be revised as appropriate to meet changing conditions and needs.

5.   Board Member Criteria

The Corporate Governance and Nominating Committee is responsible for reviewing the appropriate skills and characteristics required of directors in the context of prevailing business conditions and composition of the Board. The qualifications to be considered in the selection of director nominees include the extent of experience in business, trade, finance or management; the extent of knowledge of regional and national business affairs; and the overall judgment to advise and direct the Company in meeting its responsibilities to stockholders, customers, employees and the public. The objective is to have a Board that brings to the Company a variety of perspectives and skills derived from high quality business and professional experience.

6.   Procedure for Selecting New Director Candidates

The Board is responsible for selecting its members, subject to shareholder approval, but delegates the screening process to the Corporate Governance and Nominating Committee. The Corporate Governance and Nominating Committee is expected to work closely with the chief executive officer to determine the characteristics and qualifications desired in new members of the Board and to make recommendations of candidates to the entire Board.

7.   Board Member Orientation

Orientation materials will be made available and appropriate meetings will be held to acquaint new directors with the business, history, current circumstances, key issues and top managers of the Company.

8.   Frequency of Board Meetings; Attendance

Currently, the Board has [_____] regular meeting each year, with additional meetings as required. The Board considers its current meeting schedule to be adequate, but the number of regular meetings may be adjusted as necessary to meet changing conditions and needs. A calendar of Board meetings will be developed and circulated as far in advance as practicable. Members are expected to attend all meetings barring special circumstances.

9.   Briefing Materials Distributed in Advance

As much information and data as practical on the meeting agenda items and the Company's financial performance is sent to Board members in advance of Board and

BUSINESS STRUCTURES AND INCORPORATION

Committee meetings.

10. Executive Sessions of Independent Directors

At each meeting of the Board, the agenda includes time for an executive session with only independent directors and the chief executive officer present, and time for another executive session of independent directors without the chief executive officer present. The chairperson may participate in all executive sessions.

11. Board Access to Senior Management

All Board members have access to senior management, with the expectation that such contact would be minimally disruptive to the business operation of the Company. The chief executive officer is encouraged to invite to Board meetings senior managers who can provide additional insight into business matters being discussed and those with high future potential who should be given personal exposure to members of the Board.

12. Assignment of Committee Members

The Corporate Governance and Nominating Committee is responsible for reviewing and recommending to the Board the assignment of directors to various committees, subject to applicable membership requirements to ensure diversity of Board member experience and variety of exposure to the affairs of the Company.

13. Frequency and Length of Committee Meetings

Generally, committees meet in conjunction with regular Board meetings. Committee chairpersons may also call meetings when they deem it necessary. Committee meetings may be as frequent and as long as needed.

14. Committee Agenda

The agenda for Committee meetings is developed by Committee Chairpersons in consultation with appropriate members of management. The agenda for each meeting is circulated in advance and Committee members may suggest additional items for consideration.

15. Assessing the Board's Performance

The Corporate Governance and Nominating Committee will conduct an annual assessment of the overall effectiveness of the organization of the Board and the Board's performance of its governance responsibilities. The Committee will report its findings to the whole Board for discussion.

16. Directors Who Change Their Job Responsibilities

A Board member, including the chief executive officer, who ceases to be actively employed in his/her principal business or profession, or experiences other changed circumstances that could pose a conflict of interest, diminish his/her effectiveness as a Board member, or otherwise be detrimental to the Company, is expected to offer his/her resignation to the Board. The Board in its discretion will determine whether such member should continue to serve as a director for an unexpired term or any future terms.

17. Term Limits/Retirement Age

No term limits for directors have been established. The Board expects that no member of the Board shall stand for reelection after his or her 70th birthday.

18. Selection of the Chairman and Chief Executive Officer

The Board elects the chairman and chief executive officer in the manner and based on the criteria that it deems appropriate and in the best interests of the Company given the circumstances at the time of such election.

19. Formal Evaluation of the Chief Executive Officer

CORPORATE MANAGEMENT

Each year, the chairpersons of the Corporate Governance and Nominating Committee and the Compensation Committee will conduct a formal evaluation of the chief executive officer's performance based on appropriate quantitative and qualitative criteria.

20. <u>Succession Planning</u>

The chief executive officer will annually review succession planning with the Compensation and Executive Development Committee, and provide the Board with a continuing current recommendation as to succession in the event of that officer's termination of employment, disability or death.

21. <u>Board Interaction with Institutional Investors, the Media and Customers</u>

The responsibility for communications and relationships on behalf of the Company with institutional investors, the media, and customers should be management's.

22. <u>Authorization Guidelines</u>

The Board will establish, and periodically update, guidelines for authorization of expenditures or other corporate actions, including the acquisition or disposition of capital assets, and these will periodically be reviewed with management.

CHAPTER 9

CORPORATE RECORDS

Corporate Formalities and Records

You must be careful to observe the proper corporate formalities so that your entity will not be attacked by any governmental authority (the most common example being the Internal Revenue Service) or other creditor as being no more than a sham entity created to give you tax benefits or to protect you from personal liability.

In addition to the issue of proper capitalization, the most important "corporate formalities" which should be observed (i) the timely filings of corporate forms, (ii) the writing of corporate minutes which reflect the various actions of the corporation and the annual meeting of shareholders or action by written consent in lieu of such meeting and (iii) communicating with third parties in a manner that clearly indicates that they are doing business with the corporation and not an individual.

The corporation must keep minutes of all meetings of it shareholders, board of directors and any committee of the Board. In addition, the corporation must keep at its principal office, or at the office of its transfer agent, a shareholder list, including addresses. The minutes do not have to follow any particular form but should include information such as the date, time and place of the meeting, those persons in attendance, including a statement that a quorum of directors was in attendance, and the actions taken and considered by the Board in a clear and unambiguous fashion.

Another outward indication that the corporation is conducting business as a bona fide corporation will be the maintenance of proper books and records for the corporation. The corporation is required by statute to keep at its principal

CORPORATE RECORDS

office a copy of the current Bylaws, which are to be open to inspection by all shareholders during office hours.

The stock records of the corporation are subject to inspection by certain shareholders of the corporation, on five days' prior written demand, during usual business hours. The accounting books and minutes of the meetings of the Board of Directors and minutes of the meetings of the shareholders are subject to inspection of any shareholder, on written demand, during usual business hours, for a purpose reasonably related to the holder's interest as a shareholder. These documents need not be kept at the corporation's principal office; in many instances, it is more expedient for these records to be maintained by legal counsel, with the corporation keeping copies for its records. Finally, each director of the corporation has the right, at any reasonable time, to inspect and copy any corporate records and documents, which inspection may be made by the director's agent or attorney.

The annual meeting of shareholders or action by written consent in lieu of such meeting is significant in maintaining the on-going nature of the corporation and confirming that you and the other members of management are respecting the separate existence of the corporation. The corporation should hold a meeting of shareholders at least annually to elect the Board of Directors, to ratify the appointment of accountants (if desired) and to transact any other business properly brought before the shareholders. Special meetings of shareholders may also be held for specific purposes that require shareholder approval.

Generally, a corporation must send an annual report to its shareholders within 120 days after the end of its fiscal year and at least 15 days prior to its annual meeting (if sent by first class mail), setting forth a balance sheet, annual income statement, and statement of changes in financial position. The annual report is not required for corporations with fewer than 100 shareholders if waived in the Bylaws.

The law considers the Corporation to be a separate "person" and therefore its financial affairs and all assets and funds should be kept separate from any individual's or other entities' assets and funds. You should take care always to execute legal documents and take other action on behalf of the corporation in a way that makes clear that the corporation is the party taking the action. For example, always use corporate stationery when communicating in writing. The proper way to sign legal documents and other important papers on behalf of your corporation is illustrated by the following example:

BUSINESS STRUCTURES AND INCORPORATION

[NAME OF CORPORATION]

By: _____
Title: _____

In summary, to reduce the risk that shareholders of the corporation will be liable for its debts and obligations, all officers, directors and shareholders should observe the corporate procedures set forth in the California Corporations Code and in the Bylaws of the corporation. In addition, you should:

- ❖ Carefully maintain written consents of directors and shareholders, stock records, Bylaws, Articles of Incorporation, and other corporate records.
- ❖ Hold meetings of directors and shareholders as necessary or appropriate and keep minutes of those meetings.
- ❖ Make it clear to third parties that they are transacting business with the corporation rather than any individual.
- ❖ Execute documents and instruments on behalf of and in the name of the corporation rather than in the name of any individual.
- ❖ Carefully segregate corporate assets and funds from personal assets and funds.
- ❖ Use corporate assets and funds only for corporate purposes and not use personal assets or funds for corporate purposes.
- ❖ Carefully document all personal dealings with the corporation.

Formation Summary Checklist

- ✓ Articles/Certification of Incorporation:
- ✓ State:
- ✓ Date of Incorporation:
- ✓ Last Amended/Why:
- ✓ Includes Indemnification:
- ✓ Registered Agent:
- ✓ Bylaws:
- ✓ Annual Meeting Date:
- ✓ Number of Directors:
- ✓ Bylaw Right of First Refusal:
- ✓ Expiration:
- ✓ Includes Indemnification:

CORPORATE RECORDS

- ✓ Amendment Requirements:
- ✓ Attorney Team:
- ✓ Last Board Meeting
- ✓ Next Board Meeting
- ✓ Next Shareholder Meeting

Capitalization Summary Checklist

- ✓ Common Stock:
- ✓ Authorized:
- ✓ Issued:
- ✓ Current FMV:
- ✓ Date changed:
- ✓ Former FMV:
- ✓ Preferred Stock:
- ✓ Authorized:
- ✓ Series ___:
- ✓ Authorized:
- ✓ Outstanding:
- ✓ Date Issued:
- ✓ Price per share:
- ✓ Principal Holders:
- ✓ Stock Plans:
- ✓ Authorized:
- ✓ Balance (Date):
- ✓ Permit Expiration:
- ✓ Proforma Valuation (on a fully diluted basis):
- ✓ Updated as of:
- ✓ Accounting and Tax Data:
- ✓ Fiscal year end:
- ✓ Auditors:

Drafting Corporate Minutes

The style of minutes is determined in large part by the personal preferences of the chairman of the Board, the corporate Secretary, other senior management of the corporation, and the directors, as well as by tradition within the company. Although it is customary, the corporate Secretary is not always the person who signs the minutes, or the only person who signs. It may be the company's practice for the chairman to also sign the minutes.

BUSINESS STRUCTURES AND INCORPORATION

The argument used for short form was that with only a brief description of action taken by the directors on the agenda items, without any elaboration, there is a less risk of embarrassment in any possible litigation. However, circumstances leading to the application of the business judgment rule may require a more detailed record of the board's deliberations and actions. In those circumstances, such as the committee or board minutes dealing with an acquisition, the minutes have been written in a more detailed style, or the "mixed" form.

Many corporate Secretaries have now turned to thinking that a longer or hybrid ("mixed") form of minutes is more desirable than the traditional short form because: (1) the board wants a record that reflects information received and discussions held as a check list and to reflect its due diligence; (2) management wants a record that reflects the information provided to the board concerning recommendations, status reports; and attorneys, accountants and auditors recommend sufficient detail to show compliance with law, good faith, due diligence and business judgment that will prove a defense in possible litigation.

The National Association of Corporate Directors theorizes that the way to demonstrate the appropriateness of the corporate action is to use the same detail in the minutes as in the deliberation, accompanied by supporting memoranda and specific reports.

[NAME OF CORPORATION]
NOTICE OF MEETING OF THE BOARD OF DIRECTORS
_____, 20__

Pursuant to the call of the [office of person calling the meeting [check Bylaws to see who may call meetings of the Board] of [Name of Corporation], a [State] corporation (the "Company"), notice is hereby given that a [regular/special] meeting of the Board of Directors will be held on ____ day, _____, 20__, commencing at _____ [a.m./p.m.] at the offices of the Company at _____.

The proposed agenda for the meeting is as follows:
1.
2.
3.

Dated: _____, 20__

_____
Secretary

CORPORATE RECORDS

WAIVER OF NOTICE AND CONSENT TO HOLDING OF A SPECIAL MEETING OF THE BOARD OF DIRECTORS OF [NAME OF CORPORATION]

The undersigned, constituting the entire Board of Directors of [Name of Corporation], a [State] corporation (the "Company"), hereby waive notice and consent to the holding of the Special Meeting of the Board of Directors of the Company on _____, 20__ at the offices of the Company. The undersigned further agree that any business transacted at such meeting shall be valid, legal and of the same force and effect as though said meeting were held after notice duly given.

Dated: _____, 20__

_____
Director

_____
Director

_____
Director

_____
Director

MINUTES OF A REGULAR MEETING OF THE BOARD OF DIRECTORS OF
_____

A regular meeting of the Board of Directors (the "Board") of [Name of Corporation], a [State] corporation (the "Company"), was held at the Company's offices located at _____ on _____ day, _____, 20__, at _____ [a.m./p.m.].

DIRECTORS PRESENT:
_____

DIRECTORS ABSENT:
_____

OTHERS PRESENT:
_____

CALL TO ORDER

_____ served as Chairman of the meeting, and _____ acted as Secretary of the meeting. The Chairman called the meeting to order and announced that a quorum of directors was present and the meeting, having been duly convened, was ready to proceed with business.

APPROVAL OF MINUTES

The Board reviewed the minutes of the meeting held _____, 20__. After discussion, upon motion duly made, seconded and unanimously approved, the following resolution was adopted:

RESOLVED, that the minutes of the meeting of the Board held _____, 20__ be, and they hereby are, approved in the form distributed to the members of the Board.

BUSINESS STRUCTURES AND INCORPORATION

[INCLUDE GENERAL DESCRIPTION OF MATTERS DISCUSSED BY THE BOARD, INCLUDING RESOLUTIONS COVERING MATTERS REQUIRING BOARD APPROVAL.]

ADJOURNMENT

There being no further business to come before the meeting, the meeting was adjourned at _____ [a.m./p.m.].

Respectfully submitted,

_____
Secretary

ACTION OF THE BOARD OF DIRECTORS OF
[NAME OF CORPORATION]
BY UNANIMOUS WRITTEN CONSENT

The undersigned, being all the members of the Board of Directors of [Name of Corporation], a [California] corporation, do hereby consent by this writing, to take the following action, to adopt the following resolutions, and to transact the following business of the corporation:

ELECTION OF OFFICERS

RESOLVED, that the following named persons are elected to the offices set forth opposite their names [at the annual compensation for services to be rendered to the corporation set forth opposite their titles] to serve until the next annual meeting of the Board of Directors or until their successors are duly elected:

Name	Officer	[Annual Compensation]
_____	_____	_____
_____	_____	_____
_____	_____	_____

RATIFICATION

RESOLVED, that the [contract/lease agreement] executed on behalf of the corporation by [Name] on _____, 20__ attached hereto and marked Exhibit ___ is hereby confirmed, ratified, and approved as action taken by and for the corporation.

RESOLVED FURTHER, that all actions taken by officers of the corporation on behalf of the corporation [since the last meeting of the Board of Directors] [since _____, 20__] are hereby confirmed, ratified, and approved as actions taken by and for the corporation.

AUTHORIZATION

RESOLVED, that the officers of the corporation are hereby authorized and directed for and on behalf of the corporation to take such action and execute such documents as they deem necessary or advisable in order to carry out and perform [the purposes of the foregoing resolutions] [the proper duties of their offices].

CORPORATE RECORDS

The undersigned hereby consent to the foregoing resolutions and direct that this Written consent be filed with the minutes of the proceedings of the Board of Directors of this corporation and that pursuant to Section 307(b) of the General Corporation Law of the State of California [and the Bylaws of this corporation] said resolutions shall have the same force and effect as if they were adopted at a meeting at which the undersigned were personally present.

Dated: _____, 20__

_____
Director

_____
Director

_____
Director

_____
Director

Annual Meeting

In California, Corporation Code Chapter 6 (Section 600-605) provides statutory guidelines regarding convening of meeting, notice, quorum and procedures. Corporation Code Chapter 7 (Sections 700-711) provides statutory guidelines regarding voting of shares and record date. Bylaws provide specifics regarding meetings and should parallel applicable statutes.

The main purpose of holding annual meetings is to protect the corporate identity "corporate veil" from being pieced and corporate protections lost in certain instances where a corporation is found to not have a true corporate structure. For example, electing directors annually affords protection of corporate structure. In small corporations, a written consent in lieu of annual meeting may be desirable, if allowed by applicable law.

If an annual meeting has not been held or deemed necessary in the start-up phase of a corporation, it may be advisable to hold an annual meeting approximately one year prior to initial public offering, but this should be determined by an attorney.

Matters typically included for approval include: (i) election of directors, (ii) approval of stock option plan or amendment there to, (iii) ratification of appointment of auditors, and (iv) if not already included in the Articles, approval of indemnification and liability provisions, including: amendment of Articles, amendment of Bylaws, and approval of form of Indemnity Agreement.

Resolutions of Board of Directors

Resolutions of the Board of Directors are prepared to set date of meeting, record date, and matters to be approved by shareholders.

BUSINESS STRUCTURES AND INCORPORATION

RESOLUTIONS TO BE ADOPTED BY THE BOARD OF DIRECTORS FOR CALLING OF ANNUAL MEETING

ANNUAL MEETING OF SHAREHOLDERS/STOCKHOLDERS

RESOLVED, that the 20__ Annual Meeting of [shareholders/stockholders] of the Company (the "Annual Meeting") be, and it hereby is, set for _____, 20__, at the Company's offices at _____ [a.m./p.m.];

RESOLVED FURTHER, that the record date for persons entitled to receive notice of, and to vote at, such Annual Meeting be, and it hereby is, set at _____, 20__.

RESOLVED FURTHER, that _____, _____, _____, and _____ be recommended for nomination at the Annual Meeting to serve as directors of the Company until the next Annual Meeting of [shareholders/stockholders] or until their successors are elected and qualified; and

RESOLVED FURTHER, that the Secretary of the Company be, and [he/she] hereby is, authorized and directed cause a Notice of Annual Meeting to be sent to the Company's shareholders/stockholders of record as of the record date and to solicit proxies for the voting of their shares with respect to the following matters: (i) election of the Company's directors for the ensuing year, (ii) [approval of [an amendment to] the Company's 20__ Stock Option Plan (the "Plan") [to increase the number of shares of Common Stock available for issuance under the Plan to _____ (_____) shares], (iii) ratification of the Board's selection of _____ as the Company's auditors for the fiscal year ending _____, 20__.

SELECTION OF AUDITORS

RESOLVED, that _____, is hereby selected as the Company's auditors for the fiscal year ending _____, 20__; and

RESOLVED, that the selection of _____ as auditors for the fiscal year ending _____, 20__ be submitted to the [shareholders/stockholders] for ratification as set forth in the foregoing resolutions.

[ELECTION OF OFFICERS

RESOLVED, that the following named persons are elected to the offices set forth opposite their names [at the annual compensation for services to be rendered to the corporation set forth opposite their titles] to serve until the next annual meeting of the Board of Directors or until their successors are duly elected and qualified:

Name	Officer	[Annual Compensation]
_____	_____	_____
_____	_____	_____]

[RATIFICATION

RESOLVED, that the [contract/lease agreement] executed on behalf of the Company by _____, _____ of the Company, on _____, 20__ attached hereto as Exhibit ___ be, and it hereby is, confirmed, ratified and approved as action taken by and for the Company.]

AUTHORIZATION

RESOLVED, that the officers of the Company be, and they hereby are, authorized and directed, for and on behalf of the Company, to take such action and execute such documents as they deem necessary or advisable in order to carry out and perform the purposes of the foregoing resolutions.

CORPORATE RECORDS

Dated: _____, 20__

_____
Secretary

Notice of Annual Meeting

Note record date and prepare a shareholder list as of record date. Record date is typically fixed by Board and, if so fixed, is at least 10 days but not more than 60 days prior to meeting. Be alert to stock issuances that may be processed after record date, but have an issuance date prior to the record date.

NAME OF CORPORATION
Street Address
City, State, Zip Code

NOTICE OF ANNUAL MEETING OF SHAREHOLDERS

NOTICE IS HEREBY GIVEN that the Annual Meeting of Shareholders (the "Annual Meeting") of _____, a [California] corporation (the "Company"), will be held at the offices of the Company at _____ on _____, 20__ at _____ [a.m./p.m.] for the following purposes:

1. To elect ____ directors to the Board of Directors to serve until the next Annual Meeting of Shareholders.

2. [To approve [an amendment to] the Company's 20__ Stock Option Plan].

3. To ratify the selection by the Board of Directors of _____ as the Company's auditors for the first year ending _____, 20__.

4. [To approve provisions relating to director liability and indemnification of agents, including amendments to the Company's Articles of Incorporation and Bylaws, and to approve the related form of indemnity agreement.]

5. To transact such other business as may properly come before the meeting or any continuation or adjournment thereof.

Only shareholders of record at the close of business on _____, 20__ will be entitled to receive notice of and vote at the Annual Meeting in accordance with the number of shares of record held in the name of each shareholder on that date.

All shareholders are cordially invited to attend the meeting.

By Order of the Board of Directors

_____   _____
City and State from where notice was mailed   [Name]

_____   _____
Date of Mailing   Secretary

WHETHER OR NOT YOU EXPECT TO ATTEND THE ANNUAL MEETING, PLEASE COMPLETE, DATE AND SIGN THE ENCLOSED PROXY AND RETURN IT PROMPTLY IN THE ENCLOSED ENVELOPE TO ASSURE REPRESENTA-TION OF YOUR SHARES.

BUSINESS STRUCTURES AND INCORPORATION

Proxy Statement

The Proxy Statement is mailed with the Notice of Annual Meeting.

[NAME OF CORPORATION]
Street Address
City, State, Zip Code

**PROXY STATEMENT
FOR
ANNUAL MEETING OF SHAREHOLDERS
TO BE HELD _____, 20__**

THIS PROXY STATEMENT is furnished in connection with the solicitation of proxies by the Board of Directors of [Name of Corporation], a [California] corporation (the "Company"), for use at the Annual Meeting of Shareholders to be held on _____, 20__, at _____ [a.m./p.m.] local time or at any adjournment or postponement of that meeting. [The cost of solicitation of proxies by mail may be supplemented by telephone, telegram and personal solicitation by officers, directors or other regular employees of the Company. No additional compensation will be paid to such individuals.]

All proxies will be voted in accordance with the instructions contained in the proxy. If no choice is made on proxies signed and returned to the Company, such proxies will be voted in favor of the proposals set forth in the Notice of Annual Meeting attached to this Proxy Statement. Any proxies given pursuant to this solicitation may be revoked by the person giving it at any time before its use by delivering to the Company a written notice of revocation or a duly executed proxy bearing a later date or by attending the meeting and voting in person.

VOTING

The Board of Directors has fixed _____, 20__ as the record date for the determination of shareholders entitled to vote at the Annual Meeting of Shareholders. On _____, 20__ [record date], there were outstanding and entitled to vote _____ shares of Common Stock, _____ shares of Series A Preferred Stock (the "Series A Stock") and _____ shares of Series B Preferred Stock (the "Series B Stock"). [**OPTION 1:** Holders of Common Stock, Series A Stock and Series B Stock are entitled to one vote for each share of such stock held (on an as-converted basis).] [**OPTION 2: ALTERNATIVE FOR USE WHEN CONVERSION RATES ARE NOT EQUAL AND/OR WHEN CLASSES HAVE DIFFERENT VOTING RIGHTS TO ELECT DIRECTORS**: Each share of Common Stock is entitled to one vote; holders of Common Stock as a group are entitled to an aggregate of _____ votes. Each share of Series A Stock is entitled to _____ votes; holders of Series A Stock as a group are entitled to an aggregate of _____ votes. Each share of Series B Stock is entitled to _____ votes; holders of Series B Stock as a group are entitled to an aggregate of _____ votes.]

With respect to the election of directors, shareholders may exercise cumulative voting rights. Cumulative voting is permitted for all shareholders if at least one shareholder gives notice, at the meeting and prior to voting for the election of directors, of such shareholder's intention to cumulate his/her votes. Under cumulative voting, each shareholder will be entitled to cast [number of directors to be elected] votes for each share of stock held (on an as-converted basis). Each shareholder may give one director-nominee all the votes such shareholder is entitled to cast or may distribute such votes among as many nominees as such shareholder chooses. Voting on all other matters to be submitted at this meeting is non-cumulative. Unless the proxy-holders are otherwise instructed, shareholders, by means of the accompanying proxy, will grant the proxy-holder discretionary authority to cumulate votes.

PROPOSAL 1: ELECTION OF DIRECTORS

One of the purposes of the Annual Meeting is to elect members of the Board of Directors of the Company to serve until the next Annual Meeting of Shareholders or until their successors are elected and have qualified. Shares represented by executed proxies will be voted for the election of the nominees listed below, unless authority to vote in favor of the nominees is withheld. In the event that one or more of such nominees should become unavailable for election for whatever reason, the current Board of Directors will propose a substitute nominee.

Under the Bylaws of the Company, there are _____ authorized directors. The _____ nominees receiving the highest number of the affirmative votes cast at the meeting will be elected directors of the Company.

[OPTION 1 – FOR ONE-CLASS VOTE:

The Company's management intends to nominate the following persons, [each of whom currently is a member of the Company's Board of Directors,] to be elected as directors:

_____
_____
_____

Biographical information regarding the nominees is available from the Company upon request.]

[OPTION 2 – FOR USE WHEN VOTING RIGHTS AS TO DIRECTORS DIFFER. MODIFY LANUGAGE TO REFLECT CIRCUMSTANCES ACCURATELY:

The Articles of Incorporation of the Company provide for the election of directors as follows: the holders of Series A Stock shall be entitled, voting as a separate class, to elect _____ director(s); the holders of the Series B Stock shall be entitled voting as a separate class, to elect _____ director(s); and the holders of the Common Stock [and the Preferred Stock] shall be entitled, voting together as one class, to elect the remaining _____ directors.

The nominees to represent the respective classes as set forth above are as follows:

NAME	PRINCIPAL OCCUPATION
Series A Stock	
(_____ Director(s))	
_____	_____
_____	_____
Series B Stock	
(_____ Director(s))	
_____	_____
_____	_____

BUSINESS STRUCTURES AND INCORPORATION

Common and Preferred Stock
(_____ Director(s))

_____   _____

_____   _____

END OF OPTION 2]

THE BOARD OF DIRECTORS RECOMMENDS A VOTE IN FAVOR OF EACH NAMED NOMINEE.

[OPTION 1 – FOR NEWLY-ADOPTED PLANS:

PROPOSAL 2: APPROVAL OF THE COMPANY'S 20__ STOCK OPTION PLAN

On _____, 20__, the Board of Directors approved the 20__ Stock Option Plan (the "Plan") and reserved an aggregate of _____ shares of its Common Stock for issuance to the Company's [employees, directors and consultants] upon exercise of options granted under the Plan. The Plan was adopted to allow the Company to grant incentive stock options and supplemental stock options to attract and retain qualified persons as [employees, directors and consultants].]

[OPTION 2 – FOR AMENDMENTS/INCREASES TO PLANS:

PROPOSAL 2: APPROVAL OF AMENDMENTS TO THE COMPAN'S 20__ STOCK OPTION PLAN

On _____, 20__, the Board of Directors approved the 20__ Stock Option Plan (the "Plan") and reserved an aggregate of _____ shares of its Common Stock for issuance to the Company's [employees, directors and consultants]. On _____, 20__, the shareholders approved the adoption of the Plan. On _____, 20__, the Board of Directors amended the Plan to increase the number of shares reserved for issuance thereunder to _____ shares, which increase is for the purpose of [increasing the number of shares available for grant under the Plan].

As of _____, 20__, the Company has granted options to purchase an aggregate of _____ shares of Common Stock (net of cancellations) at exercise prices ranging between $_____ and $_____ per share. Options to purchase an aggregate of _____ shares have been exercised through _____, 20__.

END OF OPTION 2]

[DRAFTING NOTE: MAKE SURE THAT THE FOLLOWING DESCRIPTION ACCURATELY DESCRIBES THE TERMS OF THE PLAN BEING APPROVED.]

DESCRIPTION OF THE PLAN

A copy of the Plan is attached as Exhibit A hereto. The following is a summary of the essential features of the Plan, which should be read in conjunction with the Plan itself.

GENERAL

The Plan provides for the grant of both incentive and supplemental stock options. Incentive stock options granted under the Plan are intended to be "incentive stock options" as defined in Section 422A of the Internal Revenue Code of 1986, as amended. Supplemental stock options granted under the Plan are intended by the Company not to qualify as incentive stock options under the code.

ADMINISTRATION

The Plan is administered by the Board of Directors. The Board has the power to construe and interpret the Plan and, subject to the provisions of the Plan, to determine the persons to whom and the dates on which options will be granted, the number of shares to be subject to each option, the time or times during the term of each option within which all or a portion of such option may be exercised, the exercise price, the type of consideration and other terms of the option. [The Board of Directors is authorized to delegate administration of the Plan to a committee composed of not less than three members.]

ELIGIBILITY

Incentive stock options may be granted under the Plan only to employees (including directors if they are also employees) of the Company and its affiliates. Selected employees, directors and consultants are eligible to receive supplemental stock options under the Plan. Officers who are not salaried employees of or consultants to the Company or any affiliates are not eligible to participate in the Plan.

For incentive stock options granted under the Plan, the aggregate fair market value of the shares of Common Stock with respect to which such options are exercisable for the first time by an optionee during any calendar year (under all such plans of the Company or any affiliate of the Company) may not exceed $100,000. No incentive stock option may be granted under the Plan to any person who, at the time of the grant, owns (or is deemed to own) stock possessing more than 10% of the total combined voting power of the Company or any affiliate of the Company, unless the option price is at least 110% of the fair market value on the date of grant of the stock subject to the option, and the term of the option does not exceed five years from the date of grant.

TERMS OF OPTIONS

The exercise price of incentive stock options under the Plan must be equal to at least the fair market value of the underlying stock on the date of the option grant. In some cases (see "Eligibility" above), the exercise price of options under the Plan may not be less than 110% of the fair market value of the underlying stock on the date of grant. The exercise price of supplemental options under the Plan must be equal to at least 85% of the fair market value of the underlying stock on the date of the option grant. The maximum term of options under the Plan is 10 years. Options granted under the Plan become exercisable in cumulative increments as determined by the Board. Options must be exercised within specified periods of the end of a person's relationship with the Company.

DURATION, AMENDMENT AND TERMINATION

The Board may suspend or terminate the Plan without shareholder approval or ratification at any time or from time to time. Unless sooner terminated, the Plan will terminate on _____, 20__.

The Board may also amend the Plan at any time or from time to time. However, no amendment shall be effective unless approved by the shareholders of the Company within 12 months before or after its adoption by the Board if the amendment would: (i) modify materially the requirements as to eligibility for participation; (ii) increase the number of shares reserved for options; or (iii) modify the Plan in any other way if such modification requires shareholder approve

BUSINESS STRUCTURES AND INCORPORATION

in order for the Plan to satisfy the requirements of Section 422A(b) of the Code or to comply with the requirements of Rule 16b-3 promulgated under the Securities Exchange Act of 1934.

TAX CONSEQUENCES

The tax consequences of the grant and exercise of stock options and the sale of the stock acquired upon exercise of options are complex and have been changing with changes in the tax law. Option holders are generally informed of these consequences.

The favorable vote of shareholders holding a majority of the votes attributable to the Company's outstanding voting stock is required for approval of the Plan.

THE BOARD OF DIRECTORS RECOMMENDS A VOTE IN FAVOR OF PROPOSALS 2.

END OF OPTIONAL SECTION]

PROPOSAL [3]: SELECTION OF AUDITORS

The Board of Directors has approved, and is now submitting for shareholder ratification the selection of _____ as the Company's auditors for its fiscal year ending _____, 20__. [_____ has served as the Company's auditors since the Company's inception. **ALTERNATIVELY, DESCRIBE CHANGE IN AUDITORS.]**

The favorable vote of shareholders holding a majority of the votes attributable to the Company's outstanding voting stock is required for approval of the selection of the Company's auditors.

THE BOARD OF DIRECTORS RECOMMENDS A VOTE IN FAVOR OF PROPOSAL [3].

[NOTE: THE FOLLOWING OPTION APPLIES ONLY TO CALIFORNIA CORPORATIONS AND IS DESIRABLE IF THE CORPORATION HAS NOT ADOPTED INDEMNIFICATION PROVISIONS AS CURRENTLY PROVIDED FOR BY CALIFORNIA LAW:

PROPOSAL [4]: APPROVAL OF PROVISIONS REGARDING DIRECTOR LIABILITY AND INDEMNIFICATION OF AGENTS; INDEMNITY AGREEMENT

The Board of Directors of the Company has adopted a proposal to amend the Company's Articles of Incorporation to eliminate the liability of its directors for monetary damages to the fullest extent permissible under California law and to amend the Company's Articles of Incorporation and Bylaws to broaden the indemnification provided to its directors, officers, employees and other agents. The proposed amendments to the Articles of Incorporation are set forth in Article ___ of the Restated Articles attached as Exhibit ___ hereto. The proposed amendment to the Bylaws is set forth in Article ___ of Exhibit ___ attached hereto. In addition, the Board has adopted a form of indemnity agreement in the form attached hereto as Exhibit ___ to cover the Company's directors and senior executive officers. Shareholders are requested to approve Article ___ of the Restated Articles and Article ___ of the Bylaws. Although California law does not require shareholder approval or ratification of the indemnity agreements, the

Company is also submitting these agreements for shareholder ratification as a matter of good corporate practice.

The Board's actions in submitting this proposal to shareholders is prompted by changes in California law allowing the broader indemnification of agents of a corporation and the elimination of certain aspects of director liability. The Board believes approval of this proposal will enhance the Company's ability to attract and retain qualified members of the Company's Board of Directors as well as to encourage the directors, officers, employees and other agents of the Company to continue to make independent decisions in good faith on behalf of the Company.

DIRECTOR LIABILITY

Under California law, a director of a corporation is required to perform the duties of a director in good faith and in a manner the director believes to be in the best interests of the corporation and its shareholders and with the care of an ordinarily prudent person. Liability for breaches of the duty of care, including liability for monetary damages, may arise when a director has failed to exercise sufficient care and diligence in reaching decisions or in attending to his or her responsibilities to the corporation and its shareholders.

California law enables a California corporation to include a provision in its Articles of Incorporation that limits or eliminates a director's personal liability to the corporation and its shareholders for monetary damages arising out of breaches by the director of the director's duty of care.

The Company's Restated Articles include such a provision (the "Liability Provision"). The effect of the Liability Provision is to protect directors from personal liability in connection with claims made by the Company or its shareholders for negligence, gross negligence or recklessness in the directors' exercise of their duty of care. The Liability Provision does not, however, protect directors from personal liability in connection with claims made by anyone other than the Company or its shareholders.

The Liability Provision also would not protect a director if the Company or its shareholders were able to establish that the director failed to act in good faith, knowingly acted contrary to the best interests of the Company or its shareholders, engaged in intentional misconduct, knowingly violated the law, derived an improper personal benefit or illegally approved a transaction in which he/she was an interested party, approved an illegal dividend or stock repurchase, acted recklessly under circumstances where the director was aware, or should have been aware, in the ordinary course of performing his/her duties, of a risk of serious injury to the Company or its shareholder or exhibited an unexcused pattern of inattention amounting to an abdication of the director's duty to the Company. Because the Liability Provision is tied to applicable California law, the extent of the limitations with respect to the liability of directors could be expanded or otherwise modified by future changes in California law without shareholder action.

INDEMNIFICATION UNDER CALIFORNIA LAW

California law provides that a corporation may indemnify its directors, officers, employees and other agents against the expenses and cost of settlement or judgment of actions brought against such persons by third parties, provided that the person being indemnified acted in good faith and in a matter such person reasonably believed to be in the best interests of the corporation, and, in the case of a criminal proceeding, such person had no reasonable cause to believe the conduct of such person was unlawful. California law further provides that a corporation may indemnify its directors, officers, employees and other agents against the expenses of defense or settlement of actions by or in the right of the corporation (such as a shareholder derivative suit), so long as such person acted in good faith and in a manner such person believed to be in the best

BUSINESS STRUCTURES AND INCORPORATION

interest of the corporation and its shareholders, *provided* that no indemnification is payable if such person is found liable to the corporation in the performance of his/her duty to the corporation or its shareholders (except to the extent that the court involved expressly authorizes such indemnification) or if the action is settled or otherwise disposed of without court approval. Indemnification in either instance may be paid only if the director, officer, employee or other agent is successful on the merits of his/her defense in court or the indemnification is specifically authorized after a determination that indemnification is proper under the circumstances because the director, officer, employee or other agent has met the applicable standard of case described above. This determination must be made by one of the following: (1) a majority vote of a quorum of directors who are not parties to the action; (2) if such quorum is not obtainable, by independent legal counsel in a written opinion; (3) by a vote of the shareholders, with the shares of the person to be indemnified not being entitled to vote thereon; or (4) by the court in which the action is or was pending.

California law further provides that a corporation may indemnify its directors, officers, employees and other agents for breach of duty to the corporation and its shareholder beyond the limits expressly provided by California law if the corporation's Articles of Incorporation are amended to expressly permit such indemnification. If a corporation's Articles of Incorporation are so amended, indemnification remains unavailable for prohibited acts or omissions and to the extent expressly prohibited by California law. The proposed Restated Articles of the Company permit indemnification beyond that expressly permitted by the statute.

The Board of Directors has also amended indemnification provisions of the Company's Bylaws to provide that the Company shall indemnify its directors to the fullest extent not prohibited by California law and to permit the Company to provide similar indemnification to officers, employees and other agents. Such indemnification is intended to provide the full flexibility available under California law and may, under certain circumstances, include indemnification for negligence, gross negligence and certain types of recklessness.

Article ___ of the Bylaws, as amended, provides that the rights to indemnification provided in the Bylaws are not limited to those expressly provided by the California statute to the extent permitted by the Company's Articles of Incorporation. As a result, under California law and the Company's Bylaws, the Company will be permitted to indemnify its directors, officers, employees and other agents, within the limits established by law and public policy, pursuant to an express contract, Bylaw provision, shareholder vote or otherwise, any or all of which could provide indemnification rights broader than those expressly available under California law. The Board of Directors has authorized the Company to enter into such agreements should this proposal be approved.

The current Bylaws also provide that expenses will be advanced to a director upon such person's delivery of an undertaking to repay such advances if it shall be determined that the director is ultimately not entitled to indemnification under the Bylaws. Because the indemnification provisions of the Bylaws are tied to applicable California law, they may be modified by future changes in such law without further shareholder action.

In the same spirit, the Board approved indemnity agreements for the Company's directors providing them with similar protections. The form of the agreement is attached as Exhibit ___ hereto.

California corporate law and the Bylaws of the Company may permit indemnification for liabilities arising under the Securities Act of 1933 or the Securities Exchange Act of 1934. The Board of Directors has been advised that, in the opinion of the Securities and Exchange

CORPORATE RECORDS

Commission, indemnification for liabilities arising under those Acts is contrary to public policy and is therefore unenforceable, absent a decision to the contrary by a court of appropriate jurisdiction.

The affirmative vote of the holders of a majority of the outstanding shares of the Company is required to approve the amendment to the Articles of Incorporation and Bylaws.

THE BOARD OF DIRECTORS RECOMMENDS A VOTE IN FAVOR OF PROPOSAL [4].

END OF OPTIONAL SECTION]

OTHER MATTERS

The Board of Directors knows of no other matters that may come before the Annual Meeting. If any other matters are properly presented at the Annual Meeting, it is the intention of the persons named in the accompanying proxy to vote, or otherwise to act, in accordance with their best judgment on such matters.

_____, 20__   BY ORDER OF THE BOARD OF DIRECTORS
[Date of mailing.]   _____
                                Secretary

THE BOARD OF DIRECTORS HOPES THAT THE COMPANY'S SHAREHOLDERS WILL ATTEND THE ANNUAL MEETING. WHETHER OR NOT YOU PLAN TO ATTEND, HOWEVER, YOU ARE URGED TO COMPLETE, SIGN AND RETURN THE ENCLOSED PROXY IN THE ACCOMPANYING ENVELOPE.

Proxy

The Proxy is mailed with the Proxy Statement and the Notice of Annual Meeting.

[NAME OF CORPORATION]
Street Address
City, State, Zip Code

PROXY

The undersigned hereby appoints _____ and _____ and each of them, as the attorneys and proxies of the undersigned, with power of substitution, to vote all shares of the stock of _____, a [California] corporation (the "Company"), which the undersigned is entitled to vote at the Annual Meeting of Shareholders of the Company to be held at the offices of the Company, _____, on _____, 20__ at _____ [a.m./p.m.], and at any continuation or adjournment thereof, with the same force and effect as the undersigned might or could do if personally present thereat, as set forth below and in their discretion upon any other business that may properly come before the meeting.

   1.   To elect directors of the Company, whether by cumulative voting or otherwise, to serve until the next Annual Meeting of Shareholders and until their successors are elected.

Nominees:

_____

_____

BUSINESS STRUCTURES AND INCORPORATION

_____

_____

[OPTION 1: WHEN ALL SHAREHOLDERS VOTE AS ONE CLASS:

☐   WITH AUTHORITY to vote for nominees listed above (except as marked below)

☐   WITHHOLD AUTHORITY as to the following nominees:

END OF OPTION 1]

[OPTION 2: DIFFERENT VOTING RIGHTS AMONG CLASSES:

☐   WITH AUTHORITY to vote for all nominees listed above (unless such authority is withheld below), as applicable pursuant to the Proxy Statement distributed to the Shareholders herewith (the "Proxy Statement").

☐   WITHHOLD AUTHORITY as to the following nominees, as applicable pursuant to the Proxy Statement:

END OF OPTION 2]

1. [To approve [the amendment of] the Company's 20__ Stock Option Plan (check one box).

☐   FOR   ☐   AGAINST   ☐   ABSTAIN]

2. [To ratify the appointment of _____ as auditors for the Company for the fiscal year ending _____, 20__ (check one box).

☐   FOR   ☐   AGAINST   ☐   ABSTAIN]

3. [To approve the provisions regarding director liability and indemnification of agents as fully described in the Proxy Statement.

☐   FOR   ☐   AGAINST   ☐   ABSTAIN]

THIS PROXY IS SOLCITED ON BEHALF OF THE BOARD OF DIRECTORS. SHARES REPRESENTED BY THIS PROXY WILL BE VOTED IN ACCORDANCE WITH SPECIFICATIONS MADE HEREIN. IF NO SPECIFICATION IS MADE AS TO ANY INDIVIDUAL ITEM HEREIN, IT IS INTENDED THAT SHARES REPRESENTED BY THIS PROXY WILL BE VOTED FOR THE ELECTION OF THE NAMED NOMINEES AND FOR THE OTHER PROPOSALS SPECIFIED HEREIN.

Both of said attorneys and proxies or their substitutes as shall be present and act at the meeting, or if only one be present and act then that one, shall have and may exercise all of the powers of both of said attorneys and proxies hereunder.

The undersigned hereby acknowledges receipt of (a) the Notice of Annual Meeting of the Shareholders to be held on _____, 20__ and (b) the accompanying Proxy Statement.

CORPORATE RECORDS

WITNESS the signature of the undersigned this _____ day of _____, 20___.

_____
[Name of Shareholder]

_____
[Signature]

_____
[Title, if applicable]

NUMBER OF SHARES HELD:

Common Stock   _____

Series A Preferred Stock _____

Series B Preferred Stock _____

Script

Attachment to script includes formula for calculation of cumulative voting, if allowed by applicable law, and discussion of cumulative voting ramifications.

SCRIPT FOR ANNUAL MEETING OF [SHAREHOLDERS/STOCKHOLDERS] OF [NAME OF CORPORATION]

[Annual Meeting Date]

[Chair]: Good [morning/afternoon]. I am [Name], and I am [Title] of [Name of Corporation]; and will act as chairman of this meeting. I am very happy to welcome you to the [Name of Corporation] 20__ [shareholders/stockholders] meeting. Before I call the meeting to order, I would like to introduce to you the members of the Board and the business team who are with us today.

The other members of the Board are: [Names].

The other officers of the Company here today are: [Names].

I would also like to introduce [Name of Auditors], the Company's auditors, who is/are available to respond to appropriate questions.

1. **CALL TO ORDER**

[Chair]: The meeting now officially comes to order. We propose to proceed with the formal business of the meeting set forth in your notice of annual meeting and proxy statement. After the formal part of the meeting, we will review the Company's recent business activities and give you an opportunity to ask any questions you may have.

BUSINESS STRUCTURES AND INCORPORATION

2. **LIST OF [SHAREHOLDERS/STOCKHOLDERS] AND PROOF OF MAILING OF NOTICE**

[Chair]: Will the secretary please report at this time with respect to the mailing of the notice of the meeting and the [shareholders/stockholders] list.

[Secretary]: I have at this meeting a complete list of the [shareholders/stockholders] of record of the Company's capital stock on [Record Date], the record date for this meeting.

I also have with me an affidavit certifying that on [Date], a notice of annual meeting of [shareholders/stockholders'] of the Company was deposited in the United States mail to all [shareholders/stockholders] of record at the close of business on [Record Date].

3. **INSPECTOR OF ELECTION**

[Chair]: At this time I'd like to introduce [Name of Inspector of Election]. I am appointing [Name] to act as inspector of election at this meeting. [Name] has taken and subscribed to the customary oath of office to execute his/her duties with strict impartiality, which will be filed with the records of the meeting. [His/her] function is to decide upon the qualifications of voters, accept their votes, and, when balloting on all matters are completed, to tally the final votes.

Will the Secretary please report at this time with respect to the existence of a quorum?

4. **ANNOUNCEMENT OF QUORUM PRESENT**

[Secretary]: I have been informed by the inspector of election that proxies have been received for [Number] of the [Number] shares of common stock and for [Number] of the [Number] shares of Series A Preferred Stock [on an as-converted basis] and for [Number] of the [Number] shares of Series B Preferred Stock [on an as-converted basis] outstanding on the record date, which represents approximately [Number]% of the total number of outstanding shares. This constitutes a quorum for the meeting today and we may now carry out the official business of the meeting. Are there any additional proxies to be submitted to the inspector of election at this time?

[If yes, collect and deliver to inspector.]

5. **CONSIDERATION OF BUSINESS LISTED IN NOTICE OF MEETING**

[Chair]: We will now proceed with the formal business of this meeting.

There are [Number] proposals to be considered by the [shareholders/stockholders] at this meeting.

6. **ELECTION OF DIRECTORS**

[Chair]: The first item of business today is the election of directors to serve until the next annual meeting and until their successors are elected. The nominees for directors of the Company are: [Names]. Is there any discussion? [Pause]. Nominations for director are now closed.

7.	**APPROVAL OF THE ADOPTION OF THE COMPANY'S 20__ STOCK OPTION PLAN**
[Chair]:	The second item of business today is the approval of the adoption of the Company's 20__ Stock Option Plan, as described in the proxy statement relating to this annual meeting. Is there any discussion? [Pause].
8.	**APPROVAL OF AMENDMENT TO THE ARTICLES OF INCORPORATION**
[Chair]:	The third item of business is the approval of the amendment to the Articles of Incorporation to increase the number of authorized shares of common stock of the Company to an aggregate of [Number] shares. Is there any discussion? [Pause].
9.	**AMENDMENTS TO THE COMPANY'S 20__ STOCK OPTION PLAN**
[Chair]:	The fourth item of business today is the approval of the Company's 20__ Stock Option Plan, as amended, as described in the proxy statement relating to this annual meeting. Is there any discussion? [Pause].
10.	**RATIFICATION OF INDEPENDENT AUDITORS**
[Chair]:	The fifth item of business today is the ratification of the selection of [Auditors] as the independent auditors of the company for the fiscal year ending [Date]. Is there any discussion? [Pause].
	That was the final proposal for today's meeting. The Secretary will now describe the voting procedures.
11.	**DISTRIBUTION OF BALLOTS AND VOTING**
[Secretary]:	Voting is by proxy and written ballot. You do not need to vote in person if you have already sent in your signed proxy or if you have submitted your signed proxy at this meeting. Is there anyone present, whether or not you already submitted a proxy, who now wants to vote in person? [If yes, distribute ballots and say: "After you complete your ballot, please give it to the inspector of election and register your name with [him/her]."]
[Secretary]:	Each share of common stock [and each share of Series A Preferred Stock and each share of Series B Preferred Stock] is entitled to [one] vote. [If an election to cumulate votes has been made, the following: "In voting for directors, each share of common stock is entitled to [Number of Directors being elected] votes"].
12.	**ANNOUNCEMENT OF RESULTS OF VOTING**
[Chair]:	May we have the results of the voting?
[Secretary]:	The report of the inspector of election covering the proposals presented at this meeting are as follows:

1) The proposal to elect [Names] as directors of the company are carried. [If election is by cumulative voting, say instead: "The [Number of Directors being elected] nominees with the highest number votes are: [Names]."

2) The Company's 20__ Stock Option Plan has been approved.

BUSINESS STRUCTURES AND INCORPORATION

       3)   The amendment to the Articles of Incorporation to provide for an increase in the number of authorized shares of common stock to an aggregate of [Number] shares has been approved.

       4)   The Company's 20__ Stock Option Plan, amended, has been approved.

       5)   The appointment of [Auditors] as independent auditors for the fiscal year ending [Year] has been ratified.

[Chair]:   Is there any other business to come before this meeting? [Pause]. This concludes the formal portion of our meeting. [After adjournment, we will make a presentation regarding the Company's recent business and then entertain any questions from [shareholders/stockholders].

[Chair]:   Is there any discussion? Is there any opposition to adjournment?

This meeting is adjourned.

Inspector of Election

An Oath of Inspector of Election must be prepared and signed at or prior to the annual meeting and included as an exhibit to the Minutes of the annual meeting. It is recommended that you use a tabulation worksheet to determine quorum, keeping track of returned proxies. In addition, the Certificate and Report of Inspector of Election must also be prepared and attached as an exhibit to the Minutes of the annual meeting.

OATH OF INSPECTOR OF ELECTION

STATE OF CALIFORNIA   }
                                    } ss.
COUNTY OF _____   }

_____ declares and says that:

    I, _____, the undersigned duly-appointed Inspector of Election of _____, do solemnly swear that I will fairly and impartially perform my duties as Inspector of Election at the Annual Meeting of Shareholders of _____, to be held this ____ day of _____, 20__ and will faithfully and diligently canvass the votes cast at such meeting on all matters as may be properly voted upon at such meeting and honestly and truthfully report the results of said voting.

                                                                                     _____
                                                                                        [Name]

[NAME OF CORPORATION]
CERTIFICATE AND REPORT OF INSPECTOR OF ELECTION

    I, _____, the undersigned duly-appointed Inspector of Election at the Annual Meeting of Shareholders of _____ (the "Company"), held on _____, 20__, do hereby report:

    1.   The number of shares of stock of the Company issued and outstanding and entitled to vote upon such matters as were properly brought before said meeting was _____.

CORPORATE RECORDS

shares of Common Stock, _____ shares of Series A Preferred Stock and _____ shares of Series B Preferred Stock.

    2.   There were present at said meeting, in person or by proxy, shareholders holding _____ shares of Common Stock, _____ shares of Series A Preferred Stock and _____ shares of Series B Preferred Stock, or _____ shares on as-if-converted basis, equal to ____% of all such shares outstanding and entitled to vote, which constitute a quorum.

    3.   I received the votes of the shareholders at said meeting.

    4.   I canvassed the votes and the vote on the election of the _____ nominees to serve as the Board of Directors until the next Annual Meeting of Shareholders and until their successors are elected and qualified was:

	For	**Withheld**
_____	_____	_____
_____	_____	_____
_____	_____	_____
_____	_____	_____

On that basis, the nominees were elected as directors.

    5.   I canvassed the votes, and the vote on the approval of [the amendment of] the Company's 20__ Stock Option Plan (the "Plan") was _____ votes for to _____ votes against with _____ votes abstaining; on that, the [amendment to the] Plan was approved.

    6.   I canvassed the votes and the vote on the ratification of the appointment of [Auditors] as auditors for the fiscal year ending _____, 20__, was _____ votes for to _____ votes against with _____ votes abstaining; on that basis, the appointment was ratified and approved.

    7.   I canvassed the votes and the vote on the approval of the liability and indemnification provisions, including amendments to the Articles of Incorporation and Bylaws, and the approval of the form of indemnity agreement was _____ votes for to _____ votes against with _____ votes abstaining; on that, the provisions and related amendments were ratified and approved.

_____
[Name]

[NAME OF CORPORATION]
A [CALIFORNIA] CORPORATION
ANNUAL SHAREHOLDERS MEETING
[DATE OF MEETING]

		No. of Shares	As-If-Converted
1)	Proxies received		
	(a) Common Stock	_____	_____
	(b) Series A Preferred Stock	_____	_____
	(c) Series B Preferred Stock	_____	_____
Total:		_____	_____
2)	Less: Checked shares (proxy filed, but Shareholder present and voting in Person):		
	(a) Common Stock	_____	_____

BUSINESS STRUCTURES AND INCORPORATION

	(b) Series A Preferred Stock		_____	_____
	(c) Series B Preferred Stock		_____	_____
Total:			_____	_____
3)	Total shares represented by proxy			
	(a) Common Stock		_____	_____
	(b) Series A Preferred Stock		_____	_____
	(c) Series B Preferred Stock		_____	_____
Total:			_____	_____
4)	Plus: shares at meeting voting in person:			
	(a) Common Stock		_____	_____
	(b) Series A Preferred Stock		_____	_____
	(c) Series B Preferred Stock		_____	_____
Total:			_____	_____
5)	Total shares at meeting:			
	(a) Common Stock		_____	_____
	(b) Series A Preferred Stock		_____	_____
	(c) Series B Preferred Stock		_____	_____
Total:			_____	_____
6)	Total shares issued and outstanding on [record date]			
	(a) Common Stock		_____	_____
	(b) Series A Preferred Stock		_____	_____
	(c) Series B Preferred Stock		_____	_____
Total:			_____	_____
7)	Number of shares (as-if-converted) necessary for quorum		_____	
8)	Quorum present	Yes ☐	No ☐	

Certified List of Shareholders

A list of shareholders as of record date will also be prepared and attached as an exhibit to the Minutes of the annual meeting.

STATE OF CALIFORNIA   }
                          } ss.
COUNTY OF _____   }

_____ declares and says that:

    1.   [He/she] is the Secretary of _____, a [California] corporation (the "Company"), having its principal office in the State of California.

    2.   Attached hereto is a list of shareholders of record, as of _____, 20__, of the Company, with their names and the total number of voting shares they held of record as of such date set forth opposite their names.

I declare under penalty of perjury the foregoing to be true and correct.

CORPORATE RECORDS

Executed as of _____, 20__ at _____, California.

_____
Secretary

Certificate of Mailing

A Certificate of Mailing will also need to be prepared and attached as an exhibit to the Minutes of the annual meeting.

[NAME OF CORPORATION]

**CERTIFICATE OF MAILING OF
NOTICE OF ANNUAL MEETING OF SHAREHOLDERS**

[NAME] declares and says that:

    1.   [He/she] is the Secretary of _____, a [California] corporation (the "Company");

    2.   On _____, 20__ [he/she] caused a written Notice of Annual Meeting of Shareholders of the Company, together with a Proxy Statement and Proxy, copies of which are attached hereto, to be mailed, postage prepaid, addressed to each shareholder of record on _____, 20__, entitled to vote, at the last known address appearing on the records of the Company, or given to the Company for the purpose of notice.

I declare under penalty of perjury that the foregoing is true and correct.

Executed as of _____, 20__ at _____, California.

_____
Secretary

Ballot

In California, Section 708(e) provides that ballots are optional, unless requested by a shareholder for election of directors.

**[NAME OF CORPORATION]
A [CALIFORNIA] CORPORATION
ANNUAL MEETING OF SHAREHOLDERS
_____, 20__
BALLOT**

I, the undersigned, hereby vote _____ shares of stock, on a common-equivalent basis, of _____ in the following manner:

ELECTION OF DIRECTORS

Nominees	For	Withheld
_____	_____	_____
_____	_____	_____
_____	_____	_____

[PROPOSITION]

To approve [the amendment of] the Company's 20__ Stock Option Plan.

☐ FOR ☐ AGAINST ☐ ABSTAIN]

[PROPOSITION]

To ratify the appointment by the Board of Directors of _____ as the auditors for the fiscal year ending _____, 20__.

☐ FOR ☐ AGAINST ☐ ABSTAIN]

[PROPOSITION]

To approve provisions regarding direct liability and indemnification of agents, including amendments to the Articles of Incorporation and Bylaws, and to approve the form of indemnity agreement.

☐ FOR ☐ AGAINST ☐ ABSTAIN]

_____
[Print Name]
_____
[Signature]

Minutes of Annual Meeting

The Minutes of the annual meeting are usually prepared before the actual meeting based on proxies returned. If no shareholders attend meeting, Minutes may be executed after the meeting.

MINUTES OF ANNUAL MEETING
OF SHAREHOLDERS OF
[NAME OF CORPORATION]

THE 20__ ANNUAL MEETING OF SHAREHOLDERS OF [Name of Corporation], a [California] corporation (the "Company"), was held at the offices of the Company, _____, 20__, at [Time].

CALL TO ORDER

[Name] served as Chairman of the meeting. The Chairman introduced [Officers, Directors and/or Accountants] to the shareholders present at the meeting. The meeting was called to order at [Time] by the Chairman. [Name] served as Secretary of the meeting.

PRESENTATION OF LIST OF SHAREHOLDERS

The Secretary presented to the Chairman a certified list of the shareholders of record as of the close of business on [Record Date], showing opposite each shareholder's name the number of shares held by such shareholder. A copy of the certified list is attached hereto as Exhibit A and incorporated herein by reference.

CORPORATE RECORDS

PRESENTATION OF PROOF OF DUE CALLING OF MEETING

The Secretary then presented to the Chairman a certificate, signed by the [Secretary], stating that on [Date], [Name] caused to be deposited in the United States mail, postage prepaid, addressed to each of the shareholders of record as of the close of business on [Record Date], a Notice of Annual Meeting, a Proxy Statement and Proxy, all in forms attached to said certificate. A copy of the certificate with attachments is attached hereto as Exhibit B and incorporated herein by reference.

INSPECTOR OF ELECTION

[Name] was appointed Inspector of Election. A copy of the duly subscribed oath of the Inspector of Election is attached hereto as Exhibit C and incorporated herein by reference.

ANNOUNCEMENT OF A QUORUM PRESENT

The Secretary announced that a quorum [of each class] of the Company's stock was present. The Chairman declared the meeting to be duly constituted for the transaction of business and asked if there were any additional proxies to be submitted.

CONSIDERATION OF BUSINESS

The Chairman then stated that the formal business for the meeting would proceed.

ELECTION OF DIRECTORS

The first item of business was the election of directors to serve until the [Year] Annual Meeting and until their successors are elected. [Names of Directors] were nominated as directors. [The Chairman then inquired whether there were any further nominations.] [A shareholder gave notice of his/her intention to cumulate votes.] There being no discussion, the Chairman proceeded with the next item of formal business.

APPROVAL OF [AMENDMENT TO] THE [YEAR] STOCK OPTION PLAN

The [second] item of business considered by the shareholders was the approval of the [adoption of/amendment to] the Company's [Year] Stock Option Plan. The Chairman then asked if there was any discussion. There being no discussion, the Chairman proceeded with the next item of formal business.]

RATIFICATION OF SELECTION OF INDEPENDENT AUDITORS

The [third] item of business considered by the shareholders was the ratification of the selection by the Company's Board of Directors of [Auditor] as independent auditors for the fiscal year ending [Date]. The Chairman asked if there was any discussion. There being no discussion, the Chairman proceeded with the next item of formal business.

DISTRIBUTION OF BALLOTS AND VOTING

The Chairman then asked if any persons wished to vote in person.

ANNOUNCEMENT OF RESULTS OF VOTING

The Inspector of Election then submitted the report, a copy of which is attached hereto as Exhibit D. The [Secretary] thereupon declared that:

(1) [Names] were elected directors of the Company for the ensuing year and until their successors are elected and qualified;

(2) the [approval of/amendment to the] [Year] Stock Option Plan was approved; [and]

BUSINESS STRUCTURES AND INCORPORATION

(3) the selection of [Auditors] to serve as the Company's auditors for the fiscal year ending [Date] was ratified; [and]

[The Chairman asked if there was any other business to come before the meeting.]

ADJOURNMENT OF MEETING

There being no further business to come before the meeting, the meeting was adjourned.

_____
Secretary

APPROVED:

_____
Chairman

Exhibit A – Certified List of Shareholders
Exhibit B – Certificate of Mailing
Exhibit C – Oath of Inspector of Election
Exhibit D – Report of Inspector of Election

UNANIMOUS WRITTEN CONSENT
[IN LIEU OF ANNUAL MEETING]
OF THE SHAREHOLDERS OF
[NAME OF CORPORATION]

The undersigned, as the record owners of [Number of Shares] shares of stock, being all of the outstanding shares entitled to vote of [Name of Corporation], a [California] corporation, do hereby consent by this writing to the adoption of the following resolutions:

ELECTION OF DIRECTORS

RESOLVED, that the following named persons are hereby elected to serve as the directors of the corporation to hold office until the next annual meeting of shareholders or until their successors are duly elected:

[Name of Directors]
[Name of Directors]
[Name of Directors]
[Name of Directors]

RATIFICATION

RESOLVED, that all proceedings of the Board of Directors and all acts taken by members of the Board of Directors or by officers of this corporation on behalf of the corporation [since the last annual meeting of shareholders] since _____, 20__, are hereby confirmed, ratified and approved as actions taken by and for the corporation.

The undersigned hereby consent to the foregoing resolutions and direct that this Written Consent be filed with the minutes of the proceedings of the shareholders of this corporation and that pursuant to Section 603 of the California General Corporation Law [and the Bylaws of this corporation], said resolutions shall have the same force and effect as if they were adopted at a meeting at which the undersigned were personally present.

CORPORATE RECORDS

Name	Holding Number of Shares	Signature
_____	_____	_____
_____	_____	_____
_____	_____	_____
_____	_____	_____

CHAPTER 10

CHANGES IN CORPORATE STRUCTURE

Most jurisdictions authorize fundamental corporate changes with the approval of the shareholders. The procedures for the several types of fundamental changes are virtually identical, subject to minor variations noted later in the appropriate places. For example, most jurisdictions consider the following modifications to the corporate structure to be fundamental changes: merger, consolidation, sale, mortgage, or other disposition of substantially all corporate assets other than in the regular course of business; amendments to the Articles of Incorporation and Bylaws; and dissolution and revocation of dissolution proceedings.

Corporate Structure Changes

To affect changes in corporate structure, the board must perform corporate procedures, including:

- ❖ **Board Resolutions** – The board of directors must adopt a resolution setting forth the proposed action and directing that it be submitted for a vote at a shareholders' meeting.

- ❖ **Notice** – Written notice stating the purpose of the meeting (to take the proposed action) must be sent not less than 10 days before the scheduled shareholders' meeting to each shareholder of record entitled to vote thereon. Longer notice, such as 20 days before the meeting, may be required by statute for some specific fundamental changes.

- ❖ **Shareholder Approval** – The requisite number shareholders must approve the proposed fundamental change. In most states, the proposed action must be approved by the shareholders of a majority of shares entitled to vote. Some states require the approval of two-thirds or more of the shareholders entitled to vote. Classes of shares are entitled to vote as a class if the proposed action would have required a class vote had it been submitted as an amendment to the Articles of Incorporation. Certain shares, therefore, which may otherwise not be entitled to vote, will be permitted to express an opinion on fundamental changes.
- ❖ **Filing of Articles** – A document setting forth the action taken, must be executed in duplicate by the president or vice president, and by the secretary or any assistant secretary and be filed with the state. Verification by oath of the signing officer may also be required.

The action is legally effective upon the issuance of the certificate for the approved action under the traditional view, although some states provide for legal effectiveness upon filing.

Amendments to Articles of Incorporation

The corporation may amend its Articles of Incorporation in any and as many respects as desired, but only with provisions that would be lawful in the original Articles of Incorporation. If the amendment involves certain matters that could not be lawfully contained in the original Articles, the amendment is improper.

Most modern statutes contain reservations of power to authorize changes in the Articles of Incorporation. These reservations of power permit modifications in the contract between the shareholders and their corporation.

The standard procedure, described above, is followed for amendments to the Articles of Incorporation and the notice of the shareholders' meeting is usually the same as that required for regular shareholders' meetings. Once the requisite director and shareholder approval has been obtained, a certificate of amendment is filed with the appropriate state officials. However, many jurisdictions allow the directors to amend certain provisions, such as deleting the name and address of the corporation's initial registered agents, without shareholder approval.

Statutes spell out the types of amendments a corporation may make to its Articles. Amendments may be relatively insignificant (such as changing the corporation's name), or extremely important (such as removing pre-emptive rights or cumulative voting).

ARTICLES OF AMENDMENT TO
[RESTATED] ARTICES OF INCORPORATION
OF

_____

Pursuant to the provisions of the California Corporations Code, the undersigned corporation adopts the following Articles of Amendment in its **[Restated]** Articles of Incorporation, as amended (the "Articles"):

FIRST: The name of the corporation is _____ (the "Company" or the "Corporation").

SECOND: Article ____ of the Articles is amended **[Description of Amendment]**:

THIRD: The manner in which any exchange, reclassification or cancellation of issued shares, or provisions for implementing the Amendment if not contained in the Amendment itself is as follows: NONE.

FOURTH: The Amendment was adopted by the Board of Directors of the corporation [**The Amendment was adopted by a vote of the shareholders on** _____, ____. **The number of shares voted for the Amendment was sufficient for approval.**] [Shareholder action was not required pursuant to Section 902 of the California Corporations Code.]

IN WITNESS WHEREOF, the corporation has caused these Articles of Amendment to the [Restated] Articles of Incorporation to be executed as of the ____ day of _____, 20__.

By: _____
Name: _____
Title: _____

CERTIFICATE OF AMENDMENT OF
ARTICLES OF INCORPORAITON
OF

_____

The undersigned certify that:

1. They are the President and the Secretary, respectively, of _____, a California corporation.

2. Article ____ of the Articles of Incorporation of this corporation is amended to read in full as follows:
   ["_____"]

3. The foregoing amendment of the Articles of Incorporation has been duly approved by the Board of Directors.

4. The foregoing amendment of the Articles of Incorporation has been duly approved by the required vote of shareholders in accordance with Section 902 of the California Corporations Code. The total number of outstanding shares of the corporation is _____ shares of Common Stock [and _____ shares of Series A Preferred

CHANGES IN CORPORATE STRUCTURE

Stock]. The number of shares voting in favor of the amendment equaled or exceeded the vote required. The percentage vote required was more than 50% of the outstanding shares of Common Stock [and more than 50% of the outstanding shares of Series A Preferred Stock].

  We further declare under penalty of perjury under the laws of the State of California that the matters set forth in this certificate are true and correct of our own knowledge.

Date: _____

                _____
                President

                _____
                Secretary

A Certificate of Correction is a document filed for the purpose of correcting any misstatement of fact, or any other error, contained in, or any defect in the execution of any agreement, certificate or other instrument previously filed with the Secretary of State on behalf of a domestic or foreign corporation.

A Certificate of Correction cannot alter the wording of any resolution or written consent which was in fact adopted by directors or shareholders, nor can it effect a corrected amendment of Articles of Incorporation, if the amendment as so corrected would not have complied in all respects with the statutory requirements at the time when the document being corrected was filed.

The Certificate of Correction must be signed and verified and shall set forth: (i) the name of the corporation, (ii) the date when the document being corrected was filed with the Secretary of State, and (iii) the provision in the document as corrected.

The only matters deemed 'errors' in original Articles of Incorporation are those in the names or addresses of the initial agent for service of process or of the first directors and they may be corrected with a Certificate of Correction. Any other matters which in retrospect are considered 'mistakes', including the style or spelling of the corporate name, may not be the subject of a Certificate of Correction, but must be accomplished by the filing of a Certificate of Amendment.

The Secretary of State will certify two copies of the filed Certificate of Correction without charge, provided that the copies are submitted to the Secretary of State with the original to be filed. Additional copies submitted with the original will be certified upon request and the prepayment of a nominal fee per copy.

CERTIFICATE OF CORRECTION OF AMENDED AND RESTATED ARTICLES OF INCORPORATION OF

_____

_____ and _____ certify that:

1. They are _____ and _____, respectively, of _____, a California corporation.

2. The name of the corporation filing this certificate is _____ and it is a California corporation.

3. The instrument being corrected is entitled "AMENDED AND RESTATED ARTICLES OF INCORPORATION OF _____" and said instrument was filed in the office of the Secretary of State of the State of California on _____, 20__.

4. Article ___ of said AMENDED AND RESTATED ARTICLES OF INCORPORATION, as corrected, should read in its entirety as follows:
["_____"]

5. Said AMENDED AND RESTATED ARTICLES OF INCORPORATION when corrected as herein specified, will conform in wording to the wording of the AMENDED AND RESTATED ARTICLES OF INCORPORATION in the resolutions adopted by the Board of Directors and Shareholders approving the AMENDED AND RESTATED ARTICLES OF INCORPORATION.

Each of the undersigned declares under penalty of perjury under the laws of the State of California that the matters set forth in this certificate are true and correct of his/her own knowledge and that this declaration was executed on _____.

Title: _____

Title: _____

Amendment of Bylaws

A number of jurisdictions allow the corporation's board of directors to amend or repeal the corporation's Bylaws unless the Articles of Incorporation reserve this power exclusively to the shareholders, or the shareholders in amending or repealing a particular bylaw provide expressly that the board of directors may not amend or repeal that bylaw. In any case, the shareholders always have a right to amend or repeal the Bylaws.

Merger and Consolidation

Most statutes authorize the merger and consolidation procedure, and the statutory procedure, when followed, results in a statutory merger or a statutory consolidation. Many statutes also authorize a short form merger involving a merger of a subsidiary corporation into its parent.

CHANGES IN CORPORATE STRUCTURE

A merger involves one or more corporations merging into another corporation, and the latter corporation survives the merger and continues in existence. The merging corporations cease to exist following the merger.

Two or more corporations may consolidate by forming a new corporation and transferring all assets and liabilities to the new consolidated corporation. All consolidating corporations cease to exist following the consolidation and the new corporation is the only one remaining.

A number of jurisdictions provide that a corporation owning at least 90% of the outstanding shares of each class of another corporation may merge that other corporation into itself without the approval of the shareholders of either corporation. This is a short form merger whereby a parent corporation merges its subsidiary into itself, and the normal statutory procedure need not be followed. Thus, the merger need be approved only the by the directors of the parent corporation.

The standard procedure described above is followed to accomplish a merger, except for short form mergers, where no shareholder vote is required. In some states shareholders must receive advance notice (e.g., 20 days before the meeting) in order to approve the transaction. In addition, most statutes authorize shareholders' dissenting rights for merger and consolidation transactions. Moreover, most statutes authorize shareholders' dissenting rights for merger and consolidation transactions.

Share Exchange

A share exchange is a transaction in which one corporation acquires all of the outstanding shares of one or more classes of stock of another corporation. Both corporations continue to exist as separate entities. Some jurisdictions statutorily provide for share exchanges. In such jurisdictions, the share exchange is a fundamental change for the acquired corporation. Thus, shareholders of the acquired corporation must consent under the fundamental change procedure. Where there is no statutory provision, share exchanges are often treated as de facto mergers, and so the requirements for approval are exactly the same as the requirements for approval of a merger.

Transfer of Assets

If the sale, lease, or exchange of substantially all of the corporate assets is outside the ordinary course of business, it is a fundamental corporate change. Whether a transfer of assets is within the regular course of business of the corporation is sometimes defined by statute, and sometimes requires judicial interpretation.

BUSINESS STRUCTURES AND INCORPORATION

For example, most state statutes, including the Model Act, permit a corporation to mortgage or pledge its assets without compliance with the fundamental change procedure. Yet, other transfers, whether a transfer of assets is within the ordinary course of business of a corporation may be determined, in part, by the purpose clause of the Articles of Incorporation. There is authority that the transfer of assets must actually be authorized by the purpose clause in the Articles of Incorporation, and will not be tested by the actual business conducted, even though the actual business has consistently exceeded the purpose clauses.

The transfer of assets, except by mortgage or pledge, if outside the ordinary course of business, requires a resolution of the board of directors and approval of the shareholders in accordance with the standard procedure for fundamental corporate changes. In a majority of states, there is no appraisal right in the event of a sale of assets. Some states provide appraisal rights in this situation for shareholders of the selling, but not the buying, corporation.

A corporation may attempt to sell or otherwise transfer its assets to another corporation in a transaction resembling a merger, but which is characterized as a sale of the assets for procedural purposes. In many jurisdictions, whether the transaction is called a sale of assets or a merger makes no difference. Particularly, under the Revised Model Business Corporation Act, the statutory procedure for approval of both transactions is substantially the same, and dissenting shareholders are entitled to their appraisal remedy for mergers, but not for the sale or exchange of assets in the regular course of business. Furthermore, statutes may differ in the statutory procedure required for approval of the respective transactions. In these cases, if a corporation characterizes the transaction as a sale of assets, rather than a merger, the shareholders' protection will be limited. Consequently, some courts have ignored the form of the transaction to interpret its substance, and have determined that a sale of assets may be a de facto merger, requiring full compliance with the appropriate merger statute.

Courts adopting the de facto merger doctrine have stressed a number of factors that can cause an ostensible sale of assets or stock to be re-characterized as a merger: (i) The fact that the acquiring corporation used its own stock as consideration rather than cash or promissory notes; (ii) The fact that the acquired corporation was required to dissolve; (iii) In the case of an acquisition of stock, the fact that the acquired corporation was merged into the acquiring corporation after its stock had been acquired; and (iv) The fact that the smaller corporation was buying the assets of the larger corporation (rather than the converse). Some states (especially Delaware) have rejected the de facto merger doctrine, holding that all methods of acquiring a corporation are of equal dignity, and that the legislature intended corporate planners to have a free choice in deciding which route to adopt.

One consequence of a de facto merger is that the transaction may be rescinded (for failure to comply with required formalities for a merger), or the complaining shareholders may be given appraisal rights. Another consequence of holding the acquisition to be a de facto merger is that the acquiring corporation becomes liable for all debts of the acquired corporation. Again, the majority of jurisdictions permit shareholder appraisal remedies for those shareholders who dissent to the transfer of assets transaction. However, the dissenting shareholder appraisal remedies are afforded to mergers and consolidations more readily than to a transfer of assets.

As a general rule, when one company sells or otherwise transfers all of its assets to another company, the transferee is not liable for the debts and liabilities of the transferor. Circumstances under which liability will be recognized are limited to those in which the purchaser expressly or impliedly agrees to assume debts, the transaction amounts to a consolidation or merger of the corporation, the purchasing corporation is merely a continuation of the selling corporation, the transaction is entered into fraudulently to escape liability for debts, or there is inadequate consideration for the sale or transfer of assets.

Dissolution

Dissolution is another fundamental corporate change. Dissolution is the termination of the corporate existence. To dissolve the corporation, some act must be taken, which may be voluntary by the corporation or its aggregate members, or may be involuntary through judicial proceedings. Dissolution also automatically occurs when a corporation is merged into another corporation.

Voluntary Dissolution

Dissolution by corporate action without judicial proceedings is termed voluntary dissolution and may be accomplished in a number of ways, including: (i) dissolution by incorporators, (ii) dissolution by shareholder consent, (iii) dissolution by corporate act, or (iv) revocation of voluntary dissolution proceedings.

Dissolution by Incorporators

A corporation may be voluntarily dissolved by its incorporators providing that the following requirements are met: (1) No shares of the corporation's stock may have been issued. If the corporation has merely accepted stock subscriptions, but has not issued the shares, the incorporators may dissolve. (2) All monies paid on subscriptions less any necessary expenses must have been returned to the subscribers. (3) All corporate debts must be paid. (4) The incorporators may only dissolve a corporation that has not commenced business. (5) A majority of the incorporators must agree on dissolution.

Duplicate verified Articles of Dissolution signed by a majority of the incorporators must be filed with the Secretary of State. The Secretary of State will issue a Certificate of Dissolution if the Articles of Dissolution conform to law and all fees have been paid.

Dissolution by Shareholder Consent

The shareholders may agree to voluntarily dissolve the corporation if all shareholders consent in writing. The procedures to be followed for shareholder dissolution are the same as those for dissolution by corporate act.

Dissolution by Corporate Act

The corporation may dissolve voluntarily by an act of the corporation, involving both board of directors and shareholder approval. The standard procedure for fundamental corporate change is followed: the board of directors adopts a resolution and submits it to a vote of the shareholders, who must approve the resolution by either a majority or two-thirds of the outstanding shares of the corporation entitled to vote.

In addition, the corporation must file in duplicate a Statement of Intent to Dissolve with the Secretary of State, and thereafter cease all business activity except as is necessary to wind up its affairs. Corporate existence remains unaffected; however, until a Certificate of Dissolution is issued.

To wind up its affairs, the corporation must send a Notice of Intent to Dissolve to all creditors. It must also collect all of its assets, discharge all of its obligations, and distribute the remainder of its assets, in cash or in kind, to its shareholders.

After the winding-up is completed, the president and secretary execute verified Articles of Dissolution and file them with the Secretary of State. In addition to other facts about the corporation, the Articles must include: (i) a statement that the winding-up has been completed; and (ii) a statement that no suits are pending against the company or that adequate provision has been made for any judgments that may be entered.

If the Secretary of State finds that the Articles conform to law, the Secretary of State will issue a Certificate of Dissolution.

CHANGES IN CORPORATE STRUCTURE

Revocation of Voluntary Dissolution Proceeding
At any time prior to the issuance of the Certificate of Dissolution, the dissolution may be revoked if it was authorized by either the consent of the shareholders or the act of the corporation. There is a two-step procedure: (i) the revocation must first be authorized, and (ii) then a Statement of Revocation must be filed. Upon filing of a Statement of Revocation, the revocation is effective and the corporation may again carry on its regular business.

Involuntary Dissolution
A court of equity has no inherent power to dissolve a corporation. However, the Model Act and most other state statutes provide that a corporation may be dissolved involuntarily in an action brought by: (i) the attorney general, (ii) a shareholder, or (iii) a creditor.

Action by Attorney General
A corporation may be dissolved in a proceeding instituted by the attorney general of the state. Such a proceeding may be instituted for the following reasons in most jurisdictions: (i) acquiring Articles of Incorporation through fraud; (ii) exceeding or abusing authority conferred upon the corporation in its charter; (iii) failing to appoint a registered agent in the state within 30 days; (iv) failing to file a change of registered agent within 30 days; or (v) failing to file required reports or to pay taxes.

Shareholder Action
Any shareholder may apply to a court for liquidation of the corporation in the following situations: (i) if the directors are deadlocked in the management of the corporation, the shareholders are unable to break the deadlock, and the corporation is suffering or is threatened with irreparable injury, a shareholder may apply for a liquidation; (ii) if the shareholders are deadlocked in voting power and have failed, for a specified statutory period (usually two years), to elect successors to the directors whose terms have expired or would have expired upon the election of successors, a court may order liquidation; (iii) if the acts of the directors or those in control are illegal, oppressive, or fraudulent to the shareholders, the shareholders may apply for equitable relief in dissolution; and (iv) if the corporate assets are being misapplied or wasted by the directors or controlling shareholders, other shareholders may petition a court for dissolution. Dissolution, in this case, is discretionary with the court.

Creditor

A creditor may institute proceedings to dissolve the corporation if it is insolvent (unable to pay debts as they mature), and either: (i) the creditor has a claim that has been reduced to judgment and execution has been returned unsatisfied; or (ii) the corporation has admitted in writing that the claim of the creditor is due and owing.

Liquidation

Although dissolved by judicial decree or voluntary dissolution, the corporation nevertheless continues in existence for purposes of winding up. Liquidation, or winding up, involves the process of collecting the corporate assets, paying the expenses involved, satisfying creditors' claims, and distributing the net assets of the corporation. Thus, even though legally dissolved, the corporation continues to function throughout the liquidation period, and a number of problems rise with regard to actions involving the corporation, individual directors, and shareholders.

Since the corporation continues in existence for purposes of liquidation, the corporation may sue or be sued in its own name. Under most state statutes the corporation may sue or be sued in its corporate name within two years from the date of dissolution. A suit is deemed commenced upon the filing of the complaint, rather than when service is obtained, for purposes of measuring this period. However, the general rule today is that neither voluntary nor involuntary dissolution excuses contract performance.

In addition, actions may be brought by shareholders on corporate claims more than two years after dissolution. A creditor is barred from bringing a suit against a shareholder if he/she has failed to sue the corporation within two years after dissolution. This bar is absolute only if the creditor received proper notice of dissolution. If he/she received no notice, he/she may have a claim against former directors.

The directors will be personally liable for any claims brought within the two-year time period for which they failed to make adequate provisions. The directors will be personally liable for any claims that were not brought within the two year time period by reason of their failure to notify the creditors.

All shareholders participate pro rata in the net assets upon liquidation except as otherwise provided by the Articles of Incorporation. For any class of shares to enjoy a liquidation preference, the Articles of Incorporation must so provide.

CHANGES IN CORPORATE STRUCTURE

Therefore, if the Articles of Incorporation do not provide otherwise, preferred shares are not entitled to any special priority upon liquidation.

CHAPTER 11

CORPORATE STOCK MATTERS

In order to protect the investing public, corporations that plan to issue stock in California must have the issuance qualified with the California Department of Corporations and obtain a permit in conjunction with the sale of any stock, unless an exemption from such qualification is available.

Founder Stock Issuances

Section 25102(f) of the California Corporations Code exempts certain transactions in which the investors generally have access to information that will enable them to make a reasoned judgment with respect to the desirability of the investment. Typically, this exemption is available for stock issuances to the founders of a corporation. In an effort to properly document the qualification of the founder to purchase the stock, a Stock Purchase Agreement or investment letter should be executed by the founders.

If your Corporation meets the formal requirements for the exemption for the issuance of common stock to the founders, the required Notice of Transaction Pursuant to Corporations Code Section 25102(f) ("Notice") should be filed with the Commissioner of Corporations within 15 calendar days following receipt by the Corporation of the consideration for its stock. Thereafter, the notice and stock certificates should be prepared. If stock will be issued to someone residing outside of California, the securities laws of that state should be reviewed before to assure that no filings or other items are required.

CORPORATE STOCK MATTERS

SAMPLE

NOTICE OF TRANSACTION PURSUANT TO CORPORATIONS CODE SECTION 25102(F) FORM

(Department of Corporations Use Only)
Fee paid $ _____

Receipt No. _____

DEPARTMENT OF CORPORATIONS FILE NO., if any:
_____

Insert File number(s) of Previous Filings Before the Department, if any.

Fee: $25.00 $35.00 $50.00 $150.00 $300.00
(Circle the appropriate amount of fee. See Corporations Code Section 25608(c))

COMMISSIONER OF CORPORATIONS
STATE OF CALIFORNIA

NOTICE OF TRANSACTION PURSUANT TO CORPORATIONS CODE SECTION 25102(f)
A. Check one: Transaction under ( ) Section 25102(f)   ( ) Rule 260.103.

ELECTRONIC FILING REQUIREMENT AND HARDSHIP EXCEPTION:
This notice must be filed electronically through the Internet process made available by the Department of Corporations on www.corp.ca.gov, **unless the issuer claims the hardship exception as described in Number 8 below.**

1. Name of Issuer: _____

2. Address of Issuer: _____

	Street	City	State	Zip
Mailing Address:	Street	City	State	Zip

3. Area Code and Telephone Number: _____

4. Issuer's state (or other jurisdiction) of incorporation or organization: _____

5. Title of class or classes of securities sold in transaction: _____

6. The value of the securities sold or proposed to be sold in the transaction, determined in accordance with Corporations Code Sec. 25608(g) in connection with the fee required upon filing this notice, is (fee based on amount shown in line (iii) under "Total Offering"):

	California	Total Offering
(a)(i) in money	$ _____	$ _____
(ii) in consideration other than money	$ _____	$ _____
(iii) total of (i) and (ii)	$ _____	$ _____

(b) ( ) Change in rights, preferences, privileges or restrictions of or on outstanding securities ($25.00 fee.) (See Rule 260.103.)

260.102.14(c) (8-05)

BUSINESS STRUCTURES AND INCORPORATION

SAMPLE
NOTICE OF TRANSACTION PURSUANT TO CORPORATIONS CODE SECTION 25102(F)
FORM CONTINUED

7. Type of filing under Securities Act of 1933, if applicable: _____

8. **Hardship Exception for electronic filing.** An issuer may file this paper notice in person or by mail only if either of the following exceptions apply. The issuer shall check applicable box and include the reason(s) and description(s) for the hardship exception in the space provided.

    ☐ Computer equipment including hardware and software is unavailable to the issuer without unreasonable burden or expense. If this is the case, describe below both of the following: the reason(s) that the computer equipment including hardware and software is unavailable without unreasonable burden or expense, and the description(s) of the unreasonable burden or expense.

    ☐ The issuer cannot obtain and provide information (including credit card or other identifying information) requested on the Department's electronic notice or through the Internet filing process. If this is the case, describe below both of the following: the reason(s) that the issuer cannot obtain and provide the requested information on the electronic notice or through the Internet filing process without unreasonable burden or expense, and the description(s) of the unreasonable burden or expense to the issuer to make the electronic filing.

    After checking the applicable hardship exception above, the issuer shall describe below the reason(s) and description(s) for that hardship exception. (If additional space is needed, attach a separate sheet to this notice.)

    _____
    _____
    _____
    _____

9. ( ) Check if issuer already has a consent to service of process on file with the Commissioner. (Instruction: Each issuer (other than a California Corporation) filing a notice under Section 25102(f) must file a consent to service of process (Form 260.165), unless it already has a consent to service on file with the Commissioner. If no consent to service of process is on file with the Commissioner, attach the consent to this notice.)

10. _____
    Authorized Signature on behalf of issuer

    _____
    Print name and title of signatory

    _____
    Date

    Name, Address and Phone number of contact person:
    _____
    _____

260.102.14(c) (8-05)

CORPORATE STOCK MATTERS

Federal Securities Law

With respect to the federal securities laws, an exemption from the registration requirements of the Securities Act of 1933, as amended (the "Act"), is available pursuant to Rule 701 of the Act for the initial stock issuances to the founders. There is no filing requirement for this exemption.

Stock Purchase Agreement

The following agreement is not intended to be comprehensive or an absolute statement of the governing law. This agreement is not legal advice. It does not analyze any specific fact patterns from any parties but rather discusses broadly points of law, which may or may not be the most accurate, according to current case law interpretation or even case law interpretation that is very in-depth on very narrowly-presented issues. Sound legal advice arises from interaction between client and attorney in a question-and-answer dialogue where facts are provided by a client as the attorney probes for issues and then conducts appropriate research if need be to ascertain the applicable law. Anyone seeking specific advice to specific legal questions should present their facts to an attorney.

SAMPLE STOCK PURCHASE AGREEMENT
OF
_____

THIS FOUNDER STOCK PURCHASE AGREEMENT (the "Agreement") is made as of the _____ day of _____, 20__, by and between _____, a CALIFORNIA corporation (the "Company"), and _____ ("Purchaser").

WHEREAS, the Company desires to issue, and Purchaser desires to acquire, stock of the Company as herein described, on the terms and conditions hereinafter set forth; and

WHEREAS, the issuance of common stock hereby is in connection with a compensatory benefit plan for the employees, directors, officers, advisors or consultants of the Company and is intended to comply with Rule 701 promulgated by the Securities and Exchange Commission under the Securities Act of 1933, as amended (the "Act").

NOW, THEREFORE, IT IS AGREED between the parties as follows:

1.   PURCHASE AND SALE OF STOCK. Purchaser hereby agrees to purchase from the Company, and the Company hereby agrees to sell to Purchaser, an aggregate of _____ shares of the Common Stock of the Company (the "Stock") at _____ per share, for an aggregate purchase price of _____ payable in cash.

The closing hereunder, including payment for and delivery of the Stock shall occur at the offices of the Company immediately following the execution of this Agreement, or at such other time and place as the parties may mutually agree.

2. **REPURCHASE OPTION**

(a) In the event Purchaser's relationship with the Company (or a parent or subsidiary of the Company), whether as an employee, director or consultant, terminates for any reason (including death or disability), or for no reason, with or without cause, then the Company shall have an irrevocable option (the "Repurchase Option"), for a period of ninety (90) days after said termination, or such longer period as may be agreed to by the Company and the Purchaser, to repurchase from Purchaser or Purchaser's personal representative, as the case may be, at the original price per share indicated above paid by the Purchaser for such Stock ("Option Price"), up to but not exceeding the number of shares of Stock that have not vested as of such termination date in accordance with the provisions of Section 2b below as of such termination date.

(b) _____ (_____) shares of the Stock will vest immediately upon issuance thereof to Purchaser. The remaining _____ (_____) shares will initially be subject to the Repurchase Option. On _____, 20__ (the "Vesting Anniversary Date") _____ (_____) shares of the Stock shall vest and be released from the Repurchase Option. Thereafter, ____ of _____ (_____) shares of the Stock shall vest and be released from the Repurchase Option on a monthly basis measured from the Vesting Anniversary Date, until all the Stock is released from the Repurchase Option (provided in each case that the Purchaser's relationship as an employee, director or consultant of the Company (or a parent or subsidiary of the Company) has not been terminated prior to the date of such release).

3. **EXERCISE OF REPURCHASE OPTION.** The Repurchase Option shall be exercised by written notice signed by an officer of the Company or by any assignee or assignees of the Company and delivered or mailed as provided in Section 16a. Such notice shall identify the number of shares of Stock to be purchased and shall notify Purchaser of the time, place and date for settlement of such purchase, which shall be scheduled by the Company within the term of the Repurchase Option set forth in Section 2a above. The Company shall be entitled to pay for any shares of Stock purchased pursuant to its Repurchase Option at the Company's option in cash or by offset against any indebtedness owing to the Company by Purchaser (including without limitation any Note given in payment for the Stock), or by a combination of both. Upon delivery of such notice and payment of the purchase price in any of the ways described above, the Company shall become the legal and beneficial owner of the Stock being repurchased and all rights and interest therein or related thereto, and the Company shall have the right to transfer to its own name the Stock being repurchased by the Company, without further action by Purchaser.

4. **ADJUSTMENTS TO STOCK.** If, from time to time, during the term of the Purchase Option there is any change affecting the Company's outstanding Common Stock as a class that is effected without the receipt of consideration by the Company (through merger, consolidation, reorganization, reincorporation, stock dividend, dividend in property other than cash, stock split, liquidating, dividend, combination of shares, change in corporation structure or other transaction not involving the receipt of consideration by the Company), then any and all new, substituted or additional securities or other property to which Purchaser is entitled by reason of Purchaser's ownership of Stock shall be immediately subject to the Repurchase Option and be included in the word "Stock" for all purposes of the Repurchase Option with the same force and effect as the shares of the Stock presently subject to the Repurchase Option, but only to the extent the Stock is, at the time, covered

by such Repurchase Option. While the total Option Price shall remain the same after each such event, the Option Price per share of Stock upon exercise of the Repurchase Option shall be appropriately adjusted.

5. **CORPORATE TRANSACTION.** In the event of (a) a sale of substantially all of the assets of the Company; (b) a merger or consolidation in which the Company is not the surviving corporation (other than a merger or consolidation in which shareholders immediately before the merger or consolidation have, immediately after the merger or consolidation, greater stock voting power); (c) a reverse merger in which the company is the surviving corporation but the shares of the Company's common stock outstanding immediately preceding the merger are converted by virtue of the merger into other property, whether in the form of securities, cash or otherwise (other than a reverse merger in which stockholders immediately before the merger have, immediately after the merger, greater stock voting power); or (d) any transaction or series of related transactions in which in excess of 50% of the Company's voting power is transferred ((a) through (d) being collectively referred to herein as a "Corporate Transaction"), then the Repurchase Option may be assigned by the Company to any successor of the Company (or the successor's parent) in connection with such Corporate Transaction. To the extent that the Repurchase Option remains in effect following such a Corporate Transaction, it shall apply to the new capital stock or other property received in exchange for the Stock in consummation of the Corporate Transaction, but only to the extent the Stock is at the time covered by such right. Appropriate adjustments shall be made to the price per share payable upon exercise of the Repurchase Option to reflect the effect of the Corporate Transaction upon the Company's capital structure; provided, however, that the aggregate Option Price shall remain the same.

6. **TERMINATION OF REPURCHASE OPTION.** Sections 2, 3, 4 and 5 of this Agreement shall terminate upon the exercise in full or expiration of the Repurchase Option, whichever first occurs.

7. **ESCROW OF UNVESTED STOCK.** As security for Purchaser's faithful performance of the terms of this Agreement and to insure the availability for delivery of Purchaser's stock upon exercise of the Repurchase Option herein provided for, Purchaser agrees, at the closing hereunder, to deliver to and deposit with the Secretary of the Company or the Secretary's designee ("Escrow Agent"), as Escrow Agent in this transaction, three (3) stock assignments duly endorsed (with date and number of shares blank) in the form attached hereto as **Exhibit A**, together with a certificate or certificates evidencing all of the Stock subject to the Repurchase Option; said documents are to be held by the Escrow Agent and delivered by said Escrow Agent pursuant to the Joint Escrow Instructions of the Company and Purchaser set forth in **Exhibit B**, attached hereto and incorporated by this reference, which instructions shall also be delivered to the Escrow Agent at the closing hereunder.

8. **RIGHTS OF PURCHASER.** Subject to the provisions of Sections 7, 9, 12 and 14 herein, Purchaser shall exercise all rights and privileges of a shareholder of the Company with respect to the Stock deposited in escrow. Purchaser shall be deemed to be the holder for purposes of receiving any dividends that may be paid with respect to such shares of Stock and for the purpose of exercising any voting rights relating to such shares of Stock, even if some or all of such shares of stock have not yet vested and been released from the Repurchase Option.

9. **LIMITATIONS ON TRANSFER.** In addition to any other limitation on transfer created by applicable securities laws, Purchaser shall not assign, hypothecate,

BUSINESS STRUCTURES AND INCORPORATION

donate, encumber or otherwise dispose of any interest in the Stock while the Stock is subject to the Repurchase Option. After any Stock has been released from the Repurchase Option, Purchaser shall not assign, hypothecate, donate, encumber or otherwise dispose of any interest in the Stock except in compliance with the provisions herein and applicable securities laws. Furthermore, the Stock shall be subject to any right of first refusal in favor of the Company or its assignees that may be contained in the Company's Bylaws.

10. RESTRICTIVE LEGENDS. All certificates representing the Stock shall have endorsed thereon legends in substantially the following forms (in addition to any other legend which may be required by other agreements between the parties hereto):

(a) "THE SHARES REPRESENTED BY THIS CERTIFICATE ARE SUBJECT TO AN OPTION SET FORTH IN AN AGREEMENT BETWEEN THE COMPANY AND THE REGISTERED HOLDER, OR SUCH HOLDER'S PREDECESSOR IN INTEREST. A COPY OF WHICH IS ON FILE AT THE PRINCIPAL OFFICE OF THIS COMPANY. ANY TRANSFER OR ATTEMPTED TRANSFER OF ANY SHARES SUBJECT TO SUCH OPTION IS VOID WITHOUT THE PRIOR EXPRESS WRITTEN CONSENT OF THE COMPANY."

(b) "THE SHARES REPRESENTED BY THIS CERTIFICATE HAVE NOT BEEN REGISTERED UNDER THE SECURITIES ACT OF 1933 AS AMENDED. THEY MAY NOT BE SOLD, OFFERED FOR SALE, PLEDGED OR HYPOTHECATED IN THE ABSENCE OF AN EFFECTIVE REGISTRATION STATEMENT AS TO THE SECURITIES UNDER SAID ACT OR AN OPINION OF COUNSEL SATISFACTORY TO THE COMPANY THAT SUCH REGISTRATION IS NOT REQUIRED."

(c) "THE SHARES REPRESENTED BY THIS CERTIFICATE ARE SUBJECT TO A RIGHT OF FIRST REFUSAL OPTION IN FAVOR OF THE COMPANY AND/OR ITS ASSIGNEE(S) AS PROVIDED IN THE BYLAWS OF THE COMPANY."

(d) Any legend required by law.

11. INVESTMENT REPRESENTATIONS. In connection with the purchase of the Stock, Purchaser represents to the Company the following:

(a) Purchaser is aware of the Company's business affairs and financial condition and has acquired sufficient information about the Company to reach an informed and knowledgeable decision to acquire the Stock. Purchaser is purchasing the Stock for investment for Purchaser's own account only and not with a view to, or for resale in connection with, any "distribution" thereof within the meaning of the Act.

(b) Purchaser understands that the Stock has not been registered under the Act by reason of a specific exemption therefrom, which exemption depends upon, among other things, the bona fide nature of Purchaser's investment intent as expressed herein.

(c) Purchaser further acknowledges and understands that the Stock must be held indefinitely unless the Stock is subsequently registered under the Act or an exemption from such registration is available. Purchaser further acknowledges and understands that the Company is under no obligation to register the Stock. Purchaser understands that the certificate evidencing the Stock will be imprinted with a legend which prohibits the transfer of the Stock unless the Stock is registered or such registration is not required in the opinion of counsel for the Company.

CORPORATE STOCK MATTERS

(d) Purchaser is familiar with the provisions of Rules 144 and 701, under the Act, as in effect from time to time, which, in substance, permit limited public resale of "restricted securities" acquired, directly or indirectly, from the issuer thereof (or from an affiliate of such issuer), in a non-public offering subject to the satisfaction of certain conditions. Rule 701 provides that if the issuer qualifies under Rule 701 at the time of issuance of the securities, such issuance will be exempt from registration under the Act. In the event the Company becomes subject to the reporting requirements of Section 13 or 15(d) of the Securities Exchange Act of 1934, the securities exempt under Rule 701 may be sold by Purchaser ninety (90) days thereafter, subject to the satisfaction of certain of the conditions specified by Rule 144 and the market stand-off provision described in Section 12 below.

In the event that the sale of the Stock does not qualify under Rule 701 at the time of purchase, then the Stock may be resold by Purchaser in certain limited circumstances subject to the provisions of Rule 144, which requires, among other things: (i) the availability of certain public information about the Company and (ii) the resale occurring following the required holding period under Rule 144 after the Purchaser has purchased, and made full payment of (within the meaning of Rule 144), the securities to be sold.

(e) Purchaser further understands that at the time Purchaser wishes to sell the Stock there may be no public market upon which to make such a sale, and that, even if such a public market then exists, the Company may not be satisfying the current public current information requirements of Rule 144 or 701, and that, in such event, Purchaser would be precluded from selling the Stock under Rule 144 or 701 even if the minimum holding period requirement had been satisfied.

(f) Purchaser further warrants and represents that Purchaser has either (i) preexisting personal or business relationships, with the Company or any of its officers, directors or controlling persons, or (ii) the capacity to protect his own interests in connection with the purchase of the Stock by virtue of the business or financial expertise of himself or herself or of professional advisors to Purchaser who are unaffiliated with and who are not compensated by the Company or any of its affiliates, directly or indirectly.

12. **MARKET STAND-OFF AGREEMENT.** Purchaser shall not sell, dispose of, transfer, make any short sale of, grant any option for the purchase of, or enter into any hedging or similar transaction with the same economic effect as a sale, any Common Stock or other securities of the Company held by Purchaser, including the Stock (the "Restricted Securities"), for a period of time specified by the underwriter(s) (not to exceed one hundred eighty (180) days) following the effective date of a registration statement of the Company filed under the Act. Purchaser agrees to execute and deliver such other agreements as may be reasonably requested by the Company and/or the underwriter(s) which are consistent with the foregoing or which are necessary to give further effect thereto. In order to enforce the foregoing covenant, the Company may impose stop-transfer instructions with respect to Purchaser's Restricted Securities until the end of such period.

13. **SECTION 83(B) ELECTION.** Purchaser understands that Section 83(a) of the Code, taxes as ordinary income the difference between the amount paid for the Stock and the fair market value of the Stock as of the date any restrictions on the Stock lapse. In this context, "restriction" includes the right of the Company to buy back the Stock pursuant to the Repurchase Option set forth in Section 2a above. Purchaser understands that Purchaser may elect to be taxed at the time the Stock is purchased, rather than when and as the Repurchase Option expires, by filing an election under Section 83(b) (an "83(b)

Election") of the Code with the Internal Revenue Service within thirty (30) days from the date of purchase. Even if the fair market value of the Stock at the time of the execution of this Agreement equals the amount paid for the Stock, the 83(b) Election must be made to avoid income under Section 83(a) in the future. **Purchaser understands that failure to file such an 83(b) Election in a timely manner may result in adverse tax consequences for Purchaser**. Purchaser further understands that an additional copy of such 83(b) Election is required to be filed with his/her federal income tax return for the calendar year in which the date of this Agreement falls. Purchaser acknowledges that the foregoing is only a summary of the effect of United States federal income taxation with respect to purchase of the Stock hereunder, and does not purport to be complete. Purchaser further acknowledges that the Company has directed Purchaser to seek independent advice regarding the applicable provisions of the Code, the income tax laws of any municipality, state or foreign country in which Purchaser may reside, and the tax consequences of Purchaser's death. Purchaser assumes all responsibility for filing an 83(b) Election and paying all taxes resulting from such election or the lapse of the restrictions on the Stock.

      14.   **REFUSAL TO TRANSFER.** The Company shall not be required (a) to transfer on its books any shares of Stock of the Company which shall have been transferred in violation of any of the provisions set forth in this Agreement or (b) to treat as owner of such shares or to accord the right to vote as such owner or to pay dividends to any transferee to whom such shares shall have been so transferred.

      15.   **NO EMPLOYMENT RIGHTS.** This Agreement is not an employment contract and nothing in this Agreement shall affect in any manner whatsoever the right or power of the Company (or a parent or subsidiary of the Company) to terminate Purchaser's employment for any reason at any time, with or without cause and with or without notice.

    ❖   **MISCELLANEOUS.**

      (a)   **Notices.** Any notice required or permitted hereunder shall be given in writing and shall be deemed effectively given upon personal delivery or sent by telegram or fax or upon deposit in the United States Post Office, by registered or certified mail with postage and fees prepaid, addressed to the other party hereto at his address hereinafter shown below its signature or at such other address as such party may designate by ten (10) days' advance written notice to the other party hereto.

      (b)   **Successors and Assigns.** This Agreement shall inure to the benefit of the successors and assigns of the Company and, subject to the restrictions on transfer herein set forth, be binding upon Purchaser, Purchaser's successors, and assigns. The Repurchase Option of the Company hereunder shall be assignable by the Company at any time or from time to time, in whole or in part.

      (c)   **Attorneys' Fees; Specific Performance.** Purchaser shall reimburse the Company for all costs incurred by the Company in enforcing the performance of, or protecting its rights under, any part of this Agreement, including reasonable costs of investigation and attorneys' fees. It is the intention of the parties that the Company, upon exercise of the Repurchase Option and payment of the Option Price, pursuant to the terms of this Agreement, shall be entitled to receive the Stock, in specie, in order to have such Stock available for future issuance without dilution of the holdings of other shareholders. Furthermore, it is expressly agreed between the parties that money damages are inadequate to compensate the Company for the Stock and that the Company shall, upon proper exercise of the Repurchase Option, be entitled to specific enforcement of its rights to purchase and receive said Stock.

(d) Governing Law; Venue. This Agreement shall be governed by and construed in accordance with the laws of the State of California. The parties agree that any action brought by either party to interpret or enforce any provision of this Agreement shall be brought in, and each party agrees to, and does hereby, submit to the jurisdiction and venue of, the appropriate state or federal court for the district encompassing the Company's principal place of business.

(e) Further Execution. The parties agree to take all such further action(s) as may reasonably be necessary to carry out and consummate this Agreement as soon as practicable, and to take whatever steps may be necessary to obtain any governmental approval in connection with or otherwise qualify the issuance of the securities that are the subject of this Agreement.

(f) Independent Counsel. Purchaser acknowledges that this Agreement has been prepared on behalf of the Company by the Chief Executive Officer of the Company, and that the Chief Executive Officer does not represent, and is not acting on behalf of, Purchaser. Purchaser has been provided with an opportunity to consult with Purchaser's own counsel with respect to this Agreement.

(g) Entire Agreement; Amendment. This Agreement constitutes the entire agreement between the parties with respect to the subject matter hereof and supersedes and merges all prior agreements or understandings, whether written or oral. This Agreement may not be amended, modified or revoked, in whole or in part, except by an agreement in writing signed by each of the parties hereto.

(h) Severability. If one or more provisions of this Agreement are held to be unenforceable under applicable law, the parties agree to renegotiate such provision in good faith. In the event that the parties cannot reach a mutually agreeable and enforceable replacement for such provision, then (i) such provision shall be excluded from this Agreement, (ii) the balance of the Agreement shall be interpreted as if such provision were so excluded and (iii) the balance of the Agreement shall be enforceable in accordance with its terms.

(i) Counterparts. This Agreement may be executed in two or more counterparts, each of which shall be deemed an original and all of which together shall constitute one instrument.

IN WITNESS WHEREOF, the parties hereto have executed this Agreement as of the day and year first written above.

NAME OF CORPORATION
By:

_____

PURCHASER:
By:

_____

BUSINESS STRUCTURES AND INCORPORATION

EXHIBIT A
JOINT ESCROW INSTRUCTIONS

_____
_____
_____

Ladies and Gentlemen:

As Escrow Agent for _____, a California corporation ("Corporation") and _____ ("Purchaser"), you are hereby authorized and directed to hold the documents delivered to you pursuant to the terms of that certain Founder Stock Purchase Agreement dated as of _____, 20__ ("Agreement"), to which a copy of these Joint Escrow Instructions is attached as Exhibit A, in accordance with the following instructions:

    1.   In the event Corporation or an assignee shall elect to exercise the Repurchase Option set forth in the Agreement, the Corporation or its assignee will give to Purchaser and you a written notice specifying the number of shares of stock to be purchased, the purchase price, and the time for a closing thereunder at the principal office of the Corporation. Purchaser and the Corporation hereby irrevocably authorize and direct you to close the transaction contemplated by such notice in accordance with the terms of said notice.

    2.   At the closing, you are directed (a) to date the stock assignments necessary for the transfer in question, (b) to fill in the umber of shares being transferred, and (c) to deliver the same, together with the certificate evidencing the shares of stock to be transferred, to the Corporation against the simultaneous delivery to you of the purchase price (which may include suitable acknowledgment of cancellation of indebtedness) for the number of shares of stock being purchased pursuant to the exercise of the Repurchase Option.

    3.   Purchaser irrevocably authorizes the Corporation to deposit with you any certificates evidencing shares of stock to be held by you hereunder and any additions and substitutions to said shares as specified in the Agreement. Purchaser does hereby irrevocably constitute and appoint you as his/her attorney-in-fact and agent for the term of this escrow to execute with respect to such securities all documents necessary or appropriate to make such securities negotiable and complete any transaction herein contemplated, including but not limited to any appropriate filing with state or government officials or bank officials. Subject to the provisions of this paragraph 3, Purchaser shall exercise all rights and privileges of a shareholder of the Corporation while the stock is held by you.

    4.   This escrow shall terminate upon the exercise in full or expiration of the Repurchase Option, whichever occurs first.

    5.   If at the time of termination of this escrow you should have in your possession any documents, securities, or other property belonging to Purchaser, you shall delver all of the same to Purchaser and shall be discharged of all further obligations hereunder; provided, however, that if at the time of termination of this escrow you are advised by the Corporation that any property subject to this escrow is the subject of a pledge or other security agreement, you shall deliver all such property to the pledge holder or other person designated by the Corporation.

CORPORATE STOCK MATTERS

6. Except as otherwise provided in these Joint Escrow Instructions, your duties hereunder may be altered, amended, modified or revoked only by a writing signed by all of the parties hereto.

7. You shall be obligated only for the performance of such duties as are specifically set forth herein and may rely and shall be protected in relying or refraining from acting on any instrument reasonably believed by you to be genuine ad to have been signed or presented by the proper party or parties. You shall not be personally liable for any act you may do or omit to do hereunder as Escrow Agent or as attorney-in-fact for Purchaser while acting in good faith and in the exercise of your own good judgment, and any act done or omitted by you pursuant to the advice of your own attorneys shall be conclusive evidence of such good faith.

8. You are hereby expressly authorized to disregard any and all warnings given by any of the parties hereto or by any other person or corporation, excepting only orders or process of courts of law, and are hereby expressly authorized to comply with and obey orders, judgments or decrees of any court. In case you obey or comply with any such order, judgment or decree of any court, you shall not be liable to any of the parties hereto or to any other person, firm or corporation by reason of such compliance, notwithstanding any such order, judgment or decree being subsequently reversed, modified, annulled, set aside, vacated or found to have been entered without jurisdiction.

9. You shall not be liable in any respect on account of the identity, authorities or rights of the parties executing or delivering or purporting to execute or deliver the Agreement or any documents or papers deposited or called for hereunder.

10. You shall not be liable for the outlawing of any rights under any statute of limitations with respect to these Joint Escrow Instructions or any documents deposited with you.

11. Your responsibilities as Escrow Agent hereunder shall terminate if you shall cease to be Secretary of the Corporation or if you shall resign by written notice to each party. In the event of any such termination, the Corporation shall appoint any officer or assistant officer of the Corporation as successor Escrow Agent and Purchaser hereby confirms the appointment of such successor as his/her attorney-in-fact and agent to the full extent of your appointment.

12. If you reasonably require other or further instruments in connection with these Joint Escrow Instructions or obligations in respect hereto, the necessary parties hereto shall join in furnishing such instruments.

13. It is understood and agreed that should any dispute arise with respect to the delivery and/or ownership or right of possession of the securities held by you hereunder, you are authorized and directed to retain in your possession without liability to anyone all or any part of said securities until such dispute shall have been settled either by mutual written agreement of the parties concerned or by a final order, decree or judgment of a court of competent jurisdiction after the time for appeal has expired and no appeal has been perfected, but you shall be under no duty whatsoever to institute or defend any such proceedings.

14. Any notice required or permitted hereunder shall be given in writing and shall be deemed effectively given upon personal delivery, including delivery by express courier, or five (5) days after deposit in the United States Post Office, by registered or certified mail with postage and fees prepaid, addressed to each of the other parties entitled

BUSINESS STRUCTURES AND INCORPORATION

to such notice at the following addresses, or at such other addresses as a party may designate by ten (10) days' advance written notice to each of the other parties hereto.

CORPORATION: _____
_____
_____

PURCHASER: _____
_____
_____

ESCROW AGENT(S): _____
_____
_____

    15.   By signing these Joint Escrow Instructions, you become a party hereto only for the purpose of said Joint Escrow Instructions; you do not become a party to the Agreement.

    16.   You shall be entitled to employ such legal counsel and other experts as you may deem necessary to properly advise you in connection with your obligations hereunder. You may rely upon the advice of such counsel, and you may pay such counsel reasonable compensation therefore. The Corporation shall be responsible for all fees generated by such legal counsel in connection with your obligations hereunder.

    17.   This instrument shall be binding upon and inure to the benefit of the parties hereto and their respective successors and permitted assigns. It is understood and agreed that references to "you" and "your" herein refer to the original Escrow Agents. It is understood and agreed that the Corporation may at any time or from time to time assign its rights under the Agreement and these Joint Escrow Instructions.

    18.   This Agreement shall be governed by and interpreted and determined in accordance with the laws of the State of California, as such laws are applied by California courts to contracts made and to be performed entirely in California by residents of that state.

Very truly yours,

NAME OF CORPORATION

By _____

PURCHASER

_____

ESCROW AGENT(S):

_____

AND

_____

CORPORATE STOCK MATTERS

EXHIBIT B
STOCK ASSIGNMENT SEPARATE FROM CERTIFICATE

FOR VALUE RECEIVED, _____ hereby sells, assigns and transfers unto _____, a California corporation (the "Company"), pursuant to the Repurchase Option under that certain Founder Stock Purchase Agreement, dated _____ by and between the undersigned and the Company (the "Agreement"), _____ (_____) shares of Common Stock of the Company standing in the undersigned's name on the books of the Company represented by Certificate No. ____ and does hereby irrevocably constitute and appoint the Company's Secretary to transfer said stock on the books of the Company with full power of substitution in the premises. This Assignment may be used only in accordance with and subject to the terms and conditions of the Agreement, in connection with the repurchase of shares of Common Stock issued to the undersigned pursuant to the Agreement, and only to the extent that such shares remain subject to the Company's Repurchase Option under the Agreement.

Dated: _____, 20__

_____
(Signature)

_____
(Print Name)

EXHIBIT C
ELECTION UNDER SECTION 83(b)

Director of Internal Revenue
Internal Revenue Service
Fresno, CA 93888

Re: Election under Section 83(b) of the Internal Revenue Code of 1986, as amended

Gentlemen:

After consulting with, or having had the opportunity to consult with, my personal tax advisor this statement constitutes an election pursuant to Section 83(b) of the Internal Revenue Code of 1986, as amended from time to time (the "***Code***").

If this election also or only relates to the receipt of property from the exercise of an "incentive stock option" as defined in Section 422(b) of the Code, then the undersigned hereby elects, pursuant to the provisions of Sections 55-56 and 83(b) of the Code to include in alternative minimum taxable income for the undersigned's current taxable year, as compensation for services, the excess, if any, of the fair market value of that portion of the property described below that is property received from the exercise of an "incentive stock option" at the time of transfer over the amount paid for such property.

The undersigned also elects pursuant to Section 83(b) of the Code to include in gross income for the taxable year in which the undersigned disposes of some or all of the property described below that is property received from the exercise of an "incentive stock option" in a transaction which fails to satisfy the requirements of Section 422(a)(l) of the Code (a "disqualifying disposition"), as compensation for services, the excess, if any, of the fair market value of the disposed property at the time of transfer to the undersigned over the amount paid for such property.

BUSINESS STRUCTURES AND INCORPORATION

The undersigned intends that this election has the maximum permissible effect and only apply to property for which the election can be made. If the description of the property overstates the property that can be covered by this election, then this election shall only apply to that portion of the property described below for which this election can be made.

Pursuant to Treasury Regulation Section 1.83-2, the following information is submitted:

1. **Name:** _____

   Lesley Jones ("***Purchaser***")

   Address: _____

   123 Santana Row, #2343

   Social Security Number:

2. **Property Description:** _____ shares of Common Stock (the "***Stock***") of _____ (the "***Corporation***").

3. The date on which property was transferred is _____.

4. The taxable year for which the election is made is the calendar year 20__.

5. **Restrictions:** If, on or before _____, 20__ the employment of the Purchaser by the Corporation terminates for any reason, the Corporation shall have the option to repurchase some or all of the property (depending upon the date of such termination) for a price equal to the cost of the property repurchased.

6. The fair market value at the time of transfer of the Stock, determined without regard to any restriction other than a restriction which by its terms will never lapse, is _____ (_____ shares having a fair market value of _____ per share).

7. **Purchase Price:** _____ shares at _____ per share.

A copy of this statement has been furnished to the Corporation and the transferee of the Stock, if different than Purchaser.

Dated: _____, 20__

Very truly yours,

_____

Founders' Common Stock

As an additional consideration, in order to avoid possible adverse tax consequences, it is important to consummate the founders' Common Stock issuance well in advance of the issuance of any Preferred Stock to investors. The pricing of the founders' Common Stock could be put in issue if the proper documentation and payment of the purchase price of such stock is not done in a timely manner. Be advised that the pricing of the Common Stock is a matter requiring significant consideration and should be determined after discussion with your attorneys and accountants about factors involved in valuation of the Corporation's shares.

Section 83(b) Elections

Typically, the founders' Common Stock will be subject to vesting over a specified time period, with any unvested shares being subject to a repurchase option in favor of the Corporation. Certain tax consequences result from this arrangement. In many cases, it may produce advantageous tax consequences to the shareholder to file an election pursuant to Section 83(b) of the Code at the time of the stock purchase. Summarized briefly, if the taxpayer makes a proper and timely election, the taxpayer will not be taxed at the time the stock vests. Instead, the excess, if any, of the fair market value of the stock at the time of purchase over the purchase price will be ordinary income subject to tax in the year of purchase. The election must be filed within 30 days of purchase of the stock; no exceptions are allowed. If an election is not filed, a tax may be imposed at each vesting date, even if the taxpayer continues to hold the stock. Please consult either your attorney or personal tax advisor regarding any 83(b) election issues.

Additional Stock Issuances

If you decide to issue additional stock, or adopt employee stock purchase or option plans, care must be taken to comply with all federal and state laws, rules and regulations.

CHAPTER 12

CAPITAL STOCK STRUCTURES

Corporate capital comes from the issuance of many types of securities. The word security is used generically to describe many obligations, including equity obligations or shares of stock and debt obligations or bonds. A debt security (such as a bond) represents a creditor-debtor relationship with the corporation, whereby the corporation has borrowed funds from an outside creditor and promises to repay the creditor. The creditor is a lender rather than an owner. An equity security (such as a share of stock) is an instrument representing an investment in the corporation whereby its holder becomes a part owner of the business. Equity securities are shares of the corporation, and the investor is called a shareholder.

Debt Securities

Debt obligations, such as bonds, may be secured or unsecured (a debenture), and may be payable either to the holder of the bond (a bearer or coupon bond) or to the owner registered on the corporation's records (a registered bond). A debt obligation may also have special features; e.g., it may provide that it is convertible into equity securities at the option of the holder, or it might provide that the corporation may redeem the obligation at a specified price before the obligation matures.

Equity Securities – Shares

The shares described in the corporation's Articles of Incorporation are the authorized shares. Shares that have been sold to investors are issued shares. Shares that have been reacquired by the corporation from investors through either redemption or repurchase are deemed treasury shares under the

CAPITAL STOCK STRUCTURES

traditional approach, but under modern statutes such shares revert to authorized but unissued shares. If the shares are authorized in the Articles but there has been some irregularity in their issuance, the stock transaction may be rescinded or the defect may be cured by subsequent ratification.

If the shares in question were not authorized in the Articles, they would be void; and no subsequent ratification would help. In this case, any amount paid would be recoverable by the purchaser from the corporation.

Characteristics of Equity Securities

- ❖ Unless provided otherwise, shares give their holders the right to vote to elect directors and to approve extraordinary measures, the right to receive dividends when declared by the board, and the right to a share of the corporation's net assets if the corporation is dissolved.

- ❖ As stated above, equity securities represent an ownership interest in the corporation. A corporation may choose to issue only one type of shares, giving each shareholder an equal ownership right (in which case the shares are generally called common shares). Alternatively, ownership rights may be varied if the Articles provide that the corporation's stock is to be divided into classes or series within a class.

- ❖ Traditionally, the Articles of Incorporation would indicate whether the shares are to be issued with a stated par value or for no par value. Modern statutes, such as the Revised Model Business Corporation Act, have eliminated the concept of par value and allow shares to be issued for such consideration as the directors determine. The traditional distinction between par and no par stock involves the consideration required to be given for their purchase, the rates of capital franchise fees that must be paid upon incorporation, and the accounting classifications used in allocating the amount received in exchange for the shares. Many states still allow for an optional issuance of par value shares. The following is a brief review of the traditional concepts.

Subscriptions for Stock

Promises from subscribers to buy stock in the corporation are called subscription agreements. Subscription agreements are solicited in pre-incorporation activity (to be accepted when the corporation is formed) and are also used by existing corporations to sell new issues of stock. The rules governing acceptance and revocation differ between the pre-incorporation subscription agreement and a subscription agreement with an existing corporation.

Revocation and Acceptance

Judicially, a pre-incorporation share subscription is an offer to the corporation that does not become an enforceable contract until the corporation has accepted the offer. Until acceptance, the offer may be revoked. Most jurisdictions have enacted statutes regulating the revocability of pre-incorporation share subscriptions. Many states provide that pre-incorporation subscriptions are accepted by act of the board of directors (a board resolution), usually at the organizational meeting. Other states provide that the share subscriptions will be automatically accepted when the Articles of Incorporation are filed or when the Certificate of Incorporation is issued.

Subscriptions for shares of existing corporations are usually revocable at any time prior to acceptance. (Some jurisdictions, such as California – when a stock subscription is entered into after incorporation, it is an irrevocable contract obligating the corporation to issue and the subscriber to purchase the shares in question.) Subscriptions must be accepted by an act of the corporation, which normally is a resolution of the board of directors.

Contract of Sale

A post-incorporation agreement to sell stock may be interpreted as a contract of sale rather than a subscription. In a contract of sale, the corporation retains title to the stock until the full subscription price is paid. The intentions of the parties determine whether the agreement will be treated as a subscription or as a contract of sale. The purchaser does not attain shareholder status until all payments are made.

Payment

Unless otherwise provided in the subscription agreement, subscriptions for shares are payable on demand by the board of directors. In most jurisdictions, notice of the amount, time, and place of payment must be given personally, by mail, or by publication. Note, however, that once the subscription is accepted by the corporation, the subscriber becomes a shareholder. Consequently, he/she is entitled to vote and receive dividends, even though he/she has not yet paid for the stock or received the certificates.

Fraud as Defense

Where the stock subscription was induced by fraud, the subscriber may be able to have the transaction set aside. The corporation cannot take advantage of its

CAPITAL STOCK STRUCTURES

promoters' fraud. If the corporation accepted the subscription with knowledge of its fraudulent inducement, the subscriber may rescind the transaction or defend against any suit (by the corporation or its creditors) to enforce the subscription. If the promoters' fraud is not imputed to the corporation, the subscriber must pay for the stock; his/her only remedy is to sue the promoter for damages. Several states permit a fraud defense to be asserted at any time, but others cut off the defense after a reasonable time or after insolvency proceedings have been filed.

Consideration for Shares

Most state statutes prescribe certain rules for determining the amount and type of consideration that must be given in exchange for stock issued by a corporation.

Forms of Consideration

Under the traditional view, still followed by a large minority of states, shares being issued by the corporation may be paid for with: (i) money; (ii) tangible property; (iii) intangible property; and (iv) services already performed for the corporation. Modern statutes have expanded acceptable consideration to also include: (v) contracts for services to be performed; and (vi) promissory notes.

As between the corporation and the purchaser, shares issued in exchange for unlawful consideration are voidable. Such shares are subject to cancellation by the corporation or their issuance may be enjoined. Most courts hold that the corporation cannot cancel the shares if they have been transferred to a bona fide purchaser without notice of the unlawful consideration. If the corporation becomes insolvent, its creditors may be able to recover in cash the agreed price of shares purchased with improper consideration.

Amount of Consideration

The price at which the corporation will sell its shares is normally determined by the board of directors subject to the following rules:

- ❖ Generally, shares with par value may not be sold for less than par value. The par value of a share of stock is the amount, specified in the Articles of Incorporation that must be received by the corporation before the stock can be issued as fully paid.

- ❖ Shares without par value may be sold for any amount fixed by the board of directors, unless the Articles of Incorporation reserve the right to fix the consideration to the shareholders.

BUSINESS STRUCTURES AND INCORPORATION

❖ About half of the states still recognize treasury stock (shares issued and subsequently repurchased by the corporation). Treasury stock may be sold at any price fixed by the board, whether or not the shares have a par value.

Valuation of Property

If property is given in exchange for shares, the board of directors must determine the value of the property in good faith. Absent fraud, this good faith valuation is conclusive as to the adequacy of the consideration paid for shares and, thus, the shares are considered to be validly issued, fully paid, and non-assessable.

Unpaid Stock

Where a subscriber or shareholder has promised, but failed, to pay the corporation a fixed amount for a specified number of corporate shares, those shares are referred to as unpaid stock. The subscriber or shareholder may be liable to either the corporation or its creditors, but only for the consideration that the shareholder agreed to pay. Liability to the corporation is based on simple contract law and, absent fraud or misrepresentation, the subscriber or shareholder would normally have no defense. If the corporation is insolvent, the receiver or trustee in bankruptcy may enforce the corporation's contract claim.

Watered or Discount Stock

Although the concept of watered stock has been abolished by modern statutes such as the Revised Model Business Corporation Act, in states retaining the concept of par value, if the corporation issues par value stock for consideration worth less than the par value of the shares, the shares are considered watered. Of course, if the shareholder has given property in exchange for his/her shares, and the board of directors complies with the appropriate test in determining the value of the property to be in excess of the par value of the shares, there is no watered stock problem.

Regulation of Stock Transactions

There are two major pieces of securities legislation that regulate stock transactions: the Securities Act of 1933 and the Securities Exchange Act of 1934. The 1933 Act regulates original issuance of securities, while the 1934 Act regulates purchases and sales after initial issuance.

The courts have defined the term security very broadly so as to maximize the scope of the securities laws. A good rule of thumb for determining whether something is a security is to ask whether the investor expects to take part in the management of the business being invested in. If the investor is passive – i.e., is relying solely on the management of others – the investment most likely is a security. Thus, stocks, bonds, debentures, stock options, and stock warrants are considered securities.

The Securities Act of 1933

The Securities Act of 1933 regulates the original distribution of securities. Its goal is to assure that investors have sufficient information on which to make an informed investment decision. It accomplishes this goal by requiring most issuers to (i) register most new issues of securities with the Securities Exchange Commission and (ii) provide prospectuses containing material information regarding the securities to prospective investors.

The 1933 Act is targeted primarily at sales by issuers (entities whose securities are to be sold), underwriters (entities who undertake to sell the issuer's securities), and dealers (people who sell or trade securities on a full- or part-time basis).

Registration Requirement

As stated above, most securities cannot be sold unless they are first registered with the Securities Exchange Commission. The purpose of registration is to put on file all information that a reasonable investor would consider important in deciding whether to invest (e.g., a balance sheet and profit and loss statement, facts affecting the security's price or risk, remuneration of directors, etc.). The registration must include a copy of the statutory prospectus. The prospectus summarizes the detailed information required for registration and must be given to purchasers of the security prior to or contemporaneously with any sale.

Exemptions from the Registration Requirement

Not every sale of securities is covered by the 1933 Act. The Act is concerned only with sales by issuers, underwriters, or dealers. Other sales are casual sales and are not covered. The Act also has two other types of exemptions: securities exemptions (which exempt issuances of certain types of securities) and transaction exemptions (which exempt securities issued in certain types of transactions). For example, Section 3 of the 1933 Act specifically exempts certain securities, such as those issued by banks, governments, or charitable organizations. If a security qualifies for a securities exemption, it will continue to be exempt no matter how or when sold.

While the availability of securities exemptions (discussed above) depends primarily on the nature of the issuer, transaction exemptions depend on the nature of the offer. Transaction exemptions are specific to the transaction in question, so if the securities are reissued they have to be registered unless the reissuance itself qualifies for another exemption.

Civil Liabilities under the 1933 Act

Section 11 is perhaps the most important remedy under the 1933 Act. It potentially makes anyone who signs a registration statement liable for any damages caused by any misstatement of material fact in the registration statement. To bring a cause of action under section 11, a plaintiff need show only two things: (i) a material misstatement of fact in a registration statement signed by the defendant; and (ii) damages. Liability is extended to every person who signed the registration statement, every director, every expert who made a statement in the registration statement, and every underwriter.

Prospectuses and Communications

Section 12(a)(1) imposes liability upon any person who offers or sells a security in violation of the registration provisions, and section 12(a)(2) imposes liability upon any person who offers or sells a security by means of an untrue statement or omission of a material fact in a prospectus (here meaning most any written or oral communication, not just the statutory prospectus referred to above).

Safe Harbor for Forward Looking Statements

There is a safe harbor provision relieving issuers, persons acting on behalf of issuers (including underwriters passing on information from issuers), and outside reviewers (e.g., attorneys) from liability arising from forward looking statements (i.e., statements that set forth plans for the future or that project future economic performance). The safe harbor applies only in a private action for securities fraud based on an untrue statement or omission of material fact. Two forms of protection are provided: (1) The above persons cannot be found liable for forward looking statements unless the plaintiff can show that the statement was made with actual knowledge of its falsity. (2) Even if the plaintiff can show such knowledge, a protected person cannot be held liable if the forward looking statement is accompanied by a meaningful cautionary statement identifying factors that could cause results to differ materially from those in the statement. Note that the safe harbor is not available for statements made in connection with an initial public offering.

CAPITAL STOCK STRUCTURES

The Securities Act of 1934

Under rule 10b-5, it is unlawful for any person, directly or indirectly, by the use of any means or instrumentality of interstate commerce or the mails, or of any facility of any national securities exchange to: (i) employ any device, scheme, or artifice to defraud; (ii) make any untrue statement of a material fact or omit to state a material fact necessary in order to make the statements made, in light of the circumstances under which they were made, not misleading; or (iii) engage in any act, practice, or course of business that operates or would operate as a fraud or a deceit upon any person, in connection with the purchase or sale of any security. A violation of the rule can result in a private suit for damages, a Securities Exchange Commission suit for injunctive relief, or criminal prosecution.

General Elements of Cause of Action

A private plaintiff must show the following elements to recover damages under rule 10b-5:

- ❖ The plaintiff must show that the defendant engaged in some fraudulent conduct. This can take a number of forms, e.g., making a material misstatement or making a material omission;

- ❖ If the plaintiff is a private person, the fraudulent conduct must be connected to the purchase or sale of a security by the plaintiff. This includes transactions such as exchanges of stock for assets, mergers, contracts to sell, etc. It excludes potential purchasers who did not buy (because of the fraud) and people who already own shares and refrain from selling (because of the fraud);

- ❖ The fraudulent conduct must involve the use of some means of interstate commerce; something as simple as use of the telephone or the mail will suffice;

- ❖ A private plaintiff must prove that she relied on the defendant's fraudulent statement, omission, or conduct. But note that in cases based on omissions, reliance generally will be presumed if the plaintiff proves that the omission was material; and

- ❖ A private plaintiff must show that the defendant's fraud cause the plaintiff damages. Damages are limited to the difference between the price paid (or received) and the average share price in the 90-day period after corrective information is disseminated.

Insider Trading

While it may not be obvious, rule 10b-5's greatest impact is to prohibit most instances of trading securities on the basis of inside information (i.e., information not known by the general public and intended to be available only for business purposes and not for the personal benefit of anyone). The Court has adopted a rule that certain persons with inside information must either abstain from trading or disclose the information while trading (the abstain or disclose rule).

Special Relationship Required

Because rule 10b-5 is intended to curb deceit rather than mere unfairness, the duty to abstain or disclose does not apply to everyone with knowledge of inside information. Generally, there is a duty to disclose only where the person with the inside information has a fiduciary relationship with the issuer of the securities, such as a traditional insider (director, officer, manager, or other person in a confidential relationship with the company, such as banker, attorney, or accountant).

Where an insider gives a tip of inside information to someone else who trades on the basis of the inside information, the tipper can be liable under rule 10b-5 if the tip was made for any improper purpose (e.g., in exchange for money or a kickback, as a gift, for a reputational benefit, etc.). The tippee can be held liable only if the tipper breached a duty and the tippee knew that the tipper was breaching the duty.

Misappropriation Theory

In an action brought by the government, a person can be liable under rule 10b-5 for trading on market information (i.e., information about the supply of or demand for stock of a particular company) misappropriated from any source. The misappropriation need not breach a duty owed to the issuer or person with whom the mis-appropriator trades.

Inadvertent Discovery

As stated above, rule 10b-5 is aimed at curbing deceit rather than mere unfairness. Thus, no duty to disclose will be implied (i.e., there is no actionable insider trading) when a person inadvertently stumbles across inside information, such as when a person over hears material information at a restaurant and purchases or sells on the basis of the information.

CAPITAL STOCK STRUCTURES

Safe Harbor for Forward Looking Statements
There is a safe harbor provision under the 1934 Act for forward looking statements similar to the safe harbor provision for forward looking statements under the 1933 Act.

Section 16(b)
Section 16(b) of the Securities Exchange Act of 1934 provides that any profit realized by a director, officer, or shareholder owning 10% or more of the outstanding shares of the corporation from any purchase and sale, or sale and purchase, of any equity security of his corporation within a period of less than six months must be returned to the corporation. The section applies to publicly held corporations whose shares are traded on a national exchange or that have at least 500 shareholders in any outstanding class and at least $10 million in assets.

Strict Liability Imposed
The purpose of section 16(b) is to prevent unfair use of inside information and internal manipulation of price. This is accomplished by imposing strict liability for covered transactions whether or not there is any material fact that should or could have been disclosed. No proof of use of inside information is required.

Elements of Cause of Action
Section 16(b) applies only to profits from purchases and sales made within a six-month period. In most instances, it is easy to define a purchase or sale. However, there are some areas of corporate stock transactions – such as reclassification, conversion, and exercise of stock options – where the time and event of purchase or sale is uncertain. The test normally applied to determine whether there is a purchase or sale is whether this is the kind of transaction in which abuse of inside information is likely to occur.

- ❖ Section 16(b) applies only to purchases and sales of equity securities. An equity security is any security other than a pure debt instrument, including options, warrants, preferred stock, common stock, etc.

- ❖ Section 16(b) applies only to purchases and sales made by officers, directors, or 10% shareholders. Ordinarily, it is easy to identify the officers, directors, and 10% shareholders of a corporation. In some instances, however, a person may deputize another person to act as his representative on the board. In these cases, securities transactions of the principal will come within section 16(b).

- Purchases or sales made by persons before becoming an officer or director generally are excluded from the scope of section 16(b), because a person generally does not have access to the inside information sought to be protected from abuse under section 16(b) before becoming an officer or director. On the other hand, purchases and sales made within six months after ceasing to be an officer or director can come within section 16(b).

A person is a 10% shareholder if he/she directly or indirectly owns 10% of any class of equity security of the corporation at the time immediately before both the purchase and the sale. Thus, the purchase that brings a shareholder over the 10% threshold is not within the scope of section 16(b).

Profit Realized

The profit recoverable under section 16(b), known as short swing profits, includes not only traditional profits, but also losses avoided. Profit is determined by matching the highest sales price against the lowest purchase price during any six-month period. Remember that use of inside information is not material to this recovery.

CHAPTER 13

EMPLOYEE AND OTHER MATTERS

Independent Contractors

Whether an individual is an employee or contractor is a question of fact and depends on a number of criteria, irrespective of how the contract characterizes the relationship. In the event an independent contractor is determined to be an employee, the employer will, among other things, be liable for both its and the employee's income tax withholding obligations and for penalties if the contractor did not remit such amounts to the taxing authority, as well as for workers' compensation. Criteria of a "true" independent contractor relationship, includes:

- ❖ The contractor controls the manner and means by which it will complete the project(s), in contrast to an employee, who works under his/her employer's supervision as to manner and means (including set work hours).

- ❖ The contractor provides its own equipment, tools and other materials at its expense, whereas the employer usually provides such items for its employees.

- ❖ The contractor performs the services at a location, place and time which the contractor deems appropriate, while the employee typically works at the employer's site.

- ❖ The contractor works on a project basis in contrast to an employee, who is typically employed by the hour (non-exempt) or on a continuing salaried basis (exempt), irrespective of outstanding projects.

BUSINESS STRUCTURES AND INCORPORATION

The independent Contractor Services Agreement should typically be used for independent contractors who are providing programming and other technical services. Contractors which are providing non-technical content, such as graphic design, consulting or marketing services should enter into a Consulting Agreement, which is usually a shortened version of the independent contractor agreement.

Exempt Non-Exempt Determination

Both federal and state law assume that employees are non-exempt, that is, they are entitled to a minimum wage, specified rest breaks and meal periods and overtime compensation. In order to avoid these wage and hour requirements, an employer must establish that an employee meets one of the exemptions to the wage laws. To qualify as exempt, an employee must meet all of the criteria of one of the exemptions set forth in the federal Fair Labor Standards Act (FLSA) and applicable state wage and hour laws. The most common exemptions are the executive, administrative and professional exemptions, and exemptions for outside sales persons and computer professionals.

Employment Agreement

The following agreement is not intended to be comprehensive or an absolute statement of the governing law. This agreement is not legal advice. It does not analyze any specific fact patterns from any parties but rather discusses broadly points of law, which may or may not be the most accurate, according to current case law interpretation or even case law interpretation that is very in-depth on very narrowly-presented issues. Sound legal advice arises from interaction between client and attorney in a question-and-answer dialogue where facts are provided by a client as the attorney probes for issues and then conducts appropriate research if need be to ascertain the applicable law. Anyone seeking specific advice to specific legal questions should present their facts to an attorney.

[NAME OF COMPANY]
AT WILL EMPLOYMENT, CONFIDENTIAL INFORMATION, INVENTION ASSIGNMENT, AND ARBITRATION AGREEMENT

As a condition of my employment with [Name of Corporation], its subsidiaries, affiliates, successors or assigns (together the "Company"), and in consideration of my employment with the Company and my receipt of the compensation now and hereafter paid to me by Company, I agree to the following:

EMPLOYEE AND OTHER MATTERS

1. At-Will Employment.

I UNDERSTAND AND ACKNOWLEDGE THAT MY EMPLOYMENT WITH THE COMPANY IS FOR AN UNSPECIFIED DURATION AND CONSTITUTES "AT-WILL" EMPLOYMENT. I ALSO UNDERSTAND THAT ANY REPRESENTATION TO THE CONTRARY IS UNAUTHORIZED AND NOT VALID UNLESS OBTAINED IN WRITING AND SIGNED BY THE PRESIDENT OF THE COMPANY. I ACKNOWLEDGE THAT THIS EMPLOYMENT RELATIONSHIP MAY BE TERMINATED AT ANY TIME, WITH OR WITHOUT GOOD CAUSE OR FOR ANY OR NO CAUSE, AT THE OPTION EITHER OF THE COMPANY OR MYSELF, WITH OR WITHOUT NOTICE.

2. Confidential Information.

A. <u>Company Information</u>. I agree at all times during the term of my employment and thereafter, to hold in strictest confidence, and not to use, except for the benefit of the Company, or to disclose to any person, firm or corporation without written authorization of the Board of Directors of the Company, any Confidential Information of the Company, except under a non-disclosure agreement duly authorized and executed by the Company. I understand that "Confidential Information" means any non-public information that relates to the actual or anticipated business or research and development of the Company, technical data, trade secrets or know-how, including, but not limited to, research, product plans or other information regarding Company's products or services and markets therefor, customer lists and customers (including, but not limited to, customers of the Company on whom I called or with whom I became acquainted during the term of my employment), software, developments, inventions, processes, formulas, technology, designs, drawings, engineering, hardware configuration information, marketing, finances or other business information. I further understand that Confidential Information does not include any of the foregoing items which have become publicly known and made generally available through no wrongful act of mine or of others who were under confidentiality obligations as to the item or items involved or improvements or new versions thereof.

B. <u>Former Employer Information</u>. I agree that I will not, during my employment with the Company, improperly use or disclose any proprietary information or trade secrets of any former or concurrent employer or other person or entity and that I will not bring onto the premises of the Company any unpublished document or proprietary information belonging to any such employer, person or entity unless consented to in writing by such employer, person or entity.

C. <u>Third Party Information</u>. I recognize that the Company has received and in the future will receive from third parties their confidential or proprietary information subject to a duty on the Company's part to maintain the confidentiality of such information and to use it only for certain limited purposes. I agree to hold all such confidential or proprietary information in the strictest confidence and not to disclose it to any person, firm or corporation or to use it except as necessary in carrying out my work for the Company consistent with the Company's agreement with such third party.

3. Inventions.

A. <u>Inventions Retained and Licensed</u>. I have attached hereto, as <u>Exhibit A</u>, a list describing all inventions, original works of authorship, developments, improvements, and trade secrets which were made by me prior to my employment with the Company (collectively referred to as "Prior Inventions"), which belong to me, which relate to the Company's proposed business, products or research and development, and which are

BUSINESS STRUCTURES AND INCORPORATION

not assigned to the Company hereunder; or, if no such list is attached, I represent that there are no such Prior Inventions. If in the course of my employment with the Company, I incorporate into a Company product, process or service a Prior Invention owned by me or in which I have an interest, I hereby grant to the Company a nonexclusive, royalty-free, fully paid-up, irrevocable, perpetual, worldwide license to make, have made, modify, use and sell such Prior Invention as part of or in connection with such product, process or service, and to practice any method related thereto.

B. <u>Assignment of Inventions</u>. I agree that I will promptly make full written disclosure to the Company, will hold in trust for the sole right and benefit of the Company, and hereby assign to the Company, or its designee, all my right, title, and interest in and to any and all inventions, original works of authorship, developments, concepts, improvements, designs, discoveries, ideas, trademarks or trade secrets, whether or not patentable or registrable under copyright or similar laws, which I may solely or jointly conceive or develop or reduce to practice, or cause to be conceived or developed or reduced to practice, during the period of time I am in the employ of the Company (collectively referred to as "Inventions"), except as provided in Section 3.F below. I further acknowledge that all original works of authorship which are made by me (solely or jointly with others) within the scope of and during the period of my employment with the Company and which are protectable by copyright are "works made for hire," as that term is defined in the United States Copyright Act. I understand and agree that the decision whether or not to commercialize or market any invention developed by me solely or jointly with others is within the Company's sole discretion and for the Company's sole benefit and that no royalty will be due to me as a result of the Company's efforts to commercialize or market any such invention.

C. <u>Inventions Assigned to the United States</u>. I agree to assign to the United States government all my right, title, and interest in and to any and all Inventions whenever such full title is required to be in the United States by a contract between the Company and the United States or any of its agencies.

D. <u>Maintenance of Records</u>. I agree to keep and maintain adequate and current written records of all Inventions made by me (solely or jointly with others) during the term of my employment with the Company. The records will be in the form of notes, sketches, drawings, and any other format that may be specified by the Company. The records will be available to and remain the sole property of the Company at all times.

E. <u>Patent and Copyright Registrations</u>. I agree to assist the Company, or its designee, at the Company's expense, in every proper way to secure the Company's rights in the Inventions and any copyrights, patents, mask work rights or other intellectual property rights relating thereto in any and all countries, including the disclosure to the Company of all pertinent information and data with respect thereto, the execution of all applications, specifications, oaths, assignments and all other instruments which the Company shall deem necessary in order to apply for and obtain such rights and in order to assign and convey to the Company, its successors, assigns, and nominees the sole and exclusive rights, title and interest in and to such Inventions, and any copyrights, patents, mask work rights or other intellectual property rights relating thereto. I further agree that my obligation to execute or cause to be executed, when it is in my power to do so, any such instrument or papers shall continue after the termination of this Agreement. If the Company is unable because of my mental or physical incapacity or for any other reason to secure my signature to apply for or to pursue any application for any United States or foreign patents or copyright registrations

EMPLOYEE AND OTHER MATTERS

covering Inventions or original works of authorship assigned to the Company as above, then I hereby irrevocably designate and appoint the Company and its duly authorized officers and agents as my agent and attorney in fact, to act for and in my behalf and stead to execute and file any such applications and to do all other lawfully permitted acts to further the prosecution and issuance of letters patent or copyright registrations thereon with the same legal force and effect as if executed by me.

    F.   Exception to Assignments. I understand that the provisions of this Agreement requiring assignment of Inventions to the Company do not apply to any invention which qualifies fully under the provisions of California Labor Code Section 2870 (attached hereto as Exhibit B). I will advise the Company promptly in writing of any inventions that I believe meet the criteria in California Labor Code Section 2870 and not otherwise disclosed on Exhibit A.

4.   Conflicting Employment.

I agree that, during the term of my employment with the Company, I will not engage in any other employment, occupation or consulting directly related to the business in which the Company is now involved or becomes involved during the term of my employment, nor will I engage in any other activities that conflict with my obligations to the Company.

5.   Returning Company Documents.

I agree that, at the time of leaving the employ of the Company, I will deliver to the Company (and will not keep in my possession, recreate or deliver to anyone else) any and all devices, records, data, notes, reports, proposals, lists, correspondence, specifications, drawings blueprints, sketches, materials, equipment, other documents or property, or reproductions of any aforementioned items developed by me pursuant to my employment with the Company or otherwise belonging to the Company, its successors or assigns, including, without limitation, those records maintained pursuant to paragraph 3.D. In the event of the termination of my employment, I agree to sign and deliver the "Termination Certification" attached hereto as Exhibit C.

6.   Notification of New Employer.

In the event that I leave the employ of the Company, I hereby grant consent to notification by the Company to my new employer about my rights and obligations under this Agreement.

7.   Solicitation of Employees.

I agree that for a period of twelve (12) months immediately following the termination of my relationship with the Company for any reason, whether with or without cause, I shall not either directly or indirectly solicit, induce, recruit or encourage any of the Company's employees to leave their employment, or take away such employees, or attempt to solicit, induce, recruit, encourage or take away employees of the Company, either for myself or for any other person or entity.

8.   Conflict of Interest Guidelines.

I agree to diligently adhere to the Conflict of Interest Guidelines attached as Exhibit D hereto.

BUSINESS STRUCTURES AND INCORPORATION

9. **Representations.**

I agree to execute any proper oath or verify any proper document required to carry out the terms of this Agreement. I represent that my performance of all the terms of this Agreement will not breach any agreement to keep in confidence proprietary information acquired by me in confidence or in trust prior to my employment by the Company. I hereby represent and warrant that I have not entered into, and I will not enter into, any oral or written agreement in conflict herewith.

10. **Arbitration and Equitable Relief.**

A. Arbitration. IN CONSIDERATION OF MY EMPLOYMENT WITH THE COMPANY, ITS PROMISE TO ARBITRATE ALL EMPLOYMENT-RELATED DISPUTES AND MY RECEIPT OF THE COMPENSATION, PAY RAISES AND OTHER BENEFITS PAID TO ME BY THE COMPANY, AT PRESENT AND IN THE FUTURE, I AGREE THAT ANY AND ALL CONTROVERSIES, CLAIMS, OR DISPUTES WITH ANYONE (INCLUDING THE COMPANY AND ANY EMPLOYEE, OFFICER, DIRECTOR, SHAREHOLDER OR BENEFIT PLAN OF THE COMPANY IN THEIR CAPACITY AS SUCH OR OTHERWISE) ARISING OUT OF, RELATING TO, OR RESULTING FROM MY EMPLOYMENT WITH THE COMPANY OR THE TERMINATION OF MY EMPLOYMENT WITH THE COMPANY, INCLUDING ANY BREACH OF THIS AGREEMENT, SHALL BE SUBJECT TO BINDING ARBITRATION UNDER THE ARBITRATION RULES SET FORTH IN CALIFORNIA CODE OF CIVIL PROCEDURE SECTION 1280 THROUGH 1294.2, INCLUDING SECTION 1283.05 (THE "RULES") AND PURSUANT TO CALIFORNIA LAW. DISPUTES WHICH I AGREE TO ARBITRATE, AND THEREBY AGREE TO WAIVE ANY RIGHT TO A TRIAL BY JURY, INCLUDE ANY STATUTORY CLAIMS UNDER STATE OR FEDERAL LAW, INCLUDING, BUT NOT LIMITED TO, CLAIMS UNDER TITLE VII OF THE CIVIL RIGHTS ACT OF 1964, THE AMERICANS WITH DISABILITIES ACT OF 1990, THE AGE DISCRIMINATION IN EMPLOYMENT ACT OF 1967, THE OLDER WORKERS BENEFIT PROTECTION ACT, THE CALIFORNIA FAIR EMPLOYMENT AND HOUSING ACT, THE CALIFORNIA LABOR CODE, CLAIMS OF HARASSMENT, DISCRIMINATION OR WRONGFUL TERMINATION AND ANY STATUTORY CLAIMS. I FURTHER UNDERSTAND THAT THIS AGREEMENT TO ARBITRATE ALSO APPLIES TO ANY DISPUTES THAT THE COMPANY MAY HAVE WITH ME.

B. Procedure. I AGREE THAT ANY ARBITRATION WILL BE ADMINISTERED BY THE AMERICAN ARBITRATION ASSOCIATION ("AAA") AND THAT THE NEUTRAL ARBITRATOR WILL BE SELECTED IN A MANNER CONSISTENT WITH ITS NATIONAL RULES FOR THE RESOLUTION OF EMPLOYMENT DISPUTES. I AGREE THAT THE ARBITRATOR SHALL HAVE THE POWER TO DECIDE ANY MOTIONS BROUGHT BY ANY PARTY TO THE ARBITRATION, INCLUDING MOTIONS FOR SUMMARY JUDGMENT AND/OR ADJUDICATION AND MOTIONS TO DISMISS AND DEMURRERS, PRIOR TO ANY ARBITRATION HEARING. I ALSO AGREE THAT THE ARBITRATOR SHALL HAVE THE POWER TO AWARD ANY REMEDIES, INCLUDING ATTORNEYS' FEES AND COSTS, AVAILABLE UNDER APPLICABLE LAW. I UNDERSTAND THE COMPANY WILL PAY FOR ANY ADMINISTRATIVE OR HEARING FEES CHARGED BY THE ARBITRATOR OR AAA EXCEPT THAT I

EMPLOYEE AND OTHER MATTERS

SHALL PAY THE FIRST $200.00 OF ANY FILING FEES ASSOCIATED WITH ANY ARBITRATION I INITIATE. I AGREE THAT THE ARBITRATOR SHALL ADMINISTER AND CONDUCT ANY ARBITRATION IN A MANNER CONSISTENT WITH THE RULES AND THAT TO THE EXTENT THAT THE AAA'S NATIONAL RULES FOR THE RESOLUTION OF EMPLOYMENT DISPUTES CONFLICT WITH THE RULES, THE RULES SHALL TAKE PRECEDENCE. I AGREE THAT THE DECISION OF THE ARBITRATOR SHALL BE IN WRITING.

C. Remedy. EXCEPT AS PROVIDED BY THE RULES AND THIS AGREEMENT, ARBITRATION SHALL BE THE SOLE, EXCLUSIVE AND FINAL REMEDY FOR ANY DISPUTE BETWEEN ME AND THE COMPANY. ACCORDINGLY, EXCEPT AS PROVIDED FOR BY THE RULES AND THIS AGREEMENT, NEITHER I NOR THE COMPANY WILL BE PERMITTED TO PURSUE COURT ACTION REGARDING CLAIMS THAT ARE SUBJECT TO ARBITRATION. NOTWITHSTANDING, THE ARBITRATOR WILL NOT HAVE THE AUTHORITY TO DISREGARD OR REFUSE TO ENFORCE ANY LAWFUL COMPANY POLICY, AND THE ARBITRATOR SHALL NOT ORDER OR REQUIRE THE COMPANY TO ADOPT A POLICY NOT OTHERWISE REQUIRED BY LAW WHICH THE COMPANY HAS NOT ADOPTED.

D. Availability of Injunctive Relief. IN ADDITION TO THE RIGHT UNDER THE RULES TO PETITION THE COURT FOR PROVISIONAL RELIEF, I AGREE THAT ANY PARTY MAY ALSO PETITION THE COURT FOR INJUNCTIVE RELIEF WHERE EITHER PARTY ALLEGES OR CLAIMS A VIOLATION OF THE EMPLOYMENT, CONFIDENTIAL INFORMATION, INVENTION ASSIGNMENT AGREEMENT BETWEEN ME AND THE COMPANY OR ANY OTHER AGREEMENT REGARDING TRADE SECRETS, CONFIDENTIAL INFORMATION, NONSOLICITATION OR LABOR CODE SECTION 2870. I UNDERSTAND THAT ANY BREACH OR THREATENED BREACH OF SUCH AN AGREEMENT WILL CAUSE IRREPARABLE INJURY AND THAT MONEY DAMAGES WILL NOT PROVIDE AN ADEQUATE REMEDY THEREFOR AND BOTH PARTIES HEREBY CONSENT TO THE ISSUANCE OF AN INJUNCTION. IN THE EVENT EITHER PARTY SEEKS INJUNCTIVE RELIEF, THE PREVAILING PARTY SHALL BE ENTITLED TO RECOVER REASONABLE COSTS AND ATTORNEYS FEES.

E. Administrative Relief. I UNDERSTAND THAT THIS AGREEMENT DOES NOT PROHIBIT ME FROM PURSUING AN ADMINISTRATIVE CLAIM WITH A LOCAL, STATE OR FEDERAL ADMINISTRATIVE BODY SUCH AS THE DEPARTMENT OF FAIR EMPLOYMENT AND HOUSING, THE EQUAL EMPLOYMENT OPPORTUNITY COMMISSION OR THE WORKERS' COMPENSATION BOARD. THIS AGREEMENT DOES, HOWEVER, PRECLUDE ME FROM PURSUING COURT ACTION REGARDING ANY SUCH CLAIM.

F. Voluntary Nature of Agreement. I ACKNOWLEDGE AND AGREE THAT I AM EXECUTING THIS AGREEMENT VOLUNTARILY AND WITHOUT ANY DURESS OR UNDUE INFLUENCE BY THE COMPANY OR ANYONE ELSE. I FURTHER ACKNOWLEDGE AND AGREE THAT I HAVE CAREFULLY READ THIS AGREEMENT AND THAT I HAVE ASKED ANY

BUSINESS STRUCTURES AND INCORPORATION

QUESTIONS NEEDED FOR ME TO UNDERSTAND THE TERMS, CONSEQUENCES AND BINDING EFFECT OF THIS AGREEMENT AND FULLY UNDERSTAND IT, INCLUDING THAT *I AM WAIVING MY RIGHT TO A JURY TRIAL*. FINALLY, I AGREE THAT I HAVE BEEN PROVIDED AN OPPORTUNITY TO SEEK THE ADVICE OF AN ATTORNEY OF MY CHOICE BEFORE SIGNING THIS AGREEMENT.

11. General Provisions.

    A.   Governing Law; Consent to Personal Jurisdiction. This Agreement will be governed by the laws of the State of California. I hereby expressly consent to the personal jurisdiction of the state and federal courts located in California for any lawsuit filed there against me by the Company arising from or relating to this Agreement.

    B.   Entire Agreement. This Agreement sets forth the entire agreement and understanding between the Company and me relating to the subject matter herein and supersedes all prior discussions or representations between us including, but not limited to, any representations made during my interview(s) or relocation negotiations, whether written or oral. No modification of or amendment to this Agreement, nor any waiver of any rights under this Agreement, will be effective unless in writing signed by the President of the Company and me. Any subsequent change or changes in my duties, salary or compensation will not affect the validity or scope of this Agreement.

    C.   Severability. If one or more of the provisions in this Agreement are deemed void by law, then the remaining provisions will continue in full force and effect.

    D.   Successors and Assigns. This Agreement will be binding upon my heirs, executors, administrators and other legal representatives and will be for the benefit of the Company, its successors, and its assigns.

Date: _____   _____
                                                              Signature

                                                             _____
                                                             Print Name

Exhibit A

LIST OF PRIOR INVENTIONS
AND ORIGINAL WORKS OF AUTHORSHIP

___ No inventions or improvements
___ Additional Sheets Attached

Signature of Employee: _____
Print Name of Employee: _____
Date: _____

EMPLOYEE AND OTHER MATTERS

Exhibit B
CALIFORNIA LABOR CODE SECTION 2870
INVENTION ON OWN TIME-EXEMPTION FROM AGREEMENT

"(a) Any provision in an employment agreement which provides that an employee shall assign, or offer to assign, any of his or her rights in an invention to his/her employer shall not apply to an invention that the employee developed entirely on his/her own time without using the employer's equipment, supplies, facilities, or trade secret information except for those inventions that either:

(1) Relate at the time of conception or reduction to practice of the invention to the employer's business, or actual or demonstrably anticipated research or development of the employer; or

(2) Result from any work performed by the employee for the employer.

(b) To the extent a provision in an employment agreement purports to require an employee to assign an invention otherwise excluded from being required to be assigned under subdivision (a), the provision is against the public policy of this state and is unenforceable."

Exhibit C
[NAME OF COMPANY]
TERMINATION CERTIFICATION

This is to certify that I do not have in my possession, nor have I failed to return, any devices, records, data, notes, reports, proposals, lists, correspondence, specifications, drawings, blueprints, sketches, materials, equipment, other documents or property, or reproductions of any aforementioned items belonging to _____, its subsidiaries, affiliates, successors or assigns (together, the "Company").

I further certify that I have complied with all the terms of the Company's Employment, Confidential Information, Invention Assignment and Arbitration Agreement signed by me, including the reporting of any inventions and original works of authorship (as defined therein), conceived or made by me (solely or jointly with others) covered by that agreement.

I further agree that, in compliance with the Employment, Confidential Information, Invention Assignment, and Arbitration Agreement, I will preserve as confidential all trade secrets, confidential knowledge, data or other proprietary information relating to products, processes, know-how, designs, formulas, developmental or experimental work, computer programs, data bases, other original works of authorship, customer lists, business plans, financial information or other subject matter pertaining to any business of the Company or any of its employees, associates, consultants or licensees.

I further agree that for twelve (12) months from this date, I will not solicit, induce, recruit or encourage any of the Company's employees to leave their employment.

Date: _____   _____
                                                                         [Employee's Signature]

                                                                         _____

                                                                         [Print Name]

BUSINESS STRUCTURES AND INCORPORATION

<u>Exhibit D</u>
**[NAME OF COMPANY]
CONFLICT OF INTEREST GUIDELINES**

It is the policy _____ to conduct its affairs in strict compliance with the letter and spirit of the law and to adhere to the highest principles of business ethics. Accordingly, all officers, employees and independent contractors must avoid activities which are in conflict, or give the appearance of being in conflict, with these principles and with the interests of the Company. The following are potentially compromising situations which must be avoided. Any exceptions must be reported to the President and written approval for continuation must be obtained.

1. Revealing confidential information to outsiders or misusing confidential information. Unauthorized divulging of information is a violation of this policy whether or not for personal gain and whether or not harm to the Company is intended. (The At Will Employment, Confidential Information, Invention Assignment and Arbitration Agreement elaborates on this principle and is a binding agreement.)

2. Accepting or offering substantial gifts, excessive entertainment, favors or payments which may be deemed to constitute undue influence or otherwise be improper or embarrassing to the Company.

3. Participating in civic or professional organizations that might involve divulging confidential information of the Company.

4. Initiating or approving personnel actions affecting reward or punishment of employees or applicants where there is a family relationship or is or appears to be a personal or social involvement.

5. Initiating or approving any form of personal or social harassment of employees.

6. Investing or holding outside directorship in suppliers, customers, or competing companies, including financial speculations, where such investment or directorship might influence in any manner a decision or course of action of the Company.

7. Borrowing from or lending to employees, customers or suppliers.

8. Acquiring real estate of interest to the Company.

9. Improperly using or disclosing to the Company any proprietary information or trade secrets of any former or concurrent employer or other person or entity with whom obligations of confidentiality exist.

10. Unlawfully discussing prices, costs, customers, sales or markets with competing companies or their employees.

11. Making any unlawful agreement with distributors with respect to prices.

12. Improperly using or authorizing the use of any inventions which are the subject of patent claims of any other person or entity.

13. Engaging in any conduct which is not in the best interest of the Company.

Each officer, employee and independent contractor must take every necessary action to ensure compliance with these guidelines and to bring problem areas to the attention of higher management for review. Violations of this conflict of interest policy may result in discharge without warning.

EMPLOYEE AND OTHER MATTERS

Indemnity Agreement

The following agreement is not intended to be comprehensive or an absolute statement of the governing law. This agreement is not legal advice. It does not analyze any specific fact patterns from any parties but rather discusses broadly points of law, which may or may not be the most accurate, according to current case law interpretation or even case law interpretation that is very in-depth on very narrowly-presented issues. Sound legal advice arises from interaction between party and attorney in a question-and-answer dialogue where facts are provided by a party as the attorney probes for issues and then conducts appropriate research if need be to ascertain the applicable law. Anyone seeking specific advice to specific legal questions should present their facts to an attorney.

SAMPLE INDEMNITY AGREEMENT

THIS AGREEMENT is made and entered into this ___ day of _____, 20__ by and between **[NAME OF CORPORATION]**, a California corporation (the "*Corporation*"), and _____ ("*Agent*").

RECITALS

WHEREAS, Agent performs a valuable service to the Corporation in his/her capacity as a/an **[director/officer]** of the Corporation;

WHEREAS, the shareholders of the Corporation have adopted Bylaws (the "*Bylaws*") providing for the indemnification of the directors, officers, employees and other agents of the Corporation, including persons serving at the request of the Corporation in such capacities with other corporations or enterprises, as authorized by the California General Corporation Law, as amended (the "*Code*");

WHEREAS, the Bylaws and the Code, by their non-exclusive nature, permit contracts between the Corporation and its agents, officers, employees and other agents with respect to indemnification of such persons; and

WHEREAS, in order to induce Agent to serve as a/an **[director/officer]** of the Corporation, the Corporation has determined and agreed to enter into this Agreement with Agent;

NOW, THEREFORE, in consideration of Agent's service as a/an **[director/officer]** after the date hereof, the parties hereto agree as follows:

AGREEMENT

1. **Services to the Corporation.** Agent will serve, at the will of the Corporation or under separate contract, if any such contract exists, as a/an **[director/officer]** of the Corporation or as a director, officer or other fiduciary of an affiliate of the Corporation (including any employee benefit plan of the Corporation) faithfully and to the best of Agent's ability so long as Agent **[is duly elected and qualified in accordance with the provisions of the Bylaws or other applicable charter documents/is a duly appointed officer]** of the Corporation or such affiliate; *provided, however,* that Agent may at any time and for any reason resign from such position (subject to

any contractual obligation that Agent may have assumed apart from this Agreement) and that the Corporation or any affiliate shall have no obligation under this Agreement to continue Agent in any such position.

2. **Indemnity of Agent.** The Corporation hereby agrees to hold harmless and indemnify Agent to the fullest extent authorized or permitted by the provisions of the Bylaws and the Code, as the same may be amended from time to time (but, only to the extent that such amendment permits the Corporation to provide broader indemnification rights than the Bylaws or the Code permitted prior to adoption of such amendment).

3. **Additional Indemnity.** In addition to and not in limitation of the indemnification otherwise provided for herein, and subject only to the exclusions set forth in Section 4 hereof, the Corporation hereby further agrees to hold harmless and indemnify Agent:

(a) against any and all expenses (including attorneys' fees), witness fees, damages, judgments, fines and amounts paid in settlement and any other amounts that Agent becomes legally obligated to pay because of any claim or claims made against or by Agent in connection with any threatened, pending or completed action, suit or proceeding, whether civil, criminal, arbitrational, administrative or investigative (including an action by or in the right of the Corporation) to which Agent is, was or at any time becomes a party, or is threatened to be made a party, by reason of the fact that Agent is, was or at any time becomes a director, officer, employee or other agent of Corporation, or is or was serving or at any time serves at the request of the Corporation as a director, officer, employee or other agent of another corporation, partnership, joint venture, trust, employee benefit plan or other enterprise; and

(b) otherwise to the fullest extent as may be provided to Agent by the Corporation under the non-exclusivity provisions of the Code and Section 43 of the Bylaws.

4. **Limitations on Additional Indemnity.** No indemnity pursuant to Section 3 hereof shall be paid by the Corporation:

(a) on account of any claim against Agent for an accounting of profits made from the purchase or sale by Agent of securities of the Corporation pursuant to the provisions of Section 16(b) of the Securities Exchange Act of 1934 and amendments thereto or similar provisions of any federal, state or local statutory law;

(b) on account of Agent's conduct that is established by a final judgment as knowingly fraudulent or deliberately dishonest or that constituted willful misconduct;

(c) on account of Agent's conduct that is established by a final judgment as constituting a breach of Agent's duty of loyalty to the Corporation or resulting in any personal profit or advantage to which Agent was not legally entitled;

(d) for which payment is actually made to Agent under a valid and collectible insurance policy or under a valid and enforceable indemnity clause, bylaw or agreement, except in respect of any excess beyond payment under such insurance, clause, bylaw or agreement;

(e) if indemnification is not lawful (and, in this respect, both the Corporation and Agent have been advised that the Securities and Exchange Commission believes that indemnification for liabilities arising under the federal securities laws is against public policy and is, therefore, unenforceable and that claims for indemnification should be submitted to appropriate courts for adjudication); or

EMPLOYEE AND OTHER MATTERS

(f) in connection with any proceeding (or part thereof) initiated by Agent, or any proceeding by Agent against the Corporation or its directors, officers, employees or other agents, unless (i) such indemnification is expressly required to be made by law, (ii) the proceeding was authorized by the Board of Directors of the Corporation, (iii) such indemnification is provided by the Corporation, in its sole discretion, pursuant to the powers vested in the Corporation under the Code, or (iv) the proceeding is initiated pursuant to Section 9 hereof.

 5. **Continuation of Indemnity.** All agreements and obligations of the Corporation contained herein shall continue during the period Agent is a director, officer, employee or other agent of the Corporation (or is or was serving at the request of the Corporation as a director, officer, employee or other agent of another corporation, partnership, joint venture, trust, employee benefit plan or other enterprise) and shall continue thereafter so long as Agent shall be subject to any possible claim or threatened, pending or completed action, suit or proceeding, whether civil, criminal, arbitrational, administrative or investigative, by reason of the fact that Agent was serving in the capacity referred to herein.

 6. **Partial Indemnification.** Agent shall be entitled under this Agreement to indemnification by the Corporation for a portion of the expenses (including attorneys' fees), witness fees, damages, judgments, fines and amounts paid in settlement and any other amounts that Agent becomes legally obligated to pay in connection with any action, suit or proceeding referred to in Section 3 hereof even if not entitled hereunder to indemnification for the total amount thereof, and the Corporation shall indemnify Agent for the portion thereof to which Agent is entitled.

 7. **Notification and Defense of Claim.** Not later than thirty (30) days after Agent becomes aware, by written or other overt communication, of any pending or threatened litigation, claim or assessment, Agent will, if a claim in respect thereof is to be made against the Corporation under this Agreement, notify the Corporation of such pending or threatened litigation, claim or assessment; but the omission so to notify the Corporation will not relieve it from any liability which it may have to Agent otherwise than under this Agreement. With respect to any such pending or threatened litigation, claim or assessment as to which Agent notifies the Corporation of the commencement thereof:

 (a) the Corporation will be entitled to participate therein at its own expense;

 (b) except as otherwise provided below, the Corporation may, at its option and jointly with any other indemnifying party similarly notified and electing to assume such defense, assume the defense thereof, with counsel reasonably satisfactory to Agent. After notice from the Corporation to Agent of its election to assume the defense thereof, the Corporation will not be liable to Agent under this Agreement for any legal or other expenses subsequently incurred by Agent in connection with the defense thereof except for reasonable costs of investigation or otherwise as provided below. Agent shall have the right to employ separate counsel in such action, suit or proceeding but the fees and expenses of such counsel incurred after notice from the Corporation of its assumption of the defense thereof shall be at the expense of Agent unless (i) the employment of counsel by Agent has been authorized by the Corporation, (ii) Agent shall have reasonably concluded, and so notified the Corporation, that there is an actual conflict of interest between the Corporation and Agent in the conduct of the defense of such action or (iii) the Corporation shall not in fact have employed counsel to assume the defense of such action, in each of which cases the fees and expenses of Agent's separate counsel shall be at the expense of the Corporation. The Corporation shall not be entitled to assume the defense of any action, suit or proceeding brought by or on behalf of the Corporation or as to which Agent shall have made the conclusion provided for in clause (ii) above; and

(c) the Corporation shall not be liable to indemnify Agent under this Agreement for any amounts paid in settlement of any action or claim effected without its written consent, which shall not be unreasonably withheld. The Corporation shall be permitted to settle any action or claim except that it shall not settle any action or claim in any manner which would impose any penalty or limitation on Agent without Agent's written consent, which may be given or withheld in Agent's sole discretion.

8. **Expenses.** The Corporation shall advance, prior to the final disposition of any proceeding, promptly following request therefor, all expenses incurred by Agent in connection with such proceeding upon receipt of an undertaking by or on behalf of Agent to repay said amounts if it shall be determined ultimately that Agent is not entitled to be indemnified under the provisions of this Agreement, the Bylaws, the Code or otherwise.

9. **Enforcement.** Any right to indemnification or advances granted by this Agreement to Agent shall be enforceable by or on behalf of Agent in any court of competent jurisdiction if (i) the claim for indemnification or advances is denied, in whole or in part, or (ii) no disposition of such claim is made within ninety (90) days of request therefor. Agent, in such enforcement action, if successful in whole or in part, shall be entitled to be paid also the expense of prosecuting Agent's claim. It shall be a defense to any action for which a claim for indemnification is made under Section 3 hereof (other than an action brought to enforce a claim for expenses pursuant to Section 8 hereof, *provided that* the required undertaking has been tendered to the Corporation) that Agent is not entitled to indemnification because of the limitations set forth in Section 4 hereof. Neither the failure of the Corporation (including its Board of Directors or its shareholders) to have made a determination prior to the commencement of such enforcement action that indemnification of Agent is proper in the circumstances, nor an actual determination by the Corporation (including its Board of Directors or its shareholders) that such indemnification is improper shall be a defense to the action or create a presumption that Agent is not entitled to indemnification under this Agreement or otherwise.

10. **Subrogation.** In the event of payment under this Agreement, the Corporation shall be subrogated to the extent of such payment to all of the rights of recovery of Agent, who shall execute all documents required and shall do all acts that may be necessary to secure such rights and to enable the Corporation effectively to bring suit to enforce such rights.

11. **Non-Exclusivity of Rights.** The rights conferred on Agent by this Agreement shall not be exclusive of any other right which Agent may have or hereafter acquire under any statute, provision of the Corporation's Articles of Incorporation or Bylaws, agreement, vote of stockholders or directors, or otherwise, both as to action in Agent's official capacity and as to action in another capacity while holding office.

EMPLOYEE AND OTHER MATTERS

12. Survival of Rights.

(a) The rights conferred on Agent by this Agreement shall continue after Agent has ceased to be a director, officer, employee or other agent of the Corporation or to serve at the request of the Corporation as a director, officer, employee or other agent of another corporation, partnership, joint venture, trust, employee benefit plan or other enterprise and shall inure to the benefit of Agent's heirs, executors and administrators.

(b) The Corporation shall require any successor (whether direct or indirect, by purchase, merger, consolidation or otherwise) to all or substantially all of the business or assets of the Corporation, expressly to assume and agree to perform this Agreement in the same manner and to the same extent that the Corporation would be required to perform if no such succession had taken place.

13. Separability. Each of the provisions of this Agreement is a separate and distinct agreement and independent of the others, so that if any provision hereof shall be held to be invalid for any reason, such invalidity or unenforceability shall not affect the validity or enforceability of the other provisions hereof. Furthermore, if this Agreement shall be invalidated in its entirety on any ground, then the Corporation shall nevertheless indemnify Agent to the fullest extent provided by the Bylaws, the Code or any other applicable law.

14. Governing Law. This Agreement shall be interpreted and enforced in accordance with the laws of the State of California.

15. Amendment and Termination. No amendment, modification, termination or cancellation of this Agreement shall be effective unless in writing signed by both parties hereto.

16. Identical Counterparts. This Agreement may be executed in one or more counterparts, each of which shall for all purposes be deemed to be an original but all of which together shall constitute but one and the same Agreement. Only one such counterpart need be produced to evidence the existence of this Agreement.

17. Headings. The headings of the sections of this Agreement are inserted for convenience only and shall not be deemed to constitute part of this Agreement or to affect the construction hereof.

18. Notices. All notices, requests, demands and other communications hereunder shall be in writing and shall be deemed to have been duly given (i) upon delivery if delivered by hand to the party to whom such communication was directed or (ii) upon the third business day after the date on which such communication was mailed if mailed by certified or registered mail with postage prepaid: (a) if to Agent, at the address indicated on the signature page hereof, and (b) if to the Corporation, to _____, or (c) to such other address as may have been furnished to Agent by the Corporation.

19. Entire Agreement. This Agreement constitutes the full and complete agreement of the Corporation and Agent and supersedes all prior written or oral agreements between the parties with respect to the Corporation's indemnification of Agent.

BUSINESS STRUCTURES AND INCORPORATION

IN WITNESS WHEREOF, the parties hereto have executed this Agreement on and as of the day and year first above written.

[NAME OF CORPORATION]
By: _____
AGENT

_____
[Name]
Address:

_____
_____

Workers' Compensation

Almost every California employer is subject to the state workers' compensation laws, even if it has only one part-time employee. The coverage is provided by an authorized issuer, and you should make arrangements with your insurance agent. For additional information, you should get in touch with the State Compensation Insurance Fund.

Other Labor Laws

Discussion of all laws and regulations governing wages and conditions of employment is beyond the scope of this book; a few of the more important are noted. These matters may also be governed by union contracts. In addition, employers are required to post a number of notices regarding employees' rights. For example, some of the notices most commonly required in the state of California, and the agencies from which copies may be obtained, are:

- ❖ Industrial Welfare Commission Orders – California Department of Industrial Relations, Division of Labor Standards Enforcement.
- ❖ Federal minimum wage notice – Wage and Hour Division, United States Department of Labor.
- ❖ A notice entitled "Safety and Health Protection on the Job" – California Department of Industrial Relations, Division of Occupational Safety and Health.
- ❖ A notice regarding the Fair Employment and Housing Act – California Fair Employment and Housing Commission.
- ❖ Federal civil rights notices – United States Equal Opportunity Commission.

- ❖ A notice of paydays and time and place of payment – California Department of Industrial Relations.

- ❖ Workers' compensation notices – California Employment Development Department.

- ❖ Unemployment insurance and disability compensation notice – California Employment Development Department.

The Immigration Reform and Control Act of 1986 requires that employers verify employment eligibility (generally American citizens and aliens who are authorized to work in the United States) of anyone hired after November 8, 1986 and complete and retain a form entitled "Employment Eligibility Verification" (Form I-9). Additional information, including instructions for completing Form I-9, can be obtained from the local office of the U.S. Immigration and Naturalization Service.

The California Fair Employment Practices Act, Title VII of the federal Civil Rights Act and the federal Age Discrimination in Employment Act of 1967 regulate discrimination in hiring practices. The federal Fair Labor Standards Act of 1938, as amended, sets the minimum wages that apply to practically all employees who are engaged in interstate commerce, with exemptions for executive, administrative and professional personnel and outside sales persons. If the person in charge of hiring and firing employees and negotiating wages fails to see that the required minimum wages are paid, he/she may be personally liable.

In addition, the officers and directors of the Corporation should bear in mind that employees in California are bringing claims, including wrongful discharge suits, against employers in unprecedented numbers. Officers and directors of the corporation should be cautious when making representations, either orally or in writing, to employees or prospective employees.

Insurance

As you have probably considered, the corporation should obtain standard insurance coverage for anticipated contingencies. The corporation's coverage may include general liability insurance, fire and casualty insurance, automobile insurance, business interruption insurance, key-personnel death and disability insurance and workers' compensation insurance.

As an employer, the corporation may be subject to California workers' compensation laws. These laws impose liability on employers for certain job-related accidents, regardless of the employer's or employee's negligence, and provide a schedule of benefits to be paid to the injured employee. These laws may require the corporation either to be insured against workers' compensation liability by an authorized insurer or to obtain from the Director of Industrial Relations a Certificate of Consent to Self-Insure. The required insurance may be obtained through the nearest local offices of the State Compensation Insurance Fund, or it may be placed with a licensed workers' compensation private carrier. There are penalties for noncompliance.

There are certain other employee benefit actions which should be considered such as the acquisition of group life and medical insurance, directors' and officers' liability insurance and the adoption of deferred compensation and retirement programs.

Employment Litigation Risk Management

In today's legal climate, you cannot entirely eliminate the risk that your company will be sued by an employee or former employee. You can, however, take steps to reduce that risk and increase your chances of winning any lawsuit. Take steps now to prevent litigation. If you wait until your company is sued, you're too late. Moreover, the steps you take may also increase the productivity of your workforce and decrease turnover.

Recruiting and Hiring

- ❖ **Target the appropriate candidates**. Make sure all recruiting materials accurately describe job requirements and omit non job-related criteria.

- ❖ **Review your application form**. Make sure the application does not ask for information identifying protected characteristics such as age, race, religion, national origin, gender, disability, sexual orientation or marital status.

- ❖ **Interview wisely**. Avoid questions that may elicit information regarding protected characteristics. Ask only about the applicant's ability to perform the essential functions of the job.

- ❖ **Know the applicant**. Check references and other relevant background information.

- ❖ **Implement an at-will employment policy**. Include at-will language in all employment applications, offer letters, employment agreements, confidentiality agreements, stock option agreements, employee handbooks and proprietary information agreements.

- ❖ **Standardize your documents.** Coordinate offer letters and all other forms of employment-related agreements with your Human Resources department. Use confidentiality agreements to protect proprietary information. Seek advice from legal counsel.

- ❖ **Be consistent.** Make sure all written and oral statements regarding the terms and conditions of employment are consistent. Don't make promises you can't keep.

Maintaining the At-Will Relationship

- ❖ **Review employment policies.** Review and update all existing policies and handbooks. Make sure all policies are consistent with the at-will relationship.

- ❖ **Review personnel files.** Confirm that all employees have completed and signed appropriate employee agreements and acknowledgement forms that contain at-will language.

- ❖ **Maintain flexibility.** Don't commit to a specific progressive discipline policy. Keep any policy flexible and discretionary.

- ❖ **Train your managers.** Managers must know and understand Company policies and procedures, and apply them consistently. Educate your managers about the dangers of making promises they do not have the authority or ability to keep.

Evaluating Employee Performance

- ❖ **Be timely.** Establish a performance review schedule and stick to it.

- ❖ **Be honest.** Give the good news and the bad news.

- ❖ **Be tactful.** Ensure that written appraisals and review meetings are professional and constructive.

- ❖ **Review evaluation criteria.** Use only objective and job-related performance criteria and standards.

- ❖ **Document the file.** Ask employees to sign the performance appraisal form, and keep copies in the appropriate files.

Employee Grievances

- **Establish a grievance resolution policy.** Implement and adhere to grievance procedures.
- **Investigate all complaints.** A prompt and thorough investigation is the best defense to discrimination, harassment and other claims.
- **Choose an appropriate investigator.** Both the employee and the jury must believe and trust the investigator.
- **Close the loop.** Document the results of the investigation, and report the results to the employee.

Employee Discipline

- **Understand the issues.** Make sure the basis for possible discipline is well-founded.
- **Provide notice.** An employee can only improve if he/she is aware of the problem and the employer's expectations.
- **Provide an opportunity to be heard.** Let the employee tell his/her side of the story.
- **Provide an opportunity to improve.** Give the employee the tools and time necessary to meet expectations.
- **Act promptly.** Implement and document your decision in a timely manner. Delays may look suspicious later.

Termination of Employment

- **Review at-will status.** Consider the employee's length of service, any representations made to the employee regarding continued employment, and any relevant agreements and policies.
- **Analyze the reasons for termination.** Make sure the reasons are fair, legitimate and objectively business-related. Confirm that the termination is consistent with established company policy and practice as well as the treatment of other employees in similar situations.
- **Consider discrimination risk factors.** Determine what, if any, protected classifications apply to the employee: age, race, religion, national origin, gender, disability, sexual orientation or marital status.

Analyze whether any of these factors might be part of the termination decision.

- **Analyze public policy risk factors**. Determine whether the employee has complained about alleged violations of law. Make sure the termination is not retaliatory.

- **Analyze ERISA risk factors**. Consider whether termination of the employee will prevent the vesting of retirement, health or stock option benefits in the immediate future.

- **Meet with the employee**. Conduct the termination interview privately in a sensitive manner, and have a witness present. Document the meeting and keep all information confidential.

- **Be prepared**. Have ready all necessary documentation, including the employee's final pay check, a check-list of company property to be returned, and information about COBRA benefits. Consider whether severance pay and a release are appropriate.

References

- **Give only basic information**. All reference checks should be referred to human resources. Limit information given to title, dates of employment and confirmation of final salary.

CHAPTER 14

TAX MATTERS

After issuing the employer identification number, the Internal Revenue Service will automatically mail to you each year the forms for filing the corporation's federal income tax return. However, even if the forms are not received from the Internal Revenue Service, the corporation remains obligated to file any required return by the applicable due date. Quarterly payments of federal income taxes for the corporation may be required.

Further information can be obtained online or by telephoning the local office of the Internal Revenue Service. The federal income tax return (Form 1120) for corporations, for instance, must be filed on or before the fifteenth day of the third month following the close of the taxable year. Also, most corporations are required to pay estimated federal income tax installments. The first installment is due on the fifteenth day of the fourth month of a corporation's taxable year and should be deposited in an authorized bank depository or Federal Reserve Bank. Instructions are provided in Internal Revenue Service Form 1120-W (Worksheet), "Corporation Estimated Income Tax."

Start-Up Costs and Organizational Expenses

The company may elect to amortize its organizational expenses and certain start-up costs over a period of not less than sixty months, beginning with the month in which it begins doing business. A separate election may be made for the particular expenses and costs. Organizational expenses are incidental to the creation of the company, are chargeable to Capital Account and are of a type that would be amortized over the company's life if the company had only a limited life. Start-up costs are expenses incurred in setting up an active trade or business, or for investigating the possibility of setting up or acquiring such a business.

TAX MATTERS

The election to amortize organization expenses must be made on Form 4562 attached to the return for the year in which the company begins business, including any extensions of time that may have been allowed. If you elect to amortize both organizational expenses and start-up costs, a separate statement must set forth a description and the amount of the expenditures involved, the date the expenditures were incurred, the month in which the company began business, and the number of months (not less than sixty) over which the ratable deduction is to be taken. You should consult with your accountants to ensure that the election is properly made if your company desires to take advantage of this election.

Federal Taxes

In addition to federal income tax forms, after issuance of the federal employer identification number, the Internal Revenue Service will automatically mail you on a periodic basis the necessary forms for filing the quarterly and annually reports covering the withholdings of federal income taxes and other employment taxes on the wages of the company's employees. The procedures for withholding may be found in Circular E, "Employer's Tax Guide," which should be obtained directly from the Internal Revenue Service, and includes guidelines for determining who qualifies as an "employee."

Generally, if an employer controls the services performed and the manner in which they are performed, the individual is deemed an employee. You should go online or telephone the local Internal Revenue Service office at once and request the computer forms for making the monthly or quarterly deposits at your bank of amounts to be withheld on employees' wages. At this time you should also request that the Internal Revenue Service send you the businessman's kit that explains the intricacies of employer tax withholdings.

It should be noted that the officers of a corporation may be held personally liable for failure to properly withhold applicable taxes.

State Taxes

For example, in California, the Franchise Tax Board will automatically send you annually the forms for filing the corporation's California franchise tax (Franchise Tax Board Form 100-ES, California Bank and Corporation Estimated Tax) and return (Franchise Tax Board Form 100). The minimum $800 tax is due at the time the Articles of Incorporation are filed and functions as a prepayment against the corporation's last tax liability. The corporation then must pay estimated tax payments for the current year on a quarterly basis using Form 100-

ES discussed above. The first installment of the estimated tax is due by the fifteenth day of the fourth month after incorporation. Certain "qualified new corporations" may pay only a $300 tax at the time of incorporation. New corporations are generally not subject to the minimum tax for their first and second taxable years.

Every corporation must file an annual return regardless of whether or not there was taxable income for that year. The first return is due on or before the fifteenth day of the third month following the close of the income year. Any prepayment is then credited against any taxes owed or is refunded. Forms and information are described in the "Guide for Filing Franchise Tax Returns by Commencing Corporation" which is sent to the corporation at its first mailing address.

Payroll Taxes

For example, in California, if your company will be paying wages to employees, it will need a California employer identification number and will be required to withhold amounts from employees' wages, make periodic deposits and file periodic returns with the Employment Development Department (EDD). Employers must register with the EDD within fifteen days after becoming subject to the income tax withholding provisions, the Unemployment Insurance Code (discussed below), or both. Form DE-8001 should be used if the employer is subject to withholding provisions only; Form DE-1 should be used if the employer is subject to both provisions. You should obtain information on these matters immediately upon commencement of your company by going online or telephoning the local office of the EDD and refer to the "Employer's Tax Guide" which provides more detailed information.

Unemployment Taxes

In California, for example, if the company has one or more employees and will pay wages and salaries of more than $100 in any calendar quarter, it must register with the nearest office of the California EDD within fifteen days after becoming subject to the Unemployment Insurance Code. This registration is the same as that required for state income tax withholding discussed earlier. Taxes will be due at least quarterly, and in some cases monthly.

Sales and Use Taxes

With certain specified exceptions, California, like most states, imposes a sales tax on business for the privilege of selling tangible personal property at retail. The tax must be collected by the retailer from the consumer insofar as it can be done, but the obligation to pay it is imposed on the retailer. The use tax is imposed upon the storage, use or consumption in the state of tangible personal property which is purchased from a retailer. While the consumer is liable for the use tax, it must be collected by the retailer if the retailer is engaged in business in the state. The use tax is not imposed if the transaction is subject to the sales tax.

The use tax will apply primarily where property is purchased or delivered outside of California, for instance, for eventual use in the state. With certain limited exceptions, the granting of possession of tangible personal property by a lessor or a lessee is considered a continuing sale in California, and the possession of such property by a lessee is considered a continuing purchase for use in California. As a result, the lessor is obligated to collect a sales or use tax at the time of each payment pursuant to the lease.

All persons engaged in California in the business of selling tangible property of the kind subject to the sales or use tax must obtain a Seller's Permit from the State Board of Equalization. Such Seller's Permit is usually required even though the business itself sells such property at wholesale or is a manufacturer. A business which holds a valid Seller's Permit is able to purchase tangible personal property for resale without paying the sales tax, provided it gives the seller a Resale Certificate certifying in good faith that resale will occur. The Board has authority to require the posting of collateral to secure the collection of the tax in an amount not to exceed the lesser of: (i) twice the estimated average tax as to taxpayers required to report quarterly, (ii) three times the estimated average tax as to taxpayers required to report monthly or (iii) $10,000.

The holder of a Seller's Permit is required to file a combined state, local and district tax return and to pay the taxes collected on a quarterly basis. If the estimated measure of tax averages $17,000 or more per month, a prepayment is required for each of the first two months of each quarterly period.

A separate Seller's Permit must be obtained for each place of business, and must be conspicuously displayed at the place for which it is issued. In addition to the sales and use tax, certain businesses may be subject to excise and other taxes (i.e., for sale of alcoholic beverages and cigarettes).

Property Taxes

The business will be subject to taxation by the appropriate city and/or county on the value of its real and personal property. The assessor usually requests payment by sending a tax return form to the taxpayer.

Business Licenses

The business may require one or more business licenses. Some trades, occupations and businesses are directly regulated by the State of California, for example. The state licenses a variety of businesses that may typically be conducted by a business entity. Two sources of information on this topic are the "California License Handbook" published by the California Department of Economic and Business Development, and the "California Permit Handbook" which discusses certain permits affecting businesses, including pollution control. Information may be obtained from the appropriate city or county clerk.

It should be noted that some cities impose taxes based on gross receipts and employees' payroll and care should be taken to ensure that the business is adequately complying with all applicable state, county and city licensing and taxing authorities.

CHAPTER 15

DOING BUSINESS IN OTHER STATES

A corporation does not have the right to transact intrastate business in another state unless it obtains a certificate of authority to do so from the Secretary of State of such state. Failure to obtain such a certificate could result in fines and the denial of access to the state's courts. Generally, intrastate business does not include activities in other states limited to taking orders or entering into contracts with residents of other states where the contracts are subject to acceptance and approval by the business, for example, in California and will be performed in California. Before commencing activities in other states (including hiring employees or renting office space), you should notify legal counsel so that the facts and circumstances of such actions can be analyzed to determine if the business needs to qualify to do business in such state.

Doing Business in States Foreign to State of Incorporation

When a corporation does business outside of the state in which it was organized, it may be required to "qualify" – to obtain a certificate of authority and to appoint a resident agent upon whom process may be served. Although the corporation laws of every state require foreign corporations doing business in the state to qualify, no law contains a comprehensive definition of the term "doing business". The risks of failure to qualify are great. In all states, unqualified foreign corporations doing business are denied access to state courts. An unqualified foreign corporation is also subject to fines, and, in several states, its directors, officers or agents may be fined.

The statutes of most states list certain activities in which a corporation may engage without qualifying. Some states also define activities which will require qualification. Consequently, most states have adopted either the Model Business Corporation Act or the Revised Model Business Corporation Act. Nonetheless, to a very large extent, the answers to doing business questions are found in court decisions.

There are three kinds of doing business questions:

- ❖ Whether a foreign corporation doing business in a state will be subject to service of process in that state.
- ❖ Whether a foreign corporation will be subject to taxation.
- ❖ Whether a foreign corporation will be subject to the state's qualification requirements.

When a corporation does business outside of its state of incorporation, it may find itself: (i) subject to taxation by the state, (ii) subject to service of process and suit in the state, or (iii) required to qualify to do business in the state (as stated above). The level of business activity that will constitute doing business is different for each category. Therefore, where a corporation's activities in a state are sufficient to require qualification, it follows that the corporation will also be amenable to service of process and to being taxed by the state.

Some corporation laws specifically state that there doing business definitions should not be used in determining if a corporation is doing business for any other purpose. For example, the Michigan qualification statute contains a provision that "This section does not apply in determining the contacts or activities which may subject a foreign corporation to service of process or taxation in this state…" Georgia, Nebraska, New Jersey, North Dakota, Oklahoma, Pennsylvania and Vermont have similar provisions. Colorado, Delaware, Florida and Utah state that their doing business definitions do not apply to the question of whether a foreign corporation is subject to service of process and suit. Virginia excludes personal jurisdiction from its definition. Minnesota and New Hampshire exclude taxation. The District of Columbia, Maine and New York exclude service of process. Tennessee simply states that its doing business definition applies only for purposes of its qualification requirement, "and for no other purpose".

A state's power to tax or to assert jurisdiction over a nonresident corporation is limited by the Constitution. Generally, it can be stated that the question of service of process on an unqualified foreign corporation turns on "traditional notions of fair play and substantial justice".

DOING BUSINESS IN OTHER STATES

Whether a state may tax an unqualified foreign corporation engaged in interstate commerce generally depends on the corporation's "nexus" with the state. In *Northwestern States Portland Cement Co. v. Minnesota*, the Supreme Court sustained Minnesota's right to impose property apportioned nondiscriminatory net income tax on an unlicensed foreign corporation operating exclusively in interstate commerce, where the corporation had a sufficient nexus or connection with the state. Without "some definite link, some minimum connection" between the state and the corporation's activities therein, the imposition of such a tax would violate the due process clause of the Fourteenth Amendment. Since that decision, local activities, such as the maintenance of an office, have been relied upon by the courts as constituting the necessary nexus.

As a result of the court's decision in the *Northwestern* case cited above, and its denial in other cases, Congress enacted the Federal Interstate Income Law, which places a limitation on the states' power to tax purely interstate commerce. It specifically prohibits states and political subdivisions thereof from imposing a net income tax on income derived within the state from interstate commerce where the activities of the taxpayer in the state were limited to the solicitation of orders.

The general rule concerning what constitutes doing business so as to require a foreign corporation to qualify has been stated as follows: "It is established by well considered general authorities that a foreign corporation is doing, transacting, carrying on, or engaging in business within a state when it transacts some substantial part of its ordinary business therein." Doing business is really not subject to definition and each case must be considered and decided in the light of its distinctive factual situation.

The first step to determining if a corporation must qualify in a state is to examine the state's corporation law. Most state laws list certain intrastate activities, such as maintaining bank accounts or holding board meetings that a foreign corporation may engage in without having to qualify. When there is a statutory statement covering the corporation's particular situation, the statute will hold. Otherwise, the issue is for judicial determination.

The issue of whether a foreign corporation is required to qualify in a state usually comes before a court when the corporation brings an action in the state's courts. Because unqualified foreign corporations transacting intrastate business may be barred from maintaining an action in a state's courts, the defendant will assert the plaintiff's unqualified status as a defense. The court must then determine if the plaintiff's activities in the state constituted "doing business" so that the corporation would have been required to qualify under the corporation law.

Internet Activities

To limit where your corporation can be sued, you should make sure that your corporation with an Internet site insert a click-through in your site containing a forum selection clause that the user must agree to as part of the terms and conditions for using your site.

Still, it is generally understood that less activity is required (a lower standard) to subject a foreign corporation to suit than the level of activity required to establish "doing business" in that state. So a corporation can be subject to suit in a state based on the sliding scale of internet activity, but the corporation may not be considered "doing business" in that same state such that it would have to qualify as a foreign corporation.

Inasmuch, the Internet presence appears to be exactly the same as a mail order presence, which does not trigger any obligation to qualify to do business – based on the "solicitation" exception adopted by almost all of the states, and the "interstate business" exception adopted by almost all of the states (and as dictated by the Constitution's Commerce Clause.

DOING BUSINESS IN OTHER STATES

SAMPLE
STATEMENT OF DESIGNATION BY FOREIGN CORPORATION

Statement and Designation by Foreign Corporation

_____
(Name of Corporation)

_____, a corporation organized and existing under the laws of _____, makes the following statements and designation:
(State or Place of Incorporation)

1. The address of its principal executive office is _____
_____.

2. The address of its principal office in the State of California is _____
(If none, leave Item 2 blank.)
_____

Designation of Agent for Service of Process in the State of California
(Complete either Item 3 or Item 4.)

3. (Use this paragraph if the process **agent is a natural person**.)

   _____, a natural person residing in the State of California, whose complete street address is _____

   _____, is designated as agent upon whom process directed to this corporation may be served within the State of California, in the manner provided by law.

4. (Use this paragraph if the process **agent is another corporation**.)

   _____,
   a corporation organized and existing under the laws of _____,
   is designated as agent upon whom process directed to this corporation may be served within the State of California, in the manner provided by law.

5. It irrevocably consents to service of process directed to it upon the agent designated above, and to service of process on the Secretary of State of the State of California if the agent so designated or the agent's successor is no longer authorized to act or cannot be found at the address given.

_____   _____
(Signature of Corporate Officer)   (Typed Name and Title of Officer Signing)

If an individual is designated as the agent for service of process, include the agent's business or residential **street** address in California (a P.O. Box address is not acceptable). If another corporation is designated as the agent for service of process, do not include the address of the designated corporation. **Note:** Corporate agents must have complied with California Corporations Code section 1505 prior to designation, and a corporation cannot act as its own agent.

Secretary of State **Form**
S&DC-STOCK/NONPROFIT (REV 04/2010)

[Clear Form] [Print Form]

BUSINESS STRUCTURES AND INCORPORATION

Penalties for Unqualified Foreign Corporations

Few corporations confine their activities to their home state. In order to protect their interests in foreign states, corporations must have access to those states' courts. However, an unqualified foreign corporation may be prevented from bringing or maintaining an action in the courts of a state in which it does intrastate business. Because of the Constitution's Commerce Clause, a state may not prevent an unqualified corporation from using its courts if the corporation is engaged exclusively in interstate commerce.

Every state has enacted a statute denying unqualified foreign corporations access to state courts. Some states have provisions similar to Section 124 of the Model Business Corporation Act, which states that "No foreign corporation transacting business in this State without a certificate of authority shall be permitted to maintain any action, suit or proceeding in any court of this State, until such corporation shall have obtained a certificate of authority." The states that have adopted similar provisions are Alaska, Colorado, the District of Columbia, Hawaii, Illinois, Maine, Minnesota, New Jersey, New Mexico, North Carolina, North Dakota, Rhode Island, South Dakota, Texas, and West Virginia.

Other states have adopted a provision similar to Section 15.02 of the Revised Model Business Corporation Act which provides that "A foreign corporation transacting business in this state without a certificate of authority may not maintain a proceeding in any court in this state until it obtains a certificate of authority." The states that adopted similar provisions are Alabama, Arizona, Arkansas, Florida, Georgia, Idaho, Indiana, Iowa, Kentucky, Michigan, Mississippi, Missouri, Montana, Nebraska, New Hampshire, Oregon, South Carolina, Tennessee, Utah, Vermont, Virginia, Washington, Wisconsin, and Wyoming.

The statutes of California, Delaware, Kansas, Louisiana, Maryland, Massachusetts, Nevada, New York, Ohio, Oklahoma, and Pennsylvania also provide that unqualified foreign corporations doing business in their states may not use their courts. However, their statutes are not based on either the Model Act or Revised Model Act provisions.

Because an unqualified corporation is denied access to state courts, it cannot enforce contracts it made in the state. But an unqualified corporation doing intrastate business may be permitted to enforce a contract in a state court if the contract was entered into outside of that state. However, in an Alabama case, the plaintiff contracted to provide advertisements to be broadcast in Alabama. The court held that where the primary purpose of contract between the plaintiff and defendant was for services that had to be performed in Alabama, the unqualified corporate plaintiff could not use Alabama's courts even though the contract was entered into out of state. A contract made in the forum state which would not be enforceable because of the disabling statute is not made enforceable by a provision in the contract stating that is shall be deemed to have been made outside that state.

Many states have held that a defense asserting that an unqualified foreign corporation is barred from maintaining an action must be timely interposed or it will be deemed waived. Some courts have also held that a defense asserting that the plaintiff is an unqualified foreign corporation is an affirmative defense and must be pleaded as such or it will be waived.

Where a corporation is duly qualified in a state while it transacts business there and then gives up its qualification after ceasing to operate in that state, the penalty of losing access to the state's courts is inapplicable. It is intended to punish a foreign corporation for doing business without authority – if no business is done, no authority is needed.

ABOUT THE AUTHOR

New book by California lawyer, Ann Carrington, Business Structures and Incorporation — How-To and Do-It-Yourself. Carrington has brought her expertise as a lawyer to numerous startup businesses. A graduate of Lincoln Law School, she spent her career in the heart of Silicon Valley. Ann Carrington is also the author of two other books: Trademark Protection and Prosecution and Writing Winning Business Plans and Investor Presentations. Working in corporate law for more than 20 years, she had written many articles about business processes and procedures, corporate governance, and legal matters. Along the way, she became fascinated by the large number of "mom and pop" businesses not properly structured, protected, or planned because of lack of knowledge or money to afford an attorney; subsequently, she spent time organizing her articles, and the main information in her books is loosely based on those articles.

ABOUT AUTHORSDOOR GROUP

AuthorsDoor Group is an imprint of The Ridge Publishing Group, and publisher of the Roadmap Strategies for Startups series by Ann Carrington: (1) Business Structures and Incorporation, (2) Trademark Protection and Prosecution, and (3) Writing Winning Business Plans and Investor Presentations; the EntrepreneursOpen series by Melania Patterson: (1) Independent Publishing Website Platform, (2) Independent Publishing Must Haves: Blogsite and Social Media Platforms, and (3) Independent Publishing with Amazon, IngramSpark, and Others; and The Millionaire Mindset series and four Companion books by Lori Ann Moeszinger: (1) The Millionaire Writing and Publishing Mindset, (2) The Millionaire Marketing Mindset, (3) The Millionaire Sales and Advertising Mindset, (4) The Millionaire Branding Mindset, and (5) The Millionaire Public Relations Mindset. For more information, visit our website at https://www.AuthorsDoor.com.

ABOUT THE RIDGE PUBLISHING GROUP

The Ridge Publishing Group is an up-and-coming American worldwide book, film and board game Company. It's positioned to become the largest theology teaching resource in the world in terms of books, textbooks, documentaries, board games and card decks. The Ridge Publishing Group owns the trademarks and copyrights of the Guardians of Biblical Truth Publishing Group and the New Narrated Study Bible series; the Hoyle Theology Publishing Group and the Hoyle Theology Encyclopedia seminary textbooks series (independent study program); Documentaries in Print Publishing Group and the Defending the Faith – Two Worlds, Lost World, New World series; and Educations in Games Publishing Group and the Heaven's Seminary board games and card decks. For more information, visit our website at https://www.RidgePublishingGroup.com.

www.ingramcontent.com/pod-product-compliance
Lightning Source LLC
Chambersburg PA
CBHW071559080526
44588CB00010B/964